SHARI'A AS DISCOURSE

Cultural Diversity and Law

Series Editor:
Prakash Shah, School of Law, Queen Mary, University of London, UK

Around the world, most states are faced with difficult issues arising out of cultural diversity in their territories. Within the legal field, such issues span across matters of private law through to public and constitutional law. At international level too there is now considerable jurisprudence regarding ethnic, religious and cultural diversity. In addition, there are several layers of legal control – from communal and religious regulation to state and international regulation. This multiplicity of norm setting has been variously termed legal pluralism, inter-legality or inter-normativity and provides a fascinating lens for academic analysis that links up to cultural diversity in new and interesting ways. The umbrella of cultural diversity encompasses various population groups throughout the world ranging from national, ethnic, religious or indigenous groupings. This series particularly welcomes work that is of comparative interest, concerning various state jurisdictions as well as different population groups.

Also in the Series

Legal Practice and Cultural Diversity
Edited by Ralph Grillo, Roger Ballard, Alessandro Ferrari, André J. Hoekema, Marcel Maussen and Prakash Shah
ISBN 978-0-7546-7547-1

Shari'a As Discourse
Legal Traditions and the Encounter with Europe

Edited by

JØRGEN S. NIELSEN
University of Copenhagen, Denmark

LISBET CHRISTOFFERSEN
University of Roskilde and University of Copenhagen, Denmark

'Religion in the 21st Century',
University of Copenhagen

The Danish Institute in Damascus

RELIGION IN THE 21ST CENTURY
UNIVERSITY OF COPENHAGEN

المعهد الدنماركي بدمشق
THE DANISH INSTITUTE IN DAMASCUS

ASHGATE

Published in cooperation with the University of Copenhagen and The Danish Institute in Damascus.

Published by
Ashgate Publishing Limited
Wey Court East
Union Road
Farnham
Surrey, GU9 7PT
England

Ashgate Publishing Company
Suite 420
101 Cherry Street
Burlington
VT 05401-4405
USA

www.ashgate.com

British Library Cataloguing in Publication Data
Shari'a as discourse : legal traditions and the encounter
with Europe.--(Cultural diversity and law)
1. Islamic law--Europe. 2. Islamic law--Interpretation
and construction. 3. Conflict of laws--Europe.
I. Series II. Nielsen, Jørgen S. III. Christoffersen,
Lisbet.
340.5'9-dc22

Library of Congress Cataloging-in-Publication Data
Nielsen, Jørgen S.
Shari'a as discourse : legal traditions and the encounter with Europe / by Jørgen S. Nielsen and Lisbet Christoffersen.
p. cm. -- (Cultural diversity and law)
Includes bibliographical references and index.
ISBN 978-0-7546-7955-4 (hardback) -- ISBN 978-0-7546-9895-1 (ebook)
1. Conflict of laws--Europe. 2. Conflict of laws (Islamic law) 3. Islamic law--Europe. 4. Muslims--Legal status, laws, etc.--Europe 5. Religion and law--Europe. 6. Legal polycentricity--Europe. I. Christoffersen, Lisbet. II. Title.

KJC969.N54 2009
340.5'9--dc22

2009031369

ISBN 9780754679554 (hbk)
ISBN 9780754698951 (ebk)

Mixed Sources
Product group from well-managed forests and other controlled sources
www.fsc.org Cert no. SA-COC-1565
© 1996 Forest Stewardship Council
FSC

Printed and bound in Great Britain by
MPG Books Group, UK

Contents

PART 2: LOCAL EXPERIENCES

PART 3: SHARI'A AND DISCOURSE

List of Figures

Box

Figures

Notes on Contributors

Asma Afsaruddin is Professor of Islamic Studies in the Department of Near Eastern Languages and Cultures at Indiana University, Bloomington, Indiana, USA. She is the author and/or editor of four books, including *The First Muslims: History and Memory* (2008) and *Excellence and Precedence: Medieval Islamic Discourse on Legitimate Lea*dership (2002), as well as of numerous articles dealing with various aspects of Islamic thought. Afsaruddin is currently completing her research on jihad and martyrdom in Islamic thought and practice, for which she has received grants from the Guggenheim Foundation and the Carnegie Corporation.

Matilda Arvidsson is a doctoral candidate, LLM, BA, and lecturer at the Faculty of Law at the University of Lund. Her current research project is 'Constitution-making post bellum – the Iraqi example', and focuses on what happens when constitutional law, theories of democracy and international law meet after military interventions. She has previously worked as a junior judge at a Swedish district court and has specialized on Swedish judicial culture and the encounter with Islamic law. She wrote her Master's thesis on 'Ijtihad – reformation of Islamic law in the 21st century. The case of Sudan'.

Dorthe Bramsen holds a PhD in Islamic studies from the University of Copenhagen, Denmark, with the dissertation on interpreting Shari'a within the institutions of ifta' and qada' in Saudi Arabia. She has been Visiting Researcher at Harvard Law School and has written several articles on Islamic law in Danish. Since 2008 she has edited a book series on Islam and Islamic culture and history at Vandkunsten Publishers, Copenhagen.

Lisbet Christoffersen is Associate Professor in Public Law at the University of Roskilde and Professor in Law and Religion, Faculty of Theology, University of Copenhagen. She holds a PhD in ecclesiastical law from Copenhagen. She has been research coordinator in the cross-disciplinary research priority area 'Religion in the 21st century' at the University of Copenhagen and is leader of the Nordic research network 'Religion, ethic and law in Nordic society' funded by the Scandinavian Research Academy. She is among others the co-editor of *Law and Religion in the Nordic Countries* (Leuven: Peeters, forthcoming), and has written 'Religion as a factor in multi-layered European Union legislation' in Rubya Mehdi, Hanne Petersen, Erik Reenberg Sand and Gordon R. Woodman (eds), *Law and Religion in Multicultural Societies* (Copenhagen: DJØF Publishing, 2008), pp.111–30, and

'Intertwinement. A new concept for understanding religion-law-relations', *Nordic Journal of Religion and Society*, 2006, pp.107 –26.

Manni Crone is Senior Researcher at the Danish Institute for International Studies. She studied her Master's in political science at the Institut d'Études Politiques in Paris and her PhD at the Department of Sociology, University of Copenhagen. Previously, she was Head of Section at the Danish Ministry for Foreign Affairs. Her research focus is Salafism in Denmark and Europe, Islamic secularism, religion and security studies. Recent publications include: '"There's a wind from the Orient": Salafism and jihadism in Denmark', *Økonomi og Politik*, Copenhagen, 2009 (in Danish); 'Religious secularism', in Louay Hussein (ed.), *Secularism in the Arab Levant*, Damascus: Atlas Books, 2007 (in Arabic); and 'The disenchantment of an Islamic state. Perspectives on secularism in Iran', *Nordic Journal of Religion and Society*, 19, 2, 2006.

Dima Dabbous-Sensenig is Director of the Institute for Women's Studies in the Arab World (IWSAW) and Assistant Professor of Communication at the Lebanese American University, Beirut, Lebanon, where she teaches media law and ethics courses. She holds a BA in communication and an MA in media studies. Her PhD thesis, completed at Sheffield Hallam University, UK, applied methods and theories of policy analysis to the Lebanese broadcast law of 1994. Her research interests include media regulation in the Arab world, Lebanese media coverage of confessional violence, and gender and religion in Arab talk shows. She has published several scholarly articles and book chapters on broadcast policies and regulation in Lebanon and the Arab world. Her more recent publications applied critical discourse analysis to religious talk shows on Arab satellites.

Mark van Hoecke is Research Professor in Legal Theory and Comparative Law at the University of Ghent (Belgium) and Research Professor in the Methodology of Comparative Law at the University of Tilburg (The Netherlands). Dr Van Hoecke wrote his doctoral thesis on the freedom of interpretation of the judge (1979). He was previously Dean of the Faculty of Law and Rector (2002–2007) of the Katholieke Universiteit Brussel. His research focuses, among other themes, on comparative legal cultures. His publications include *Epistemology and Methodology of Comparative Law* (as editor, Oxford: Hart Publishing, 2004) and *Law as Communication* (Oxford: Hart Publishing, 2002).

Peter Madsen is Professor of Comparative Literature at the Department of Cultural Studies and the Arts, University of Copenhagen. He has written on censorship in 'Offence. Literature in the public sphere', in Kirsten Hastrup (ed.), *Discrimination and Toleration, New Perspectives* (Leiden: Martinus Nijhoff, 2002), pp. 44–9) and has published a selection of the *Arabian Nights* (translated by Johannes Østrup) with a postscript (2005). He currently leads a research project on Islam in European literary history.

Kjell-Åke Modéer is Professor of Legal History at the University of Lund and holds degrees in theology from Lund and in law from Greifswald, Germany. He is an internationally renowned legal historian who operates between legal theory and legal praxis, between law and history of religions, both Islam and Christianity, and between law and theology. In his current research the focus is on de-sacralization and re-traditionalization in late-modern perspectives on law.

Mogens Müller is Professor at the Department of Biblical Exegesis and Deputy Dean at the Faculty of Theology at the University of Copenhagen. His research centres on the meaning of the expression 'Son of man' in the gospels, but during his 25 years as professor, he has published a wide range of books and articles covering everything from core gospel theology to the ancient Jewish literature and the interpretation of history.

Jørgen S. Nielsen is Professor of Islamic Studies and Director of the Centre for European Islamic Thought, Faculty of Theology, University of Copenhagen, Denmark; previously he was a lecturer and professor at the University of Birmingham, UK. He studied Arabic and Islamic law at London, and his PhD in Arab history from the American University in Beirut was on medieval legal administration in Egypt. Since 1978 his research has been focused on Islam in Europe. He is the author of *Secular Justice in an Islamic State: Mazalim under the Bahri Mamluks, 662/1264–789/1387* (Leiden: Netherlands Institute for the Near East, 1985) and *Muslims in Western Europe*, 3rd edition (Edinburgh, 2004) and chief editor of *Yearbook of Muslims in Europe* (Leiden, 2009).

Hanne Petersen is Professor of Law and part of the management team of the Centre for Studies of Legal Culture at the Faculty of Law, University of Copenhagen. She received her doctoral degree on a dissertation about labour law, informal law, women's law and legal theory. She has worked as a consultant and facilitator since the1990s on courses concerned with human rights, women's law and methodology in African countries, Pakistan and the Middle East. She was Professor of Jurisprudence and Sociology of Law in Greenland 1995–9. She has published *Home Knitted Law. Norms and Values in Gendered Rule-Making* (Aldershot: Dartmouth, 1995). She has also edited *Love and Law in Europe* (Aldershot: Ashgate, 1998) and co-edited *Paradoxes of European Legal Integration* (Aldershot: Ashgate, 2008) and *Law and Religion in Multicultural Societies* (Copenhagen: DJØF Publishing, 2008).

Prakash Shah is Senior Lecturer in Law, Queen Mary's College, University of London, UK. He holds degrees in law completed with a PhD from the School of Oriental and African Studies, London. His interests lie mainly in the fields of migration law, ethnic minorities and diasporas in law, and comparative laws of Asia and Africa, including Islamic law. Publications include *Refugees, Race and the Legal Concept of Asylum in Britain* (London: Cavendish, 2000); *Legal Pluralism* *in Conflict: Coping with Cultural Diversity in Law* (London: Glass House, 2005); *Migration, Diasporas and Legal Systems in Europe* (ed, with W. Menski, London: Cavendish, 2006); and *Law and Ethnic Plurality: Socio-legal Perspectives* (ed., Leiden: Martinus Nijhoff, 2007).

Mona Siddiqui is Professor of Islamic Studies and Public Understanding, Department of Theology and Religious Studies, and Director of the Centre for the Study of Islam, University of Glasgow, UK. She has studied Arabic, French and Middle East Studies and holds a PhD in classical Islamic law (Manchester, UK). Among her publications are 'Defective marriage in classical Hanafi law: issues of form and validity', in Hawting, Mojaddedi and Samely (eds), *Texts and Traditions in Memory of Norman Calder* (Oxford: Oxford University Press, 2000, pp.271–86), and 'The ethics of gender discourse in Islam', in Michael Ipgrave (ed.), *Scriptures in Dialogue* (London: Church House Publishing, 2004, pp.72–80).

Jakob Skovgaard-Petersen, DrPhil, is Professor and Leader of the New Islamic Public Sphere Programme, Department of Cross-Cultural and Regional Studies, University of Copenhagen. His field of research is modern Islam with a focus on the establishment of modern Muslim media and the role of Muslim writers and intellectual in the modern Muslim states. Lately, his research has primarily focused on the place of Islam in the new pan-Arab television networks, and on renewal of the classical Islamic literary genres, especially the interpretation of the Qur'an and of fatawa. Among his publications are *Defining Islam for the Egyptian State – Muftis and Fatwas of the Dār al-Iftā* (Leiden: Brill, 1997) and as co-editor, *Global Mufti: The Phenomenon of Yusuf al-Qaradawi* (London, New York: Hurst/Columbia University Press, 2009).

Preface

Jørgen S. Nielsen and Lisbet Christoffersen

The chapters in this volume arise out of an ongoing discussion among specialists in Islamic studies on the one hand and, on the other, various kinds of legal experts with a continuing interest in the interaction between European legal systems and Muslim communities. It has been argued that, in some sections of the Muslim communities in Europe, aspects of custom related in some way to Islam – Marshall Hodgson invented the term 'islamicate' to cover this relationship (Hodgson, 1974, I, 177) – remain so persistent that for the legislator and the judge to ignore them is tantamount to institutionalizing severe injustice and, especially, leaves women at the mercy of male-dominated practice. This would, for example, be the case in a marriage conducted Islamically but not recognized by European family law jurisdictions, which could therefore find such jurisdictions unable to hear any arising dispute and thus often leave a woman at the mercy of informal systems of social control. From a Muslim perspective the discussion refers to the wider contests taking place about the nature and role of Shari'a within the Muslim world, contests which can be traced in various ways to the early generations of Islamic learning and which are to be found all over the Muslim world today, often formulated in the context of a response to the ominous 'other' associated with the dominant, ex- and post-imperial 'West'. From a European perspective we are witnessing an engagement with a religious/legal/cultural complex of traditions which have until the last couple of generations been located outside Europe, or at least outside the western and northern parts of the European subcontinent, and which certain European institutions had some experience of engaging with but only as the external, colonial 'other'. These two perspectives have now become engaged within the boundaries of Europe, often in a contest of some virulence both in their mutual relationship and in their respective internal negotiations and arguments.

The chapters in this book are an attempt to expose some of the various issues thus raised and to put the two intellectual and legal traditions into some form of dialogue and to explore how the encounter is working out in practice in selected locations both in Europe and in the Arab Muslim world. The starting point, as is indicated in the first chapter by *Jørgen Nielsen*, is that too much polemical attention has been given to certain sets of rules associated with Shari'a. More interesting and more productive, it is suggested, is to look at how the processes of theological-legal interpretation have been expressed and are being expressed in a more or less common intellectual framework and to do so in a dialogue with similar processes in Europe – and to record how certain more polemical contemporary approaches close off possibilities of change. So the volume brings together a number of scholars of Shari'a and Islamic law with counterparts from parallel European disciplines: hermeneutics, philosophy and jurisprudence.

Part 1 of the book focuses on legal theory in the broad sense. *Mona Siddiqui* uses some specific themes to show how the '*ulama*' of the developed *fiqh* writings of the classical period were concerned with logical coherence but in the process could reach a number of varying and equally valid solutions to the problems they posited, in contrast to the modern trend towards codification and mistrust of diversity of opinion. *Asma Afsaruddin* develops this theme with reference to the contest between those she calls 'modernists' and 'hardliners'. It is suggested that one of the central elements of that contest is the approach to and use of history – history as context for the interpretations of earlier generations, and history as itself contested territory – as well as, from some quarters, an implicit or explicit assertion of the irrelevance of history. In the encounter with Europe, Shari'a discussion meets a new context with its own history, and *Mark van Hoecke* considers the implications both in terms of comparisons and in terms of consequential challenges each to the other. On the way he touches on the growing awareness of a contemporary European legal pluralism, which *Lisbet Christoffersen* explores in greater depth. Her starting point, as it is also in Chapter 1 by *Jørgen Nielsen*, is the Refah case at the European Court of Human Rights. She proceeds to debate the nature of law in its European context and thence to discuss how, and how far, Shari'a can be regarded as law in such a sense. She ends on a transitory note: the field is changing, and it is changing in unpredictable ways over which the present generation of experts, practitioners and observers have only limited influence. One of the most sharply controversial fields, and one of those which often drives the controversies, is the place of women, and we examine this in the rest of Part 1. *Hanne Petersen* shows how conditional Scandinavian feminism and the moves towards equality for women are located in a particular cultural, religious and political history. The continuing process of 'gender neutralizing' the more or less secularized countries of Scandinavia appears to run parallel to a process of 'gendering' Shari'a. *Kjell-Åke Modéer* considers the Scandinavian legal tradition and the contested relationship between its strong nation-state tradition and the growing internal social pluralism and the related contest between the monopoly of territorial jurisdictions and the impact of discussions about legal pluralism and polycentricity in the context of pressures related to Muslim communities and their concepts of Shari'a.

Part 2 transfers the more theoretical discussions to particular local experiences. *Matilda Arvidsson* takes us to the very local experience of the functioning of a Swedish family court dealing with one particular case involving the child custody claim of one woman of Iranian origin. She shows how the quite separate cultural enclaves of the Swedish judge and court administrators and the Iranian Muslim family in its local Malmö context meet and interpret each other within a strongly asymmetrical power relationship. Britain is probably that European country which has most extensively engaged with Shari'a in its legal system. *Prakash*

Shah shows how far as well as the limits for such engagement, limits which have become more marked and, he suggests, more discriminatory in relation to Islam and Muslims in time with the growth in political controversy surrounding Muslims both internationally and domestically. This controversial focus on Islam has been earlier and, in some ways, more marked in France, but *Manni Crone* also shows how some French Muslim leaders, in particular Tareq Oubrou of Bordeaux, have been engaged in developing an understanding of Shari'a more attuned to the situation of Muslims in a French minority situation. She concludes that there are forms of Shari'a which can accommodate to the European situation by emphasizing the ethical dimensions. Contrary to that is Shari'a as predominantly a legal phenomenon, primarily viable in the traditionally majority Muslim countries, which is treated in the remaining three chapters in Part 2. *Dorthe Bramsen* takes us to what is often considered to be the opposite end of the spectrum, namely the legal practice of Saudi Arabia. Here the official debate is around the process of what amounts to a codification of Shari'a as Islamic law. This is illustrated with reference to a number of opinions expounded by two leading representatives of the conservative end of the Saudi legal establishment, namely the shaykhs Ibn Baz (d. 1999) and Ibn 'Uthaymin. The status of women inevitably enters this debate, and *Dima Dabbous-Sensenig* selects one particular expression of this discussion in the form of a discourse analysis of two broadcasts on the subject on Al Jazeera satellite television by the renowned Egyptian-Qatari shaykh Yusuf al-Qaradawi. His way of discussing the subject, she concludes, is one which closes off options with which he disagrees, in a manner which is unlike more traditional forms of discussion. *Jakob Skovgaard-Petersen* rounds off this part with an analysis of the way in which Islam has become a contested theme also in constitutional politics, here with Egypt as the case study. Through a series of constitutional documents during the 20th century, the place of Islam has moved from the end to the beginning, most recently in the document adopted in 2007. Also in these most recent debates much public discussion and political negotiation took place before the status of the Shari'a was reconfirmed as being 'the principle source of legislation'.

The short final part of the volume includes two chapters which, each in their own way, recapitulate the main themes running through this book. *Mogens Müller* illustrates both the shared and the disparate approaches to scriptural hermeneutics in the Western Judaeo-Christian tradition and the Muslim tradition. *Peter Madsen* surveys the 20th-century development of discourse analysis as a method for understanding language and applies it to the controversy surrounding the publication in Spain in 2003 of a book by the Malaga imam Mohamed Kamal Mostafa. He shows how this attempt internally to regulate Muslim interpretations of Qur'an 4:34 was interpreted – and politicized – in quite different ways within a much broader public Spanish frame of reference.

The draft chapters were discussed in some detail at a conference organized as a joint project between the Danish Institute in Damascus under its then director, Jørgen S. Nielsen, who has since moved to the Faculty of Theology, University of Copenhagen, and the University of Copenhagen's Research Priority Area 'Religion in the 21st Century', whose research director Lisbet Christoffersen is now based at the Department of Society and Globalization at the Roskilde University Centre since the Research Priority Area concluded its work at the end of 2007. The editors are extremely grateful to these institutions for their support for this conference and the production of this volume. Finally, the editors wish to recognize their debt of gratitude to Mr Niels Valdemar Vinding whose work as student assistant to the conference and the subsequent assembly of the revised chapters was invaluable.

Chapter 1
Shari'a Between Renewal and Tradition

Jørgen S. Nielsen

Shari'a: Immutable or Adaptable?

Shari'a is one of the main focuses of current attention on Islam from the side of the European public, often accompanied by a manner which betrays alternatively ignorance and misapprehension. At the same time Shari'a is one of the central resources in the search by many parts of the Muslim world for ways of dealing with modernity and globalization. And in those trends, whether self-declared Muslim or secular, which do not regard the Shari'a as such a resource, the Shari'a is often regarded as the main obstacle to progress. Whichever way one looks at it, a discussion of Shari'a cannot be avoided.

One of the key problems in such a discussion is what the various protagonists mean by Shari'a. Many Muslim radicals as well as Western critics tend to view Shari'a as a code characterized by certain notorious features, particularly in the field of criminal law and the position of women. This tends to lock most Western debates about Shari'a onto a narrow positive law track, while the equivalent Muslim debate tends to become intolerant and exclusive of others.

A recent example of the resultant confusion was the series of court cases arising out of the initiative of the Turkish military establishment in 1995 to ban the Refah Party, a party with a self-declared Islamically based ideology. The accusation was that members of the party, including its then leader Necmettin Erbakan, had expressed themselves in terms which breached the secular nature of the Turkish constitution. Among other things, these individuals were reported as having called for introduction of Shari'a law in parallel with other codes. In response to legal appeals the Turkish Constitutional Court had upheld the banning of the party, which then appealed to the European Court of Human Rights in Strasbourg, Turkey being a signatory to the European Convention on Human Rights (ECHR).

In its first treatment of the Refah case, the chamber of the European Court rejected Refah's appeal against the Turkish Constitutional Court's decision to dissolve the party. Among other things the court concluded that the Shari'a which Refah was allegedly attempting to introduce 'would oblige individuals to obey … static rules of law imposed by the religion concerned.'[1]

1 *European Court of Human Rights, Case of Refah Partisi (The Welfare Party) and others* v. *Turkey* (applications nos. 41340/98, 41342/98 and 41344/98), 31 July 2001, para. 70.

Further, it quoted with approval the Turkish Constitutional Court's view that

> sharia was the antithesis of democracy in that it was based on dogmatic values and was the opposite of the supremacy of reason and of the concepts of freedom, independence and the ideal of humanity developed in the light of science.[2]

The Strasbourg court concluded

> that sharia, which faithfully reflects the dogmas and divine rules laid down by religion, is stable and invariable … It is difficult to declare one's respect for democracy and human rights while at the same time supporting a regime based on sharia, which clearly diverges from Convention values …[3]

This view was confirmed just over 18 months later by the Strasbourg court meeting in Grand Chamber.[4]

It is clear here that the European Court of Human Rights accepted the view of the Turkish courts that the Shari'a is essentially a non-negotiable code whose authority lies outside the human plane, and certainly outside the authority of a modern state. It therefore conflicts fundamentally with the requirements and the sovereignty of the nation and the state. Presented as a set of immutable rules resting on the authority of divine revelation the Shari'a must therefore be incompatible with democracy.

It is not difficult to find Islamic sources presenting a similar view of the Shari'a. Take one quote off the internet:

> Our love for Allah (Subhanahu Wa Ta'aala) and His Messenger (Sall Allahu Alaihi Wasallam) makes it haram to keep silent while man made kufr ideas and solutions exist in society. Islam obliges us to accept the Sovereignty of Allah (Subhanahu Wa Ta'aala) in all of life's affairs from the individual to social, economic and political affairs.[5]

This is recognizable from media portrayals of Islam – and from the speech of certain noisy individuals presenting themselves as speaking for Islam. In fact, the source is Hizb al-Tahrir, a small but very vociferous movement which originated in Jordan in the 1950s as a radical offshoot of the Muslim Brotherhood (Taji-Farouki, 1996) and which since the early 1990s has found some limited but highly profiled support in parts of Europe, especially among Muslim students whose

---

2 *Ibid.* para. 71.

3 *Ibid.* para. 72.

4 *European Court of Human Rights, Case of Refah Partisi (The Welfare Party) and others* v. *Turkey* (applications nos. 41340/98, 41342/98 and 41344/98), 13 February 2003.

5 <http://www.khilafah.com/home/category.php?DocumentID=6454&TagID=2>, accessed 13 May 2005.

parents immigrated from parts of the Muslim world in the 1960s and 1970s (see Grøndahl et al., 2003; Husain, 2007).

The coinciding views of the European Court and Hizb al-Tahrir reflect only one of several understandings of the nature of Shari'a to be found in both its classical forms and in much serious modern Islamic discussion. Is Shari'a primarily a law code or is it rather a framework for thinking, a discourse, under cover of which a wide variety of practical solutions to existential problems and the ordering of individual and social life has been and can be developed? In his study *Between God and the Sultan: A History of Islamic Law*, Knut Vikør points out that 'the central factor was that the law was common and had the proper authority, not necessarily what it said'. (Vikør, 2005, 30). Indeed, the American legal anthropologist Lawrence Rosen holds the view that Islamic law fits into a classification of 'common law' systems in contrast to 'codified' legal systems (Rosen, 1989).

An older school of Western research on Shari'a has tended towards the view that after the formative and classical periods of development the Shari'a tended to stagnate (e.g. Schacht, 1964; Coulson, 1964). However, more recent research has shown that this picture is too simplistic, and Coulson showed later that his own ideas about Islamic law were more dynamic than had previously appeared (Coulson, 1969). In Hanafi *fiqh* in India, significant change took place in the 16th and 17th centuries, a period when the forms of Hanafi law, which have since become dominant in the subcontinent, were laid down by al-Marghinani (1791) and in the *Fatawa Alamghiriyyah* (Bazmee Ansari, 2008). In a quite technical but at the same time theoretically ground-breaking study, Professor Baber Johansen has shown, using a case study of land tax and rent in the late Mamluk and Ottoman period (Johansen, 1988), that through much of Islamic history, it was not the specific solutions or legal rulings (*ahkam*) which were considered legitimate or illegitimate, the key was rather whether they had been arrived at within the generally accepted framework of thought using the generally accepted intellectual tools.

The ground is much more contested in modern times, as much on political, social and cultural grounds, as on intellectual, legal or theological grounds. For this reason, it is also the case that Muslim thinkers today are much quicker to condemn each others' views than they were in the past, just as it is the case that Western observers very often are ignorant of this aspect of the nature of Shari'a. It is thus no surprise that the views of, for example, the shaykhs of Al-Azhar University in Cairo have become much more contested over the last century (see Zebiri, 1993).

Returning to summary presentations of the nature of the Shari'a, here is a statement which the majority of Muslims today would recognize:

> This religion consists of belief and Shari'a (Islamic Law), and the latter is application of the former. The difference between Shari'a and fiqh (Islamic jurisprudence) is that Shari'a is set by Allah; whereas fiqh is the human

> comprehension of Shari'a. In addition, religion has been perfectly completed by the message of Muhammad (peace and blessings be upon him).[6]

A more classical, but potentially quite radical view, is that of Abu Ishaq al-Shatibi, a North African Maliki scholar who died in 1388. He simply equated the Shari'a with the revelation, i.e. the Qur'an is the Shari'a (Masud, 1997, 247f.). Everything else is human interpretation. In his study of al-Shatibi, Masud (1997) draws the conclusion and heads his last chapter 'Shari'a: the source of Islamic law', in other words, in this view Shari'a and Islamic law are two distinct entities.

Shari'a, *Fiqh* and the Challenges of Modernity

It is clear that we need to deal with a number of different concepts here, in particular Shari'a and *fiqh*, but also the concept of *usul al-fiqh*, the 'roots' of the *fiqh*. It could be said, at its simplest, that the Shari'a expresses God's will for human behaviour. This is what is immutable. *Fiqh* is the process of human interpretation of that revealed will, the extrapolation of the immutable Shari'a into the rules of everyday living. This goes well beyond what is normally understood as legislation in the contemporary sense in Western societies including, as it does, the dimensions of worship (*'ibadat*) as well as human transactions (*mu'amalat*), the latter resembling more closely a modern understanding of 'law'. *Usul al-fiqh*, the 'roots' of the law, is then the complex interaction of the primary textual sources, namely the Qur'an and the Sunna (the model behaviour of the Prophet Muhammad as recorded in the anecdotes of his sayings and actions called *hadith*), plus the principles of interpretation and establishment of authority where independent reasoning (*ijtihad*) and its various techniques, particularly the application of analogy (*qiyas*), expresses the former and (in Sunni Islam) the consensus (*ijma'*) of the community, primarily formulated by the scholars (*'ulama'*), expresses the latter. *Usul al-fiqh* is often depicted as Islamic jurisprudence or the 'philosophy' of Islamic law.

How one then views the Shari'a depends crucially on three questions:

1. Where is the demarcation line between immutable Shari'a and human interpretation?
2. How do the intellectual interpretation and the impact of the community implied in *ijtihad* and *ijma'* relate to the textual sources?
3. Who has the authority to engage in *fiqh*?

Further questions follow. How are intellectual disagreements argued? How do Shari'a and *fiqh* deal with change? Traditionally, one way has been casuistic and piecemeal with little consideration for the consequences of one view or decision

---

6 <http://www.islamonline.net/English/In_Depth/ShariahAndHumanity/Articles/2005-04/09.shtml>, accessed 13 May 2005.

on other aspects of the system – as if it is not really a system. That still goes on extensively. Another way is to take a more systematic approach, using certain principles which have been deduced from Qur'an and Sunna as foundational, as the hermeneutical keys by which other aspects must be understood.

There have tended to be two major responses to modernity in Shari'a thinking. At the risk of oversimplification, one range of responses has been to demand that reality change to conform with the perceived expectations of the Shari'a – the world has strayed and must be put right. The other range of responses has been to acknowledge that Shari'a thinking has become isolated from the community's concerns and the realities of the modern world. It therefore needs reforming itself before it can again speak to the needs of humanity, Muslim or otherwise.

The former approach has attracted most attention in recent years in the form of trends commonly grouped under the term 'Salafi'. *Salaf*, more correctly *al-salaf al-salih*, refers to the first pious generations of the companions of the Prophet Muhammad and their immediate heirs. The early community of the faithful is considered to have been closest to the prophet and the revelation, and it can therefore be assumed to have the best knowledge of the divine will. Since the term was first applied in the modern period to the reformists of Egypt and the Middle East in the late 19th century, it has changed meaning in a more strict and inward-looking direction. One of the early modern Salafis was Muhammad 'Abduh (d. 1905), who became a reforming Shaykh al-Azhar towards the end of a controversial career which included being exiled to Paris by the British occupiers (Hourani, 1962, ch.6). But today Salafism is broadly associated with the theological traditions identified with political movements arising out of the intellectual tradition of Ibn Taymiyya (d. 1328), in particular as transmitted through Abu'l-A'la Maududi, Sayyid Qutb and the official Saudi tradition of Ibn 'Abd al-Wahhab (Ende, 2008; ICG, 2005).

From the other side of this internal debate, let me point to two different methods, which are increasingly widely referred to as means of adjusting *fiqh* to contemporary lived realities.

1. *Maqasid*, the intentions of the Shari'a, is occasionally also referred to as the divine intention, although for many this gets too close to claiming that one can read God's mind from the Qur'an. It was a native of Granada, Abu Ishaq Ibrahim al-Shatibi (d. 1388), who first expounded in a developed fashion on this concept, although the basic idea that God had certain intentions in the revelation of his will appears quite early in the development of Islamic theological debate: it is at the core of the Mu'tazilite controversies of the 8th and 9th centuries (Gleave, 2008). In his work *Al.Muwafaqat fi usul al-Shari'a* al-Shatibi identifies three categories of such intentions, of which the five essential ones are the preservation of life, property, progeny, mind and religion. This he builds on the concept of the classically more widely accepted *maslaha*, common good, often considered one of the supplementary roots of the law, especially in the Maliki school (Kamali, 1991, ch.13). In the modern period, the Tunisian scholar Muhammad ibn

'Ashur (d.1868) was among the first to focus on the *maqasid* as a route to adapting the *fiqh* to changed times, writing a book entitled *Maqasid al-Shari'a al-islamiyyah* (Ibn 'Ashur, 2005). The concept was taken up in particular by the well-known reformist Rashid Rida (d.1935) and has gained growing impact since then.

2. Another, more procedural route is the identification of *qawa'id*, or legal principles or maxims. Kamali (1991, 2–6) is at pains to stress that the maxims of *fiqh* are categorically different from the *usul al-fiqh*. The latter comprises the system of rules of interpretation of the sources and deal with the practice of human reasoning (*ijtihad*) which leads to the detailed rules and judgements which make up the *fiqh*. The maxims are part of the *fiqh* and 'refer to a body of abstract rules …' which 'consist of theoretical guidelines in the different areas of *fiqh* such as evidence, transactions, matrimonial law, etc.' (Kamali, 1991, 5). Some 200 such maxims have been collected, and many of them were incorporated into the first section of the Ottoman law code, the *Mecelleh*, promulgated in the period 1869–76, which remains part of the legal foundations of a number of Arab states today. Typical examples of legal maxims would be:

    - acts are judged by their intentions
    - when the receiving of something is forbidden, giving it is also forbidden.

Maxims have received less attention in recent research than has the study of *maqasid* (but see al-'Amiri, 2003), but what they have in common, even if they are, as Kamali insists, categorically distinct, is that they are an attempt to identify some common methods or principles which allow the jurist to discern some order or degree of system in a field which is in danger of becoming unpredictable or chaotic if it is left to theologians, such as those of the Ash'ari school, who reject any search for principle in the divine will, or legal literalists such as those of the Zahiri school, which has not survived.

So far this discussion has sought to keep within the bounds of the Shari'a discourse. Some modernists would say that this approach will always have its limitations, and that only by breaking out of what they regard as a straitjacket, even if it may feel spacious, can the Muslim world move forward. Bassam Tibi represents basically a secularist, if not *laïcist*, view (Tibi, 2002 and 2005). Muhammad Arkoun from a philosophical angle calls for a radical new approach to understanding the revealed text (Arkoun, 1994), while Nasr Hamid Abu Zayd calls for the same but via the disciplines of historical and literary criticism (Abu Zayd, 2006). Here the basic question is to what extent techniques and disciplines can be successfully imported from outside the tradition, especially from the West – but that is equally a question which cannot be answered without resort to political, economic and social analysis.

What I am interested in here is the extent to which renewal and reform are possible from within the tradition. I would argue that this limitation is not just an intellectual exercise. For historical, cultural, social and political reasons it seems reasonable to suggest that arguments coming from within the tradition are much more likely to carry weight among ordinary practising Muslims than are arguments based on imported techniques and disciplines, at least until such time as the political, institutional and demographic balances in the Muslim world may have changed radically from what they at present. Even in Europe, where one might expect that the depth of the encounter between Muslim populations and Western traditions and structures would lead to a process of broad fusion, the resilience and flexibility of aspects of Muslim cultural traditions is a source of regular surprise to expert observers (see Menski, 2008, 43).

Let me take one frequently controversial example: the place of women. The position of women is one the currently most contested topics in Muslim societies, both in outsiders' approaches to Islam as well as among Muslims themselves. A number of well-known writers have sought to move the debate forward: in the Arab world women like Nawal Saadawi, Leila Ahmad and Fatima Mernissi, and in North America, Aminah Wadud. On the other hand, the Islamic faculties of universities in the Arab world continue to teach traditional views, views which in some social sectors are increasingly regarded as stifling if not irrelevant. Such traditional views are particularly difficult for educated young professional women to accept (see e.g. Droeber, 2005). This is especially the case among the recently immigrated Muslim communities in Europe and North America. Here, Anne Sofie Roald argues that there are two cultural patterns which can be identified, namely what she calls the 'Arab cultural base pattern' and the 'Western cultural base pattern'. She has broadly defined 'these two cultural patterns as the *patriarchal* versus the *equality* pattern respectively' (Roald, 2001, 295). She relates a move among Muslim thinkers in Europe towards the latter directly to the experience of interacting with a European context but provides an Islamic justification by reference to the legitimacy in the jurisprudential tradition (*usul al-fiqh*) of local custom (*'urf*) as a source of permitted Islamic practice, a view which has been particularly strong in the Hanafi tradition (former Ottoman regions, Central and South Asia) and in the Maliki tradition (North Africa and parts of the Arabian Gulf):

> As *'urf* is an acceptable legal concept in the broader Islamic law … I believe that European *'urf* which are compatible with Islamic principles might, in the creation of a 'minority *fiqh*' in European society, be accorded a strong position on a conscious level as well. (Roald, 2001, 296)

Other researchers have sought from within the Islamic tradition to discover possible Islamic conceptions of the position of women alternative to the traditional. A basic argument which is often made in this discussion is that the traditional position, as laid down in the classical textbooks of *fiqh*, represents male elaborations of Qur'an and Sunna in a social and political environment in which male superiority was taken for granted. It is against such tradition that writers like Ahmad, Mernissi, Wadud and others suggest alternative approaches.

That it is possible to make a radical break with the past, purely from within the traditions of Islamic sciences and without reference to modern disciplines such as sociology or psychology is illustrated by a PhD study completed in 2004 (Fino, 2004). The key text in Dr Fino's analysis is in Surah 4:34:

> Al-rijal qawwamun 'ala al-nisa′ bi-ma faddala Allah ba'dahum 'ala ba'd wa-bi-ma anfaqu min amwalihim …

This verse has traditionally been cited to reinforce the claims of traditional Muslim scholars that male social pre-eminence is divinely ordained, as is reflected in most commonly used English translations:

> Men are in charge of women, because Allah hath made the one of them excel the other, and because they spend of their property (for the support of women) … (Qur'an, 1930)

> Men have authority over women because Allah has made the one superior to the other, and because they spend their wealth to maintain them. (Qur'an, 1966, 360)

> Men are the ones who support women since God has given some persons advantages over others, and because they spend their wealth [on them]. (Qur'an, 1979, 202)

> Men are the managers of the affairs of women for that God has preferred in bounty one of them over the other, and for that they have expended of their property. (Qur'an, 1955, 105)

> Men are the protectors
> And maintainers of women,
> Because Allah has given
> The one more (strength)
> Than the other, and because
> They support them
> From their means. (Qur'an, 1411 AH, 219)

However, a recent and increasingly widely used translation, that of Abdel Haleem, takes a different approach:

> Husbands should take good care of their wives, with [the bounties] God has

> given to some more than others and with what they spend out of their own money. (Qur'an, 2004, 54)

Fino's own translation is similar:

> Men shall take full care of women with the bounties (with) which God has favoured some of them more abundantly than others, and what they may spend of their own wealth … (Fino, 2004, 96)

It is in her analysis of the passage that Fino becomes interesting. She starts by asserting that the verse does not have to be normative, as it has traditionally been read. It can be descriptive, which would mean that the social fact that men usually controlled the economic resources at the time of the revelation is that which alone gives them the upper hand. By reading the whole of the Qur'anic text she then reaches two further conclusions. Firstly, the 'superiority' (*qawwama*) of the traditional interpretations, when it exists, cannot be unrestrained. Nowhere in the Qur'an is any divine favour unlimited and unconditional. Secondly, taken as a whole, the Qur'an is clear, she says, about equality between men and women – this is the divine intention (*maqsad*, pl. *maqasid*). To support this she refers to the many verses which explicitly place male and female believers on the same level, such as 9:71–2, 24:12, 33:35 and 71:28. She then proceeds to argue that the divine intention of such equality could not be achieved within the period of revelation – the society of the Hijaz was not ready for it – but the direction is clearly pointed out in the measures which the Qur'an indicates: men's right to dispose freely over women as chattel is abolished; limits to polygamy are imposed both in numbers and in conditionality; a preference for monogamy is explicit (referring to Qur. 4:129); and inheritance and public rights are asserted where none existed before.

Reforms initiated by the revelation take place, if necessary, in gradual steps, as in the prohibition of alcohol which took place in three stages before the full ban was revealed. This process of progression is called *tadarruj*. Where Fino goes further than most is when she argues that those steps do not stop with the end of the revelation. They can continue beyond along the path already pointed out. As an example she points to slavery, a status socially and legally analogous to that of women in the Hijaz and in the Qur'an in the sense that the position of both prior to the revelation was fully subject to the whim of the owner in the one case and the husband or male guardian in the other. In both cases the Qur'an sought to limit and regulate and made it clear that the remains of the traditional practices were the subject of divine displeasure. Today slavery has been accepted as illegitimate by the vast majority of scholars and countries (for a detailed discussion see Clarence-Smith, 2006), and there should be no theological reason why similarly the position of women cannot be advanced beyond the restrictions of the Qur'anic text.

None of the intellectual techniques used by Fino in constructing her argument are new in Islamic terms, and many of her conclusions are shared by thinkers across the Islamic spectrum. It is the combination of these various techniques into a cohesive argument from within the Islamic intellectual tradition which is unusual. The question remains, of course, what impact this will have in the realities of everyday life, and again the answer cannot be other than that this depends less on the strength of the argument than on the social, cultural, economic and political circumstances.

Islam Comes to Europe – Does the Shari'a?

When we turn our attention to Europe, such circumstances become a crucial dimension of our analysis (for detail see Maréchal et al., 2003). A characteristic of the immigration into western Europe which took off during the 1960s and 1970s was that the immigrants overwhelmingly came from the countryside: villages and small provincial towns. Their background was mostly agricultural, and the educational level tended to be poor with a high rate of illiteracy, especially among women. In fact, this stage of the immigration was but a minor dimension of the remarkable immigration from countryside to city which was and still is taking place throughout the developing world (Clarke, 1980; Hershlag, 1979; UNDP, 2002, 45f.). But Bergen, Birmingham and Brussels are different from Karachi, Cairo and Ankara. The mere move from village to city has driven changes which have found expression in economic and political but also in religious terms. But the move to European cities represents also a move to a world in which religion as such was moving to the margins in the peculiarly European process of secularization. And what religion there was in the public space, whether implicit in culture and discourse or explicit in institutionalized civic and state religion, was not Islam but some form of Christianity.

It was the process of family reunion which brought Islam into Europe. Before that the mainly male single migrant workers had had little practical connection with their culture and religion. It was as if this was being taken care of by the family back home on their behalf. The arrival of wives and children was initially provoked by the closing of the gates of labour migration, in Britain from 1962 and in mainland Europe in response to the recession sparked by the oil crisis of 1972–4. With the family came the full panoply of cultural traditions increasingly expressed in Islamic terms, especially around the encounters with European public services in connection with childbirth, women's health and children's education. Here was the motivation for local communities to establish places of worship and facilities for bringing children up in the basic tenets of Islam in so-called Qur'an schools. Communities often brought in their own imams according to their traditional expectations of an imam, so many of these were seriously undereducated and had no experience and few resources for providing guidance to their congregations in an environment which bore no resemblance to what they were used to.

Soon Islamic movements and their organizations saw the needs – and the opportunities. Coming from the countries of origin, it was often movements which had grown up in opposition to European colonial powers and to European cultural and educational dominance that were best placed to join the migration. From the Indian subcontinent it was movements such as Deoband, Jama'at-i-islami and Tablighi Jamaat, and from North Africa movements which had grown out of the Muslim Brotherhood. In the case of Turks the situation was different. Here there was a distinct rivalry between the movements which had emerged in opposition to the secular state, movements such as the Nursis and the Milli Görüş, on the one hand, and, on the other, the structures sponsored by the Diyanet, the government's religious affairs department.

For many Muslims in those early phases, it was probably in their encounters with other Muslims from different backgrounds that the realization dawned that seeking refuge in Islam as a source of reassurance and identity in the face of all this strangeness was problematical. One of my first research students in Birmingham, at the end of the 1970s, reported an incident in a mosque where she had asked a group of men about Muslim expectations of burial. Quickly the discussion degenerated into an internal argument about two different ways of burying a body, both of which were claiming authority in the Qur'an. It turned out that the men came from two distinct districts of Pakistan, and each was seeking to explain their own custom in Islamic terms. The Qur'an has nothing to say about how to perform a burial. The whole complex of customs was in this way open to internal challenge. Muslims needed to find out more about their own faith tradition because of the new situation they found themselves in.

In this process it was the younger people, and especially the women, who had the strongest motivation to push ahead. They also increasingly had the personal experience and the intellectual skills learned as they grew through European school systems. Their own personal priorities challenged them to explore what was essential to being a Muslim, to seek for practices and ways of living which were functional in the European environment, and in the process to determine what of their parents' culture was non-essential. They entered into a process of stripping the essence of Islam of its local cultural accretions and re-clothing it in ways which made sense in their new environment.

But this process does not mean that there is one way forward. Different people follow different paths for a complex variety of reasons. A decade ago I suggested six possible routes young people might take (Nielsen, 1997, 139):

1. *random retaliation*, representing the disaffected youth moving into youth gangs and criminality;
2. *collective isolation*, in which communities find protection in collective retrenchment;
3. *limited participation*, preserving a separation between participation in economic life but preserving cultural tradition in the private sphere;
4. *high-profile separation*, in which tradition is maintained within the community but active collective participation takes place outside;

5. *high-profile integration*, seeking visible participation in public life while also critically reviewing the Muslim tradition as it affects religion and cultural tradition;
6. *aggressive action*, whose purpose is to change society towards an Islamic model.

Young Muslims are faced with a number of ready-made paths on offer from various parts of the Muslim world, a range of choices from the rejection of Hizb al-Tahrir or the violence of al-Qa'ida at one end to this at the other:

> a new and constructive posture which relies on a fine comprehension of Islam's priorities, a clear vision of what is absolute, definitively fixed and what is subject to change and adaptation and, finally, on an appropriate understanding of the Western environment. The objective being to shape a European-Islamic identity out of the crisis. Before disputing the secondary aspects of Islamic legislation, it was thus imperative to protect the five elements constituting maqasid ash-Shari'a: namely, Religion, life, intellect, lineage and property. (Ramadan, 1999, 101)

And one should not forget that substantial numbers simply want to be left in peace to get on with their lives!

To analyse the processes being reviewed here it might, in fact, be more helpful to put aside, at least for the time being, the temptation to develop typologies of the kind just discussed – the processes are simply too complex and fluid to fit neatly into any such system. Instead it could be more helpful to identify the fields of contestation as a number of distinct spectra with no prior expectations as to how those fields interrelate and interact. Different individuals, organizations or movements are likely to place themselves at different points between each of these contested pairs, and it cannot be taken for granted that the location in one pair is predictive of the location on another. Such fields of contestation should probably include the following, but others may be added:

1. *Understanding of text*, especially Qur'an and Hadith, but also other texts which may be imbued with special authority by particular groups. Are such texts to be understood literally and is their authority unquestioned, or can they be interpreted with reference to current needs, and do current needs require the reinterpretation of the nature of their authority? It may be more useful to consider this as two interrelated fields of contestation, namely one referring to interpretation of the text and the other to do with the nature of its authority.
2. *Priority of principles or specifics*: In the process of interpretation and the ordering of ethics and daily life, are choices made with reference to some basic principles, or is the focus on a large number of specific rules?

3. *The role of tradition/heritage*: What is the function of the accumulated tradition in relation to contemporary needs? How far does it offer an authoritative base line for choices and how far can it be ignored?
4. *Tension between the individual and the collective*: In any given issue or movement what is the balance between the authority of a particular individual or group of individuals and that of the larger community, however defined, and how large is the space within which individuals are free to make their own choices?
5. *Global versus local priorities of reference*: This will clearly consider the degree to which global principles and priorities can be adapted or even give way to local perceptions of authority and needs but also how far local experience and priorities will impact on the global.
6. *Essence versus cultural relativity* entails some complex considerations of definitions of culture and its relationship with religion in terms of both ideas and practice, and this field may, on further thought, have to be deconstructed into more than one.

On closer examination it may, for example, emerge that in the case of some intellectual movements that the fields of contestation are nested within each other in such a way that the movement's teaching may place it towards one end of a line while the place of the individual within such a movement may be closer to the other end. This might be a movement whose teachings take a relatively liberal view of authoritative traditions but whose individual members are bound comparatively tightly by the views currently adopted by the leadership.

A reading of the chapters in this volume shows the usefulness of such an approach to analysing specific collations of ideas. If this were applied to the two broad tendencies discussed in Chapter 3 by Afsaruddin, namely the 'modernists' and the 'hardline Islamists', the following analysis could be suggested. The 'modernists' tend towards interpretative flexibility, give priority to the application of principles, are ready to challenge tradition, give more space for individual intellectual activity, appear to be balanced between global and local perspectives, as also between essential teachings and the cultural milieu. The 'hardline Islamists', on the other hand, tend towards a literal interpretation of the foundational texts, are selective as between certain deduced principles and a focus on particular specifics, often strongly challenge the tradition, tend to prefer the primacy of the interests of the collective, prioritize global perspectives and reject adaptation to local cultural milieux.

A similar exercise can be conducted in the European environment with reference to, for example, Tariq Oubrou as discussed by Crone in Chapter 10 or Mohamed Kamal Mostafa as discussed by Madsen in Chapter 15 of this volume. Oubrou interprets the text flexibly with a preference for a focus on principles, but he also lends some weight to the authority of the *'ulama'* and the tradition of the Hanafi *madhhab*. This implies a balance between the interests of the individual and of the collective, but this has to be achieved in practice within a French context and with reference to the French cultural environment. Kamal differs markedly. He adheres more closely to the text within the traditional bounds of interpretation, is more focused on the specifics than on general principles. In his view the authority of the *'ulama'* seems to be central, and the freedom for individual interpretation limited. He sees the law (*fiqh*) as a global Islamic entity which can make only limited reference to local cultures. Neither of these two fit neatly into the more general classifications of 'modernist' or 'hardline Islamist'.

The approach clearly needs refining, but the point is that it is flexible and therefore can be refined and adapted. The key advantage, however, is that it makes space for the sometimes sharp variations of approach within apparently common trends, variations which tends otherwise to be marginalized or suppressed by most conventional systems of categorization. It therefore also makes space for a more refined contextualization of the narrower and more focused analyses which specialist observers of such movements and individuals engage in, so the scholar who is primarily interested in the Qur'anic understanding of a particular movement's discourse is not forced into a taxonomy determined by, for example, attitudes to political activism.

PART 1
An Encounter of Legal Theories

Chapter 2
Clarity or Confusion – Classical *Fiqh* and the Issue of Logic

Mona Siddiqui

Many years ago when I was embarking on my doctoral studies, my late supervisor Norman Calder pointed out that logic and humour were central aspects of *fiqh*. Inherent in the literary style of these vast complex texts was a play on words and ideas that had its own life force. At the time I had no idea what he meant. My own thesis looked at the juristic approach to marriage laws as compiled in the Hanafi collection *al-Fatawa al-Alamgiri*.[1] I had embarked on this study with little more than a personal knowledge of what a Muslim wedding was and presumed that the law would present the written account of the practice with which I was already culturally familiar. I realized immediately how wrong I was. Even as I tried to understand the concept of *nikah*, it took some time to fully comprehend how its literal meaning of 'intercourse' unravelled into the complexities of the juristic notion of 'contract'. Marriage laws did not talk about love, companionship or honour but sexual status, affinity and financial rights. This was further complicated with the growing awareness that many of the institutions within the law of marriage had conceptual and linguistic similarities to the Islamic law of sale. Not only could contracts be valid or invalid, they could also be defective, i.e. neither valid nor void, determining some rights but not others. In all of these contractual variances, sexual intercourse between a man and woman triggered off various changes in status and obligation of payments. It gradually emerged that what I was really exploring in *fiqh* was a process, a process of thinking about the marital contract rather than the nature of marriage itself.

Such revelations, as they were for me, necessitated a dramatic shift in my approach to much of Islamic practice and to the study of *fiqh*. The study of this work was not a study of a concise illustration of simple religious rules and principles which is a modernist vision of law – in fact there were hardly any principles. *Fiqh* was first and foremost a process of reasoning, and to study it carefully, it was

1 The *Fatawa Alamgiri* is also known as the *Fatawa Hindiyya* and was compiled under the patronage of the emperor Aurangzeb during the years 1664–72. Aurangzeb had appointed a team of scholars to put together a collection of legal opinions with the aim of achieving an authoritative body of Hanafi law. Shaykh Nizam Burhanpur was the chief jurist and this chapter uses the 1973 edition published in six volumes in Beirut. The quotes are taken from *kitab al-nikah* and references will be made to the book in this chapter.

important to see both the individual piety and the literary ingenuity contained within the text. The study of *fiqh* is a way of exploring the religion through the dimension of literature, more specifically legal literature.

The tradition of *fiqh* holds a prominent place in Islamic literature and the development of Muslim thought because it was within the creation of this literature that many pious and learned Muslim scholars found self-realization. Historically, it was the creative aspect of legal thinking which made the literary output so extensive. Writing was about thinking and rethinking and books were the end product of the process of expounding rules and laws. They revealed the literary skills involved in presenting legal values through the process of juristic speculation.

In tracing the history of *fiqh*, it would be fair to say that the process by which the words of the early Islamic scholars acquired written form is still relatively unknown, and the original formulation of the genre in its written form may remain elusive. While several Western scholars locate the formation of the four Sunni schools of law (*madhahib*) to around the middle of the 8th century, it still remains unclear when the schools of law emerged as distinct schools with their distinctly transmitted doctrines. But it appears that the use of *taqlid*, speaking on the authority of a previous jurist, became the main stylistic methodology of *fiqh*. This meant that jurists of individual schools had to write according to the particular literary disciplines of their schools despite spatial and temporal difference. There were two methods by which the views of different writers from various eras were united. One was through the exploration of those problems which each generation of jurists inherited from its ancestors; the study of these cases meant that certain concepts and rulings were revived constantly, thereby maintaining a continuity of thought. The other was through the process of citing past authorities. George Makdisi has used this premise to explain why only four schools remained, claiming that a school of law died out when it had no more advocates practising *taqlid* (Makdisi, 1981, 4f.). The major stylistic differences between the schools appear to rest on their respective uses of Hadith reports or *ra'y*, personal opinion. In his study of the origins of the four Sunni schools, Melchert concludes:

> At the beginning of the ninth century, Muslim jurisprudents had not clearly divided themselves amongst the Hanafiyah, the Malikiyah and the Shafi`iyah, but rather between the adherents of *ra'y* and the adherents of *hadith*. Mutual suspicions ran deep: the adherents of *ra'y* doubted whether the adherents of *hadith* were competent to make out the divine law, the adherents of *hadith* doubted even whether the adherents of *ra'y* were proper Muslims. (Melchert, 1997, 198)

Whether the jurists relied on Hadith or *ra'y*, the written law became a body of literature that reflected both doctrine and practice. Law is not only illustrative of the legal norms of a culture but provides an insight into those very ideas and institutions which a civilization accepts and those which it rejects. When the law is also a reflection of a faith, its study becomes even more challenging, for the social, legal and religious dimensions become inextricably intertwined. *Fiqh* is the result of both religious piety and literary ingenuity. In their writing of *fiqh*, the jurists used language for the purpose of stamping conduct with approval or disapproval. I would contest whether the jurists had the intention of creating any desired social order. But the texts do more than just reflect desirable or undesirable behaviour; they reveal the interaction between Islamic religious values, how they determine legal principles and how these principles subsequently formulate their own life forms. In the end the law responds to its own structures. The preservation of diverse but related viewpoints on a single issue is a careful construction of pushing a single argument to its logical limits. Here the analysis of the hypothetical and the real carry equal significance. The methodology, however, aims to highlight the principle by such an excessive use of logical reasoning that clarity often gives way to confusion. The purpose of the written text is not to formulate a body of concise rules but to open the debate to exploration. In this chapter, I have taken a selection of examples from different areas of law to illustrate this stylistic feature of *fiqh*.

The works cited here are what I call 'mature' works which appeared after the 11th century, the refined and defined end products of the different *madhahib* or schools. They appeared after decades of deliberation about recension, canonization and what constituted legal authority and legal principles.

Marriage Contract and Verbal Formalism

The word *'aqd* literally means an obligation or an agreement binding two parties but in legal works has assumed a precise and more technical meaning of contract. However, there is no discussion of this concept of *'aqd* with reference to marriage and as Chehata points out, any theoretical discussion of the word 'contract' is absent from *fiqh* works in general:

> La Notion generale de contrat n'a jamais fait l'object, dans les ouvrages de doctrine, d'une theorie generale. (Chehata, 1971, 157)

The closest we get to a definition of the word *'aqd* to denote marriage is contained in the *Fath al-Qadir*:

> The intention of a contract is completion, whether it be a marriage contract or otherwise, comprising the offer of one of the two speakers followed by the acceptance of the other. (Ibn al-Humam, 1970, 187)

The manner whereby the marriage contract comes into effect is primarily through a verbal agreement. Hanafi works explore in some detail the words and expressions which can constitute a marriage contract:

> *Nikah* takes effect with offer and acceptance where both are expressed in the past or where one of them is expressed in the past and the other in another tense in the future, like the imperative or the imperfect according to the *Nahr al-Fa'iq*. (*al-Fatawa al-Alamgiri*, 1973, 270)

The agreement reached as a result assumes *a priori* the significance of 'performative utterances' where to say something is to do something (Austin, 1975, 6–7). Acceptance of the marriage contract can be declared by either the man or the woman as long as the acceptance is made in the past tense. If the words used for marriage imply a future sense then the contract is not valid. However, a contract which is *mu'allaq* is one which is dependent on a condition which may or may not be in the future. In such a marriage if the condition has not yet been met and refers to an action or event in the future, the contract would be invalid. If however the dependence is on an event already passed, the contract is considered valid. Certainty is the central issue so that the marriage contract becomes legally effective when the set of words expresses perfection rather than intention of deed. A curious example of this is taken from *al-Nahr al-Fa'iq:*

> Hence if a person whose daughter has been asked in marriage should falsely inform the applicant that he has already married her to someone and say, 'If I had not married her to him, I would have married her to your son.' In such a case, if the father of the son should accept in the presence of witnesses and it should subsequently transpire that the daughter had not been married to anyone, the marriage would be valid. (*al-Fatawa al-Alamgiri*, 1973, 272)

As the daughter has not actually been married to anyone else, the condition becomes irrelevant and the contract acquires validity because of the declaration in the past tense and the subsequent acceptance by the other party in the presence of witnesses. Here, neither the intention nor the reasoning behind the father's words are taken into account; what matters is to present an example that shows how the tense and sequence of the words uttered allow for a marriage contract to be initiated and concluded.

The formalism of a verbal contract demands distinction between a reply and a promise. Thus if a man asks a woman 'Do you give yourself to be my wife for a thousand dirhams?' and she replies, 'I hear and obey,' the contract is valid. But if she says, 'I am grateful to you', the *nikah* is not valid. The reason is that whereas the first is a reply the second is merely a promise. As promise implies future time, the contract cannot be legally valid.

For the Hanafis, if marriage was not constituted by the use of words which clearly expressed marriage such as *nikah or tazwij*, marriage could also be constituted by the use of words which denoted the creation of immediate ownership or possession in the substance of a thing. The notion of ownership contains vestiges of a concept that has its roots in pre-Islamic society in which it appears that captivity was an important concept of marriage. Robertson Smith provides an interesting discussion on the issue of purchase in Arab marriages stating that marriage by capture preceded marriage by contract. He explains that the subjection of Arab women to their husbands was regarded by the Arabs as 'virtual captivity', and that marriage originated in bondage (Smith, 1885, 81–5). In incorporating words of ownership to convey the marital contract, the Hanafis show an acceptance of vocabulary that reflected the varying concepts of matrimony throughout social history.

Logic demanded that this concept had to be present in a language other than Arabic, e.g. Persian:

> A man and a woman say in front of two witnesses in Persian, 'We are husband and wife', the *nikah* is not valid. If he says, 'This is my wife,' and she says, 'This is my husband,' and there has not actually been a *nikah* preceding this, then the learned are disagreed upon this matter. According to the Zahiriyya, what is correct is that no marriage will take place. (*al-Fatawa al-Alamgiri*, 1973, 272)

It would seem that the dispute arises as a result of the possessive pronouns which imply that both the man and the woman 'belong to each other.' Therefore, technically there does not need to be a formal declaration of offer and acceptance, as possession or ownership is implied in a choice of words which satisfies the verbal demands of the contract. On this basis there are two ways of confirming the *nikah*: the decision of the *qadi* is the first option and, secondly, if the man and the woman answer in the affirmative to the following question by the witness, 'Did you make this contract?'. This shows that a mutual agreement expressed in front of witnesses has the force of transforming an assumed marital status into a legally valid marriage contract; the *qadi*'s authority is only optional, not obligatory.

It is a curious phenomenon of the marriage contract that despite its verbal formalism, the addition of words which imply a condition to the contract does not affect the validity of the declaration; the conditional element is quite simply ignored. In Hanafi law, neither the man nor the woman has the right to put forward conditions in the marriage contract on the assumption that if the conditions are not met, they have the option of rescinding the contract. If a condition is stated then the contract remains valid, only the condition becomes void. The only exception to this rule is if the husband is physically incapable of consummating the marriage, i.e. he is either a eunuch or impotent. Since the legitimization of sexual intercourse is the principle objective of marriage, any impediment to this provides adequate grounds for the annulment of the contract.

Issues of *Mahr*

Although there are several forms of separation in Islamic law, death and divorce are the most commonly cited for the discussion of legal and financial consequences. *Talaq*, which is any form of separation initiated by the husband, is problematic as there are various forms of divorce. Furthermore, divorce before consummation may have financial implications, especially in relation to *mahr*.[2] The problem cited in most of the Hanafi works is that, if divorce takes place before consummation, the woman is entitled to only half the *mahr*:

> Objection – it would appear here that the whole dower should of right drop because the object of the contract reverts to the woman untouched, the same as in sale, where the whole price drops if the buyer and seller break off the contract.
>
> Reply – There are two analogical conclusions applicable to the subject. First what is cited in the above objection; secondly it would appear that the whole dower is due because the husband did not make use of this possession but suffered it to pass from him untouched of his own choice. (Hamilton, 1989, 44)

Both stances are logical conclusions emerging from the essential premise of the contract which contains the element of transfer and possession. Yet a further question is raised in the *Hidaya* regarding a castrated eunuch who retires with his wife and then divorces her. *Khalwa*, or valid privacy between husband and wife, usually necessitates payment of *mahr* on the assumption that consummation could have taken place. Here the problem lies with the fact that the man is castrated and therefore does not have the wherewithal needed for intercourse (Hamilton, 1989, 128). While his two disciples, Abu Yusuf and al-Shaybani, maintain that only half the dower is payable to the woman, analogous to a wife being divorced when there has been no consummation, Abu Hanifa disagrees:

> All that is due on the part of the woman is the delivery of her person and this being to the extent of her ability, completely performed, it follows that the consideration is completely due to her. (Hamilton, 1989, 129)

The logic of both arguments stands but no overall preference is stated. *Fiqh* allows for either of the two conclusions to be drawn and no moral superiority is attached to the respective views.

The following case presents issues related to both *mahr* and affinity:

> Two brothers marry, one of them marries a woman, the other marries her mother. Each of them is taken to the husband of the other and intercourse takes place in both cases. Abu Yusuf says that each woman becomes absolutely separated from her husband and each husband is liable to his wife for half the *mahr* and to the woman with whom he has had intercourse for her *'uqr* (compensation paid to a

2 *Mahr* is the sum of money or gift owed by a husband to his wife. It becomes binding on the husband in every valid contract of marriage, whether or not it has been expressly mentioned at the time of the contract.

> woman with whom intercourse took place by mistake). Moreover it will not be lawful for either of them after this to marry his own wife. However, the husband of the mother may marry her daughter with whom he has had intercourse though the husband of the daughter may not marry her mother. (*al-Fatawa al-Alamgiri*, 1973, 325)

At first reading this case seems like an improbable, indeed absurd situation but the issue here is the discussion of legal impediments to marriage. Islamic law prohibits certain marriages on the grounds of affinity. Both men will not be able to marry their wives since he who married the mother had intercourse with the daughter and therefore cannot remarry the mother; he who married the daughter had intercourse with the mother and cannot marry the daughter again. Prohibition of marriage becomes established by intercourse with the woman with whom he had intercourse. The interesting exception to this is that a man may marry the descendant of a wife with whom marriage has not been consummated. Thus, the husband of the mother may marry her daughter with whom he had intercourse because the legal ruling is that a woman's daughter becomes unlawful not by mere marriage with the woman but by intercourse with her. As regards the *mahr*, each of the wives would be entitled to half the *mahr* since separation took place before intercourse with the wives (Siddiqui, 1995).

Intoxicants in Islamic Law

The prohibition of the consumption of intoxicants, specifically alcohol, has always been a definitive marker of the Islamic faith. Despite some variances in practice, it is generally understood that the practising Muslim should not drink alcohol. Over the last few years there has also been a growing emphasis also on abstaining from food products which may contain even traces of alcohol. Yet a close look at *fiqh* texts shows that the jurists were more concerned with the definition of an intoxicant rather than the moral defect implied in its consumption and the appropriate punishment. The lengthy discussions around intoxicants and the state of being intoxicated was complex and carried legal consequences. The following extract is a paraphrase of an argument taken from Ibn Rushd's *Bidayat al-Mujtahid* from the Book of Foods and Beverages (Siddiqui, 2007).

With respect to *khamr* (i.e. drink derived from grape juice) they agreed about its prohibition in small or large quantities, I mean that which is derived from grape juice. In the case of the other intoxicating beverages they disagreed about a small quantity that does not intoxicate. They agreed that the amount which intoxicates is prohibited. The majority of the jurists of Hijaz as well as the majority of the traditionalists maintained that small and large quantities of intoxicating liquor are prohibited. The Iraqis – Abu Hanifa and all the remaining jurists of Kufa as well as the majority of jurists of Basra – maintained that what is prohibited in all the remaining drinks (that is, besides wines derived from grape juice) is intoxication itself and not the substance of the drink. The reason for their disagreement springs from the conflict of traditions and analogies on the issue. The first is through the traditions laid down on the issue. The second is by designating all the intoxicating drinks in their totality by the name *khamr.* One of the best known traditions that the jurists of Hijaz used as evidence is, 'The Messenger of Allah was asked about *bita'* (wine from honey and dates) and *nabidh* from honey and he said, "Any drink that intoxicates is prohibited."' There is also the tradition: 'Every intoxicant is *khamr* and each *khamr* is prohibited' and a third tradition: 'If something intoxicates in a large quantity its small quantity is prohibited'.

The second argument is that all drinks are called *khamr* in the legal sense. They argued for this on the basis of a tradition that the Messenger of Allah said, '*Khamr* is from grapes, *khamr* is from honey, *khamr* is from raisins, *khamr* is from wheat and I forbid you from using all intoxicants'.

The Kufans rely on the apparent meaning: 'And of the fruits of the date palm, and grapes, whence you derive strong drink, *sakar* and good nourishment.' They argue that *sakar* is an intoxicant and if it had been prohibited in its substance, God would not have designated it as good nourishment.

Such passages are concerned with the extent of the debate around an issue which in popular Islam usually receives only one assessment, which is that all intoxicants are completely forbidden. Indeed the word *haram* is used to convey the stringency of prohibition, though the Qur'an does not use this term. Despite the relative ambivalence towards alcohol in the Qur'an, legal works looked at all the possible meanings and effects of any pronouncement. Even with the use of varying *hadith* reports, *fiqh* had to deal with the formal structure of the arguments not just the jurist's own leaning towards any particular position. Ibn Rushd builds a very careful argument on both sides but does lean in the end towards the complete prohibition of anything which intoxicates either in small or large quantities. This is partially in keeping with *hadith* reports and early commentaries which saw wine and all intoxicants as having the capacity to corrupt both personal piety and proper social behaviour. Consumption of wine was not just considered profligate behaviour for which repentance had to be sought, but both drinking and the state of intoxication eventually came to be regarded as ritually impure and ultimately a crime against God. However, a careful legal distinction had to be maintained between the intake of alcohol and the state of inebriety. The issue at hand is that alcohol affects the legal capacity of a person. Thus, are the prayers held behind an intoxicated imam valid, and is the smell of alcohol on a person enough evidence for the application of the *hadd* punishment? Such are the dominant concerns of the jurists. How relevant these issues were socially is, however, not discussed.

Yet it is perfectly clear that this kind of reasoning can lead to a variety of conclusions about permissible behaviour. In the Book of Purification in the *Bidayat* it is related that Abu Hanifa uses a *hadith* from Ibn Abbas to permit ritual ablutions with *nabidh*. *Nabidh* is a problematic drink in legal texts because it understood both as a fermented drink popular amongst the Arabs and also as a nourishing fruit drink. In the tradition, whilst on a journey, the Prophet tells Ibn Mas'ud to pour out the *nabidh* he has in his container to perform the ablutions because *nabidh* is 'a drink and purifying'. This view is problematic for Ibn Rushd and he claims weak transmission of the *hadith* and doubt over the likelihood of Ibn Mas'ud being with the Prophet on this occasion to be two of the reasons why this *hadith* and therefore the permissibility of *nabidh* should be rejected. Ibn Rushd uses Qur'an 4:43, 'And if you do not find water then take resort in clean soil/dust passing lightly over your face and your hands', to argue that the majority saw ablutions as being permissible only with water or clean soil. But equally interesting is the point made that all the disciples of Abu Hanifa and all the other jurists of the regions opposed this opinion by Abu Hanifa.

What we are therefore left with in such arguments is the question of relevance. While we may contest the tension between law and practice, my concern is not whether *nabidh* was actually used to perform ablutions, but rather how relevant was this debate then and how relevant is this kind of debate today? While varying evidence allows for different perspectives on the use of *nabidh*, how important is this kind of reasoning for the ordinary Muslim who sees all intoxicants as prohibited for both internal and external use? How can that which is legally impure or about which there is doubt, purify? Both Muslim discourse and popular perceptions of Muslim law is that it is definitive and concise, that *fiqh* is Shari'a and has the objective of setting strict moral boundaries. But I would argue that much of *fiqh* was simply not concerned with setting moral boundaries of behaviour but with exploring possible boundaries of argumentation.

'Aqiqa

While much of Muslim ritual practice is regarded as a reflection of faith and piety, emulation of prophetic deeds or implementation of divine mandates, some subject matters yield surprising results when analysed in the *fiqh* debates. One such area is that of *'aqiqa* or the sacrifice given for newborn babies. In the *Bidaya*, Ibn Rushd lays out an extensive analysis of different opinions of the various rites associated with *'aqiqa* but he begins the discussion:

> With regard to its *hukm* (legal category), a group of jurists including the Zahirites maintained that it is obligatory. The majority of jurists say that it is a *sunna* (recommended). Abu Hanifa says that it is neither an obligation nor a *sunna* and it is said that in his view in the end, it is voluntary.

The *hadith* which is the basis for this difference of opinion is quoted in the *Bidaya*, wherein the Prophet says, 'I do not like disobedience, and he to whom a child is born if he wishes to perform the rite for it, he may do so' (Ibn Rushd, 1992, 568). As this implies both recommendation and permissibility, those who understood these words as a recommendation, said that *'aqiqa* is a *sunna*, while those who understood it as permissibility said that *'aqiqa* is neither a *sunna* nor an obligation. There is disagreement over every issue of *'aqiqa*, though it is recognised as a *nusuk* or sacrifice. Two conflicting *hadith*s pose the question: How many sheep or rams are to be sacrificed? Ibn Abbas related that the Prophet offered one ram each for his grandsons but he is also reported to have said, 'For a girl it is one sheep and for a boy two' (Ibn Rushd, 1992, 568). Though the majority of jurists claim that the *'aqiqa* is to be offered for every newborn infant, male and female, al-Hasan deviated and said that the *'aqiqa* is not to be performed for the girl. The *hadith* used for this view is, 'Each boy (*ghulam*) is held in pledge for his *'aqiqa*' (Ibn Rushd, 1992, 568). While some jurists allow for the *'aqiqa* to be performed for grown-ups, the majority restrict its use to infants on the basis of a *hadith*: 'On the seventh day.' The other *hadith* which makes the *'aqiqa* applicable to a girl is the *hadith*: 'For a girl it is one sheep and for a boy two'(Ibn Rushd, 1992, 569).

Malik also narrates two views about the shaving of the infant's head on the seventh day and giving alms worth the value of the weight of his hair in silver. Ibn Rushd says that Malik quotes both views, 'It is said that this is desirable while it is also said that it is not desirable' (Ibn Rushd, 1992, 570). On the authority of Malik's *al-Muwatta*, Ibn Rushd cites the *hadith* suggesting the preference for this practice: 'Fatima, the daughter of the Prophet shaved the hair of al-Hasan and al-Husayn, Zaynab and Umm Kulthum and gave alms equal to the weight of the hair' (Ibn Rushd, 1992, 570).

As with so many Islamic rituals, one can trace their origins to pre-Islamic times. In those days, the head of the newborn was smeared with the blood of the sacrificed animal. With the arrival of Islam, this practice was abolished and the newborn was smeared with saffron (Ibn Rushd, 1992, 570). Taking and breaking from the traditions of the pre-Islamic (*jahiliyya*) period is part of the narrative of Muslim history and the *'aqiqa* is an excellent example of the fluid relationship between Muslim legal prescriptions and the existing social customs. The observance of *'aqiqa* is recognized as essential to Muslim practice yet it would appear that the differing *hadith*s on the subject allow for huge variances of interpretation over both the necessity and manner of observance. The obvious question is how certain practices became entrenched in Muslim cultures despite conflict of both the oral and written *hadith* reports on the subject? Furthermore, how essential are these practices to Muslim piety? The conflict of traditions on *'aqiqa* would indicate that for Abu Hanifa the whole practice was neither obligatory nor desirable, simply a voluntary choice. Compared with the prevalence of this practice in most Muslim countries including those where the Hanafi school is predominant, how did this practice coexist and firmly establish itself alongside conflicting legal opinion?

The above examples show that diversity of opinion is the fundamental characteristic of *fiqh*. In order to maintain diversity, conflicting opinions are juxtaposed with little intention of providing any clear principles. But these examples also reflect the ambiguity of authority. The reader remains ambivalent about authority because the opinions stated are not conclusive. Abu Hanifa's students often disagreed with him while recognising him as their teacher. Whether the jurists used *hadith*s or *ra'y*, it is difficult to ascertain how the varying opinions competed with one another. Prophetic practices are often cited as precedent, but the *hadith*s citing these practices often conflict with one another with little or no guidance as to juristic preference.

Conclusion

The above examples show how the content of the law develops. What does this tell us about the nature of law? At a time when many Muslims express a desire to return to 'Shari'a made simple', a codification of law which would serve as a moral paradigm for society, how can the complexity of these arguments serve as a directive in both practice and piety? How can such diversity of opinion, all of which are considered to varying degrees 'sacred', lead to realistic and practicable norms? I would argue that in many of these examples all we really glimpse is evidence of some kind of perspective and practice and the rest is left to the believer; guidance may be suggested but is rarely conclusive.

In contemporary discourses on *fiqh*, we are aware that colonialism and the expansion and influence of European codes of law on Muslim countries have had a profound influence on Muslim law. In addition the increasing secularization of societal structures poses a fundamental challenge. The nature of *fiqh* does not lend itself to providing a paradigm for a systematic and normative ethics for Muslims globally. Muslims can continue to look for guidance on issues of formalism in ritual such as purity rules or ritual prayers. But ritual observation is about practical conduct and not necessarily about ethical norms. Ethical suppositions demand that human progress and moral agency be factors framing the constant challenges of our contemporary social and moral contexts.

Chapter 3
Demarcating Fault-lines within Islam: Muslim Modernists and Hardline Islamists Engage the Shari‘a

Asma Afsaruddin

There are competing discourses among Muslims today concerning what constitutes ‘authentic’ Islam and who may be considered qualified to speak on behalf of Muslims. Strands of these discourses are often at loggerheads with one another and struggle to gain centre stage, creating ideological fault-lines within the *umma*, the transnational Muslim community. Such faultlines are invariably constructed around competing perceptions of the nature and role of the Shari‘a or the religious law and contested notions of religious and political authority among Muslims.

Authenticity is predicated on historicity. In order to demonstrate the legitimacy of their claims and counter-claims, contemporary Muslim discourses, whether in the Islamic heartlands or in Western diaspora communities, often invoke the concept of *al-salaf al-salih.* This Arabic term means ‘the pious or virtuous forebears or ancestors’, and usually refers to the first three generations of Muslims. Reverence for these early Muslims as moral exemplars developed quite early among the Muslim faithful since, as the generations closest to the Prophet Muhammad, they were assumed to have replicated his practices and beliefs as faithfully as possible. Ascription of certain principles and practices to these pious forebears attests to their early origin, and thus their authenticity, and justifies their implementation by Muslims today. This tendency arose early. The oldest reference to the *salaf* as paradigmatic role models appears to be a statement ascribed to Abu Hanifa (d. 767) recorded by the fifteenth century polymath Jalal al-Din al-Suyuti (d. 1505) in one of his works. According to this statement, Abu Hanifa counsels, ‘Follow the traditions and the way of the *salaf* and be on your guard against new-fangled matters (*bid‘a*) for all of that constitutes a departure from the norm’ (Suyuti, 1947, 32). Here we have the express purpose in following the *salaf* clearly articulated – to guard against undesirable innovation and preserve the integrity of the custom of the Prophet and his closest associates. Today, the association of the *salaf al-salih*, or in short *salaf*, with certain beliefs and practices has become highly evocative of authenticity and legitimacy.

In this chapter, I discuss two primary groups of Muslims today who have constructed competing world-views based on how they ‘read’ the Pious Forebearers and their lives, particularly in connection with their conceptualization of the Shari‘a and their understanding of the nature of *jihad*. These two groups are the Muslim modernists and reformists and the hardline Islamists. My focus on these two polar camps is not intended to narrow or elide other possible intermediate views on this spectrum. It rather serves the heuristic purpose of allowing me to highlight the most dominant and contentious views on these critical topics.

For our purpose, the term 'Islamist' refers to activist individuals and groups in various contemporary Islamic societies whose primary wish is to govern and be governed politically only by Islamic principles, understood by them to be immutably enshrined in the Shari'a or the religious law. Islamism refers to a highly politicized version of Islam whose genesis occurred in the early 20th century largely as a reaction to the abolition of the caliphate by republican Turks in 1924 and to the debilitating effects of Western colonialism in the Islamic world. In 1928, Hasan al-Banna in Egypt established the Muslim Brotherhood (*al-Ikhwan al-Muslimun*) as a countervailing response to both British colonial rule and secular nationalist politics which unchecked, it was feared, would undermine the traditional Islamic character of Egyptian society. In the Indian sub-continent, Abul A'la Mawdudi established the Jamaat-i-Islami ('the Islamic Society') party in 1941 to effectively articulate and galvanize a new Muslim political consciousness in reaction to British occupation and Hindu nationalism. Mawdudi migrated to newly created Pakistan in 1947 and continued to agitate for the establishment of an Islamic state there until his death in 1979. Among such politically activist individuals and groups today, we are using this term to refer to particularly hardline Islamists, who have been considerably influenced by the thought of Abul A'la Maududi and his disciple, the Egyptian activist Sayyid Qutb (d. 1966), and whose attitude towards modernity and its epistemic foundations can fairly be described as rejectionist. It should be pointed out though that not all radical Islamists are influenced by Qutb's thought; in fact, there are some who specifically reject it (Roy, 2004, 250). There are also 'moderate' Islamists (as they are usually termed), who, while also committed to a highly politicized form of Islam, subscribe to democratic norms and embrace modern notions of gender equality and human rights to a considerable extent. The moderate Islamists are generally not included in my use of the term Islamist in this discussion, unless specifically stated to the contrary.

Modernist and reformist Muslims, in our usage, refers to observant Muslims who, starting roughly in the 18th century, began to emphasize the inherent adaptability of Islamic principles and thought to modernity, partially in response to the beginning of the European colonial onslaught. For the most part, I will be using these terms interchangeably. Thus, the modernists argue, certain freshly interpreted Islamic principles can reveal their congruence with modern liberal principles of democratic government, civil society, gender equality, etc., without necessarily being identical to their formulations in the Western context. Like the Islamists, they too would like to usher in social change but their means of effecting change are essentially hermeneutic, that is interpretive, and educational. Accordingly, they stress the rereading of religious texts, primarily the Qur'an and *hadith*, as a legitimate exercise in *ijtihad* (independent reasoning) to arrive at interpretations appropriate to their historical circumstances without jettisoning the classical heritage and to foster a sense of a continuous critical and dynamic process of engagement with this heritage through education (Rahman, 1982a; Kurzman, 2002). Despite their respect for tradition in general, modernists tend to be critical of traditionalists who are perceived as unthinkingly following precedent and stymieing the efforts of Muslims to adapt to the modern world in an ethical and critical manner. Modernists and reformists are also called liberals and moderates by some.

In this chapter, I deal with two prominent issues in which modernists and hardline Islamists have developed distinctive positions, based on their competing readings of the Shari'a and evaluation of the praxis of the early Muslim community as recorded in extant sources. These two issues are: (1) the conception of the so-called Islamic state; and (2) the nature of *jihad*. I then proceed to discuss how the concept of the Shari'a itself and its nature remains highly contested among these groups in particular.

Institution of the Islamic State

A highly politicized version of Islam is the cornerstone of most, if not all, Islamist discourses. According to this version, a full-blown concept of what most Islamists call the Islamic state and Islamic government is articulated by the religious law. Such a state, they affirm, has existed since the time of the Prophet and was elaborated by particularly Abu Bakr and 'Umar, the first two Rightly Guided caliphs. The primary characteristic of the Islamic state, according to this school of thought, is 'divine sovereignty' or 'divine governance,' termed in Arabic *al-hakimiyya* by the Islamist thinker Abu'l-A'la al-Mawdudi. In his writings on political Islam, Mawdudi has maintained in regard to the Islamic state (Ar. *al-dawla al-islamiyya*) that 'the basic conception underlying all its outward manifestations is the idea of divine sovereignty' (Mawdudi, 1979, 13). In this Islamic state, its ideal leaders and servants 'will all work with a sense of individual and collective responsibility to God [alone], not to the electorate, neither to the king nor the dictator' (Mawdudi, 1979, 13f).

These ideas greatly influenced his ideological disciple, the Egyptian activist Sayyid Qutb, who made *al-hakimiyya* the linchpin of his Islamist agenda. In his strident political manifesto *Ma'alim fi'l-Tariq* ('Signposts on the Path'), Qutb invokes the latter part of Qur'an 4:59 which states, 'If you should differ in regard to anything, then refer it to God and the Messenger' (Qutb, 1982, 105) and understands it to place an absolute limitation on the authority of human beings. It moreover establishes, according to Qutb, that no one may arbitrarily promulgate a piece of legislation without acknowledging 'the supreme sovereignty' (*al-hakimiyya al-'ulya*) of God. This entails recognition that the only source of political authority (*al-sultah*) is 'God, the Almighty, not the people, not the [political] party, not any individual'. The verse also makes clear, Qutb asserts, that no human being can claim to speak or to have spoken in the name of God except the Prophet; thus there is no resemblance here to European notions of theocracy or of divine kingship.

While modernist Muslim scholars and activists have argued vigorously in favour of a basic ideational compatibility between the concept of *shura* or consultation (about which I will say more later) and Western-style democracy, many Islamists of particularly the Mawdudian/Qutbian school of thought tend to see fundamental differences between the two. They argue that since a democratic government derives its authority from the will of the people and laws enacted by humans, it is immediately at odds with an 'Islamic government' which is understood to derive its authority from God and His revealed laws. Thus Mawdudi states, 'Wherever this system [sc. democracy] exists, we do not consider Islam to exist, and wherever Islam exists, there is no room for this system' (Mawdudi, 1978, 42). Members of the Islamic polity are required to obey their ruler as long as he follows Qur'anic and sunnaic regulations, in accordance with their understanding of Qur'an 4:59. Mawdudi further adds that such a ruler in turn derives his legitimacy from the consent and freedom of the Muslims (Mawdudi, 1976, 25).

Although this last statement sounds quite democratic on the surface, it should be remembered that Mawdudi (and Qutb) had very specific and exclusivist notions of exactly who qualifies as a 'true' Muslim (see further Shepard, 1992, 217ff). Mawdudi in fact subscribed to what he described as 'theo-democracy' or a 'democratic caliphate'. In this conceptualization, the ideal Islamic state is headed by virtuous rulers who govern its contented obedient citizenry consensually and perfectly in accordance with the assumed transparent political mandate provided by the Qur'an and the *sunna* (Nasr, 1996, 80–106) (the *sunna* refers to the customs, practices and sayings of the Prophet Muhammad). Needless to say, the transparency of such a scriptural political mandate is only evident to 'true' Muslims like Mawdudi and his cohorts, and only they are able to implement it.

Nowhere is the hardline Islamists' perception of the Shari'a as absolute and unchanging more evident than in their construction of religious and political authority. In their political discourse the Qur'anic verse (4:59), which states in its first part, 'O those who believe, obey God and the Messenger and those who possess authority (Ar. *ulu'l-amr*) among you,' is frequently invoked. Sayyid Qutb's exegesis of 4:59 in his *Ma'alim* must be supplemented by his commentary in his exegetical work *Fi Zilal al-Qur'an* ('In the Shade of the Qur'an') for us to determine whom he intends by the *ulu'l-amr* and what role they play in his political schema. These two works taken together tell us that Qutb, like Mawdudi before him, described the *ulu'l-amr*, that is those who possess authority, as those who acknowledged the sovereignty of God in the Muslim polity. As a consequence, they are the best qualified to implement the divine laws conveyed to humankind by the Prophet Muhammad and elaborated upon comprehensively in his *sunna*. Unlike classical Islamic jurisprudence which added analogical reasoning and consensus of the community as supplemental sources of jurisprudence in the absence of explicit texts, Islamists usually recognize no other authoritative sources besides the Qur'an and *sunna* for legislative activity. For them the Shari'a, simply put, is a legal code which 'enacted as it is by God, is unchangeable' (Mawdudi, 1976, 31).

This view allows hardline Islamists to insist, for example, on the literal application of the *hudud* penalties as spelled out in classical Islamic jurisprudence for major infractions and crimes, such as theft and adultery, in their Islamic state. No leniency is to be permitted in such matters. The immediate implementation of *hudud* laws is of burning importance for them, since that is for them in many ways the most visible manifestation of an Islamic/Islamist identity. In their ahistorical reification of the religious law, there is no room for accommodation of customary and cultural practices (*'urf*) nor for multiple readings of scripture and ancillary texts. Nor is there room for the historical contextualization of legal rulings as they developed over time nor for the appeal to the public common good (*maslaha*) as grounds for legal reasoning, as actually occurred in the praxis of Muslim communities throughout time (such anti-intellectualism is excoriated by el-Fadl, 2001, 170–208; also Albertini, 2003). The slogan 'Islam is the solution' is meant to convey to the world that Islam, reduced to a monolithic unchanging corpus of religious and political commandments, has left nothing unaddressed. Not surprisingly then, Qutb and those following him frequently refer to Islam as a 'system' (Shepard, 1989). The *ulu 'l-amr*, among whom Qutb undoubtedly places himself and his cohorts, and who, therefore, constitute the vanguard (*tali'a*) of the 'Islamic Revolution' in the making, have all the pre-packaged answers yielded by this 'system' in the service of the Islamic utopia they ultimately hope to establish (Afsaruddin, 2006c, 45–6).

Nature of *Jihad*

The extremist Islamist view of the world holds that Islam represents a drastic rupture with everything that went before, effaces the validity of prior religious traditions, and mandates its political hegemony over all. Hardline Islamists signal this kind of 'historical' view by their contemptuous use of the term *jahiliyya* which signifies everything that antedated Islam and is not Islamic, as they define it, and therefore morally worthless in their evaluation (Mawdudi, 1980b; Shepard, 2003). What reeks of *jahiliyya* and is assumed to be an obstacle to the spread of Islam must be ruthlessly stamped out. The vehicle for doing this is the 'Islamic state' and the means for achieving this goal is *jihad.* Since, according to many radical Islamists, 'Islam is a revolutionary ideology and programme which seeks to alter the social order of the whole world and rebuild it in conformity with its own tenets and ideals,' *jihad* then 'refers to that revolutionary struggle and utmost exertion which the Islamic Party brings into play to achieve this objective' (Mawdudi, 1977, 5).

Jihad in this sense is arguably the most controversial issue that dominates activist Islamist rhetoric. Of course, not all Islamists (or modern Salafis in general) are militants who advocate the use of violence for political gain. Those who are militants, however, tend to understand *jihad* as the waging of unrelenting military activity against non-Muslims deemed hostile to Islam and against those perceived as 'lapsed' Muslims until they are politically vanquished (for example with reference to Jordan, Wiktorowicz, 2000). The 'true' Muslims, namely themselves, who die waging militant activity against their adversaries, are martyrs who are promised bounteous rewards in the hereafter. Once again, these militant Islamists attempt to justify their positions and rhetoric by asserting that they reflect 7th-century views regarding *jihad* and martyrdom. They refer in particular to the so-called sword verses (9:5 and 9:29) in the Qur'an without any contextualization as scriptural warrants for their militant position. They have developed a cult of martyrdom in justification of which they appeal to the *hadith* genre known as the 'excellences of *jihad*' (Ar. *fada'il al-jihad*), which tends to contain unreliable and spurious reports in fulsome praise of military activity and which hold out the promise of abundant posthumous rewards for such activity.

The militant Islamists' novel conception of *jihad* as armed combat directed against other Muslims is predicated on their doctrine of *takfir* (see art. 'Takfir' in Esposito, 1995, 4: 178f.), the declaration of Muslims, whom they regard as lukewarm or lapsed, to be unbelievers. A particularly unsavoury militant tract titled 'The Lapsed Duty' (Ar. *al-Farida al-gha'iba*), was penned by an Egyptian extremist 'Abd al-Salam Faraj, who is said to have inspired the assassins of Egyptian president Anwar al-Sadat. His screed scathingly criticizes various Muslim rulers for having apostasized from Islam, on which account they must be fought against.

The binary vision of the world articulated by jurists of the 9th century, which divided it into the 'abode of Islam' and 'abode of war', finds considerable resonance among radical Islamists. Despite the fact that these divisions are not to be found either in the Qur'an or the *sunna* (a fact that may not be known to many among them), they tend to promote these categories and the world-view behind them as normatively mandated. They thus appeal to the legal opinions of the 9th-century jurist al-Shafi'i (d. 820) who fully articulated this dichotomous conception of the world, which, however, he had qualified by the addition of a third domain, the abode of treaty or reconciliation (Ar. *dar al-'ahd*).[1]

By the 12th century, this notion of a bifurcated world had become quite passé as it no longer matched the political realities of the time. However, militant Islamists have resurrected the 9th-century concepts of opposed dual spheres or abodes in the contemporary period, preferring to ignore the period before the late 8th century (from the time of the early *salaf*) when these notions had not existed, as well as ignoring the later period when these concepts fell into disuse. They also prefer the

1 Even though we pointed out earlier that many Islamists eschew the interpretations of the pre-modern jurists based on independent reasoning for which method they claim to have scant regard, they have embraced, however, this particular Shafi'i postulate, despite its not having a Qur'anic nor sunnaic antecedent, since it accords very nicely with their 'fundamentalist' Manichaean view of the world.

understanding of *jihad* as exclusively 'armed combat', a meaning that had gained ascendancy from roughly the 9th century on, once again bypassing the earlier period when this was a much more diverse and polyvalent term, reflecting its Qur'anic usage (Afsaruddin, 2006a). They also skip over the later period when its spiritual significations became considerably heightened, especially in Sufi circles. Radical Islamists in fact are dismissive of *hadith*s which speak more highly of spiritual and non-militant *jihad* than the military one, such as the famous one, popular especially among Sufis, which divides *jihad* into the greater and lesser one (Nakamura, 1975, 167; Renard, 1988). They generally tend to denigrate Sufism in general which is too other-worldly and self-abnegating for them (Johansen, 1996; Ernst, 1997, 211–14). The military *jihad* may bring these Islamists untold pleasures in the next world, if they should expire in its midst, but the kingdom of this world is their most coveted and preferred prize. The term *jihad* for them primarily serves to yoke the religious to their temporal, political ambitions.

Modernist and Reformist Views

We now proceed to delineate typical modernist (others may say 'liberal' or 'moderate') positions on the two issues of the Islamic state and the nature of *jihad* discussed in relation to the hardline Islamists.

Establishment of the 'Islamic State'

Modernists and reformists do not necessarily have a consistent position on this issue. Some modernists may advocate the establishment of a state that would be recognisably Islamic, primarily by upholding the Shari'a, which however, unlike the Islamists, is understood by them to be adaptable to and accommodating of modern life and its complexities. In contrast to the traditionalist Salafiyya and hardline Islamists, the revival of the caliphate as an institution is not necessarily an integral part of the modernist project, although the revival of the ethical and political principles and the general ethos associated with the Rightly Guided caliphate usually is. Furthermore, unlike the hardline Islamists, the modernists do not believe that there is a pre-conceived blueprint specifying the structural format of an 'Islamic state' as such. Modernists tend to regard any state which guarantees certain basic individual and communal rights and liberties as being in accordance with broad Islamic moral parameters and thus meeting the Islamic litmus test. The actual mode of governance may be decided upon by consultation with knowledgeable people, the consent of the public, and the prevailing historical circumstances, since they believe that there are no specific religious directives concerning this matter (Afsaruddin, 2006b). They point, for example, to the views of the 11th century rationalist theologian 'Abd al-Jabbar (d. 1095) who identified three broad trends of thought in his time on the issue of the caliphate. The first, a minority, held that the caliphate was not necessary; the second believed that it was required on the basis of reason; and the third maintained that it was necessary according to the religious law.[2] This range of thought testifies to the active engagement of many thinkers with the critical issues of sound governance and socio-political administration, unfettered by an assumed religious mandate for a specific political institution. Their suggestions and solutions were clearly the product of rational deliberation and philosophical reflection, based on the needs of their own times and circumstances.

With regard to legitimate government, modernists tend to insist on three cardinal tenets that are defining of consultative and accountable government, an ideal pursued by the *salaf*, and actually implemented by the Rightly Guided caliphs, as they maintain. These three tenets are: (a) *shura* ('consultation'); (b) *bay'a* ('allegiance'; 'ratification'); and (c) *ijma'* ('consensus') (Mousalli, 2001, ch.1, and Esposito and Voll, 1996, 25–30). *Shura* in fact is a Qur'anic concept and thus sanctified by revelation and rooted in prophetic practice. There are two Qur'anic verses advocating consultation which are frequently quoted in this context. The first (3:158–9) states, 'So pass over [their faults], and ask for [God's] forgiveness and consult them in matters; then, when you have made a decision, put your trust in God'. The second verse (42:38) runs, '[The believers are] those who answer the call of their Lord and perform prayer, and who conduct their affairs by mutual consultation, and who spend of what We have bestowed upon them'. The predominant sentiment in the sources – theological, juridical, ethical and administrative – is that *shura* as mutual consultation in various spheres is the preferred and desirable method of resolving matters. Modernists derive examples from the time of the Prophet through the Rightly Guided period in order to bolster their argument that consultation is a mandated practice in all matters, and particularly in the political realm. Modernists point to these historical instances to make their case that a representative and accountable government which upholds justice and equitable treatment for all its citizens is the only kind permissible within Islam, regardless of what its actual structure and mode may be.[3] Modernists tend to be strong proponents of democracy today, whether in its procedural, constitutional or liberal forms, since in their perception democratic processes today best satisfy

2 See Abd al-Jabbar, n.d., 20:16. I owe this reference to Hayrettin Yucesoy, 2003. Thus 'Ali 'Abd al-Raziq, the Egyptian scholar of the early 1920s, was hardly expressing an original point of view when he stated, to the consternation of many, in his book *al Islam wa Usul al-Hukm* ('Islam and the Principles of Government') (Beirut, 1966) that the caliphate was not a religious requirement. This was an early opinion among a spectrum of opinions regarding the nature of the office of the caliph which fell out of favour by the 10th century of the Common Era.

3 Ghannouchi, 1993; 'Imara, 1979; Ashmawy, 1987; Hibri, 1992; Ramadan, 2001, 81–91; Osman, 2002, 85–97, among others, see no problems with recasting and focusing on *shura* as the organizational principle for a modern democratic polity. Among the cluster of choices available to modern Muslims, they regard democracy as the system of government that offers the best opportunity for consultative and collective political decision-making.

Islamic standards of popular enfranchisement and accountability established in the earliest period (el-Fadl, 2003a).

With regard to the political concept of 'divine sovereignty', modernists point to many of the defining characteristics of the early political culture of Islam to counter the hardline Islamist understanding of this concept as a divine mandate for a complete way of life with a set of prescribed answers for nearly every imaginable situation, a scenario that leaves little room for human input and interpretation. While acknowledging God's sovereignty over all creation, modernists do not view this as impeding in any way human freedom in determining their course of action in particularly the political sphere under the guidance of broad moral imperatives.[4] The well-known modernist scholar of Islamic thought Fazlur Rahman stressed that the Qur'anic concept of God's sovereignty has nothing to with political or legal sovereignty but rather means that 'God has bestowed a certain constitution both to this universe and to man ...'(Rahman, 1982b, 264).

The Qur'anic designation of human beings as 'God's vicegerent' (Ar. *khalifa*) on earth is emphasized by modernists as investing humans with the right and authority to assume custodianship of earth. The example of the Rightly Guided caliphs, the modernists assert, clearly establishes that such custodianship was understood in the early period to be predicated on human agency and deliberative reasoning while safeguarding the moral objectives and the spirit of the religious law. The caliph 'Umar's bold innovations, for example, in instituting the state register of pensions (*diwan*), abrogating temporary marriage, establishing the Islamic (*hijri*) calendar and modifying inheritance laws are lauded by posterity as reasoned measures whose adoption was prompted by both moral and practical considerations.

Modernists also question hardline Islamist readings of divinely formulated government into scripture. With regard to the critical Qur'anic phrase *ulu'l-'amr* that has figured prominently in discussions of religious and political authority, the late-19th/early-20th-century reformist intellectual Rashid Rida (d. 1935), close friend and disciple of Muhammad 'Abduh (d. 1905), the famous modernist scholar and rector of al-Azhar University in Cairo, glossed the phrase as referring to 'the people who loosen and bind' (Ar. *ahl al-hall wa-'l-'aqd*) among Muslims. The 'people who loosen and bind' include the political rulers, judges, the religious scholars (*al-'ulama'*), the leaders of the army and the rest of the rulers and leaders 'whom people resort to in their need and for their general welfare' ('Abduh, 1999, 5:147; also el-Fadl, 2003a, 11f. and Afsaruddin, 2006c, 42–6). They further include leaders of various sectors of society who promote the general interests (*al-masalih al-'amma*) of the people; among these sectors are trade, industry and agriculture.

4 Among modernist writers on political Islam who have vigorously and convincingly challenged the notion of *hakimiyyat Allah* and its presumed Qur'anic lineage is Muhammad Sa'id al-'Ashmawi who, in his work *al-Islam al-siyasi*, states that this concept is actually un-Islamic and contrary to the Qur'an and *sunna*. Similar views were expressed earlier by Hudaybi, 1965. On al-Hudaybi, see el Fadl, 2005, 84–5.

Therefore, labour union leaders, political party leaders, members of the editorial boards of respectable newspapers and their chief editors are all included in the category of the people 'who loosen and bind'.[5] Unlike hardline Islamists, Rida does not see authoritarianism being mandated by an exclusively political reading of Qur'an 4:59. Rather, he understands the verse as referring to different kinds of authority – moral, intellectual, administrative, financial as well as political – dispersed among different groups of people who, with the consensus of the majority, wield collective, benevolent influence for the welfare of the community. On that account they are owed voluntary obedience by the people, which is liable to be withdrawn if the *ulu'l-amr* fail to live up to their obligations. This kind of non-authoritarian reading of key Qur'anic verses directly challenges the radical Islamist hermeneutic enterprise which leads to political authoritarianism.

Nature of Jihad

Modernists find the radical Islamist conception of *jihad* to be anathema and also have trouble with a considerable portion of the classical juridical conception of *jihad* and related concepts. I mentioned earlier that the distinguished jurist al-Shafi'i divided the world into three realms of war, peace and treaty/armistice and that he did so on his own initiative without any scriptural basis. Modernists point to this as an example of independent *ijtihad* on al-Shafi'i's part in order to make sense, from an Islamo-centric point of view, of the conflict-ridden world that he inhabited, which has no bearing on the contemporary world (al-Ghunaimi, 1968, 104).

Muslim reformists have pointed to the diversity of opinions throughout the classical and post-classical period to point to the contested and historically contingent nature of many of the classical pronouncements on *jihad* and related issues. Once again, modernists and reformists have turned to accounts of the views and practices of the *salaf* that have a bearing on these topics to challenge the legitimacy of the Islamist position, particularly in its radical form. A favourite example of modernists drawn from the 1st century of Islam is the treatment of the Christian Abyssinians by the Prophet and various Muslim administrators after him. The Christian Abyssinians under the devout ruler, the Negus, became famous in early Islam for having harboured a group of destitute Muslims fleeing from the persecution of the pagan Meccans before the emigration to Medina by Muhammad and his followers in 622. As a consequence of this exceptional act of goodwill and religious fellowship, various Muslim authorities in the early period, following the example of the Prophet, exempted the Abyssinians from the payment of any taxes (*jizya*) that would otherwise be expected and automatically considered them to

5 We must not forget that Rida was the editor of the highly regarded periodical *al-Manar* ('The Beacon') and his mentor Muhammad 'Abduh was one of the key figures associated with the influential journal *al-'Urwa al-wuthqa*; no doubt he was including himself and 'Abduh among the *ulu'l-amr*.

be part of the abode of treaty/peace. The Nubians of North Africa, despite being non-Muslims, were also exempted from the *jizya* and not considered *dhimmis* ('protected people'). Instead they entered into a trade agreement (*baqt*) with the Muslims according to the terms of which they mutually traded goods (Khadduri, 1955, 257–61). Modernist Muslims are particularly heartened by these concrete historical instances, which they invoke to bolster their argument that in an era of an international commonwealth of nations subscribing to shared values of human rights and peaceful coexistence, these examples of Muslim and non-Muslim interaction yield a much more pertinent and appropriate model for international relations today. It further underscores the fact that relations with non-Muslims are governed not on the basis of religious affiliation but on the goodwill and peaceableness of the people involved.

Jizya or the head-tax, they point out, was not always consistently imposed on non-Muslims. Women, the elderly, the poor, religious clerics and monks were routinely exempted from its payment. There are also instances when non-Muslims requested to pay the *zakat*, the poor-tax enjoined on Muslims, in lieu of the *jizya* and the request was granted. Thus, 'Umar ibn al-Khattab exempted the Christian tribe Banu Taghlib from the *jizya* when they protested its imposition on them and allowed them to pay *zakat* instead; the Christians of Tanukh were treated similarly. The Jarajima tribe agreed to serve in the military in lieu of paying the *jizya* (Khadduri, 1955, 198f.). Modernists point to these historical instances to underscore the contingent nature of *jizya* and its imposition.

The division of the world into two mutually opposed spheres requiring the subjugation of one by the other is regarded as being completely obsolete by the modernists. Thus Muhammad 'Abduh and Rashid Rida recognized that the assumed bipolar division of the world had been defunct for centuries and explicitly affirmed that peaceful co-existence was the normal state of affairs between Islamic and non-Islamic nations (Esposito, 1995, 2:369–73). Mahmud Shaltut (d. 1963), the reformer who, like Abduh became the rector of al-Azhar University, expressed a similar conviction. He further stated that Muslims and non Muslims were equal with regard to rights and duties in a Muslim-majority state, and that only defensive wars are permissible in response to external aggression (Zebiri, 1993, 68).

Modernists also wish to foreground the spiritual and social reformist aspects inherent in *jihad* and restore its full semantic purview, compromised by hawkish medieval jurists who were reacting to a violent, adversarial world that was part real, part imaginary. They reject the abrogating status of the so-called sword verses, which would result in the abrogation (*naskh*) of numerous Qur'anic verses that counsel peace and reconciliation.[6] Besides emphasizing the multiple significations of the term *jihad* in the Qur'an, modernists point to the broad range of views among the early *salaf* on what constitutes *jihad* and martyrdom. Thus modernists stress various reports recorded in early *hadith* collections like the *Musannaf* of 'Abd al-

6 Al-Suyuti, 1993, 2:714, where he says disapprovingly that the sword verse would effectively abrogate 124 conciliatory verses.

Razzaq which defines *jihad* in terms of striving daily to live righteously through acts of worship, earning a licit livelihood, and serving one's family, in addition to military defence of Islamic realms (el-Fadl, 2005, 220-249; Afsaruddin, 2006a). These reports are used by them as proof-texts to support their position that the multifaceted aspects of *jihad* informed the lives of the early *salaf* and that the monolithic, military conception of *jihad* promoted by many of the classical jurists was a historically contingent development and lacking any normative function today (Dakake, 2004; Shah-Kazemi, 2004). The position of contemporary radical Islamists that *jihad* refers to unrelenting military activity against all those unlike them, Muslim and non-Muslim, until the latter come around to their view of things is regarded by modernists as a desperate and grotesque distortion of a noble and morally uplifting concept, whose reclamation from the extremists is necessary and long overdue.

The Nature of the Shari'a

Unlike radical Islamists, modernists tend to emphasize the application of the intent and overall objectives (Ar. *maqasid*) of the religious law more than its literal injunctions, especially when the literal understanding of a specific dictum in a particular circumstance would result in unusual hardship and/or violation of an inviolable broader moral imperative. Thus, many of them argue, since the Shari'a must uphold certain ethical values such as justice and mercy at all times, specific legal injunctions may never violate these fundamental objectives in any given historical and social circumstance (Crane, 2005; Ramadan, 2004, 147–52; el-Fadl, 2001, 27–30; Sachedina, 2001, 109–12; Khadduri, 1984). Those injunctions that appear to do so need to be re-examined and reinterpreted (el-Fadl, 2002, 11–23). They also place more emphasis on the discernment of the *ratio legis* (underlying cause; Ar. *'illa*) of specific legal precepts than on their literal, textual meaning (Hallaq, 1999, 83–95).

Modernists further believe that since the Shari'a is essentially flexible and invariably just, it has enough checks and balances built into it to prevent miscarriage of justice. Punitive sanctions that appear on the surface to be harsh are usually difficult to implement since the conditions for proving the commission of the crime for which these sanctions exist are practically impossible to fulfil. Modernists thus hold that *hudud* punishments, for example, are essentially deterrent in nature and have been carried out infrequently in Muslim societies throughout history (Ashmawi, 1998). The law as interpreted in the pre-modern period, say the modernists, should not be understood nor applied in a literal manner in modern societies (Shahrour, 1990, 454–64).

Modernists argue against the assumed all-pervasive, reified nature of the Shari'a as maintained by the Islamists and against the notion that the Shari'a comes with ready-made answers to every imaginable circumstance. They tend to affirm that the reach of the religious law extends to many aspects of human existence while not directly addressing others. Outside of worship (*'ibadat*) the

Shari'a offers broad guidelines rather than detailed precepts for proper conduct in various spheres of social and other forms of interaction (*mu'amalat*) (Ramadan, 2004, 31–61). The religious law certainly does not, and cannot, have a specific injunction in advance for every possible human situation or contingency. The Qur'an, the principle source of the religious law, 'is not a lawbook but is primarily a moral code from which a legal system may be derived' (Rahman, 1980, 47). This derived legal system is the result of human reasoning and effort which allows specific legal precepts to be extrapolated from the Qur'anic moral code, as well as from the *sunna*.

The science or the study of law (that is, jurisprudence) which leads to the derivation of legal rulings is called *fiqh* in Arabic. In its basic semantic signification, *fiqh* broadly refers to human understanding and rational discernment. Islamists and modernists are essentially in agreement that the Shari'a must always be respected but they tend to talk past one another when the former mistake *fiqh* for Shari'a and/or use the terms interchangeably. Jurisprudence (*fiqh*) is a human intellectual activity and, therefore, fallible and changeable. Specific legal interpretations resulting from the deliberations of jurists were crafted in response to specific historical and social contingencies. Changed circumstances, the modernists insist, necessitate changed interpretations in conformity with the objectives (*maqasid*) of the law. Modernists see a fatal epistemological problem arising from the conflation of jurisprudence with the religious law itself, that is, of *fiqh* with Shari'a by hardline Islamists (and often by traditionalists as well).

Thus in opposition to hardline Islamists, modernists typically emphasize the flexibility of the Shari'a which allows the faithful to relate to it in creative interpretive ways in different circumstances. The broad parameters of the religious law, they maintain, leave ample room for negotiation and accommodation of its fundamental moral objectives as well as for considerations of the common good (*maslaha*) through recourse to independent reasoning (*ijtihad*). Like *maqasid* ('objectives'), *maslaha* is another key term associated with modernist discourses on the relevance of the Shari'a in the contemporary period that harks back to the Shafi'i jurist and theologian Abu Hamid Muhammad al-Ghazali's (d. 1111) exposition of this legal principle (Hallaq, 1990). This principle would be further elaborated upon by Najm al-Din al-Tufi (d. 1316) (al-Tufi, 1993) and Abu Ishaq al-Shatibi (d. 1388), whose rational juristic thought has enjoyed a revival among modernists (Shatibi, 2000; see also Masud, 1977).

Within the hierarchical ordering of the sources of law, modernists and reformists emphasise the supremacy of the Qur'an over the *sunna*, sometimes even the former's sole supremacy *vis-à-vis* the latter. Thus Rashid Rida maintained that the Qur'an is the main source (*asl*) of religion and that rules derived from the *sunna*, if not directly bearing on religious matters, need not be followed. Such non-religious sunnaic rulings, which have to do with civil, political and military matters, are the result of the Prophet's fallible personal *ijtihad* and are consequently non-binding on the believer. He cites in this context Qur'an 5:101 which states, 'O those who believe! Do not ask questions about things which, if made known to you, would cause you harm'. Rida comments that this verse implies that the Qur'an deliberately did not address many things, since detailed rulings about a large number of matters would prove cumbersome for humans. Religion should lead to ease and well-being of the people, as indicated in Qur'an 87:8, which says, 'We will make it easy for you [to follow] the Easy [Path]'. According to Rida, pre-modern jurists often flouted this basic legal objective (*maqsad*) – to ensure ease in the practice of religion – by devising difficult and arduous applications of the law in matters where Qur'anically speaking, it had no jurisdiction (Rida, 1984, 12–23).

The 'Abduh and Rida school of thought have enjoyed a resurgence among contemporary Muslim modernists and reformists. Their rational, critical and thoughtful approach to the religious and historical sources resonate among today's leading Muslim modernist and reformist thinkers, many of whom are in the West, particularly in the US. This would include academics and activists like Khaled Abou el-Fadl, Azizah al-Hibri and Muqtedar Khan in the US, and Tariq Ramadan, for example, in Europe.

Conclusion

Beyond certain core beliefs and precepts, many Muslims throughout time have negotiated and contested almost every issue related to their spiritual, material and cognitive well-being, a process which has led to dynamic processes of engagement with and interrogation of the Shari'a and its objectives, among other things. On the other hand, resistance to such enterprises on the part of others has led to stultifying stalemates in turns. The *salaf*, configured and reconfigured, have remained germane to such intense theological, legal, and political discussions since the early pre-modern period. The relevance of the lives and examples of the *salaf* as both historical and 'iconic' figures in these processes of negotiation and engagement continues unabated for contemporary Muslims. How the *salaf* are constructed has a very important bearing on the modern Muslim's perceptions of the religious law, political and religious authority, and inter-faith and inter-cultural relations, as we have seen. The *salaf* when viewed through an illiberal prism, as through some of the later sources, can and have been implicated in intolerant and repressive social and political policies, which they believe are mandated by the religious law. The *salaf*, when viewed through a liberal lens, as through quite a number of early and now modernist sources, can generate interpretations of the Shari'a that are conducive to tolerant, magnanimous and boldly innovative measures while claiming to remain true to the intent of the law and its spirit. To some degree, how one 'reads' the *salaf*, then, is contingent on the kind of sources one chooses to consult and how one proceeds to interpret them. This has important consequences as well for how each camp understands the function of the Shari'a and the most effective way to implement its objectives as defined by them in their given socio-historical circumstances. Legal and textual hermeneutics of this type continue to undergird Muslim discursive engagements with the Shari'a today, whether in the Islamic heartlands or in diaspora.

Chapter 4
Islamic Jurisprudence and Western Legal History

Mark van Hoecke

Legal cultures and legal traditions are often seen as coherent and very stable over time. However, a closer look at different such traditions shows how similar tensions between opposite views are to be found in seemingly quite different legal traditions. The difference lies sometimes more in the chronology of the debates and of the choices made than in the nature of the respective legal cultures. An example is the approach to the interpretation of contracts in Common Law when compared to the French and German approaches. It transpires that in each of those legal traditions there has always been a tension between an 'objective', rather text-bound, literal interpretation, on the one hand, and a 'subjective' interpretation, focusing on the intent of the contracting party, on the other, with some intermediate positions, which tend to focus more on reasonableness and on the role of contract in society. At some moment in the course of history one view has been dominating, whereas, as a reaction, the opposite view, or a more balanced intermediate position, may have become more popular some decades or centuries later. The debate is often the same in varying legal traditions, but its chronology is not, neither are the dominating positions the same in the same periods of history (Van Hoecke, 2004).

It looks as if this is also largely true when we compare the Islamic legal tradition(s) with the Western one(s). Moreover, it is only at the surface that both legal cultures seem to be completely different. When taking a closer look at them, one may sometimes notice larger divergences among legal systems within each of those traditions than some of them may show when compared to a legal system of the other legal culture.

In this chapter I would like to point to commonalities among both legal traditions, be it at a different moment in their respective histories.

Legal Epistemology

Since the early Middle Ages, Western legal thinking has been dominated by some idea of 'natural law', that took different shapes: first as God's law (Middle Ages), later on as a rational law (17th–18th centuries), occasionally even as an empirical conclusion of what all legal systems would have in common (19th century). Today, the natural law idea is present in the human rights discourses. In all cases some 'ideal law' is used as a touchstone for checking the quality of imperfect, human-made, positive law.

As long as one sees natural law as having a divine origin, scholars are confronted with an epistemological problem: how can we know God's will and God's rules and principles, as there is always at least an inevitable human translation and interpretation of what one may have found e.g. in the Bible ? There is no direct contact with God and human skills and knowledge are limited. Perfection cannot be guaranteed in a human world.

Scholars in the Islamic legal tradition have been faced with similar epistemological problems. In comparison with the Bible, the Qur'an has a more authoritative status, as it is considered to represent directly the Word of God whereas the Bible is considered to represent God's Word more indirectly, through intermediate human writers. However, the Qur'an has not been written as a Code nor as a legal textbook. The number of moral or legal rules worded is very limited. In the 2nd and 3rd centuries after the death of the Prophet Muhammad his sayings (*hadith*s) were written down and constitute the *sunna*, offering more rules. But, again, this is neither a code nor a textbook but a set of sayings that sometimes point into diverging directions. This has been solved by a scholarly consensus on the internal hierarchy of such texts in the Qur'an. Because of that consensus this hierarchy is considered to be absolutely certain. Nevertheless, for this interpretation of God's Word the epistemological question is the same as with natural law as the *sunna* is based on a, possibly imperfect, communication between God, the Prophet and the subsequent generations of Islamic scholars. The *sunna*, or more broadly the *fiqh* (legal scholarship) remains a human interpretation of Gods will (Siddiqui, 2007, 1).

Legal Methodology

Law and its Historical Context

As explained by Asma Afsaruddin in Chapter 3 of this volume, there are two major approaches to Shari'a within Islam: the historical, 'modernist', 'reformist' or 'liberal' approach, as opposed to the ahistorical or 'Islamist' approach.

An ahistorical approach considers the Shari'a to be immutable and to be understood exactly as in the early times after the Prophet's death. The historical approach accepts the need for adapting rules to changed circumstances in the course of history. Translated into the Western wording of the debate one could present it as the question to what extent divine law coincides with human law or whether natural law may coincide with positive law. In the Western tradition the distinction has always been made, partly, of course, because there was no authentic text which could be considered to truly represent the divine law or the natural law. In a way the ahistorical approach is also anti-historical: in this view society *should* not change. The 'good old times' are to be preferred over the current situation. This view translates a fear for change and a strong need for certainties, which also underlie the black letter approach to interpretation.

Interpretation Theories

Actually, the opposition between historical and ahistorical views on Shari'a runs parallel to the opposition between schools of interpretation: the 'black letter' approach, as opposed to a teleological interpretation. The tension between both theories of interpretation has been present in both legal traditions ever since their early years.

The black letter approach sticks to a literal interpretation of the normative text, whereas the teleological approach sees the text as a means to express a rule or a principle, which doesn't necessarily coincide with the text or even lead to results which seem to be incompatible with the text, and are, for that reason, rejected by the black letter adepts. Through such a teleological interpretation the interpreter may adapt a rule to changed circumstances, avoid absurd results of a literal application, or fill gaps in the law.

The black letter approach seems to offer more certainty, but in fact it does not. It assumes that the meaning of a text is 'in the text' and can just be 'found' by reading it. It also assumes that the text has been written in view of all possible, present and future, circumstances and that it perfectly translates the will of the author(s) of the normative text. This is an idealistic view on meaning, which doesn't fit at all with reality (Van Hoecke, 2002).

On the other hand, a teleological interpretation bears the risk of a *gouvernement des juges*, of replacing the will of the lawgiver by the very personal view of the interpreter. In practice, this risk is to a very large extent limited by the scholarly debates where rational arguments and authoritative points of view of highly estimated scholars and higher courts lead to a consensus and to a large coherence of interpretations within the legal community. This offers another kind of certainty that, moreover, guarantees that the legal solutions are better adapted to current society.

Especially in the 2nd century of Islam, there was a strong debate between 'traditionalists', who wanted to stick to a literal interpretation, on the one hand, and 'reformists', who took a more liberal, teleological position towards the texts. See, for example, the following quotation from one of the greater jurists in the Islamic tradition, Shamsaddin al-Sarakhsi, who lived in the 11th century:

> The best that has been said about the lawyer is that he should assimilate the dispositions and meanings of the Book and the *Sunna* in its diverse forms and texts, and that he must be good in analogy and know about society. However, even then he could still have a case for which he finds no reference in the Book or in the *Sunna*. Texts are finite and cases infinite. Then he has no other means but to reason, and the way of reasoning has been alluded to in the *Hadith*: know

> the examples as well as doubts, and measure matters with them. This is the method of the jurists. Precedent is argument. Not all events are to be found in the Book and the *Sunna*, unlike what the literalists say. So turn to the closest to God and to Justice. Use the way of precedent in order to give ruling its most appropriate meaning. (Sarakhsi, xvi, 62–3)

This has led to some balance between both approaches. Since 20th century, and especially since the more fundamentalist, Islamist reactions against modernism, however, more extreme positions as to interpretation are being taken again today.

Early in the Western tradition, Roman law offered quotations for both theories, but it was especially after the 19th-century codifications in continental Europe that there was a move towards a strict application of the texts; later on, mainly in the 20th century, these were followed by more liberal approaches, as a reaction against the shortcomings of a black letter interpretation.

Legal Sources

At first sight, the legal sources of the Shari'a seem to be quite different when compared to Western legal sources: Qur'an, *sunna*, consensus and analogy are not to be found in any Western legal system in the category of 'legal sources'. Nevertheless, some parallels could be drawn.

Translated into the Western terminology, the Qur'an shows some similarities with a constitution, be it an unchangeable constitution (but also in Western legal theory there have been discussions on the normative force of constitutional dispositions that prohibit a change of this constitution). Anyway, the Qur'an is the basic text, with a binding force at the highest level in the hierarchy of legal sources in the Islamic world. But it has a somewhat ambivalent status, being both natural law and directly binding positive law at the same time. In that sense it may be compared to the international treaties on human rights, and most notably the European Convention on Human Rights. This Convention has a similar ambivalent status. On the one hand, it clearly belongs to positive law, as a legal source that may be directly invoked in courts or against public or private authorities, but, on the other hand, it is also an ideal, supranational, 'natural law', against which the quality of national legal systems may be checked.

The *sunna* could be compared with a Western Code, in the following sense. Nineteenth-century civil codes were a synthesis of customary law, a long-lasting legal scholarship and newly introduced principles. The *sunna* can be compared to customary law, as it is based on the customs and life of Muhammad, later on written down in authoritative texts and rearranged by legal scholarship, as the 'glossators' and 'post-glossators' did with customary law in the Middle Ages in Europe.

'Consensus' in the Shari'a refers to a consensus among the scholars of Islamic law. In that sense it is perfectly comparable with 'legal doctrine' or 'legal dogmatics' in the Western legal tradition. Here too, a scholarly debate may lead, and often will, to a consensus on how a text has to be interpreted, how a problem has to be solved legally or, at a more abstract level, which legal sources can be accepted, which kind of interpretation methods can be applied or how, more generally, the legal system has to be conceived. Consensus on many points is a prerequisite to construct a paradigmatical framework within which debates on more specific issues are made possible.

What, in Shari'a, is called 'analogy', actually refers to more general principles to be found behind a concrete rule with a more limited scope. If the prohibition of alcohol is, by analogy, extended to all kinds of drugs, it is because it is seen as an application of a more general principle that one should avoid the consumption of products to which one could get addicted.

In continental Europe, the use of 'unwritten general principles of law' became popular in the second half of the 20th century, partly to fill gaps in the law, partly to make it more coherent, and partly to correct the law on the basis of moral principles. A typical example is the recognition of the 'good faith principle'. In virtually all continental European countries, until recently, 'good faith' was only mentioned in a disposition that requires from the parties to a contract to execute this agreement 'according to good faith'. Courts, all over Europe, have considered this not to be a limitative area in which good faith would apply, but rather a concrete application of a more general duty of good faith. By analogy, the scope of this duty has thus been considerably extended.

Universal Law vs. State Law

Both Islamic and Western legal cultures have gone through a development from universalism to nationalism, with, more recently, trends towards new forms of globalization.

Western Legal Tradition

Western societies in the Middle Ages show a combination of local particularism with customary law, limited legislation at a regional level, universal canon law and legal science (based on Roman law). In the 19th century, a synthesis of this development, together with new views on society, led to codifications. However, the rise of the nation state also brought about a narrowing of legal systems and legal cultures to the borders of those states. In the course of the last few decades those national legal systems started to develop into the opposite direction again. There has partly been a process of regionalization, with regional parliaments, with relatively important competences, in many European countries (including Great Britain, France, Germany, Spain, Italy, Belgium), on the one hand, but more importantly a new universalism through European law, and most importantly (European) human rights law, on the other.

The law of the European Union could be seen as being still a kind of 'national' law, but at a larger geographical level, more or less comparable to the law of the United States of America. However, EU law is still largely economic law and its basic underlying principle is creating and protecting the free market. This liberal free-market model is currently dominant all over the world and, in that sense, universal. This universal free-market law often creates tensions with local, national interests, leading to national protecting regulation, such as tax law, product requirements, labour law requirements, consumer protection, etc., even if the free market model is otherwise fully accepted by those states.

As already mentioned above, human rights law replaced, in the Western tradition, metaphysical conceptions of natural law, offering an interesting combination of positive law with natural law. The claim to universalism is inherent to human rights. The tension between state interests, on the one hand, and human rights law, protecting the individual against public authorities, on the other, transpires most clearly in the jurisprudence of the European Court of Human Rights. It is the task of this court to decide on such tensions. At a wider international level such courts are lacking or have much fewer competences but, at a political level, human rights are constantly being used as a universal truth for criticizing national laws or national policies. Human rights are accepted worldwide. Even if there may be diverging interpretations of their scope, the ideas of individual freedom, equality and the like seem to be generally accepted, at least in the public discourse. Only within Islamic law do some schools and political movements seem to consider Western human rights thinking to be incompatible with the Shari'a, but at state level human rights have found recognition in all national legal systems in countries with a Muslim majority. Here, there is a potential tension between two sets of legal principles with a claim to universalism: Shari'a, on the one hand, and human rights, with a Western flavour, on the other.

Islamic Legal Tradition

Islamic law has seen a comparable development: a universal Islamic law, be it with several schools, each of them dominating some regions in the Islamic world, until the early 20th century, followed by the development of national legal systems in the course of the 20th century. This caused a tension between the universal Islamic legal sources on the one hand and the local, national legal sources on the other. Varying interpretations of Islamic law made it possible that, within one and the same Islamic tradition, such diverging legal systems could develop, such as Turkish law as compared to Saudi Arabian law, or Moroccan law as compared to Iranian law. Islamist tendencies nowadays want to restore the unity of a universal Islamic law, which would be interpreted uniformly all over the world. In practice, however, it is not only a plea for universalism as opposed to local divergences, but also a battle for traditionalism against all kinds of modern developments of the last millennium.

The varying interpretations of Shari'a are thus strongly linked to the opposition between universalism and nationalism, between traditionalism and modernism and between the epistemological and methodological oppositions mentioned above. In European law, a unity of interpretation has been guaranteed by the creation of European courts, whose decisions have an authoritative force *vis-à-vis* national courts, governments and even parliaments.

Legal Pluralism

Centralized national legal systems are a relatively recent phenomenon. In large parts of the world, including the Islamic regions, nation states were only created after decolonization in the 20th century. China has, in most of its history, been a centralized nation state, but law in that tradition never played an important role until very recently. So, notwithstanding a strong bureaucracy, there hasn't been a developed Chinese national legal system. In Western legal history centralized nation states mainly developed during the 19th century. Before that time the European map had been one of legal pluralism. Local customary law existed along regional regulation, some 'national' legislation and canon law. Moreover, legal education was, with the exception of canon law, not about those regulations, but about Roman law. Lawyers were not educated in their local positive law, but in a 'universal' Roman legal science. This legal pluralism also allowed 'person-bound' law, distinct from 'territorially bound' law. Different rules, different courts and different types of punishment applied to noblemen as compared to the average citizen. University students had their own law and courts and were immune to the local 'police', local courts and local rules. Ever since the rise of the nation states, the validity of legal systems has been strongly territorially bound, with just the exception of diplomatic immunity. Today, however, a new legal pluralism has developed. Especially in Europe, the more sophisticated distribution of competences over regional, national and European authorities has created such a new form of legal pluralism. Moreover, non-state legal systems and some of their rules have been increasingly recognized by national courts. This ranges from sports law of international sports organizations to religious rules of varying religions. By this, Western law has developed from personalism to territorialism and, today, again creating some space for person-bound legal rules. Also within state law this distinction is sometimes made. An example is the 'culture-bound' legal regulation in Brussels. For education, arts and the like, different legal systems apply to French-speaking inhabitants of Brussels than to their Flemish neighbours. Sometimes religious rules may be accepted as a valid reason for not following some specific state legal regulation, such as the prohibition to cover one's head for a picture on one's passport, when it is recognized that a person's religious rules impose the opposite. As the examples in Prakash Shah's chapter in this volume show, this is even the case in Britain, notwithstanding the strong statements of leading politicians and lawyers saying the opposite (quoted by Prakash Shah in Chapter 9).

From the 6th till the 20th century Islamic law was largely person bound rather than territorially bound. Other religions, especially the Jewish and Christian ones, were fully accepted and were allowed to follow their own rules. This was not only the case in conquered territories, such as Spain, with a large Catholic population, but in the whole Islamic world too. Pluralism has been a typical characteristic of the Islamic legal tradition. In the aftermath of colonization, nation states were established in the Muslim world in the 20th century. Law became more territorially bound. But at the same time a new form of legal pluralism has been created. Universal Shari'a, based on the Qur'an and the *sunna*, continued to be valid alongside pure national state law, issued by parliaments and governments.

Legal Scholarship

Legal scholarship has developed in varying shapes within each of the large legal traditions. In the continental European legal tradition it reached a high level of sophistication in the early centuries of Roman law, especially in the 3rd and 4th centuries. After the decline of the Roman empire it disappeared until the end of the 11th century, when the rediscovery of Roman legal texts led to the creation of the very first law school and university in Bologna. This was the start of a continuous development of legal scholarship in continental Europe until today. Britain and Ireland, however, remained largely outside this development. In those common law countries law was considered to be a matter of practice, not of science. Until the 18th century, no single course of positive law was taught at universities and it was not before the 19th century that the first law faculty was created. Legal education was carried out at the 'Inns of Court' in London, not at universities. A university degree is, still today, not required for entering legal practice. And it is only very recently that it was made possible to enter legal practice with a university degree only. For those reasons, legal scholarship in this part of Europe only developed in the course of the last few decades. This explains why UK law and Irish law are, technically speaking, less developed than their continental counterparts and are completely marginalized in the elaboration of European law.

Just as with the general development of law, legal scholarship in continental Europe has seen a shift from universalism to nationalism (as from the 19th century), with recently some new attempts at a 'Europeanization' of legal scholarship. This development also entailed consequences for the conception of 'legal science' and its methodology. In the Middle Ages, science was largely a matter of authority. Something was considered to be true because of the authority of the person who concluded it, not because of some empirical evidence. In law, it was the authority of the great Roman jurists or of the medieval glossators and post-glossators that founded and underpinned legal statements and legal reasoning. This is quite comparable to Islamic legal science during most of its history: a quite abstract scholarly analysis of authoritative legal sources, outside all kinds of parliamentary or governmental legislation, in which the authority of the interpreters strongly determines the validity of the statements and conclusions.

With the rise of the nation states in Europe and the development of purely national legal systems, legal scholarship took a very different shape. Until the 19th-century codifications, academic legal writing was a creative activity, in which a synthesis had to be made between different legal systems and approaches. For instance, Roman law was systematically used to interpret customary law in such a way that regionally diverging rules were made more compatible and more similar, so as to facilitate harmonization in the long term. Roman law offered the scientific framework for describing, interpreting and systematizing all kinds of other legal regulations. It is this long tradition of a creative, systematizing and harmonizing legal scholarship that culminated in the great codifications of the 19th century. This great success for many generations of legal scholars, however, was a disaster for legal scholarship in the following decades. As everything had now been laid down in nicely ordered, sophisticated codes, legal scholarship turned into positivism. Legal textbooks, henceforth, just repeated the texts of the codes, completed with some historical explanations and some examples from case law. All kinds of creativity and even critical attitude had been lost. These elements only slowly came back, albeit still to a lesser degree than before the 19th century, when new needs of systematization and harmonization came to life because of diverging legislation outside the codes, because of societal changes which made parts of the codes less adapted to current society and because of judicial decisions that sometimes offered interpretations of legislative texts that considerably diverged from their apparent literal meaning, but were more in line with current needs and situations. As from the second half of the 20th century, a new impetus for creativity in legal scholarship was offered by the development of European Union law and European Human Rights law. As national law had to be made compatible with those European laws, it, again, had to be reinterpreted in a creative way, apart from the interpretation of the European rules that, in their turn had to harmonize diverging national rules, principles and choices made by the national legal systems.

Legal philosophy is a typical Western product. Philosophy is clearly present in other cultures, but not 'legal philosophy' or 'legal theory'. This says something about the position of law in society. In the European tradition law has been disconnected from other normative systems, such as morals and religion and could, partly because of this, develop as a well-elaborated, relatively independent system in society. This is neither the case in the Islamic tradition, nor in African or Asian cultures. Therefore, there never has been a legal philosophy in the Islamic tradition (Mallat, 2003, 4). '*Usul*' is considered to be a kind of Islamic legal philosophy, but according to Chibli Mallat it is just a discipline which has adapted classical Greek logic to legal categories (Mallat, 2003, 4). Law, in this tradition, has always been strongly linked to religion, as its main direct sources are religious texts. This lack of systematic theoretical reflections on law, with its own concepts and methodology, makes it difficult for Islamic lawyers to elaborate theories that may help to accommodate Islamic tradition with the developments in the last century. Maybe the 21st century will offer a development of Islamic legal philosophy. This may well be necessary in order to work out alternatives to pragmatism, on the one hand, and fundamentalism, on the other. To the extent that positive law, outside the Shari'a, in all Muslim countries is influenced, at least to some extent but often to a large extent, by Western law, one may expect that such an Islamic legal philosophy will also largely build on the Western legal philosophical tradition.

If there has not been a tradition of legal philosophy or legal theory in the Islamic world, there certainly has been a legal science in the sense of legal doctrine: *fiqh*.

As from the 10th century there has been a genre of '*qadi* manuals', where detailed regulations on what happens in the courtroom is elaborated:

> In these manuals, sample cases are discussed, along with formulas, problems of evidence, how a judge deals with a judge in another jurisdiction, or in another school of law, down to the way the judge should accept or not social invitations, or gifts, the risks of corruption and how to avoid it, a rationalised use of public resources, including saving on precious paper for the registration of judgments. (Mallat, 2003, 6)

The lack of concrete and precise rules to be found in the Qur'an for most situations made legal doctrine flourish. Inevitably, a methodology of legal reasoning and legal interpretation had to be developed. Varying theories have been developed as from the early centuries, leading to different schools, both in the Shi'ite and Sunni traditions, and which have continued to develop up to now (Berger, 2006, 25). The tenets of those schools, however, have been consolidated as early as in the 9th century (3rd century of the Islamic calendar). Of course, different legal interpretations also mean different theological views. So, those jurisprudential schools are at the same time theological schools. With the exception of a limited amount of rules to be found in the Qur'an or in the *sunna*, for which only one single interpretation is accepted, the *fiqh* offers a picture of a rather liberal and pluralist approach to legal doctrine, with a lot of space for the development of a critical approach to the interpretation of texts and, hence, for adapting law to changed circumstances. This approach is certainly more open than the (continental) European ones at the heights of positivism, which mainly occurred after codification but still survive now. It is more comparable to the pre-codification period, before the 19th century, where a multitude of legal sources and their vagueness also offered a lot of space for diverging interpretations and sophisticated legal reasoning.

Just like European legal scholars in that pre-codification period, but unlike current Western legal doctrine, Islamic legal scholars are not practically oriented. They develop ways of reasoning and their methodology is closer to the one used by theologians than the one used in modern Western legal doctrine (Berger, 2006, 32). As Mona Siddiqui concludes in Chapter 2 of this volume, exploring the boundaries of argumentation seems to have been more preponderant in the history of *fiqh* than finding solutions for concrete legal cases or setting moral boundaries of behaviour.

Conclusion

When comparing the Islamic legal tradition with the Western ones, it transpires that there are more commonalities than one would expect at first sight, be it that the chronology is not the same. Legal doctrine (*fiqh*) flourished in Islam mainly in a period in which Europe was a desert in this area (7th to 9th centuries). The link between law and religion has never been as strong in the West as in the Islamic tradition, but canon law played an important role in areas such as family law (which is also the main focus of the Qur'an) in the Catholic world until the French revolution. Islamic tradition did not develop a genuine legal philosophy, apart from general philosophy or theology, but it developed parts of legal theory (legal logic, legal reasoning, legal interpretation) and a sophisticated legal doctrine. Even its methods of 'consensus' and 'analogy' are comparable to current methodology in European legal doctrine and legal practice. The classic tension between literal and teleological interpretation has always been present in both traditions. Plurality of legal sources has always been typical for the Islam, as it was also the case in the Western legal tradition during most of its history. Both traditions currently see a tension between national, positive law, on the one hand, and a kind of supranational, 'natural law'. While in Islam it is the Shari'a, in Europe this role of natural law is played by human rights law.

Chapter 5
Is Shari'a Law, Religion or a Combination? European Legal Discourses on Shari'a

Lisbet Christoffersen

When you push a cat into a corner, it might turn around as a tiger.[1]

Anglican Food for Thought

In this chapter I discuss Shari'a in relation to discursive trends within European legal thinking in order to identify dimensions of legal traditions behind some of the normative confrontations around Shari'a. I am not pretending to give a total overview of European legal discourses on Shari'a, which would be reckless in a short chapter. What I am aiming at doing here is to reveal deeper normative structures or lines of thinking beneath European jurisprudence, structures that are basic to some of the difficulties regarding Shari'a as such in a European legal context.

1 I was in, June 2004, invited to speak at a seminar at the European University in Budapest, discussing the Refah Partisi case because the organizer of the seminar, W. Cole Durham, Jr, who is a professor of comparative law and religion at Brigham Young University, was told by a Scandinavian colleague of both of us, Tore Lindholm from the Centre of Human Rights in Oslo, that I was in favour of the court's decision. At that time a scholar of that opinion seemed to be rare within the European or international law and religion discourse. The two of them have in collaboration with others furthered their discussions at the Strasbourg Conference on Freedom of Religion and Belief (see www.strasbourgconference.org). One of the participants in the Budapest seminar, a Bulgarian colleague, told me the sentence I quoted as an epigram to this chapter referred to a proverb. The proverb has become a guiding principle for my growing interest in the concrete case, Shari'a and European legislation as well as broader law–religion relations in Europe and internationally. In the years after I have had several occasions to discuss Shari'a and European legal understanding with European colleagues, including particularly Richard Potz, Mark van Hoecke, Hartmut Lehmann, Charalambos Papastatis, Shaheen Sardar Ali, Grace Davie and Silvio Ferrari. I wrote my first piece on Shari'a in Danish at the request of the editors of a local yearbook *Årbog for Københavns Stift 2006,* Jesper Stange and Bente Hansen. My knowledge of Islam and Shari'a has also been enlightened by texts from and discussions with the Danish colleagues Ditlev Tamm, Jakob Skovgaard-Petersen, Nils Bredsdorff, Peter Blume, Rubya Mehdi, Hanne Petersen, Helmuth Schledermann and Jørgen S. Nielsen. I am grateful to all these colleagues for inspiration and discussions.

Such deep roots behind European legal thinking are normally not so visible that they become part of a discussion in the public sphere. But as Anglican Archbishop Rowan Williams in February 2008 published his reflections on Shari'a and English law,[2] the public was suddenly reminded of these deep roots. Dr Williams had opened a series of lectures at the Temple Church at the Inner and Middle Temple of the Inns of Court in London on the theme 'Islam in English law'. His lecture was entitled 'Civil and religious law in England: a religious perspective'. The question he confronted in his lecture was:

> the existence of what is very widely felt to be a growing challenge in our societies – that is the presence of communities which, while no less 'law-abiding' than the rest of the population, relate to something other than the British legal system alone. But the issues that arose around what level of public or legal recognition, if any, might be allowed to the legal provisions of a religious group, are not peculiar to Islam.

It followed from his speech that these issues are relevant also for the role of the Church of England, which is of course governed by the law of the land, but ruled within this legislation by the authorities of the Church, not by public authorities. In the English context the issue the archbishop raised is also relevant for the Jewish communities, since Orthodox Judaism for more than a century has had a court system of its own in England. The relevant question therefore is broader than a discourse on Shari'a. It concerns the 'rights of religious groups within a secular state' and what the archbishop calls a 'just and constructive relationship between Islamic law and the statutory law of the United Kingdom'.

He based his speech on a 'robust appeal to the rightness of the law of the land protecting individuals on the ground of their religious identity and securing their freedom to fulfil religious duties'. He presupposed that 'no kind of supplementary jurisdiction could have the power to deny access to the rights granted to other citizens (regardless of faith affiliation) or to punish its members for claiming those rights'.

On this basis he suggested, that 'it might be possible to think in terms of 'transformative accommodation': a scheme in which individuals retain the liberty to choose the jurisdiction under which they will seek to resolve certain carefully specified matters … (including) aspects of marital law, the regulation of financial transactions and authorized structures of mediation and conflict resolution'.

The reactions in the public media in at least England and Denmark were heated. An example was Peter Wivel, a widely respected and very well-informed journalist, who in an editorial in *Politiken* (a leading Danish newspaper) on 20 February 2008 wrote (with reference to Thomas Hobbes),

2 <http://www.archbishopofcanterbury.org/1575>, accessed on 19 February 2008.

> We cannot make agreements with God, they necessarily have to be made with one of His representatives, such as imams, archbishops and the like – and agreements like that are precisely what democracy categorically rejects.
>
> Our laws are our protection against imams, archbishops and other self-appointed authorities, with whom nobody should feel secure. They may have the opportunity to judge us in the world to come, but in this world they have to restrict themselves to giving us spiritual guidance. Here we are protected by the rule of law – also as regards the clergy … therefore there can be no compromise between free societies, governed by the rule of law, and Shari'a courts.

The headline of the article was 'We do not compromise with God', drawing on biblical references such as Moses' remarks at the end of his life, when he repeated the rulings of God for the Jewish people and gave them a choice between following God or following other gods (Deuteronomy 30:15–20), or St Paul's claim that the Christians of Corinth ought to let themselves be reconciled with God (2 Corinthians 5:20).[3] How come? On what grounds are these deep roots called upon in order to uphold or re-establish a clear-cut separation between law and religion and make no arrangements relating to what could be called religious law or religiously inspired legal norms at the common courts in England or Denmark? This chapter aims to contribute towards an answer to that question.

The Refah Partisi Case

One of the best places to see the aforementioned reaction towards the mere possibility of arguing with Shari'a in a European legal context is in the Refah Partisi case, a judgment published on 13 February 2003 by the European Court of Human Rights in Strasbourg.[4] The case contains leading arguments on relations between religion, law and democracy in Europe – and as a decision from the highest relevant court in Europe it not only argues or recalls a discourse; it simply lays down what European law is in this field.

The factual background was the following. After having taken part in a number of elections since its foundation in July 1983 and after having become the largest political party in Turkey at the elections in 1995 – resulting in the party coming into power by forming a coalition government with other parties – the Refah Partisi was dissolved by the Turkish Constitutional Court in January 1998 on the

3 I have asked Peter Wivel whether the biblical references were intentional – he told me the headline was taken from Hobbes (who of course was very well informed on the biblical references).

4 *Case of Refah Partisi (The Welfare Party) and others* v. *Turkey*, Appl nos 41340/98; 41342/98; 41343/98 and 41344/98, Grand Chamber.

grounds that the party 'had become a centre of activities against the principle of secularism', which is seen as basic in the Turkish constitution. The court further held that the public declarations of Refah's leaders and some named leaders in particular had collectively committed Refah as regards the constitutionality of its activities. They were therefore banned from sitting in parliament or holding certain political posts for five years.

It was this judgment on which the European Court of Human Rights took a grand chamber decision. The court held unanimously (with the votes of 17:0) that there had been no violation of article 11 of the European Convention of Human Rights (freedom of assembly and association) and that it was not necessary to examine separately the complaints under among others article 9 (freedom of thought, religion etc.).

Basically the decision is based on arguments of militant democracy. That is also how it is most widely analysed (see among others Moe, 2006; Macklem, 2006). Macklem, however, as we shall see, broadens his analysis to the very point of the possible conflict between European legal thinking and the (religiously based) concept of legal pluralism.[5] Gadirov (2006) shows that the case transgresses the militant democracy concept and must be understood on basis of an analysis of relations between freedom of religion and a plurality of legal systems. Thereby he argues along the same lines as I did already at the Budapest seminar (cf. note 1 above) and am doing in this chapter.

The reasons why the Refah Partisi was seen as anti-democratic, however, were related to an understanding of the role of Shari'a in Europe. In the press release[6] this was formulated in terms that,

> those acts and speeches revealed Refah's long-term policy of setting up a regime based on sharia in order to implement its policy and keep the system it envisaged in place. Considering that these plans were incompatible with the concept of a 'democratic society' and that the real opportunities Refah had to put them into practice made the danger to democracy more tangible and more immediate, the penalty imposed on the applicants by the Constitutional Court, even in the context of the restricted margin of appreciation left to it, might reasonably be considered to have met a 'pressing social need'.[7]

The court's evaluation was based on a combination of arguments: regarding Shari'a as being incompatible with the fundamental principles of democracy; considering a plurality of legal systems as not being compatible with the Convention

5 For a Danish analysis of the limits of democracy, based on material from World War II, see Koch (1994).

6 085 – 13.2.2003. Press release issued by the registrar, <http://www.echr.coe.int/Eng/Press/2003/feb/RefahPartisiGCjudgmenteng.htm>.

7 In this chapter I am not going deeper into the militant democracy arguments in the court's decision, since it is the freedom of religion part of the case I am focusing on.

system; and rejecting Refah's arguments that it could be seen as part of the right to a protected freedom of religion to open for an individual use of the family law dimension of Shari'a based on a free choice formulated contractually.[8]

Shari'a as a ((Inter)national) Legal System

One of the leading discourses on law is to see law as a set of normative and institutional systems, each of them upheld by a combined set of regulatory power, legislation, court systems and legal concepts. This understanding of law traditionally lies behind the discipline of comparative law, the legal discipline comparing the contents of different legal systems of the world in order to identify their basic principles, their differences and similarities, for the purpose of formulating legal solutions on concrete legal problems or for the purpose of formulating a general legal order within a broader area or within a distinct legal system. The 'state of the art' on the discipline (Reimann and Zimmermann, 2006), interestingly enough, does not define the task of the discipline of comparative law – this definition is picked up in Zweigert and Kötz (1998), where the concept, functions and aims, method and history of comparative law are discussed in detail.

Within the context of comparative law discourses, Islamic law is seen as one of the legal systems or families of the world. Zweigert and Kötz used the term 'religious legal systems' to comprise Islamic law and Hindu law. Shari'a was here defined as 'the complex of divinely revealed rules which the faithful Muslim must observe if he seeks to perform the duties of religion' (Zweigert and Kötz, 1998, 303).

In this definition is no argument as to why Shari'a should be understood as law, not as religion. The nature of the set of norms or rules is said to be that they are divinely revealed and cover all aspects of life. Its content is traditionally understood as, on the one hand, a set of rules (often called the five pillars) on the basic creed, the duty to observe regular daily prayers, periods of fasting and the distribution of alms, and the instruction to conduct the pilgrimage at least once a lifetime. As shown in the literature the concept of Shari'a is, however, wider containing law of personal status (particularly marriage, divorce and inheritance), criminal and commercial law, dress and dietary rules, and the law of evidence. Thus, on the other hand, Shari'a is said to contain a total set of norms, a full discourse, covering religion, morality and justice and with specific legal methods to formulate concrete rulings for all imaginable specific situations (Hjärpe, 2005).

In historical fact, says Zubaida, Shari'a has varied according to time and place, but its discourse is based on a claim to be eternal and coherent (Zubaida, 2006; Zweigert and Kötz, 1998, 304f). Zweigert and Kötz also take their starting point in this claim that Shari'a is eternal and coherent, but turns it around in their

8 I come back to these three basic arguments of the court when discussing Shari'a as legal system later in this chapter.

understanding of Shari'a as a 'claim to be a comprehensive ethic or doctrine of duties (*fiqh*) which controls the entire earthly existence of Muslims and shows them the way in which they must perform their religious duties in order to earn the promised reward of bliss in a better world' (Zweigert and Kötz, 1998, 304).

It is clearly such a fixed understanding of Shari'a which was influencing the European Court of Human Rights in its decision on the Refah Partisi case:

> the Court considers that sharia, which faithfully reflects the dogmas and divine rules laid down by religion, is stable and invariable. Principles such as pluralism in the political sphere or the constant evolution of the public freedoms have no place in it. The Court notes that, when read together, the offending statements, which contain explicit references to the introduction of sharia, are difficult to reconcile with the fundamental principles of democracy, as conceived in the Convention taken as a whole. It is difficult to declare one's respect for democracy and human rights while at the same time supporting a regime based on sharia, which clearly diverges from Convention values, particularly with regard to its criminal law and criminal procedure, its rules on the legal status of women and the way it intervenes in all spheres of private and public life in accordance with religious precepts. In the Court's view, a political party whose actions seem to be aimed at introducing sharia in a State party to the Convention can hardly be regarded as an association complying with the democratic ideal that underlies the whole of the Convention. (paragraph 123 with reference to an earlier court's decision paragraph 72)

For many Muslims living in Europe as immigrants it is, however, neither necessary nor relevant to think in fixed terms of religion in order to get access to Islamic rules for their family life. The existing systems of international private law leaves the door open for many of them to refer to rules of marriage, divorce and inheritance which are Islamic in their foundations because the leading international private law arrangements allow the law of nationality precedence over the law of the country of residence (Nielsen, 2004, 108ff; Foblets, 2003, ch.7; Rohe, 2007, 111–36). If the international private law regime of the country of residence points to the legal system of the parties' nationality, then it follows that the courts in such a country (e.g. Sweden) must use the private law system of, for example, Pakistan when a married couple of Pakistani nationality has private law problems in the country of residence. Thereby a legal system derived from Shari'a can become the legal system ruling the marriage for persons living in European countries. In this context the Refah Partisi case would appear to become irrelevant.

Through this international private law system of choosing the law relevant for the couple or the contract, Shari'a becomes a legal system relevant in concrete European court cases. Jørgen Nielsen and others have argued that in an age of globalization it also ought to be so, since personal legal status cannot be rigidly dependent on one's geographical location at any given moment (Nielsen, 2004, 111; Ballard, 2006, 29–56). Others would follow Marie-Claire Foblets in her preference for solutions allowing the law of the country of the habitual residence to be applied in principle as against the law of the country of nationality. Marie-Claire Foblets can only accept Shari'a as a subsidiary rule, with a limited and conditional choice. Her basic argument is that the great majority of litigants concerned, women in particular, are even today not well enough informed of their rights to be able to handle negotiations by themselves with (future) spouses and thus allow them to resist pressure or outside influence and control their own positions within the family circle (Foblets, 2003, 283). Mathias Rohe perhaps offers the solution by suggesting, that 'native' legal rules can be applied within the limits of public policy (Rohe, 2006, 57–72).

Shari'a thereby shows up, not so much in the courtrooms as in the empirical reality of Europe, when Muslims living here choose to turn their backs to the national legal system with its norms and concepts, its statutory regulations and its courts, lawyers and judges, and instead look to more or less unofficial Muslim systems for legal advice, which they themselves feel bound by.

Rubya Mehdi in her research thus shows the same development in Denmark, as has earlier been shown by Werner Menski and others for England and by Matthias Rohe and others for Germany (Mehdi, 2007; Menski, 2006, 13–28; Rivers, 2006; Rohe, 2007), namely that people within the Muslim minorities use the opportunities of the law to establish an 'optional' civil law. As Rohe formulates it:

> Private autonomy is the core value of the liberal European Civil law orders. Thus, in matters exclusively concerning the private interests of the parties involved, these parties are entitled to create and arrange their legal relations according to their preferences. Legal rules regulating such matters are 'optional' within a certain framework. (Rohe, 2007, 91)

The members of Muslim communities, who choose to follow their own, 'privatized' way of introducing Shari'a as the law of choice, are of course free to shift and let their case be brought before the common national courts with use of the common legal norms of the country of residence. They are thereby in the same situation as the members of the Catholic Church in Europe, who might choose to follow canon law for their marriage problems and let their legal problems be brought before the Catholic courts (in Scandinavia situated in Stockholm); or the members of the Jewish community, who choose to follow advice from the rabbi but are free to go to the civil law system of the country.[9]

Seen as such, one could just let people do what they want to do. There are, however, still problems in this individualized type of solution. One is that especially women very often suffer from lack of knowledge of their rights and are in reality

9 For such solutions in the Nordic countries, see the articles in Christoffersen et al. forthcoming.

bound by systems which disadvantage them.[10] This is why feminist lawyers such as Rubya Mehdi seek to bring this 'black legal economy' to the surface and get it integrated in the common legal system.

For many families it is not enough to appeal to the legal norms in force, if the religiously based norms are not followed. That counts for Catholic families and for Jewish families as well as for Muslim families. Even more, Jewish families with relations to Israel and especially many Muslim families can become split between two countries with two different legal systems following two distinct and different normative models. They will suffer, if their legal matters do not get the correct solutions. It is easy enough to tell a Muslim woman, living in Copenhagen, that she can just follow the Danish legal system, but that does not necessarily help her much if she is of Pakistani nationality and her marriage in Pakistan is only judged by Pakistani (Muslim) norms. To give her a divorce in Denmark helps her, but only in Denmark; it does not free her to remarry according to the legal norms in Pakistan, in her family background and in her religious identity.

The privatized solution, where people are outlawing themselves in order to follow Shari'a, also means areas of tensions between Islamic law and the ethical assumptions underlying international law as well as most European legal systems. Observers here mention the following four areas (see Rivers, 2006, 160; and Rohe, 2006, 62):

- the prohibition on Muslim women marrying non-Muslim men (whereas Muslim men are free to marry non-Muslim women), which infringes individual freedom of choice in marriage and is discriminatory;
- the acceptability of polygamy;
- the Islamic form of divorce known as *talaq*, since it allows a divorce without cause, juridical oversight or financial provision;
- marriage of minors under the age of puberty and without their consent.

Of course marriages following these rules in Islamic law are void under European law – but in practice the tendency to keep outside the European legal system permit these things to happen even in European countries.

This is also the reason, Jytte Klausen shows, why the 'choice' option between European and religious civil law is not attractive for the Muslim leaders in her investigation. Thus the women in Jytte Klausen's study were notably less supportive of legal pluralism and multicultural devolution of authority to Islamic scholars and imams than were the male leaders. Even women who otherwise expressed traditionalist views prefer, says Klausen, to see an accommodation between Islam

10 For a detailed analysis, showing that religious laws very often are suppressing women, see Whiting and Evans, 2006. For concrete analysis in the same field among European Muslim leaders, see Klausen, 2005, especially 193ff on balancing religious and civil law.

and European legal norms that protect women's rights. 'They want equal rights, not different rights' (Klausen, 2005, 193–9).

The *Millet* System and a Plurality of Legal Systems

Even though groups of people living in Europe are in reality basing their civil law problems on Shari'a-derived solutions, the European Court of Human Rights seems to find Shari'a totally outside the scope of European legal ruling. This has to do with an attempt to outlaw a distinct dimension of the Ottoman heritage, namely the so-called *millet* system.

In the Refah Partisi case, the court 'observed that there was already an Islamic theocratic regime under Ottoman law' and the reader can get the impression that this system was dismantled with the Ottoman regime and the introduction of the republican regime in Turkey. The dismantling also was nearly total – but not 100 per cent, as Shari'a is still behind the private law of the Muslims living in the north-eastern part of Greece (Western Thrace) (Ferrari, 2003, ch.6).

The basic idea in the *millet* system (as the Ottoman system was named) was that each person in the empire was born into an identity based on religion – not an identity based on nationality. If a person was born of parents belonging to the Jewish community, he or she became by birth member of the Jewish community of the empire, and it was the same with people born into the different Christian communities and into the large Muslim community. The private law of subjects of the empire then depended on the community to which they belonged. Jews followed Jewish law, Orthodox followed Orthodox canon law, Assyrian Christians their legal system and Muslims the Shari'a. Legal institutions were related to each legal system, which was thus fully equipped to keep the inhabitants within their *millet*.[11] If people had to make contract arrangements crossing the *millets*, Muslim law prevailed and provided solutions.

This system has been called a system of freedom of religion (cf. paragraph 126 of the Refah Partisi judgment), and it is correct that there was freedom to perform religious rituals and to follow religiously based legal norms in the system, etc. The freedom was, however, based on a collective identity. There was no individual freedom of religion in the system – on the contrary, since the whole legal system was based on each subject being linked to a religious identity. So if a person wanted to leave his or her own religious system, this would mean changing to another religious system with another related legal system – if such a change was at all possible. One of the basic discussions in current international freedom of religion discourses is related to this, since all countries (be they Orthodox, Muslim, Hindu or Western) agree on a freedom of having or adapting a religion. The problems show up when there is a wish to guarantee the freedom to change one's religion or

11 A *millet* was originally a group of 1,000 men within an army, whose leader was responsible for their keeping the rules, fulfilling their goals etc.

to be allowed to not have a religion at all. These freedoms are only secured in the European Convention of Human Rights (Evans, 2001; and Ferrari, 2000, 4ff.).

The basic conflict between this system and the European legal systems, common after Napoleonic times, is, as noted by the European Court of Human Rights, that such a system refers to religious rules as the basis for the entrance into the legal system and thereby infringes the principle of non-discrimination between individuals (paragraph 119 with reference to paragraph 70 in the former court case). The system thus distinguishes between the legal systems in force on the basis not of country of origin or nationality or country of residence, but on the basis of the individual's belonging to a religion. More simply expressed: the basic distinction is not citizenship, but the religious marker: cross (of different types), star or crescent. This system is still the basis of aspects of civil law in the Middle East, especially in Lebanon and Israel (on the latter see Cohn, 2004). In Europe it is, as mentioned, only in force in a part of Greece, based on international treaty.

When the ECHR in the Refah Partisi case finds against the party on the grounds of its 'plan to set up a plurality of legal systems', then it is the *millet* system which the court considers to be incompatible with the Convention system (paragraph 119).

As mentioned, the case was decided unanimously in grand chamber with the vote 17:0. The court was really seeking to reject the *millet* system in order to block definitively any attempt to re-introduce a religiously based legal system in Europe. There were however two concurring opinions on some of the arguments in the case, of which one is of relevance here. Judge Kovler (of Russia) in his concurring opinion gave a much more in-depth analysis of the concept of legal pluralism than the one provided in the judgment and referring to the *millet* system. He refers to legal pluralism as an internationally respected system, not only from a legal anthropological view but also in areas within modern constitutional law which under certain conditions can give members of minorities of all kinds more than one type of personal status. He admits that pluralism, which impinges mainly on an individual's private and family life, is limited by the requirements of the general interest and public order, but on the other hand he also stresses that, given the fact that it is more difficult in practice to find a compromise between the interests of the communities concerned and civil society as a whole, a judgment from an international court as the European Court of Human Rights at least ought not to reject the very idea of such a compromise.

The arguments of Judge Kovler are in line with more general trends to accept a plurality of legal systems or at least of legal norms, a trend which is surfacing increasingly often in European as well as international laws of religion, the idea being that there ought to be a link between the religion of birth or choice and the legal rulings governing family relations. This way of turning the argument around, starting with freedom of religion, was also relevant in the Refah Partisi case.

A Civil Law Dimension of Freedom of Religion?

The most central discussion in the Refah Partisi judgment concerns the scope of the concept of freedom of religion in relation to private law, especially as it relates to marriage, divorce and inheritance. This discussion is so central because the arguments combine general law-of-religion-arguments from European jurisprudence (as in the archbishop's speech discussed above) with traditional understandings not only in Islam, but also within Jewish communities and, among Christians, particularly the Catholic and Orthodox denominations.[12]

The argument from the representatives of the Refah Partisi goes as follows:

> what Mr Necmettin Erbakan had proposed, was only the introduction of a 'civil-law' system, based on the freedom to enter into contracts, which would not have affected the general sphere of public law. Frustrating such a policy in the name of the special role of secularism in Turkey amounted to discrimination against Muslims who wished to conduct their private lives in accordance with the precepts of their religion … (paragraph 72)

In response to this, the court noted that:

> Refah's policy was to apply some of sharia's private-law rules to a large part of the population in Turkey (namely Muslims), within the framework of a plurality of legal systems. Such a policy goes beyond the freedom of individuals to observe the precepts of their religion, for example by organising religious wedding ceremonies before or after a civil marriage … and according a religious marriage the effect of a civil marriage. This Refah policy falls outside the private sphere to which Turkish law confines religion and suffers from the same contradictions with the Convention system as the introduction of sharia. (paragraph 127)

> freedom of religion, including the freedom to manifest one's religion by worship and observance, is primarily a matter of individual conscience, and (the Court) stresses that the sphere of individual conscience is quite different from the field of private law, which concerns the organisation and functioning of society as whole. It has not been disputed before the Court that in Turkey everyone can observe in his private life the requirements of his religion. On the other hand, Turkey, like any other Contracting Party, may legitimately prevent the application within its jurisdiction of private-law rules of religious inspiration prejudicial to public order and the values of democracy for Convention purposes (such as rules

12 The non-Protestant denominations referred to are those dominant within Christianity: the Catholic Church, the Orthodox churches, but also some of the most conservative Protestant churches are included, as well as some of the new religious movements (Seventh Day Adventists, Mormons, etc.).

> permitting discrimination based on the gender of the parties concerned, as in polygamy and privileges for the male sex in matters of divorce and succession). The freedom to enter into contracts cannot encroach upon the State's role as the neutral and impartial organiser of the exercise of religions, faiths and beliefs. (paragraph 128)

Earlier in the judgment, the court had reminded the audience and the parties of general European law on religion on the basis of the court's own case law. It was thus reiterated that democratic pluralism depends on respect for freedom of religion as well as of the life stances of the non-religious. This freedom entails *inter alia* freedom to hold or not to hold religious beliefs and to practise or not to practise a religion. In pluralistic societies where more religions coexist, it is the state's obligation in a neutral and impartial way to reconcile the interests of the various groups and to ensure that everyone's beliefs are respected (paragraphs 90–1).

Freedom of religion is in the first place a matter of individual conscience. It does, however, also imply 'freedom to manifest one's religion alone and in private or in community with others, in public and within the circle of those whose faith one shares. Article 9 lists a number of forms which manifestation of a religion or belief may take, namely worship, teaching, practice and observance. But it does not protect every act motivated or influenced by a religion or belief (paragraph 92).

What is said here is that, legally speaking in a European context, freedom of religion concerns religion as one of the dimensions of life – not all dimensions of life, even though these wider dimensions of life for the religious observer might be influenced by the whole set of norms which a religion may offer. As Jørgen S. Nielsen has put it: 'It is inescapable that modern European legal concepts of religious freedom are based on a narrow definition of religion' (Nielsen, 1999, 88). When that was formulated, though, Jørgen S. Nielsen was not prepared 'to dismiss the demand from some Muslim quarters for Islamic family law', even though he drew attention to the need for individual, not collective choice, the rivalry among the leaders, etc. Fifteen years later, the European Court of Human Rights put its foot down in the Refah Partisi case.

There is thus no doubt that Europe is not prepared to let religious *groups* decide over family law for their adherents, already because the adherents must be allowed to change their religion or to have different degrees of being religious within the different religious groups. Europe is thus not prepared to accept segregation of people on the basis of religion, if the relevant persons have not chosen that specific consequence of being religious to a smaller or larger extent. In this sense, the Refah Partisi case simply stated what most European observers would also have held based on the freedom of religion discourses.

Several of the contributors to the recent book of Shah and Menski (2006) do not, however, share this analysis. Not only Roger Ballard in his contribution (Ballard, 2006), but also Werner Menski, points to the historical fact that the

Europeans took their legal systems with them when they went out not least in India, establishing a plurality of legal systems especially in the field of personal laws. Now, as Ballard puts it,

> like it or not, the process of globalisation is changing the character of the world in which we live, such that hubristic assumptions about the innate superiority of all things Euro-American have become increasingly threadbare. So long as Europeans continue to take it for granted that their own values, practices and conceptual constructions are *ipso facto* superior to those of all others, and hence universally applicable, they will doubtless regard the prospects of taking others seriously as an unacceptable challenge to the integrity of their own self-constructed worlds. (Ballard, 2006, 56)

Seen from Ballard's point of view, a civil law perspective of freedom of religion is only natural. Seen from the perspective of Mathias Rohe, though, it would imply a segregation or acculturation in opposition to the more desirable goal of assimilation or integration. No European state with historical memory could bear to force any member of any religious group to let his or her civil or legal rights be based on a religious identity any more – the yellow star of the Nazi period being too close to mind.

The Cross-road

This response has to do with the *forced* relationship between religious identity and civil laws. The basic argument in the Refah Partisi case was, however, that the relationship should not be forced but based on individual contract. Because a large majority of the Turkish population belongs to the Islamic faith, this argument did not convince. The weak dimension of religious pluralism in Turkey convinced the court to follow the government in thinking that the reality would be no individual freedom for big parts of the population, only giving more radical secularists the choice of using other solutions but there again possibly only for a short time. That – besides the constitutional understanding of secularism – might be the real-life context for why the court supported the Turkish government in not accepting the possibility of contracting into Shari'a-based family law.

In Britain, however, there is no lack of pluralism, on the contrary. There and possibly in some European countries the real problem seems to be that rather large groups of religious people simply outlaw themselves. In Scandinavian countries at the end of the 20th century, for example, large groups simply stopped marrying and instead co-habited without going through a formal marriage. During the first long period the courts and the legislatures did not intervene. But after a while legal problems began to surface, especially when the weaker partner turned out not to be able to get substantive rights on a par with the stronger partner, a situation which required new legal solutions.

If at the same time such groups do not trust the national court systems, as suggested by Nielsen (1999, 86), as well as the archbishop in his speech of February 2008, the legal system has to react in order to find new solutions or, as Jytte Klausen puts it:

> One of the difficulties of the multiculturalist project has been to come up with institutional solutions that provide fair solutions to the problem of how to balance the need for solidarity – for example, an equal right to social protection – against the need for self-government and cultural and political autonomy for communities that claim to have distinct identities which set them apart from the majority. (Klausen, 2005, 196f.)

Many would react to this difficulty as did Grace Davie in her remarks at the concluding seminar at the final conference of the research priority programme 'Religion in the 21st century' at the University of Copenhagen, September 2007: 'They must abide by the rule of Law'! These groups must learn that there is a distinction between law and religion and an understanding of law as secular and democratic and that it is this distinction, which rules European societies. When in Rome, do as the Romans.

In Rome, however, we already have groups arguing that their adherents on basis of individual contract combined with personal conviction should follow not the secular, but religiously based legal discourses different from secular law, and that such a solution should be allowed and legally respected by the public authorities in so far that contractually based solutions which are not contrary to public norms should be seen as legally binding.

That counts for members of Jewish communities in England, who can follow Jewish norms as far as they wish and get their matrimonial contracts on that basis respected by the public legal authorities. This applies even more to the many European Catholics, covered by a concordat between the Holy See and the state concerned, allowing the members of the Catholic Church to, for example, marry or divorce only on the basis of canon law. When in Rome, do as the Romans – why not such solutions based on individual choice also for Muslim believers in Europe?

(North) European Legal Culture

European legal culture could be seen as a combination of particularity and universality, and even though a basic confessional neutrality of the state is seen as central, that has always been combined with the acceptance of individual ways of individual religious people (Häberle, 1994, 21–32). The same applies to the legal system: even though that is seen as based on scientific analysis and a jurisprudence independent not least of religious arguments, canon law on the other hand is seen as a legitimate part of precisely the same European jurisprudence – why not the same for a scientific and non-theological jurisprudence on Shari'a?

The rule of law is seen as central to European civilization, but as Chibli Mallat (Mallat, 2006, 622) has shown, Islamic legal culture also knows the contrast between ruling by law and ruling of law, which might be one of the undesirable, but not unexpected consequences of a flat, merely numeric understanding of Western democracy, an understanding which is at least associated with Scandinavian realism. The basic difference between Islamic legal culture and European legal culture might thus not be the question of the distinction between rule of or rule by law, but rather, as Mallat also points out, the question whether law is personal or territorial – and here there is no doubt: current European law is territorial, not personal (Rohe, 2006, 70).[13] This dichotomy, Mallat argues, 'may ultimately prove more important than any traditional classification familiar to comparative jurisprudence' (Mallat, 2006, 638f.).

European legal culture is a culture of national states established, among other processes, through the acquisition by the king of regulatory power within a specific territorial area. In the Middle Ages the power struggle was between competing smaller kings or princes, but also between Roman law, canon law and the law of the land. Especially in the northern part of Europe, however – England, the Scandinavian countries and the northern part of Germany – Roman law was always seen as foreign law, inspiring the law of the land, but only in force for Roman citizens. So even though the legal systems of the Middle Ages could be seen as pluralistic and related to persons, rather than to territories, that mostly counted for the rather few Roman citizens.

From the 12th century the basic criterion was territorial: the area of a city, ruled by the legislature in the city, property and commercial laws, etc. The real legal struggle from that time was less one between the concept of person and the concept of territory as the basic concept in law and more a power struggle between the Church and the state (the princes, kings and emperors). This fight went on until the Protestant reformations. Central for all these three dimensions of the Reformation period was the question of the law, not only the content, but basically whether the Church (the pope) or the prince or king was the central ruler.

England, the northern part of Germany and the Scandinavian countries broke the superior power of canon law and of the Church, establishing the kings as the central authority. That means that from the middle of the 16th century, the territorial principle has been central, also when it comes to family laws. That became even more obvious in the Lutheran reformation with its combination of a secularized legal system run under the authority of the king who in exchange had the obligation

13 This distinction should not be misunderstood. European law is characterized by a system of civil laws, in which the concept of the person is central (see e.g. Glenn 2007). But the concept of the person is central in a civil law system set in force by the legislative within a certain territory.

to keep the inhabitants to the correct and pure religious understanding (see Witte, 2002).

Even though England has its colonial experiences, these deep roots mean that English as well as Scandinavian legal culture can be seen as rather harsh towards any support for an understanding that there should be a personal or religious basis for legal systems. It is also on this background that the Scandinavian countries have a rather narrow understanding of the concept of religion, precisely *not* covering personal laws, which Jewish communities have already realized. So when members of Jewish communities in 1814 were accepted as citizens in Denmark, they had to pay a certain price, namely to give up their religiously based personal laws. On the other hand, no real codification of civil laws was made in the Scandinavian countries, which meant that the religious formalisation of a marriage was upheld in opposition to the real civil law countries (Zweigert and Kötz, 1998, 276–86).

But this counts also in a broader European context: the Peace of Westphalia (1648) after 100 years of religious wars meant that the old Latin phrase *cujus regio, ejus religio* became the basic ruling in Europe. The national states were built on the national churches and combined with the national legislative, and even though the Catholic Church remained a transnational church, during the following centuries of remaking Europe in the mirror of the national states it learned how to deal with this reality by way of the concept of concordats and national Catholic churches. This meant, that even though canon law still was (and is) an international discourse, it was implemented in the national churches through international treaties between the different national states and the Holy See. This became the system from the Napoleonic wars and was upheld also after the Second World War and has gained new impetus after 1989 with the establishment of new European national states with large Catholic denominations.

The Western legal tradition has been called a secular-rational model and this model, as it has been stated, tends to neglect elements of law that go transcend secular rationality. But that does not mean that there are no religious elements in the western secular rational legal model – on the contrary. Berman has showed that the legal and religious thinking of the West shares the concepts of rituals, of tradition, of authority and of universality (Berman, 2007, 745–6), and, maybe even more basic, the very distinction between the concept of secularity and the concept of sacred could and maybe should be seen as Christian – at least neither Islamic nor Jewish (Berman, 2007, 746; Dan, 1998, xxiii–xxxvi).

New Common European Solutions?

No matter where the origins of the distinction between sacred and secular are to be found, these distinctions are fundamental European law, and that may in reality be the central point to be learned from the Refah Partisi case. Or put another way: Europeans, European court systems as well as European parliamentarians do not want to accept religious court systems as the final instance deciding over personal laws.

That however is not the same as to say that Europeans do not want to accept religious influence into personal law thinking. The principles are shown e.g. in a recent recommendation from the Parliamentary Assembly of the Council of Europe.[14] In it, the Assembly recommends that the Committee of Ministers:

- ensure that religious communities are able to exercise the fundamental right of freedom of religion
- rule out any interference in religious affairs, but consider religious organizations as part of civil society and call on them to play an active role
- reaffirm the principle of independence of politics and law from religion
- give thought to religious dimension of intercultural dialogue
- exclude from the consultations any grouping that does not clearly support the Council of Europe's fundamental values, namely human rights, democracy and the rule of law
- identify good practice in dialogue with leaders of religious communities
- gradually to remove from legislation elements likely to be discriminatory from the angle of democratic religious pluralism.

What is at stake is the basis for an influence from religious communities on legislation with major religious impact or with religious elements. In the Lisbon Treaty, a new paragraph opens for an open and regular dialogue between religious communities and the EU institutions (Christoffersen, 2008). This dialogue has, so for as the Roman Catholic Church is concerned, for a long time been run by the Council of European Bishops' Conferences (COMECE), and for the non-Catholic European churches by the Conference of European Churches (CEC), which has a Church and Society Committee with an office in Brussels in order to follow many different European political and legal debates. Muslim groups are also organizing themselves in order to gain access to these dialogue fora.

At the same time, European legal discourses try to find common solutions to the differences, also when it comes to marriages and other civil law dimensions. With the classic Christian phrase, 'Render therefore unto Caesar the things which are Caesar's, and unto God the things which are God's', the leading discourse is here presented as an attempt to make an even more clear distinction between religious and legal dimensions of marriage (Gerven, 2004, 137–64; cf. Krause, 2006, 1099–130). The attempts are vigorous and exercise no constraints in the

14 Recommendation 1804 (2007) on State, Religion, Secularity and Human Rights, adopted by the Assembly on 29 June 2007 (27th Setting) and related to a report on the same topic, doc 11298, 8 June 2007, adopted by the Committee on 31 May 2007, Doc 10908, Reference No 3238 of 26 June 2006.

project of codifying European private law (Gerven, 2004, 137–64, and Pylkkänen, forthcoming). No doubt, there will be given space for Christian (including Catholic and Orthodox) as well as other monotheistic religious influences on a forthcoming European family law understanding.

Shari'a – Law or Religion?

My main question in this chapter has been to investigate how different European legal discourses could contribute to a description of the firm and manifest rejection of Muslim family law in not least northern European countries. As has been shown, that has to do with European legislation as a national not a clerical legal system, which is in turn based in Christian roots of European secular legislation in the area, in the very idea of European law as being secular and not least with the historical roots of that idea. In recent European changes into a broader cooperation among the national states, the basic idea of secularity has been reiterated in order, among other things, to open a space for religious influence on the normative changes to come.

That means, in brief, that in so far as Shari'a and other religious legal systems see themselves as legal *systems*, or even as *legal*, their influence is reduced as much as possible. But the moment that these normative traditions see themselves as religions, their influence will grow very quickly. At an individual level, that could be seen as relating to the demand that any single individual must be given the right to decide on his or her own to which degree religious norms should be followed.

Mathias Rohe makes a relevant distinction among the concepts of assimilation, integration, segregation and acculturation (Rohe, 2006, 70). What is assimilated, integrated, segregated or acculturated is however not quite clear: the religion – or the religious people? This slightly fluid nature of the distinction might have to do with the fact, that European citizens are religious, secular and secular-religious at the same time. They are *intertwining* their identities and they do not necessarily behave in a rational manner in their way of intertwining (Christoffersen, 2006).

I find it helpful to raise the questions of distinction directly to Shari'a, asking whether Shari'a is to be understood as:

- A religion containing an (internal) legal system (like the Catholic or the Orthodox churches), a religion arguing the right to maintain its own legal system – covering family law, fundamentally different treatment of men and women, penal law, etc. – which is a rather problematic ethical voice in democratic societies.
- A religion containing a legal system but not covering family law matters: a religion arguing an ethical way of living following the law of the land but also religious rules such as the five pillars, different treatment of men and women, food, cemeteries, teaching religion in school, etc.

- A religion not containing a legal system and of course not covering family law matters: a religion arguing an ethical way of living following the law of the land and at the same time following the five pillars.

Perhaps there are no answers. Perhaps the period of distinction is coming to an end – either because people are following religions where the leadership decides over the distinctions (as in the classic world churches as well as, for example, in the Mormon Church); or people are following religions with little or no distinctions (as in traditional understandings of Jewish or Muslim faith); or because people are following religious trends with no idea of an external normative force (as in new Eastern-inspired religious movements).

I have already cited the admonition about the function of law in a globalized world with which Roger Ballard, an English expert in anthropologically based religious studies, ends his contribution to the book by Shah and Menski. He refers to a story which is common to the Danes and the English, namely a reference to King Canute (Ballard, 2006, 56). Ballard says that a trust in *the rule of law* in a globalized world would be 'precisely King Canute's mistake when he sought to forbid the incoming tide from swamping his throne. The growth of transnational migration, powered as it is by current processes of globalisation, is undoubtedly precipitating a similarly, unstoppable inflow; but is the result any more threatening to Britain's integrity than a rising tide?', Ballard asks, supposing that the moral lesson from King Canute would be that England survived even though he could not stop the tide.

Seen from the Danish side of the water, the story was as follows: King Canute (970–1035), a Danish king who established himself in a greater part of England, became king of England in addition to ruling over Norway and Denmark. His men saw him as the most powerful, but in order to show them the limit of his power, he asked them to set his throne out in the tide. There he ordered the tide to stop, without effect. From here, the story has several different endings. One suggests that he retired, sick of repeatedly being frustrated in trying to impose order. Another argues that he after that gave up the ruling of England and only kept Denmark, realizing that it is impossible to rule both sides of water governed by the tide. And finally one argues that seeing the tide he became a pious man, handing over power to the rising Christianity of Denmark.

No matter which of these narratives one chooses, the point in the north European experience of King Canute is that the rule of law can only prevail in a context where its interpreter realizes that legal discourses have their limitations.

Chapter 6
Women, Secular and Religious Laws and Traditions: Gendered Secularization, Gendering Shari'a

Hanne Petersen

> The battle for democracy is a battle for the mind. It is about ideas of human solidarity and dignity, about gender equality and equal rights of all human beings, irrespective of their caste, creed and colour. It will claim a lot of blood before it is won.[1]

'There's a Special Place in Hell for Women who Don't Help Each Other'[2]

In the beginning of December 2007 I bought a pocketbook in a bookshop in Sweden on the special place in hell for women who don't help each other. A few days earlier I had been asked to go to Beirut in January 2008 to participate in a conference on gender research in Denmark and the Arab region and to co-chair a workshop on 'Women, secular and religious laws and traditions'.[3] I had read about the book on several occasions, and had been puzzled by the title. Why would a punishment in hell be invoked by secular Swedish feminist authors who wanted to improve the situation of secular Swedish women? Liza Marklund, who is a famous author of detective novels, has written the tiny book together with Lotta Snickare, who researches management issues at the Royal Technical University in Stockholm. Liza Marklund was also a friend of the former Swedish Minister of Foreign affairs, Anna Lindh, who was murdered in the summer of 2003, during a visit to a shopping centre, in Stockholm by a man of Serbian origin. After the death of Anna Lindh a series of Memorial Lectures was established, and in one of these lectures Madeleine Albright in 2004 said the sentence which was to become the title of Marklund's and Sickare's book.

---

1 Ishtiaq Ahmed, 2007, 'The assassination of Ms Bhutto', Monday 31 December, <http://www.thenews.com.pk/print1.asp?id=88567>.

2 Quote by Madeleine Albright, first US female Minister of Foreign Affairs, at an Anna Lindh Memorial Lecture in Stockholm, 24 August 2004.

3 The conference was organized by KVINFO (a centre for gender and information) and the Institute for Women's Studies in the Arab World at the Lebanese American University in Beirut, 14–16 January, 2008. This chapter is an expanded and extended version of the paper given in Beirut.

Only after the horrible assassination of Benazir Bhutto a few weeks later, I thought about the connection between the murders of two prominent female politicians, one from a perceived peaceful Nordic secular background, and the other from a recently established Muslim state with a history of violence, but both women challenging their own secular and religious norms and political traditions.

I had been to Sweden for the last class of an interdisciplinary and international course, 'Law and Religion – Fragments and Crisis', taking place both in Lund and in Copenhagen, two cities in different countries in northern Europe, but both in the Öresund region – and only one hour apart by train. This joint course was one of many outcomes of the special research priority area of 'Religion in the 21st Century', which took place at the University of Copenhagen 2003–2007.

My long interest in interdisciplinary research and in issues concerning legal pluralism and women (Petersen, 1991, , 1996; Petersen and Zahle, 1995) had led to my involvement in this project from its very beginning. I had spent the years 1995–9 living in Greenland and working at the miniscule university there – in an environment of legal pluralism in practice. Having returned to the University of Copenhagen I spent another five years at the beginning of the 21st century working on a transatlantic professorship in Greenlandic sociology of law. My work with indigenous peoples and legal pluralism and especially a trip to Australia in 1998 had opened my eyes to the importance and legitimacy of religious argumentation in what was otherwise understood as a secular context.

In Danish and Nordic secular societies law is understood as positive state law. Progress has been and still is strongly related to secularism. For this reason it was – and still is – rare to meet religious arguments used by anybody who wants to convince and to be taken seriously in the public sphere. In Greenland, which had taken over a Western model for home rule and local government, cultural arguments would be heard in favour of local regulations, decisions and solution, but rarely religious ones. In Australia, however, indigenous peoples constitute a minority, but they do not have home rule. As a minority their possibilities of influencing majority-made positive state law are very limited. In order to protect their interests in relation to local and national issues, they have thus on several occasions used religious arguments referring to sites as 'sacred sites' where this sacral status would imply a special protection and a need for a stronger legitimacy for state or local authorities who wanted to intervene in these areas or issues. The legal situation and strategy of the Aborigines in Australia is thus an example of the use of religious authority in legal argumentation in a secular context, which has had an influence on Australian intellectuals, who have perhaps developed an

> increased awareness of Aboriginal spirituality, and … sense both of the need to respect and honour traditional belief systems, and of the tensions between a religious cosmology and the Enlightenment ethos, which governs, and rightly governs, our work. That tension is inescapable, and we cannot pretend not to be subject to it. Its implications are in part political: the legitimacy of Aboriginal

> claims to rights in land is based ultimately in their religious ties to country … (Frow, 2006, 81)

This awareness can also be found in the work of feminist legal academics such as that by Australian law professor Margaret Davies (Davies, 2007).

Perhaps the quote from 2004 by Catholic-raised, Jewish-born Madeleine Albright and the bestselling popular science book on the role in hell for disloyal women demonstrate both the need for non-state sanctions and the influence of traditions and expectations for the constitution of gender roles in a society as dominated by secular laws and modernity as the Swedish and the Nordic ones.

It also demonstrates the tension between the Enlightenment ethos and its seemingly limited effects in doing away with serious discrimination on a global scale not only in relation to gender and not only in the Nordic countries.

Women's Law, Secular Law and Religious Traditions

Scandinavian women's law was an outcome and a part of the international women's movement, which swept across the world especially after the 1960s. The changing role of women goes back to their role as citizens and when they got the vote in the wake of the Russian revolution and World War I.[4] The Nordic model of marriage introduced in the 1920s was characterized by egalitarianism and secularism, and the Nordic countries harmonized their marriage laws in order to avoid discrepancies, when people moved from one country to another. The professed goal was to abolish private patriarchy and furnish married women with full legal rights (Pylkkänen, forthcoming). After World War II a gradual change of marriage laws took place (Petersen, 2007), and the period in the 1970s and early 1980s is described as the most 'secular' in Denmark, although some authors would rather describe the period as characterized by an 'individualization' in the divine belief of the Danes (Lüchau, 2005).

The beginning of Scandinavian women's law is dated to the establishment of the department for Women's Law at the University of Oslo in 1975 – the only major and traditional Scandinavian university where women's law was ever institutionalized. I think it is fair to say that Scandinavian women's law and Western feminist law and lawyers have been strongly secular for a number of historical reasons.

The international women's movement was linked to the left wing in Western politics, and this wing has been secular since both the French and the Russian revolutions. The social democratic Nordic welfare states were undergoing the perhaps strongest process of secularization after World War II, and religious institutions were viewed as impediments for social change of gender relations.

4 Finland – 1906; Norway – 1913; Denmark – 1915; Iceland – 1915; Sweden – 1919.

Women were accepted as priests in Danish churches from 1947 and in Norway in 1956, in both countries against strong resistance in the clergy. The first Norwegian female priest has vividly described the strong reactions to her and her male supporters, when she was appointed the first female priest in Norway in 1961 (Bjerkås, 1966/2001).

Dominant legal theory in this period was strongly influenced by Scandinavian legal realism, which was also very anti-metaphysical as it was supporting a modern democratic state against the earlier absolutist regimes. There were and are no female professors appointed in legal philosophy in any of the Nordic countries – and very few in any Western countries at all.

One of the few exceptions, Margaret Davies, writes that

> Positivist monism is at present Western law's defining narrative with a mythical or fictional, yet incredibly powerful, truth-status: the question is therefore what other narratives contradict that picture of law, narratives which are more pluralistic, multi-faith, and practically situated in local social spaces. (Davies, 2007)

Denmark, Norway and Sweden are still monarchies, and until 1849 Denmark was a regime where everybody under the principle of *cuius regio eius religio* had to be a Lutheran Protestant. Religious freedom did not exist, and non-Lutherans were only permitted to live in the country in special cities or on special conditions (Petersen, forthcoming). Legal monism has thus been particularly strong in these countries.

Besides Scandinavian legal realism the also secular, Marxist oriented legal theories of the 1970s strongly influenced Scandinavian women's law. Women's law was concerned with issues about gender neutralizing those parts of legislation which had not been so yet, and with issues about equality and social affairs, not least child care, social welfare and mechanisms for coping with different demands in family life and work life. This last issue was my own field of interest, and the one which sparked off my interest in legal pluralism (Petersen, 1991, 1996; Petersen and Zahle, 1995). My superficial investigations of the focus of women's law over the last three decades, indicates very little interest in aspects concerning religious issues and traditions even in very recent publications (Gunnarsson et al., 2007; see Christoffersen, 2001 for an exception).

Scandinavian feminists and Scandinavian feminist lawyers have for a very long period relied on 'social engineering' and on the instrument of modern secular law to produce gender equality and to improve the social and economic situation of women. It is my impression that many Scandinavian feminists who have fought for an improvement of women's situation during the 1970s and onwards today are very sceptical of and reluctant towards an increased focus on religious issues also in gender relations.

In a paper 'Secular feminism and multi-faith legal pluralism', Margaret Davies, who has worked and published with Swedish feminist legal academics, writes that

> Mainstream western feminism has on the whole accepted the story of secularization and positioned itself as external to religion … Feminism has been critical of the emphasis which Christianity places upon marriage and heterosexual family relationship. (Davies, 2007)

She admits that feminist secularism can take on a more dogmatic form – what some have called a 'fundamentalist secularism'. She also underlines that the deep and intricate relationships between our Christian heritage and our legal and political institutions have become more apparent. I agree with this, but I think that this is an insight which is still very limited and vague amongst most modern lawyers, men and women alike. It is a fact, as Davies emphasizes, that 'Christianity is woven into the cultural and political fabric of the West both as a geo-political location and as an ideology translated into other contexts'. But it is not a fact known to many or acknowledged by many. Rather few feminists and modernists are today able to identify the 'Christian threads' in the contemporary legal fabric – or to identify its parts of what Finnish legal theorist Kaarlo Tuori has called 'deep structures' of law (see Tuori, 2006).

Some research is emerging on this field, especially in Asia, which has a heritage of religious pluralism. Carolyn Evans and Amanda Whiting write that their research in the Asia-Pacific region shows that

> for women, laws (customary, colonial, post-independence, and international) and religions (indigenous or introduced, Buddhism, Christianity, Islam and Confucianism) have been a 'mixed blessing'. These diverse legal systems and religious doctrines have variously denied women authority and the capacity to participate fully in the public organization of social, political, and religious life; they haver furthermore constructed gender and familial relations in ways that subordinate women. Yet they have also offered promises of women's empowerment, and provided rules and procedures, norms, values, and interpretations of sacred traditions to deliver those emancipatory promises. (Evans and Whiting 2006, 1)

Gendering Secularization Theory

One of the results of the Copenhagen Research Priority Area mentioned in the beginning of this chapter has been a special issue of a journal called *Kvinder, Køn & Forskning* ('Women, Gender and Research') on religion. Linda Woodhead, Senior Lecturer in Christian Studies, has an article in this journal called 'Gendering secularization theory', where she writes that the classical accounts of secularization have in mind chiefly men and the life stories of men. Industrial capitalism is characterized by a strong differentiation of male and female labour. This is particularly clear in the Nordic countries and in Denmark where it is also reflected in the gender-segregated labour markets and wage differences.

> (W)omen are not absorbed into a world dominated by rational-scientific modes of thought and action, and are so less likely to become disenchanted with the supposedly irrational or superstitious nature of religious belief. (Woodhead, 2005, 24)

Women have been more religiously active than men by the start of the 20th century both in Britain and in Sweden.[5] Up until World War II most women's experiences in the Nordic countries were shaped 'by domestic experience and the roles and duties of daughter, wife, mother, aunt, grandmother and so on. Women's mode of self-hood … was likely to be domestic-relational, whilst men's was much more likely to be atomistic-individual' (Woodhead, 2005, 24).

Norwegian women's law focused on birth law and housewives' law in two important volumes on women's law published in 1985 (Dahl, 1985, 1987). But none of these volumes dealt with the important role of Christianity in shaping the expectations for family life in Norway. As late as 2005 the Norwegian Parliament decided on an act on Norwegian kindergartens the aim of which is in article 1 described as to help to bring up children 'according to basic Christian values'.[6] Tove Stang Dahl on certain occasions also spoke about a specific 'female duty of caring'.

According to Linda Woodhead the continued differences in the patterns of male and female labour yields information about the nature of recent secularization and sacralization, by which she means the decline of traditional 'religion' and the growth of new forms of spirituality. Women are still disproportionately engaged in part-time labour, they still carry out the bulk of unpaid caring work and there is still gender segregation in the workforce (Woodhead, 2005, 28f). Women who share a typically male experience of the workplace (as female lawyers to a certain degree do) are likely to find this 'equally corrosive of religious commitment'. Women who 'juggle' work and home may privilege one over the other and thus reject either Christianity or find in it a legitimation for their domestic roles.

> Holistic spirituality caters predominantly for women, as well as being predominantly 'run' by women… What is more, such spirituality is primarily concerned with catering for the stresses and strains of female life, including

5 P.O. Enquist describes the Swedish Pentecostal Movement as the biggest women's movement in Sweden in the beginning to the 20th century in his novel *Lewis Resa*.

6 'Barnehagen skal hjelpe til med å gi barna en oppdragelse i samsvar med kristne grunnverdier.' <http://www.lovdata.no/all/tl-20050617-064-001.html#1>, accessed 10 October 2008.

> dealing with issues of overwork, stress, and lack of self-confidence. (Woodhead, 2005, 30)

These issues have been issues of clear relevance and concern for women for decades, and are increasing on a global scale (Gambles et al., 2006; Kabeer, 2008). Secular national laws oriented towards equality as well as welfare legislation in the Nordic countries have not been able to solve these issues. Also in Denmark it is clear that the rise in religiosity which takes place after 1970 is a rise primarily amongst women, who have during the period since the 1940s constantly been stronger believers than men. 'Seen from above it is clear that it is women, who stand for the innovation of the Danes' image of god, but also for a broader growth in religiosity both as self-chosen label and as ideas of belief' (Lüchau, 2005, 54).

Limits to Secularization – How to Change Normative Traditions?

Finnish feminist legal historian Anu Pylkkänen claims that in the Nordic countries 'secular law has been so much intertwined with religious norms and understandings that it does not make sense to discuss the relation of law and religion as if such a bind did not exist' (forthcoming). According to her the Protestant Nordic state churches had for centuries relied on the Lutheran interpretation that detached marriage from the realm of the sacred. Religious traditions are discernible in the underpinning in modern secular positive law. One heritage of Lutheranism may be the strong gender segregation of public life and the labour market. According to Luther women belonged to the private sphere, where the husband ruled.

> While Luther had seen men and women as equals in the spiritual sense, his heritage signified women's exclusion from education and knowledge. In the Protestant Church, everybody was educated so that they could read the Bible, but the prevalent 'truth' was that women were not capable of rational learning… Women were seen as passive and ignorant, deprived of their unique personality in spirit and deed. In sexual morals, double standard prevailed. (Pylkkänen, forthcoming)

The Swedish gender-mixed primary school has only existed since 1962, write Marklund and Snickare (Marklund and Snickare, 2007, 29). They do not discuss the role of the school as a preparation for the Christian confirmation during Absolutism in the Nordic countries, but probably this role also lies behind the continuation of a gender-segregated school for almost a century after the establishment of formal democracy and constitutional monarchy.

Pylkkänen underlines that even the seemingly neutral and secular understandings of law – especially family law – have roots in the early modern interpretations of Protestant faith and that the 'Nordic nation states are a paradigm example of the fusion of Lutheran ideas and social welfare'.

The issue of family is clearly amongst the issues with deep religious roots, she writes. This is an area where direct religious laws have most impact, or where still existing but often unconscious and unacknowledged religious values still play a very important role.

Family life has undergone considerable practical changes in the Nordic countries. Divorces have increased almost dramatically over the last decades. The family is no longer considered a union between two grown-ups of different sexuality. The important legal relationship is today not the gender relationship, but the generational relationship between parent (often single parent) and child. In this relationship there are still considerable economic and caring duties to be carried out – in the case of single-parent families most often by women, who are economically and institutionally supported by the feminized welfare state (Petersen, 2007).

Pylkkänen writes that it is especially interesting to look at four issues from the perspective of secular law/religious norms:

- monogamy, polygamy/ serial polygamy (monogamy?)
- (in)dissolubility of marriage
- contractual/functional (teleological) understanding of the marital relationship
- sexual integrity of partners.

Margaret Davies asks whether by excluding religion from political discourse 'we silence those who would challenge dominant interpretations of their faith?' She also claims that,

> Privatization of religious views provides an opportunity for a political hegemony to essentialize and normalize religions, in much the same way that cultures are essentialized, normalized, and othered by an identitarian gaze … State law is interpreted through religious norms: thus, a plurality of possible meanings arises from law's intersection with various normative worlds and subject-positions. (Davies, 2007)

In my view the over-emphasis on what is perceived as the threat of Islam in Europe and not least in the Nordic countries may perhaps lead also to a closer scrutiny of the way a religious heritage is influencing what we understand as secular laws (see Razack, 2004, 2007).[7]

Since H. Patrick Glenn in 2000 wrote his 'classic' *Legal Traditions of the World* – now in its third edition – we have begun to speak of 'legal traditions' instead of legal systems (Glenn, 2007). Glenn describes seven traditions of which four are directly or indirectly religiously inspired: the Chthonic, the Talmudic, the Islamic and the Hindu legal traditions. The other three traditions are: the Asian

7 Razack's article from 2004 'Imperilled Muslim women, dangerous Muslim men and civilised Europeans: legal and social responses to forced marriages', is a critique of especially Norwegian feminist approaches to Islam.

legal tradition, the common law tradition and the civil law tradition. Maybe we could and also need to look much more into the Christian heritage of the common law and civil law traditions. From a gendered perspective such a view would probably make more sense than upholding a strong distinction between religious and secular laws – a distinction which in itself is based upon a Western positive and positivist understanding of law, which is not necessarily useful for women. We are probably witnessing what Lisbet Christoffersen has called 'intertwinement' between law and religion in so-called secular legal regimes (2006).

Gendering Shari'a?

One might perhaps say that the attempts to 'gender-neutralize' secular laws in the West are 'parallelled' by attempts to 'gender' religious norms in Muslim countries – perhaps especially interpretations of Shari'a. This process seems to have taken off from a variety of approaches. Economical, political and educational migration and remigration, and mobility have increased in the last part of the 20th century – especially for women. Increased communication has brought different traditions closer to each other, including different local experiences with challenges of patriarchal traditions. This allows for both personal local and academic comparisons.

Women Living Under Muslim Laws, which was established in 1984, about a decade after the first UN conference on women took place, describes itself as 'an international solidarity network that provides information, support and a collective space for women whose lives are shaped, conditioned or governed by laws and customs said to derive from Islam.' The network spans about 70 different countries, but it is perhaps dealing as much with the relationships between local and global contested and controversial interpretations of the Qur'an, Shari'a and Muslim law as with national legislation. Western (feminist) jurisprudence might perhaps learn from this view of law 'beyond the state'.

The comparative practice of WLUML as well as of many individual scholars and activists, religious or secular, working under Muslim law, indicates the differences and varieties of Muslim law, and thus the different and local practices, customs and interpretations women experience. These differences between countries with different political and legal religious regimes were also demonstrated at the conference in January 2008, where parts of this chapter were originally given. The situation in Morocco and Tunis is clearly different from the situations and conditions in Syria and Yemen. Inside and outside Morocco the country's new family law, the Mudawwana, is by many considered a step in the direction of an improvement of the legal situation of women – for whom life and living conditions has changed considerably over the last decade (see Rosen, 2008; Foblets, 2008). This result has been achieved through a considerable effort of challenging interpretations of the Qur'an, Shari'a, national law and local customs. WLUML carried out Qur'anic interpretations meetings in 1990.

Box 6.1 Women Living Under Muslim Laws

WLUML focuses on laws and customs and the concrete realities of women's lives. This includes the often **diverse practices and laws classified as 'Muslim'** (resulting from different interpretations of religious texts and/or the political use of religion) and the effects these have on women, rather than on the religion of Islam itself.

The network consciously builds bridges across identities – within our contexts and internationally. We are especially concerned about marginalized women. This includes non-Muslims in Muslim majority states, especially where spaces for religious minorities is rapidly dwindling; Muslim minorities facing discrimination, oppression, or racism; women whose assertions of sexuality – including but not limited to sexual orientation – are either criminalized or are socially unacceptable.

WLUML recognises that women's struggles are interconnected and complementary, and therefore has a commitment to international solidarity.

WLUML actively endorses plurality and autonomy, and consciously reflects, recognises and values a diversity of opinions. Individuals and groups linked through the network define their own particular priorities and strategies according to their context.

The personal has always played an important part in the work of WLUML, which values the solidarity and active support that the networkers extend to each other by way of personal links.

<http://www.wluml.org/english/about.shtm>l (accessed 1 February 2008 – emphasis mine)

There is no doubt that the knowledge and expertise in how to understand, interpret and challenge religious law is much bigger in Muslim countries than in so-called secular legal traditions. This work is undertaken by female and also male Muslim legal scholars inside and outside Muslim countries and in different forms of cooperation.[8] There is also no doubt that both many Muslim (feminist) men and women consider an influence from 'moderate secularism' beneficial for Muslims living both in the West and in Muslim majority societies.[9]

In these processes, we will have to rethink models of normative interaction. Menski describes himself as a 'global legal realist' (2008). Global legal realism probably implies an acknowledgement that both religious and secular norms

8 My knowledge of this immense work is limited both for lack of studies and for lack of language skills. Authors whom I have worked with or met over the last decades are: Mehdi and Shahid (1997); Mehdi (2007); Quraishi (1997); Quraishi and Syyed-Miller (2004), Sardar Ali (forthcoming). The work by Göle and Amman (2006) has also been important.

9 As suggested by Tariq Modood in his book *Multiculturalism* (2007).

(fundamentalist and moderate) constitute the normative pattern of global world society, together with mixed legal traditions, norms, customs and practices emerging from different sources, centres, groups and schools.

I think that what we are witnessing in these processes are challenges of Western monist, positivist state law – emphasizing the national expressions of common law and civil law traditions – as well as challenges of the Islamic legal tradition – emphasizing the strong role of religious law and tradition. We are also likely to witness processes where legal traditions will gradually come much more together, and become more influenced by each other, creating forms of both local and 'surface law' (Twining, 2008) not only in Europe and in the Mediterranean area but on a global scale.

Similarly religious feminisms and feminists are contributing to challenging understandings of religious traditions across the world as well as challenging secular feminisms (see McGinty, 2007; Good, 2005; Mahmoud, 2005). There is no doubt that gender and generational relations will continue to play an important role in local societies influenced by globalization as well as in world society. The mixtures of law and religion may continue to be mixed blessings but may also create new avenues for interpretation understanding and ordering.

In the Abrahamic traditions to which both Christianity and Islam belong with their similar roots and overlapping histories there is both a heaven and a hell. Perhaps we need as both women and men to make sure that we help each other across the specific expressions of these traditions in order not to end in our own versions of hell.

Chapter 7
Shari‘a and Nordic Legal Contexts

Kjell-Åke Modéer

Scandinavian Legal Realism

At European universities law is taught as ‘valid law’. Throughout the 20th century valid law has been identified with the national law. Concepts like *nation state* and *sovereignty of the people* were the contextual frame for the concept of law that law students were taught to be able to enter the modern legal profession. In the Nordic countries these modern concepts were to a great extent related to Scandinavian legal realism, which constructed a non-value-based and anti-metaphysical dimension of the law, and which dominated the legal structure in the Nordic countries, especially Sweden and Denmark, throughout the 20th century. The legal cultures in the Nordic countries during that period were monolithic and homogeneous (Modéer, 2008).

Currently, however, academics are retreating from this monolithic position, and international legal sources are increasingly included in the concept of valid law. The incorporation in the 1990s of the European Convention of Human Rights (ECHR) and of European Union law into the national law of the Nordic countries has changed the interpretation of these concepts. The importance of the decisions from the European supranational courts in Luxembourg and Strasbourg has restricted the jurisdictions of the nation states, and the principle of the people's sovereignty has – as in many other European countries – had to compete with the principle of the separation of powers as a constitutional framework.

Contemporary multicultural Western societies, however, with their different religious elements and institutions, have created not so much a paradigm shift as an increasing disruption within the legal cultures of the Nordic countries. Today these legal cultures are becoming more and more fragmented and heterogeneous. The world religions are increasingly visible in local societies, and the citizen as well as the state has to relate to this new situation. Immigration into Europe in the post-war period has contributed to make Islam visible in the European setting. But even if a ‘euro-Islam’ – adjusted to a new geopolitical situation – is under construction there is an immediate reluctance within the secularized Nordic societies against e.g. religious symbols and religious schools.

From a Nordic perspective, however, this contextual transparency hasn't more generally changed the view of the law persistently remaining from modernity. Even if the legal cultures of the Nordic countries are on the move there is no clear direction. The main problem is whether the minority religious communities will increasingly be isolated diaspora communities in society, or will there be an interactive dialogue with mutual adjustments and compromises related to the civil religion of these societies?

This short chapter will discuss the relation between state, law and religion from a more contextual perspective in the Nordic countries. My emphasis will be on the contexts which the Shari'a as a norm system is meeting in the Nordic situations.

Constitutional Law

The decline of the monolithic nation state of the 19th–20th centuries and its transformation into multicultural and multi-religious entities has challenged the freedom of religion clauses in the Western constitutions. It has resulted not only in active interpretations bur also in legislative secularization, seeking to keep religion out of the public space. The renaissance of constitutionalism in many European countries has not only resulted in a European treaty, which is currently subject to a problematic ratification process in the member states. The importance of the national constitutions in this supra-national framework has also resulted in revisions of constitutions, and in eastern and central Europe in new constitutions. In this process of transition the main attitude has been to keep religion out of the constitutional content. This attitude, however, contradicts late-modern discourses within law, as well as the new role of religion in the public square.

The field of law and religion has redefined itself in Western jurisprudence. From having been a non-existing discipline in the modern post-war law school it has developed and acquired a reputable academic position focusing on the deep structures of the law which underpin the actual problems related to law and religion. These discourses are to a great extent founded on historical argumentation, focusing on religious principles embedded in legal traditions and cultures (Berman, 2007, xiiff; Modéer, 2004a, 3ff; Modéer, 2004b, 48ff).

This part of soft law was articulated in the late 1970s by Robert Bellah who introduced the concept of *civil religion* related to the fundamental values represented in the American Constitution as a secular bible and by its interpreters, the nine justices of the US Supreme Court (Bellah, 1967, 1ff; Bellah, 1968). This discourse has recently been revitalized both in the US and within the European Union (Semonche, 1998). The preamble of the European treaty became a very important example of the focus on fundamental constitutional values in the construction of a European constitution (Koch, 2007, 335). Danish civil religion, to a great extent related to the tradition of religion and nation (constitutional values), has also currently been in focus for a vital discourse (Gundelach et al., 2008).

In the Nordic countries the debates related to fundamental societal (and religious) values have been intense. In Denmark the Muhammad cartoon crisis in 2005–2006 demonstrated the clashes between national and religious values in a borderless global media situation. Recently, a highly hypothetical question of whether it is permissible for a female Muslim judge in Denmark to wear a headscarf on the bench has resulted in a heated debate on religious symbols in the public sphere (Christoffersen, 2006). In the recent controversial Norwegian case at European court of Human Rights, *Folgerø and others* v. *Norway* (Application no 15472/02, Judgment June 29, 2007), about religious education and teaching in public schools, has resulted in a intense domestic discourse about the role of the constitutionally secured evangelical Lutheran majority church in Norway. In Sweden problems related to the review of the constitution have also resulted in a discourse on the role of religion in the public square, especially in relation to Muslims (Modéer 2005, 193ff).

Plural Legal Systems and Polycentricity

Competing legal systems within the nation state has been one of the most important discourses in relation to modernity within late-modern jurisprudence. This discourse is to a great extent international and has to be put into a wider context.

The interpretation of the US Constitution in the US Supreme Court is in that respect of special interest. The verbal encounter between the US Supreme Court justices Sandra Day O'Connor and Antonin Scalia some years ago was related to the question of whether the court also should be able to relate its decisions to international legal sources. This struggle resulted in a victory for the conservative majority of the court.

A deeper question is to what extent external religious (legal) sources can be used and to what extent this argumentation can be used. Also in this respect the American example gives some directions. In *Wisconsin* v. *Yoder* (1972) the Supreme Court gave the Amish in Wisconsin a right to exclude their young family members from high school. In their view the values taught in high school were not in line with those of their religion and legal culture. The Amish brought the case to the Courts. The Supreme Court decided to use culture and its arguments in the relation to the argument of religious freedom mounted by the plaintiffs (Shawn Francis Peters, 2003).

In the European Union (EU) the dynamic dichotomy between the national legal systems and that of the European Communities has been legitimized in the Maastricht Treaty 1994. Within the Nordic countries a discourse related to this new dynamic situation had earlier been observed by Henrik Zahle, who in a *Festschrift* article in 1986 made an observation on *polycentricity* related to the legal sources which were used within the national legal systems (Zahle, 1986). The concept of polycentricity has in the Nordic countries been a useful instrument within late modern legal science. Especially the discourse on law and values became a part of this diverse discourse (Blume and Petersen, 1993). Together with Hanne Petersen Zahle introduced this concept some years later also to an international audience (Petersen and Zahle, 1995). This intense discourse on polycentricity within Nordic legal science demonstrates the quite new dimensions of the law relating to open boundaries and supra-national legal and political entities.

Shari'a and Comparative Law

The field of comparative law is to a great extent a Western construct. The discourses within comparative law 50 years ago were to a great extent run by legal scientists within the Western hemisphere. Those representatives generally had a universalistic perspective on the law. This concept was to harmonize the law and to include so many of the legal systems as possible into the Western *legal families*. This geopolitical construct also included the imperial and colonial entities related to the Western civil law and common law traditions. Also the first edition of the important work by Zweigert and Kötz (1969–72) looked upon the comparative private law as first of all a Western enterprise. It was to a great extent a 'we' and the 'other' perspective. In this construct also the Nordic countries were regarded as a distinct legal family. The context of the legal families was defined as 'style'. The Nordic legal family was regarded as 'in between', a special civil law family lacking modern codifications. The weaknesses of this construct in the new geopolitical situation in late modernity has been demonstrated in the third edition of Zweigert and Kötz (1998), in which the socialist legal family has been abolished but the Nordic legal family, in spite of evident divergences within the current legal cultures in the Nordic countries, is kept.

Postmodern constructs within comparative law have tended to focus on identity and differences, not similarities, between legal systems. Discourses on legal culture (Cotterrell 1996, 21ff), deep structures of law (Tuori, 1997, 432ff) and legal traditions (Glenn, 2007) have demonstrated this shift between different perspectives. The discourse on legal culture has contributed to the understanding of the cognitive structures of the legal profession (in relation to e.g. polycentricity). The discourse on the transnational deep structures of the law has given better understanding of the common historical heritage within the law and its common European principles. And the discourse on the legal tradition has brought in a better understanding of both the religious traditions in relation to the legal traditions, and of the importance of customary law as a legal source in late modernity.

In this perspective religious norms – and especially the Shari'a – have been emphasized as important and relevant norms. Patrick Glenn in his works emphasizes the role of legal systems based on oral traditions. Such an analysis ended up in the importance of religious legal norms as presented not only in Islam but also for example in Judaism and Hinduism (Glenn, 2007). His main argument is that these religious norms have to be regarded not only as legal norms but also (in relation to the national law) as equal legal systems (*cum pare*).

Even if the concept of religion as a legal tradition is very relevant also from a Nordic perspective it has difficulties in gaining a foothold due to the enduring heritage of Scandinavian legal realism. The Nordic countries of today are – even if they from an historical point of view have been nations with a homogeneous Lutheran evangelical belief – very diverse as regards legal history and legal traditions. The differences are very much related to immigration and visibility of other religions in relation to the position of the state church in some of the most secularized countries in the world. Finland has a dual system in its constitution since 1869. Sweden has broken up from the state church system in 2000 and all religious beliefs are in principle equal within the system. In Norway the politicians in June 2008 made a compromise resulting in a constitutional reform of church autonomy in relation to the government within the state church system. The effect of that reform is that the Norwegian state church model in the constitution of 1814 is brought to the standard of the Danish liberal constitution of 1849. In Iceland also a similar work on autonomy reform has been made. In Denmark, however, a reform related to church autonomy in relation to the state church model has so far not been seriously debated.

This presentation of the Nordic legal, constitutional and religious contexts is necessary to understand the relation between the religious communities and the national (state) churches in the Nordic countries. It brings us to how the Muslims and the Shari'a as norm system fits into this divergent Nordic legal family.

Shari'a as Legal Norm

The relation of the courts in the Nordic countries to the Shari'a is very much related to the Hague convention of 1904. In the countries like Sweden, which have ratified the Hague convention, the courts also have to implement the Shari'a as an international private legal system, whereas countries like Denmark, which has not ratified the convention, are not in that respect bound by the international public law. This tension between religion and law demonstrates the increasingly visible differences between the legal cultures of the Nordic countries (Christoffersen, 2008).

Problems related to Shari'a as a 'foreign' norm system have been articulated in relation to modern discrimination legislation. One example: since Muslim women are placed on the balcony in the Stockholm mosque, a member of the Swedish parliament made a request to the Office of the Ombudsman against Ethnic Discrimination (DO) and asked the ombudsman to interfere with a prohibition against this form of discrimination of women by the Muslim congregation in Stockholm. Even though the request did not result in any action from the DO it shows the ignorance and intolerance from 'secular' citizens and MPs against the 'sacred spaces' of non-Christian congregations.

Legal pluralism and polycentricity have also raised the question whether Shari'a as a family law could be implemented in Nordic legal systems. There are a couple of decisions from Swedish district courts in which Muslim male defendants have successfully pleaded mitigation in wife-beating cases due the argument that wife-beating is due to a Shari'a ruling. Those decisions from the district courts, however, have been corrected in the Courts of Appeal. It is an interesting observation that the district courts' judges, closer to the concrete conflict, also have been more open to the mitigating position in their decision-making (cf. Mehdi, 2007, 2008).

Conclusion

As long as the Nordic nation states are upholding their monopoly regarding territorial jurisdiction there will be ongoing conflicts with different forms of informal religious jurisdictions. This is in line with the legal and normative positions Patrick Glenn has related to regarding religious traditions (Glenn, 2008). There is also a possibility for the future that there will be a renaissance of the conglomerate state which ruled during the early modern times of the 17th and 18th centuries (Petersen, 2006, 129ff). The *suum cuique tribuere* principle of that time gave jurisdiction to all privileged congregations. To some extent there are those who argue that the plural legal systems within the late-modern multi-religious societies are giving the lawyers and the judges new alternatives for decision-making. The decisions – and dissenters - in the European Court of Human Rights relating to Article 9 in the European Convention on Human Rights demonstrate the cultural and religious differences between the member states (Arold, 2007). On the national level the national courts are increasingly competing with different forms of religious diaspora jurisdictions. It can also be observed that within the religious communities in the Nordic countries there are lively internal discussions related to a strengthening of the ecumenical dimension. Thus the Lutheran evangelical churches in the Nordic countries are currently open to different forms of theological encounters and dialogues with Muslim believers (religious dialogue, religious theology) (e.g. Bengtsson, 2008). We are today moving far away from the 'black–white' situation of modernity. It is not any longer *either – or*, it is *as well as* (Beck, 2004).

PART 2
Local Experiences

Chapter 8

Shari'a from Behind the Bench: Court Culture, Judicial Culture and a Judge-made Discourse on Shari'a at a Swedish District Court[1]

Matilda Arvidsson

Introduction

In January 2002 Lund District Court (Lunds Tingsrätt, hereafter 'the court') in southern Sweden received an application from a woman, Atosa Mirdamadian, regarding custody of children (Lunds tingsrätt T 43-02, aktbil 1). That is where the story about the Atosa Mirdamadian and Peivan Tavakoli cases at the court begins. In a series of seven interrelated cases involving the two of them – mainly concerning custody of children, marriage and divorce, and distribution of marital property – the story takes place over a period of five years.

There are a number of ways in which such a story could be told in a chapter like this. It could perhaps be told as a story about love and what happens 'ever after'. But that would not have been particular to the cases involving these parties, and other court cases would surely have been more illustrative of that point. What instead makes this story particular could be made clear in two main points, summarizing the two main arguments of this chapter.

Firstly, the story points to the fact that there is a multitude of legal cultures simultaneously at work in Sweden, and one of these legal cultures relates specifically to Shari'a. When this legal culture was established, and what more precisely defines it is beyond the scope of this study. These legal cultures cannot be dismissed as 'foreign' as among many others Rolf Nygren puts it (Nygren, 1999, 521ff). Their primary geographical point of reference is Sweden, and Swedish society and Swedish law and legal institutions are other important points of reference in these legal cultures.

Legal culture here refers to 'a specific way in which values, practices and concepts are integrated into the operation of legal institutions and interpretation of legal texts' (Bell, 1995, 70). Emphasis is put on both the sets of rules and concepts,

1 I would like to thank and express my respect for those individuals at the court who have supported me and who helped and took part in this study.

and the social practice within a community (Van Hoecke and Warrington, 1998, 498). Law is thus not exclusively defined on a state level but more importantly in the society where legal institutions and legal texts other than those of the nation state are at work instructing how people live and arrange their lives. This splits the definition of the legal culture in two, referring to either an internal 'professional' legal culture, as John Bell does (Bell, 1995, 70) or an external or 'lay' legal culture, as Lawrence Friedman does (Friedman, 2007, 169). The latter legal culture is 'external' insofar that it is at least partly independent of the existence of the state, as it has its own legal texts and legal institutions. These legal texts and institutions then in turn relate to other existing legal cultures within the environment where they exist. Most importantly such an 'external' or 'lay' legal culture also relates to the 'professional' legal culture of the state, its legal texts and legal institutions.

Secondly, the story of the Atosa Mirdamadian and Peivan Tavakoli cases at the court points to the fact that Swedish legal institutions such as the court and the government, when acting as an instance of legal decisions, and state agencies such as the Swedish Tax Agency (Skatteverket), seem to be ignorant of the implications of existing in a society with a multitude of legal cultures. What seems to be the problem is an inability or unwillingness to recognize and formulate the events which have taken place in the lives of Atosa Mirdamadian and Peivan Tavakoli in a way that recognizes and respects that these events did not take place exclusively in relation to a legal culture which is sanctioned by a state. As becomes evident through the story, the different legal institutions and agencies constantly get tangled up in a confusing terminology, as they do not make distinctions between arguments in relation to Shari'a and arguments in relation to Swedish law. The parties will of course use language as they see it best fits their purposes in the case. It is, however, the task of the Swedish legal institutions to recognize and distinguish in the material brought to them by the parties.

Atosa Mirdamadian and Peivan Tavakoli are Swedish Muslims, and they move between one particular legal culture instructed by Shari'a, and another instructed by Swedish law. Shari'a here stands for 'a body of sources of revelation and a methodology for making rules from these sources' (Vikør, 2005, 1), and 'thus not based on any decision from a parliament or council, but is the result of individual efforts by the scholars working with God's revelation' (Vikør, 2005, 3). The emphasis is on the divine sanction, a particular way – based on divine revelation – which leads you to arrive at particular rules of life (Hjärpe, 2005, 31). A clear distinction must be made between the body of sources and the methodology on the one hand, and the codification into statutes on the other (Layish, 2004, 96). Whereas codified law is easy for a Swedish judge at a district court to recognize – if not to interpret – the non-codified Shari'a is much more difficult to conceptualize and to make sense of.

How does the judge formulate the multitude of legal cultures within the language of law? How does he – because it is most often a he – decide the legal relevance of circumstances, and how does he recognise what law *is* when his legal training speaks of a *bonus pater familias* whose last name is Svensson and lives in the same neighbourhood as him, and 'the other' in front of him does not fit that description? How does he approach Shari'a as a Swedish legal culture, when he is trained to recognize Shari'a only in cases of Swedish international private law as part of a recognized foreign national legal system? My suggestion is that the judge's particular understanding of law and legal terminology sees law and legal terminology as an ideal form of language, purely separated from a more general understanding of society and language. In this particular understanding there is a sense of law and legal terminology being *contaminated* by society and ordinary language, when society approaches the law using an ordinary language. When society and non-legal language insist on its presence, the answer of the judge is to either misinterpret what is being said or to give no room for it by remaining silent in relation to it.

The implications of the existence of a multitude of legal cultures within Sweden go beyond the example of the particular legal culture instructed by and relating to Shari'a with which this chapter is concerned. The problems identified are thus not particular to that relation only, they are rather general problems of Swedish court culture and judicial culture – and perhaps even Swedish law. There might, however, be something to the particular example of a legal culture instructed by and relating to Shari'a, which cannot be generalized to all other existing legal cultures in Sweden. The judge-made discourse coming out of a legal culture relating to sports approaching the court would perhaps not have as strong a dimension of exclusion and subordination as the judge-made discourse on Shari'a, as comes through in this study.

The way the story in this chapter will be told, is how a Swedish district court interacts with members of a society for which it has a language of silence and misconception. In this understanding, it is a story about how a discourse on Shari'a is formulated from 'behind the bench', in other words a judge-made discourse on Shari'a.

The Study: Method, Material and Limitations

The chapter is based on two separate studies. The first study, section two in this chapter, is concerned specifically with the court cases involving Atosa Mirdamadian and Peivan Tavakoli during the years 2002 to 2007: five civil law cases (*tvistemål*), T 43-02, T 329-02, T 912-05, T 4777-05 and T 3352-06, and two court matters (*domstolsärenden*), Ä 3939-04 and Ä 4029-04.[2] The case material is comprehensive and deals with a wide range of legal questions. The study is thus focused on the case material related to the question of marriage and divorce, mainly found in T 912-05 and Ä 3939-04.

The second study, section three in this chapter, is an empirical study of the court culture and the judicial culture at the court. There are many other courts which would have been of interest to study in relation to discourses on Shari'a,

2 'Ä' refers to court matter (*domstolsärende*).

the newly established Migration Court (*Migrationsdomstolen*) being one such example. However, for the purpose of this study, it has been important to study a court which is well established within an existing legal tradition, and which deals with general questions of law. In order to establish the discourse which comes out of the meeting of different legal cultures at a court, it has been important to study a first instance court. It is at these courts that the judges – as they put it themselves – 'refine' the case and identify the legal question within the 'mish-mash' of information provided by the parties. The study was carried out during the years 2004–2006. In 2007, additional data was collected and previous data was updated. The empirical study was carried out as a participatory study, including both structured and semi-structured interviews with employees at the court. The study serves to locate important structures and values within court culture and judicial culture which instructs how the judge formulates his discourse on Shari'a. These structures and values are inaccessible to 'outsiders'. Thus in order to gain access to the inside of the court, the court had to become the physical place where the study took place during a longer period of time. During this time, the observations were made possible through participation in the daily work at the court. Unless otherwise stated, section three in this chapter, concerning court culture and judicial culture, is based on the empirical study.

In order to understand what is informing the particular discourse the judge creates on Shari'a, it is relevant to investigate the spheres that influence his understanding of law and legal language in general, namely court culture and judicial culture (Modéer, 1994; Bell, 2006). The role of legal education and professional training of judges is one important reference in relation to those cultures (Ryberg, 1988, 149), but also the reference material which the judge relies on: case law, available literature and other sources are of interest (Ryberg, 1988, 150). Thus a survey of resources and references on Shari'a and Islamic law within Swedish law schools, the formal trainee programme of Swedish judges, and in the field of Swedish legal literature – including the two most prominent Swedish law journals *Svensk Juristtidning* and *Juridisk Tidskrift*, the journal of the National Courts Administration (I) *Domkretsen* and the journal of the Swedish Union of Judges (*Sveriges Domareförbund*) *Tidskrift för Sveriges Domareförbund* – has been carried out.

One important question is of course how and in what respect court culture and judicial culture are instructed by the structure and content of Swedish law. Are some of the problems which are identified in this study, problems emanating from how Swedish law is structured, what it allows and does not allow for? However important this question is, it will not be given the attention it deserves as it is too large a question to approach in a systematic way in an essay as short as this.

While this chapter is mainly concerned with the court and its judges, let us not forget that were it not for Atosa Mirdamadian and Peivan Tavakoli there would be no story. Through the series of cases in which they involve the court in their social reality, it is not only the court approaching Shari'a, but also Shari'a approaching the court through the parties as they communications with the court.

And, as the story develops, there are the artefacts, signs and signatures which mark the narrative: there is the poor-quality fax copies of the wedding pictures, the handwritten note from the board of the Muslim congregation (*Muslimska församlingen*) in Malmö, and the signature of the then Minister of Justice, Thomas Bodström, on the government's decision disallowing the application for approval of the marriage. Photographs, handwriting and signature: these are the signs of real life and real people.

The Story of the Atosa Mirdamadian and Peivan Tavakoli Cases at the Court

The two Swedish nationals of Muslim faith Atosa Mirdamadian and Peivan Tavakoli married in 1991. The ceremony was carried out in accordance with Shari'a by an imam at the Muslim congregation in Malmö (T 912-05, aktbil 12 and 17). Atosa Mirdamadian and Peivan Tavakoli moved in together, and they had two children born in 1993 and 1998. In the mid 1990s they were granted a divorce in accordance with Shari'a from the imam at the Muslim congregation in Malmö (Ä 3939-04, aktbil 28, bil 1).

From 2002 to 2007 seven cases – mainly concerning custody of children, marriage and divorce, and distribution of marital property – were filed at the court by the two of them. Four different judges and one judge-delegate at the court have written final decisions and judgments on these cases, and numerous associate judges, assistant judges, judge-delegates, law clerks and law secretaries have been involved in the process of preparing, researching, taking minutes, drafting decisions and judgments, filing and communicating with the parties. The final decisions and judgments of previous cases in the story are attached to the dossiers of the following cases, interlinking them and making them into one continuous story at the court. In – and on the folders of – the case dossiers there are notes and scribbles left by different judges and law clerks handling the cases before the final decisions and judgments seal the cases and the dossiers are sent to the archive in the basement of the court. The notes and scribbles are as much biographies of the individual cases as they are a communication of instructions from the different judges and law clerks to the law secretaries, instructing them on how to proceed with the case and what to communicate to the parties. In both respects, the notes and scribbles are signs of the process of institutionalizing knowledge at the court. From tracking down the names of all the different judges, law clerks and law secretaries who have put their signatures on the folder of the dossiers and on the documents inside the dossiers it becomes apparent that it is not only independent individuals at the court who have been involved in this story – it is individuals acting within a shared, homogenous culture. And it is through that culture that the story of the Atosa Mirdamadian and Peivan Tavakoli cases at the court comes through.

Let us look closely at one aspect of the story – the story about marriage and divorce – to see what Atosa Mirdamadian and Peivan Tavakoli have argued, and how the court and the judges have approached the information and arguments submitted by the parties. The two cases in which this aspect of the story is dealt with – Ä 3939-04 and T 912-05 – are closely intertwined. They take place at approximately the same time, cross-references are made between them by the parties, and the case dossiers include material – put there by the judges and law clerks working with the cases – from both cases.

In the correspondence with the court, Atosa Mirdamadian maintains that she was under the impression that the she had entered into marriage as a consequence of the ceremony in 1991 (Ä 3939-04, aktbil 17; T 912-05, aktbil 1). She is not explicit as to the definition of 'marriage', i.e. if she refers to her being under that impression that the marriage was valid both in relation to Shari'a *and* Swedish law at the point of her signing the marriage contract. It is, however, certain that she at some point after the marriage ceremony assumed that the marriage was valid according to both spheres of law. In the correspondence with the court she points to the fact that the marriage was officiated within a religious body (*trossamfund*) which according to its own records had been granted competence from the government in accordance with the ordinance (1987:1017) concerning marriage officiates in religious bodies other than the Church of Sweden (*Förordning (1987:1017) angående vigselförrättare i annat trossamfund än Svenska kyrkan*)[3] to officiate marriages in accordance with Swedish law. The board of the congregation confirms this in a note, which was sent to the court. From this note it is further evident that the congregation – or at least the person representing the congregation in writing that note – was under the impression that the congregation also could perform divorces which would be valid according to Swedish law (Ä 3939-04, aktbil 34, 5).

As what might be understood as a consequence of the dispute between Atosa Mirdamadian and Peivan Tavakoli regarding marital property, she filed an application for registration of the marriage – as a marriage according to Swedish law – at the Swedish Tax Agency for matters of national registration (*folkbokföring*) in early 2005. Allegedly, she was acting on advice from her lawyer at the time (Ä 3939-04, aktbil 89, 2). Registration of marriage has no independent legal significance according to Swedish law. However, it is practically impossible to enter into marriage if the national registration records show the marital status as already married.[4] And this proved to be a problem as Peivan Tavakoli wished to

3 That ordinance is now annulled and replaced by the law (1993:305) concerning the right to officiate marriages within religious bodies other than the Church of Sweden (*lagen (1993:305) om rätt att förrätta vigsel inom andra trossamfund än Svenska kyrkan*).

4 This has to do with the fact that one of the prerequisites for entering into marriage, according to the Swedish law on marriage and divorce chapter 2 § 4, is that neither of the parties is already married. Consideration of impediments to marriage (*hindersprövning*) must be carried out, according to the law chapter 3 § 1, by the Swedish Tax Agency and

get married soon after the registration was entered into the records at the Swedish Tax Agency. As will become evident later in this story, the time of the registration of the marriage has been considered as an important circumstance in at least one of the legal decisions concerning the marital status of the parties (Regeringsbeslut 51, Ju2005/5456/L2). For reasons which are outside the scope of this study, the Swedish Tax Agency registered Atosa Mirdamadian and Peivan Tavakoli as having been married in accordance with Swedish law since 12 July 1991. About the same time, in March 2005, Atosa Mirdamadian filed an application urging the court to grant a divorce between her and Peivan Tavakoli. In August the same year, the registration of the marriage at the Swedish Tax Agency was revoked on Peivan Tavakoli's request. The reasons for revoking the registration are outside the scope of this study.

As to the divorce granted by the imam, Atosa Mirdamadian maintains in her correspondence with the court that she and Peivan Tavakoli did get a divorce, but that they had been 'together again'. 'An evidence', she argues, 'is that our common child [-] was born 980530'[5] (Ä 3939-04, aktbil 17). She is making a legal argument referring to Shari'a, arguing that the divorce is no longer valid if the parties have been 'together' within the time period of three months and ten days from the divorce, which will then nullify the divorce (T 912-05, aktbil 33, 1). Her argument was never answered or refuted by Peivan Tavakoli in any of the cases of this story.

Peivan Tavakoli maintains in his correspondence with the court that he never intended to enter into marriage in accordance with Swedish law with Atosa Mirdamadian (T 912-05, aktbil 33, 2). The marriage was strictly meant to be valid in terms of Shari'a. According to the judge's final decision in Ä 3939-04, Peivan Tavakoli has referred to the marriage as an Islamic 'engagement'[6] (*förlovning*) (Ä 3939-04, aktbil 89, 2). Peivan Tavakoli himself states in his correspondence with the court that 'I [Peivan Tavakoli] and [Atosa Mirdamadian] are not married'… '[We] are in any case divorced'[7] (T 912-05, aktbil 7, 1) referring to the letter of divorce from the Muslim congregation in Malmö (T 912-05, aktbil 11) as evidence of that. We can know nothing about what Peivan Tavakoli really intended as he signed the marriage contract in 1991. But one might wonder how he could know that the imam performing the ceremony was not authorized to officiate marriages

---

the Swedish Social Insurance Agency (*Försäkringskassan*). Without a certificate from the Swedish Tax Agency stating that there is no impediment to the marriage – as the law requires it in chapter 3 § 4 – it is not possible to get married according to Swedish law. Being registered as being married at the Swedish Tax Agency is thus an obstacle to getting married according to Swedish law.

5 Translated from Swedish '*tillsammans igen*'…'*att vårt gemensamma barn [--] föddes* 980530', i.e. born 30 May 1998.

6 Translated from Swedish '*förlovning*'.

7 Translated from Swedish '*Jag [--] och [--] är inte gifta med varandra*'… '*[Vi] är i vart fall skilda från varandra*'.

according to Swedish law, when neither the imam himself nor the congregation seems to have been aware of that circumstance.

As the story of the Atosa Mirdamadian and Peivan Tavakoli cases at the court developed over time, it became evident that the imam indeed was not competent at the time of the marriage in 1991 to officiate marriages according to Swedish law. As a consequence, Atosa Mirdamadian filed an application to the Department of Justice (*Justitiedepartementet*) for an approval of the marriage. The Swedish law on marriage and divorce (*Äktenskapsbalken*), chapter 4 § 2, section 3, states that the government – the Department of Justice – can approve a marriage which would otherwise be invalid due to the lack of competence on the side of marriage officiate. In the preparatory works – an important source of Swedish law – it is stated that approval should be granted if the parties seem to have trusted in the marriage being valid (*Sveriges riksdags proposition* 1968:136, 45f). Now, the problem is of course that the preparatory work refers to validity and trust in relation to Swedish law. There is room for some uncertainty in this story about what laws and legal institutions Atosa Mirdamadian and Peivan Tavakoli were referring to as they signed the contract of marriage in 1991. Were their legal actions directed exclusively towards Shari'a, did they intend to act in relation to both Shari'a and Swedish law, or were the differences between and implications of these two spheres of law not entirely clear to them? In relation to what legal culture did they put their trust? In any case, as the preparatory works puts it, the government should not approve the marriage if there is uncertainty to whether or not the parties intended to enter into marriage and if one of the parties contests the application. The Department of Justice rejected Atosa Mirdamadian's application, referring to four separate circumstances: Peivan Tavakoli's statement that he never intended to enter into marriage according to Swedish law, the circumstance that the marriage had not been registered at the Swedish Tax Agency until 2005, the circumstance that the parties had been registered on different addresses during a longer period of time, and the circumstance that Atosa Mirdamadian had given different statements to various Swedish agencies at different time concerning the parties' marital status (*Regeringsbeslut* 51, Ju2005/5456/L2, 2f). Peculiarly enough, the circumstance that Peivan Tavakoli contested the application, and that there was a statement from his part that he never had intended the marriage to be valid according to Swedish law, should have been enough for the government to arrive at its conclusion of disallowing the application. The additional circumstances, which are referred to in the decision, add nothing of legal value to it. They do, however, raise doubts concerning how the Department of Justice has interpreted the information and arguments submitted by the parties.

Following the Department of Justice's decision, Atosa Mirdamadian withdrew her suit in the case at the court concerning marriage and divorce (T 912-05, aktbil 32), after which the court closed the case (T 912-05, aktbil 36).

And so the story goes that in the end Atosa Mirdamadian and Peivan Tavakoli have the signature of the then Minister of Justice that there are 'no particular grounds for sanctioning the ceremony as a marriage'[8] (T 912-05, aktbil 33, 3), the signature of one judge that '[they] agree to their marriage not being valid'[9] (T 912-05, aktbil 25, 2), and the signature of another judge that they were 'engaged according to Islamic practice'[10] during a brief period of time (Ä 3939-04, aktbil 89, 2).

The material in the dossiers of the cases in this story does not give away what Atosa Mirdamadian and Peivan Tavakoli really did intend with their legal actions. That is something which will never be possible to know. It is however possible to draw some conclusions and raise some questions based on the material in this story.

It is noticeable that Atosa Mirdamadian and Peivan Tavakoli repeatedly refer to the marriage as a 'marriage' without specifying to which law and legal institutions they refer, though it is clear that they sometimes argue in reference to Shari'a and sometimes in reference to Swedish law. Thus the meaning of the term 'marriage' comes through as uncertain, as it is not always easy to follow in relation to which legal culture the term is used.

It is further noteworthy that the judge in the case on marriage and divorce – T 912-05 – refers to the parties having agreed on the marriage as being 'not valid'[11] (T 912-05, aktbil 25, 2). In writing his decision he leaves out the possible – even probable – continuation of that sentence, which would have then read 'not valid *according to Swedish law*'. Perhaps it is implicit in the sentence as the judge writes it. Perhaps it is obvious that the judge can only possibly refer to what is valid in reference to Swedish law. But having read through the entire material filed into the dossier of that case, it is apparent that the parties refer to the marriage in relation to Shari'a as often as they refer to it in relation to Swedish law. They offer arguments in relation to both spheres of law. The interesting point is not if the judge should have made himself more clear or not by distinguishing between the validity of the marriage in relation to Swedish law and Shari'a when writing his decision. The interesting point is that the law places no restriction on the judge *not* to make that distinction. On the contrary, the law has no particular instruction to the judge on this matter. So, having no particular instruction from the law, the judge silently – by informed choice or out of ignorance – does not acknowledge the existence of *the other* legal culture, its legal texts and legal institutions, to which the parties repeatedly have related and argued in the case. That is indeed both noticeable and interesting.

How did the marriage between Atosa Mirdamadian and Peivan Tavakoli translate into an 'engage[ment] according to Islamic practice'[12] (Ä 3939-04,

8 Translated from Swedish '*inte synnerliga skäl att godkänna förrättningen som vigsel*'.

9 Translated from Swedish '*ense om att deras vigsel inte är giltig*'.

10 Translated from Swedish '*förlovade enligt muslimsk sed*'.

11 Translated from Swedish '*inte är giltig*'.

12 Translated from Swedish '*förlov[ning] enligt muslimsk sed*'.

aktbil 89, 2)? In the case concerning distribution of marital property – Ä 3939-04 – the judge refers to Peivan Tavakoli presenting his suit in such a way during an oral statement at the court session preceding the judge's final decision on case. The same judge refers to Peivan Tavakoli presenting his suit referring to the marriage as 'an alleged Muslim marriage ceremony'[13] (Ä 3939-04, aktbil 89, 2). It is not possible to retrieve what Peivan Tavakoli really did say in his oral statement, as tape recordings of statements are not archived at the court for more than four weeks. The minutes of the court session only state that Peivan Tavakoli did give a statement. It remains silent on what he said (Ä 3939-04, aktbil 83, 3). Regardless of whether or not Peivan Tavakoli did speak of an 'engagement', an 'Islamic practice' or referred to the marriage as 'alleged' in his oral statement, the interesting point is that the judge in question chooses to formulate the narration in his decision using that specific terminology. In the material filed into the case dossier, Peivan Tavakoli – through his attorney – presents his suit stating that 'the parties are divorced according to Islamic law'[14] (Ä 3939-04, aktbil 15, 1), and he further invokes the divorce certificate from the imam in Malmö as evidence to that fact (Ä 3939-04, aktbil 28, 1). The only reference by Peivan Tavakoli to the marriage as being 'alleged' is found in one of the other cases, the one on marriage and divorce (T 912-05, aktbil 6).

So given the choice, the judge in this case uses the particular terminology of 'engagement' instead of marriage, and 'practice' instead of law, which is by any standard a belittling mistranslation of Shari'a, and indeed a misconception in relation to what is being argued by the parties in the case in general. Again, the interesting point is not whether the judge should have used another terminology regarding Shari'a or not when writing his decision. The interesting point is that the law has no instruction to the judge on how to narrate and, given the choice, the judge – by informed choice or out of ignorance – mistranslates *the other* legal culture, its legal texts and legal institutions, to which the parties repeatedly have related and argued in the case. That is indeed both noticeable and interesting.

Perhaps as interesting is the handwritten note from the board of the Muslim congregation in Malmö, pointing in the direction that the congregation has been under the impression – or was at least at the time the note was written in 2005 under the impression – that it could officiate marriages *or divorces* according to Swedish law during the years 1991–9 (Ä 3939-04, aktbil 34, 5; T 912-05, aktbil 18). Swedish law does not allow – and has not during the time the congregation refers to allowed – any other instances than Swedish general courts to perform divorces in accordance with Swedish law. The point is that there seem to be a specific legal culture coming out of the attitudes and beliefs in relation to both Shari'a and Swedish law at the Muslim congregation in Malmö. It is not possible from the material in this study to know much about that legal culture. Swedish law and legal institutions only seem to become relevant when, and to the degree

13 Translated from Swedish '*en påstådd muslimsk vigselakt*'.

14 Translated from Swedish '*Parterna har skiljt sig enligt islamisk rätt*'.

that the congregation and the individual members of the congregation choose to interact with Swedish law and legal institutions. The only conclusion that can be drawn is that the material in the story of the Atosa Mirdamadian and Peivan Tavakoli cases at the court gives evidence of the existence of a legal culture of Shari'a in and around the Muslim congregation in Malmö.

The story of the Atosa Mirdamadian and Peivan Tavakoli cases at the court leaves many questions unanswered. Why do the officer at the National Tax Agency, the judges at the court and the then Minister of Justice seem to be unable to approach Shari'a, and the legal culture that the Atosa Mirdamadian and Peivan Tavakoli bring into the cases, on a systematic level? Why is it that the legal language which the judges use either treat this other legal culture with silence or with a language of belittling mistranslation?

Court Culture and Judicial Culture at a Swedish District Court

My suggestion is that the discourse of misconception and silence on Shari'a which can be found in the story of the Atosa Mirdamadian and Peivan Tavakoli cases at the court is informed by a specific court culture and a judicial culture which is prevalent at the court. How are the court culture and the judicial culture formulated, and what is informing it? Those are questions to be dealt with in this part of the chapter. By answering these questions, it might be possible to get closer to understanding how the judge approaches Shari'a, how he – in practical terms – solves the problems which he encounters, and from where he draw the relevant knowledge needed in order to communicate about Shari'a in a legal context: how he formulates his discourse on Shari'a.

Court Culture

Lund District Court is a mid sized district court in the very south of Sweden, employing 61 persons.[15] The court handles an estimated 4,000 cases a year – including criminal cases (*brottmål*), civil cases (*tvistemål*) and court matters (*domstolsärenden*) – a fairly high workload considering its size. The employees[16] are divided into categories of judges: one chief judge (*lagman*), nine judges (*rådmän*), two associate Court of Appeal judges (*hovrättsassessorer*), three deputy judges (*fiskaler*), nine judge-delegates (*tingsnotarier med särskilt förordnande att döma i särskilda fall*) and 14 law clerks (*tingsnotarier*) of which some also act as judge-delegates, 22 law secretaries (*domstolssekreterare*, *beredningssekreterare*), six administrative personnel and two security personnel.

15 The number of employees varies between 55 and 60. The number given in this chapter is from October 2007.

16 Lay judges (*nämndemän*), who are not employees, are left out of the study as they do not take any significant part in the court culture or in the professional judicial culture.

All employees take part in forming a specific institutionalized court culture through their interactions in the internal organization of the work at the court. As a general rule, the employees have been working at this court or at similar workplaces for a period varying between 10 and 46 years. There are few exceptions to that rule. Judges, law clerks and law secretaries are of special interest in a study of the court's culture, because they carry out the core of the court's main activities.

With few exceptions, the judges at the court have been working exclusively at district courts within the jurisdiction of the Court of Appeal (*Hovrätten*) of Skåne and Blekinge, and within the Department of Justice as secretaries in Commissions of Inquiries (*utredningssekreterare*) – often placed at the Court of Appeal in Malmö. Consequently, judges tend to have a thorough experience of court culture, but limited experience from other workplaces. Judges take part in training younger judges and court clerks, as have been the tradition at Swedish courts since the 18th century (Bell, 2006, 249f; Modéer 2003, 151). As the judges serve as advisors to younger judges, and court clerks assist the individual judges, the younger judges and the law clerks gradually learn and adjust to the institutionalized court culture and become part of it.

The law secretaries are the institutional memory of the court. They have a thorough knowledge of, and experience in, how things are done at the court. An overwhelming majority of them started to work at the court in the 1970s, and they have been working there since. While the majority has no academic training at all, the more recently employed secretaries hold law degrees. The law secretaries register, manage and file all cases and case dossiers at the court. They assist the judges in preparing the cases, they take minutes during hearings and they sometimes draft judgments. They take part in training law clerks in a daily basis. Consequently, the law secretaries hold a key position in forming and preserving the court culture.

The court clerks are the only personnel who are employed on temporary contracts: one and a half to two years. They are often in the early stages of their professional careers. They assist the different judges in all their tasks, and work close to the law secretaries. While one could imagine that the clerks might bring new knowledge or fresh impulses to the court, this is seldom the case. The institutional structure of the court hardly allows for knowledge to emerge from bottom of the hierarchy where the law clerks are, to the top where judges – and depending on the issue, sometimes also law secretaries – are. In this respect, tradition is the key value at the court.

Thus, the court culture is quite conservative in the sense that it is instructed by a commitment to institutional knowledge. The organizational structure of the court is traditional and hierarchical – as organizational structures of district courts often are (Lindström, 1999, 473) – and has a formal as well as an informal aspect. The overwhelming majority of judges are men, and the overwhelming majority of the law secretaries are women. The current chief judge has held the same position for the last two decades. The formal organizational structure places him at the top of the hierarchy. The informal organizational structure places the chief judge at the top together with one of the law secretaries who also serves as the head of division for all law secretaries. This informal organizational structure is a praxis which has been established over the last 20 years. It is well known and respected by all employees. Both the formal and the informal organizational structures of the court centre the workplace culture on a small number of persons who hold a high level of institutional knowledge about the court and its culture.

Judicial Culture

All judges at the court hold Swedish citizenships and undergraduate LLM degrees in Swedish law from Swedish law schools. Judges must swear an oath of allegiance to the profession (*domared*) before they sit on the bench. The oath is part of the code of ethics for judges, which is found on the fourth chapter of the code of procedure (*Rättegångsbalken*). All judges who have not yet been appointed as permanent judges take part in a trainee programme managed in conjunction with the National Courts Administration, and are thus judges in training. The trainee programme takes the judge in training from being a law clerk to becoming a permanent judge. That career journey usually takes eight to 10 years to complete (Sweden, 2006, 12).

The formal training of judges consists of seminars and courses once or twice a year, ranging in length from half a day up to five weeks (Bell, 2006, 250). The formal training includes issues of substantial Swedish law, but also introduces questions of methods and ethics of the profession. In a broader understanding the trainee programme introduces and socializes (Ryberg, 1988, 149f) the individual trainee judge into the professional culture of judges. It also insures a high level of homogeneity among judges (Bell 2006, 251). The informal training is perhaps more interesting than the formal when trying to understand judicial culture at the court. It is primarily through this informal process of peer learning that the trainee judge learns the profession. The informal training takes place on an everyday basis, and it ensures an intergenerational transfer of knowledge (Zetterholm, 1994, 71)

The principal virtues taught in the informal training at the court are accuracy and efficiency (Ryberg, 1988, 110ff). This means correct spelling, a particular grammar and phraseology, a particular way of narration as well as accuracy and appropriateness in relation to the collective of judges, judicial culture and court culture. Loyalty towards the collective of judges and judicial culture (Ryberg, 1988, 111; Modéer, 1994, 15) and the virtue of judging in accordance with the praxis of the High Court (*Högsta Domstolen*) and the Courts of Appeals are other important virtues. These virtues require that the judge spend a lot of time at his workplace – as it requires a lot of time to adjust a person's language into a language which is in accordance with the standard court language. Judges perceive themselves as working very hard, and reading literature which does not have a direct impact on the cases they are working on cannot be prioritized. Thus, judges primarily read what other judges write. Acquiring a specific language plays an important role in the process of becoming a judge. By reading what other judges write, the judge is socialized into the particular understanding of language which a judge should acquire.

Having or acquiring knowledge beyond general law is not a virtue. As the chief judge at the court put it in a speech at a national conference on the reformation of the juridical system

> I for my part think that the demand for special knowledge is substantially exaggerated … the issue [in a legal case] might be complicated and touch on areas where the judge's knowledge from the beginning is *non-existent, inadequate or at best amateurish* … But when the judge has *made up his mind* on what circumstances to base his judgment on, then the legal evaluation of those circumstances is self evident in at least nine out of ten cases.[17] (Alvå, 1997, 8) (emphasis added)

By becoming socialized into the profession of judge, the trainee judge is supposed to develop a feeling which will guide him on how to 'make up his mind' as to what circumstances he should base his judgment on, when his knowledge about the issue at hand is 'non-existent, inadequate or at best amateurish'.

Court culture instructs judicial culture in the sense that the conservative and hierarchical nature of court culture instructs the trainee judge to follow the examples of the more experienced judges, law secretaries and law clerks (Modéer, 1994, 17).

Discipline and punishment are part of judicial culture primarily in the practice of shaming and self-discipline. The State Disciplinary Board (*Statens ansvarsnämnd*) and the Swedish Parliamentary Ombudsman (*Justitieombudsmannen*) are the official instances for discipline and punishment in matters of malpractice, but very few matters go that far (*Statens ansvarsnämnds verksamhetsberättelse för 2006*, 2; *Redogörelse 2006/07:JO1 Justitieombudsmännens ämbetsberättelse*). Instead discipline and punishment are often carried out through practices of shaming and self-discipline. When a judge at the court is criticized by the Ombudsman, the word spreads at the court within minutes. During the time of the study there were two such instances. The instances were taken very seriously. Not so much because what was actually stated in the critique, but in the sense of an affirmation of a feeling among the judges of being watched. The instances certainly reinforced a certain degree of fear, shame and self-discipline among judges as well as trainee judges and law clerks.

---

17 Translated from Swedish '*Jag tycker för min del att behovet för specialkunskaper är kraftigt överdrivet ... Sakfrågan [i ett mål] kan vara nog så komplicerad och beröra områden där domarens kunskaper från början är obefintliga, otillräckliga eller i bästa fall amatörmässiga ... Men när domaren väl har bestämt sig för vilka sakomständigheter som ska läggas till grund för avgörandet, blir den rättsliga bedömningen något som i minst nio fall av tio ger sig självt*'.

When the judge or trainee judge has gone 'wrong' in a judgment – the Court of Appeal has overturned it in whole or in part – he will have a copy of the Court of Appeal judgment waiting for him on the seat of his office chair as he arrives at the court in the morning. Another copy will be made available for the rest of the employees at a special box in the court library. Being 'wrong' in this sense means failing to stay true to the principal virtues of the judicial culture. As the practice of the court has it, it also means shaming both in the copy-on-the-office-chair practice and the copy-made-public-in-the-library practice. During the time of the study, there was on average less than one instance a month of this kind, and it seemed to happen to the trainee judges more often than to the judges.

Self-discipline is enforced on the judge and trainee judge in order for him to avoid the shaming at the court, but more importantly in relation to the risk of losing out on a career as a judge. The law clerk is told by his peers that he must have a 'clean record' in order to be accepted as a trainee at the Court of Appeal, meaning that he should ideally not have had any judgments overturned in whole or in part by the Court of Appeal. Thus, on an organizational level, the judicial culture is in part instructed by internal norm-senders. That the chief justices of the different courts play a major role in the processes of hiring judges as trainees in the Courts of Appeals, as well as appointing judges and justices for permanent positions (Ryberg, 1988, 110). There is thus an organizational structure supporting the fear of losing out on career opportunities.

The judicial culture at the court is in many respects a culture which evolves around the professional identity of the judge and the court as a workplace. It is in that respect very self-centred. It seems to have few worries about the society and the individuals with which the judge interacts in his daily work at the court. Finding judicial culture connecting to virtues of loyalty towards the profession rather than other possible or probable virtues – such as loyalty towards the letter of the law, any sort of idea of justice, or perhaps the society which it is put to serve – stands out as a rather unexpected finding of this study.

Professional Training of Judges, Legal Education, Court Cases and Swedish Legal Literature on Shari'a

There is no formal professional training of judges relating to Shari'a,[18] and no informal training relating to Shari'a has taken place at the court during the time

18 At the time of writing, but outside the scope of the study, there has been one try-out seminar for judges in Stockholm organized by the National Courts Administration where Shari'a has been one of the topics. A similar seminar is planned to take place in Malmö in the near future for judges working in the southern region of Sweden. A related project – although not specifically on Shari'a – was carried through out in Malmö in 2007, in conjunction with the theatre company Theatron, the district court of Malmö and the administrative court of Malmö. The aim of the project was to shed light on hidden structures in the courts' interactions with the public. The National Courts Administration supports the

of the study. As Shari'a is not, and has never been, considered part of national Swedish law, it is not taught as such in Swedish law schools. It is sometimes mentioned in conjunction with Swedish international private law and comparative law insofar that Shari'a is a recognized part of a foreign national legal system. This division of law into either Swedish law or foreign law – and nothing in between – is instructive as to how the judge thinks about law. Law only becomes recognizable to the judge when it is sanctioned by a nation state, and by its very nature Shari'a does not primarily rely on the existence of a nation state. On the contrary, national legislation often relies on Shari'a, though that is not the case in Sweden. Most jurists would recognize this bipolar distinction – as either national or foreign national law – as the only possible way to recognize law. However, this way of recognizing law becomes a problem when the social reality which approaches the judge does not fit into that bipolar distinction.

When the judge is approached by something he recognizes as relating to Shari'a, it is probable – from what we know about judicial culture – that he would rely on peer knowledge. He would try to figure out what his colleagues would have done or have already done. Most probable he would also rely on the Court of Appeal and High Court praxis for guidance. He would not want to devote much time on reading literature, and if he had to read, he would prefer legal texts written by other judges or from a judge's perspective.

There are a few Swedish cases relating explicitly to Shari'a which the judge might find useful. The cases which are most often cited and commented on in the Swedish legal literature are the Court of Appeal cases RH 1993:116[19] (Schiratzki, 2001, 73; Bogdan, 1993a, 597ff; Bogdan, 2006a, 605f; Bogdan, 2007) and RH 2005:66 (Bogdan, 2006a, 605f; Bogdan, 2007). Both cases concern *mahr* in relation to questions of Swedish international private law. Questions of custody and alimony have been dealt with in cases RH 1993:52, the Administrative Court of Appeal case Kammarrätten i Jönköping 12275-1992 (this case will not be directly relevant to the district court judge, as it is a case from the Administrative Court of Appeal) (Schiratzki, 2001, 84), and NJA 1987 s. 600[20] (Pålsson, 1992, 483), the last case only in relation to Swedish private international law.

There are of course a number of cases which deal with issues of Islamic culture, Muslim culture and ethnic cultures which Muslims are part of. Many of these cases – mainly concerning what is often labelled as 'honour killings', circumcision and discrimination – do not specifically touch on Shari'a, but rather social or cultural practices which have little or nothing to do with Shari'a or Islamic law. Examples of such cases are the Court of Appeal of Skåne and Blekinge case on discrimination (Hovrätten över Skåne och Blekinge B 505-00) concerning '*slöja*' ('veil'), the

---

project in allowing the theatre company to give the show at a number of other district courts. A similar project has been carried out in Stockholm (*Domkresten*, no. 2, 2007, 25).

19 'RH' refers to reported cases from the Courts of Appeals (*Rättsfall från Hovrätterna*).

20 'NJA' refers to reported cases from the High Court (*Nytt Juridiskt Arkiv*).

Labour Court (*Arbetsdomstolen*) case concerning discharge in relation to a *fatwa* (AD 2000 number 75[21]) and the Göta Court of Appeal case concerning 'honour killing' (Göta Hovrätt B 1339-06). These kinds of cases might prove instructive to the judge, since there are distinctions made in them between what is to be considered as Shari'a and what is to be considered as social or cultural practices.

The last 20 years of publication in law in Swedish concerning Shari'a – meaning literature published by publishers dealing mainly or specifically with law, and authored by scholars in law – do not have much to offer. There is little other than Johanna Schiratzki's *Muslimsk familjerätt – i svenskt perspektiv* (Schiratzki, 2001), a book on Islamic family law in a Swedish perspective. Schiratzki's book cannot be found in the court library, but can be sent for from the library at the Court of Appeal of Skåne and Blekinge.

When stretching the term 'legal literature' a bit, the closest the judge gets to finding a comprehensive book on Shari'a in reference to Swedish law, written in Swedish, is Jan Hjärpe's *Shari'a – Gudomlig lag i en värld i förändring* (Hjärpe, 2005). Hjärpe's book is a general introduction to Shari'a and it outlines some practical implications of Shari'a in relation to Swedish court practices and legal interpretation. As it is neither available at the court library, nor at the library of the Court of Appeal of Skåne and Blekinge, the judge will most probably not have access to it. Hjärpe is Professor Emeritus of Islamic Studies and a publicly known academic in the Swedish debate on Islam. He is one of the very few Swedish 'authorities' on Islam who have been contracted on a regular basis to write legal opinions for parties in Swedish courts, the discrimination case mentioned above being one such example (appendix to Hovrätten över Skåne och Blekinge B 505-0). Hjärpe has also served as an expert witness on Islam and Shari'a in a number of legal cases. Most famously, he testified as an expert witness for the defence in the 'Radio Islam' case, RH 1991:20. Judges at the court have noted that there is no authority on Shari'a or Islam to which they can turn for reliable information, such as they would perhaps turn to the Vatican on issues of canon law. In this respect, Hjärpe has sometimes served as an entry to Swedish discourses on Shari'a.

In *Svensk Juristtidning* – one of the journals that judges do read, and which also is available in the court library – there are 11 entries explicitly concerning Shari'a or Islamic law during the last twenty years (Pålsson, 1992; Bogdan, 1993a; Bogdan, 1993b; Schiratzki, 1994; Schött, 1994; Bogdan, 1999; Nygren, 1999; Said and Chahanedh, 2001; Bogdan, 2006a; Bogdan, 2006b). In *Juridisk Tidskrift*, another major Swedish law journal which judges are likely to read, there are three entries in reference to Shari'a (Schiratzki, 1997; Strömberg, 2001; Mahmoudi, 2002). The judges' own union's journal *Tidskrift för Sveriges Domareförbund* does not have any entries at relating to Shari'a, nor does the journal of the National Courts Administration, *Domkretsen*.

21 'AD' refers to reported cases from the Labour Court (*Arbetsdomstolen*).

Shari'a from Behind the Bench: Court Culture, Judicial Culture and a Judge-made Discourse on Shari'a at a Swedish District Court

If the judge does not have any legal training in Shari'a, and he has virtually no reference to Shari'a in the Swedish legal literature and case law, how does he approach Shari'a? How does he – in practical terms – solve the problems which he encounters? From where does he draw the relevant knowledge needed in order to recognize Shari'a and communicate about it in the legal context? These questions can only be answered against the background of the court culture and the judicial culture as these cultures have been described in this essay.

When the judge finds no particular instruction in the law, he relies on court culture and judicial culture. In approaching Shari'a he does as he has been taught: he determines if it is a question of Swedish international private law or not, and if it is not, he will simply do as he would in any other case. He will use the language with which he has made himself familiar through his years of training. If the case in front of him instead had been on murder, he would have had access to a discourse where the meaning of particular terms would have been fairly well established in Swedish legal literature, case law and among his peers. But, as has become evident through the story of the Atosa Mirdamadian and Peivan Tavakoli cases at the court, when the case involves a legal culture where language and legal terminology have meanings which are different from the meanings of language and legal terminology at the Swedish court and among Swedish judges, the result might be that the judge ignores or misinterprets the information and arguments submitted by the parties. As the legal significance and the meaning of particular words relating to Shari'a seem to be less well established within the judge-made discourse of Shari'a than in other judge-made discourses, silence and distance seems to be the predominant way of dealing with it. The judge in training is given the advice to put as little as possible into words when writing his judgments. If he follows that advice he will minimize the risk of going wrong. Choosing to treat complex issues with silence in judgments is often the result of such considerations.

The story of the Atosa Mirdamadian and Peivan Tavakoli cases at the court has pointed to yet another practice among judges. By letting the parties do the narration – as in '[Peivan Tavakoli] has presented his suit as follows' – the judge creates a notion of authenticity and of staying true to what the parties actually have argued. The judge manages to borrow ethos from the parties of the case at the same time as he is free to put into words his own interpretation of what has been argued. By simply repeating what the parties have said, or rather by placing his own words in the mouths of the parties, the judge can distance himself from the risk of going wrong in the sense of misinterpreting what is being argued by the parties in the case. While seeming not to take a stance on the meaning of language, the judge chooses – as it has been described earlier in this chapter – a belittling language, putting as much distance as possible between Swedish law and Shari'a. The judge-made discourse on Shari'a coming out of the story of the Atosa Mirdamadian and Peivan Tavakoli cases at the court seems to be the product of judges wanting to distance themselves from the meaning of Shari'a in relation to Swedish law. The institutional knowledge derived from the hierarchical and traditional court culture and the virtues of judicial culture instructs the judge to keep the legal terminology as pure as possible and as separate as possible from competing forms of understanding legal terminology. There seems to be an agreement in legal education, legal literature, case law and judicial culture on silence and distance in regard to Shari'a and the legal culture referring to Shari'a. As court culture and judicial culture come through in the study, they seem to be fairly hostile to change of cognitive structures as well as towards all types of knowledge which are not already part of the institutionalized structures. However, recent reforms of the judicial structure – the decision to open new career paths to becoming a judge, and creating new courts where the cognitive structures are not (yet) as institutionalized, such as the Migration Court, are two examples of such reforms – might create opportunities for a change for the better.

In ending this chapter, let us return to the origin of the story, to the artefacts, signs and signatures of real life and real people. That is how the story of the Atosa Mirdamadian and Peivan Tavakoli cases at the court has been told. Through the scribbles and notes, the decisions and judgments, the handwritten certificates, through all the appendices of the court dossiers, people have given evidence by declaring their identities and their wills through their signatures: the judges, the law clerks, the law secretaries, the attorneys, the then Minister of Justice, the imam, the representative of the board of the Muslim congregation in Malmö, Atosa Mirdamadian and Peivan Tavakoli. Those signatures are the evidence of the encounter at a district court in Sweden between court culture, judicial culture and a legal culture on and referring to Shari'a.

Chapter 9
Between God and the Sultana? Legal Pluralism in the British Muslim Diaspora

Prakash Shah

Nowadays in Britain we are constantly being reminded that Britishness is opposed to Islam, if Islam means adherence to Shari'a, a legal system that appears to be in competition with the official British and European legal systems for the setting out of an alternative social order. Indeed, the crisis that some detect today in the paradigm of multiculturalism appears to be occurring because of the Muslim presence in Britain.[1] In barely coded references to Muslim minorities, some commentators have criticized the multicultural ethic as having led to separatism among the various ethnic components of society and thereby argued that it is no longer appropriate as a principle for the governance of plural societies. The unease about multiculturalism among this group, some of which have included members of the West's ethnic minority populations, has led others to diagnose a crisis in, or an end to, political multiculturalism (Joppke, 2004; Grillo, 2005). Conversely, Modood (2005) argues that multiculturalism in Britain is being drawn back unfairly now that Muslims lay claim to its achievements and, indeed, are contributing to its expansion beyond 'race' to include consciousness of religious difference.

While individual responses obviously vary somewhat, a common thread that runs through a core group of public figures is their advocacy of the need for the principles holding plural societies together to draw upon what is common among people rather than what makes them different. In Britain this has led to assertions that it is in 'Britishness' that we can locate the core values, beliefs or principles which bind society together. A number of political leaders have championed this view, among them then Prime Minister Tony Blair (2006), the Conservative opposition leader David Cameron (2005) and the new Prime Minister Gordon Brown (2006). Another notable figure is Trevor Phillips, Chair of the Commission for Racial Equality and of the newly established Commission for Equality and

1 The Muslim presence is seen as problematic not just in Europe or the West generally. Many other regions of the world are seeing conflicts between Muslim minorities and the dominant social order, India, Thailand and China being examples outside the Western world. It is tempting in this context to read into such troubles the self-fulfilment of the Huntingtonian vision of a clash. Incidentally, Bernard Lewis was the originator of the phrase 'clash of civilizations' in the September 1990 issue of *Atlantic Monthly*, which was later picked up by Samuel Huntington.

Human Rights.[2] Phillips (2005) famously stated that 'we are sleepwalking our way to segregation', the principal cause of which he locates in the type of multiculturalism hitherto practised in Britain, while his remedy is also to look to Britishness as the foundation of the core values of civility linking all of the country's inhabitants.

Positing Britishness as the primary factor behind cohesion is fraught with difficulty, however, and the precise menu of items it constitutes varies from one commentator to the next, although the British generally feature as the 'good guys' in whatever (hi)story one is expected to accept. This sort of positioning indicates the continuing assumption of Europe as an 'instruction culture' (Malik, 2004, 4), teaching others how best to live.[3] It is also remarkable how discussions about Britishness tend to strongly centre on the question of law. Britishness is said by Phillips to include adherence to the rule of law, principles of democracy and looking to Parliament as the accepted authority for law making. In December 2006, Tony Blair also took up the legal theme during his lecture at the non-governmental organization (NGO) the Runnymede Trust, saying:

> we must demand allegiance to the rule of law. Nobody can legitimately ask to stand outside the law of the nation. There is thus no question of the UK allowing the introduction of religious law in the UK. Parliament sets the law, interpreted by the courts. All criminal matters should be dealt with through the criminal justice system. There may be areas where, in civil proceedings, parties consent to arbitration by a religious body. But these are arrangements based on consent and, in all cases, parties will have recourse to the UK courts.

Effectively Tony Blair was saying that there was no prospect of the principles or rules of Shari'a being generally recognized in Britain. Some months earlier, Trevor Phillips (2006) had used even stronger language in response to a question about the reportedly high number of Muslims who wish to live by the Shari'a:

> We have one set of laws; they are decided by one group of people, members of parliament that is the end of the story. And anybody who lives here has to accept that that's they way we do it, if you want to do it somewhere in another way you have to live somewhere else.

---

2 The establishment of this new 'equalities' body marks a change in official concerns about race and ethnicity to more general notions of equality of treatment, and is arguably part of the paradigm shift which questioning of multiculturalism has entailed.

3 This tendency to assume the role of an instruction culture is most clearly reflected in the state requiring English competency and 'knowledge of life in the United Kingdom' as a condition of settlement rights (i.e. a residence permit for an indefinite period) and acquisition of British citizenship. Similar conditions also apply in several other European countries.

On 14 February 2007, Lord Falconer, the Lord Chancellor and Secretary of State for Constitutional Affairs, said in pretty much the same vein:

> One law for all. This is the principle that underpins our justice system. Which is why we will not consider permitting Sharia law or any other religious law to determine what constitutes criminal behaviour. Parliament sets the law, interpreted by the courts. Allegiance to the Rule of Law is the keystone of our society. It is non-negotiable. Protection under the same law is something that every one of us shares, regardless of region or religion, background or beliefs. We are all subject to the same rules – something that has been a defining characteristic of our society and fundamental to our values.[4]

There is thus an ongoing debate about the extent to which living in an ethnically and religiously plural society can entail the possibility of people ordering their lives by parallel principles or rules of law. It is entirely welcome that such discussions are now being aired publicly, even though one gets the feeling that the tone often adopted is less that of an ongoing conversation among concerned parties and more of a unilateralist, take-it-or-leave-it – or 'take it or leave the country' – one. This situation is made worse by the virtual disenfranchisement from the mainstream media of people who can speak lucidly about alternative conceptions of law, a grave asymmetry which, in the end, penalizes the weakest members of society.

While he did not say so explicitly, in the quoted part of his speech Tony Blair seemed to be alluding to the coverage on the radio and press in the prior few days of the existence of dispute-resolution fora among different minority ethnic communities. This round in the debate was sparked off when BBC Radio 4 was about to broadcast its *Law in Action* programme on 28 November 2006 in which participants from the Jewish, Somali and other Muslim communities provided information about how certain types of disputes were being handled under communal structures of one sort or another. I also took part in the programme, as did Cassandra Balchin of the NGO Women Living Under Muslim Laws.

Most controversially, information was given about how some Somalis were organizing to solve intra-communal disputes among themselves, sometimes touching on matters that would also concern the official criminal law. Some disputes are 'delegated' to a Somali forum by agreement between the families of the perpetrator and victim respectively, and with the approval of the police. Jonathan Greenwood, a solicitor who often represents Jewish litigants, spoke about the long-standing practice among some Jews to have their intra-communal disputes resolved before the Beth Din. Faizul Aqtab Siddiqi, a commercial barrister and a member of a 'Shari'a council', the Mahkamah Council of Jurists, spoke of how Muslims in Birmingham were organizing along similar lines in civil disputes.

Meanwhile, the BBC grapevine meant that within days of recording the programme I was being asked by other radio stations to take part in their

4 I am grateful to Innes Bowen of the BBC for drawing my attention to this speech.

programmes on the same issue. Within two days of the *Law in Action* programme being broadcast, the *Daily Express* (30 November 2006) announced on its front page, 'Muslim law is here in Britain'. The newspaper article stated that:

> the Government had already allowed elements of sharia law to be introduced. The Treasury has brought in measures including interest-free loans and mortgages which comply with the Islamic law.

It also linked Muslim dispute-resolution fora ('secret courts' according to the language used in the *Daily Express* article) to stoning and amputation which occurs in some Muslim majority countries. The article was remarkably silent about the Jewish bodies which have been established as dispute processors for much longer.[5] Indeed, one interviewee in the *Law in Action* programme stated that arbitrations by the Beth Din were already enforceable by the English courts, and the courts had indeed been enforcing them for many years. On reflection it can be explained why Tony Blair had to react to such scaremongering and why he had to state clearly that there was no prospect of religious law being introduced in Britain. He made an important qualification, however, stating that civil arbitration by religious bodies, based on the consent of the parties, and subject to the official courts' jurisdiction, was a different matter.

The latest round in the controversy surrounding Shari'a was sparked by the speech of the Archbishop of Canterbury, Dr Rowan Williams, on 7 February 2008 at the Royal Courts of Justice in London in which he foresaw a 'higher level of attention to religious identity and communal rights in the practice of law' and also 'something like a delegation of certain legal functions to the religious courts of a community'.[6] Dr Williams' speech was the first in a series of lectures in London which has kept legal minds busy thinking about the implications of the Muslim presence in Britain. I have discussed the speech and some of its implications elsewhere (Shah, 2009) but for present purposes it is important to note that the discussion about Shari'a and its place within British legal order continues to be a matter of controversy and quite some ill-feeling, while it has attracted worldwide public and scholarly attention.

---

5 The *Daily Express* meanwhile appears to have a mission to highlight the legal separatism of Muslims. A more recent front page headline of 30 April 2007 announced 'Now Muslims get their own laws in Britain', with very little new information. The magazine *Der Spiegel* has meanwhile been adding to the negative coverage of Muslims and the law in Europe in an issue titled 'German justice failures: Paving the way for a parallel Muslim society', *Spiegel Online*, 29 March 2007, at <http://www.spiegel.de/international/germany/0,1518,474629,00.html>, last accessed 24 July 2007.

6 The speech can be found at <http.//www.archbishopofcanterbury.org/1575> and is linked to a fairly long question-and-answer session which followed it at <http.//www.archbishopofcanterbury.org/1594>. A radio interview was recorded the same day, but earlier, for BBC's World at One programme – text at <http.//www.archbishopofcanterbury.org/1573>.

Legal Pluralism as Social Reality

From a certain perspective the whole public debate on multiculturalism and law has an aura of 'unreality' (Nielsen, 2004, 155) about it, but it is not surprising if we consider the dominating presuppositions which operate strongly when we discuss the Western idea of 'law'. This perspective often blocks our view to legal developments occurring throughout the world, as much as they do in Britain. According to Western legal theory or 'model jurisprudence' as Japanese writer Masaji Chiba (1986) has it, law is generally considered to emanate from political authority. Many of us, lawyers and non-lawyers alike, have absorbed this powerful ideology, perhaps more properly referred to as the 'ideology of the powerful', and have rarely questioned its foundations. Open any textbook on English law today and we will hardly find a mention of laws operating outside the realm of the state authorities.

This state-centric and basically nationalist vision of law has developed over a long dureé, as aptly summarized by Nielsen (2004, 110). Otherwise described by some comparative legal scholars and theorists as being a 'myth' (Griffiths, 1986, 4) or a 'political claim' (Santos, 2002, 89–90), it makes us focus almost exclusively upon the activities of bodies like Parliament or the official courts and tribunals. We are rarely able to acknowledge that other actors – individuals or different components of society – have legal agency. Thus, the Western ideology of 'legal centralism', as Griffiths (1986) terms it, has actually developed in such a way as to reinforce the position of a minor political elite, hardly representative of the wider social sphere, but speaking and ruling on the latter's behalf, while simultaneously denying its freedom to operate by autonomous value systems. That this does not necessarily lead to outright conflict is rather surprising, but we can often take comfort from the fact that in liberalism a large space for manoeuvre is still left to the autonomous individual maximizing his, and latterly her, own happiness, whatever that may be. But conflict very soon surfaces in all sorts of spheres and is amplified considerably in an ethnically plural setting especially if those comprising that plurality organise their lives, and make sense of such organization, upon bases which are at considerable variance to those which the majority ethnic components have largely unquestioningly used to govern their own lives. The greater this variance, the greater the possibility of conflict.

While Britain has always been ethnically plural, the current condition of ethnic plurality is different to the extent that we now have considerable numbers of people living in Britain, whether full citizens or not, who have either directly migrated from outside Europe or are descended from one or more forebears who have. Those of European descent themselves have a range of histories. Some are returnee colonial settlers; others are intra-European migrants and their descendants, the Irish and Jews being their long-standing representatives, while the migrants from new member states of the EU are the latest of these groups. Each has had its own troubles in settling down to some sort of liveable compromise within Britain. However, the task of doing so successfully for those who trace their roots to some

African, Asian and, increasingly, Latin American contexts is made that much more complicated because they hold on to value systems and legal cultures based on sharply differing premises.

From a legal pluralist perspective the project of cultural reconstruction and, importantly for Muslims, religious reconstruction in Britain, in Europe or in any other Western country which migrants and their descendants have undertaken, the facts of which are now undeniable (Ballard, 1994; Nielsen, 2004), has also been accompanied by legal reconstruction, a haphazard process of transplantation of 'foreign' laws. Social psychologist, Günther Bierbrauer, drawing on his fieldwork with Kurdish and Lebanese immigrants in Germany (see Bierbrauer, 1994), explains why it is not tenable to expect their outright assimilation to the dominant legal order:

> one could argue that immigrants should try to cope with the new legal system of the dominant society by learning its rules in the same way as they learn the language and customs practised in their new environment. Why is this not tenable?
>
> … law and legal systems are cultural products like language, music or marriage arrangements and as such they form a structure of meaning that guides and organises individuals and groups in situations of conflict. Thus, legal culture refers to the layman's conception and knowledge of legal rights and duties and the way in which people solve their disputes in a particular culture … cultural norms, values and practices are internalized during socialisation and they become part of a person's identity. Legal culture is only one aspect of a person's ethnic or cultural identity. (Bierbrauer, 1998, 196)

Bierbrauer's insights on the unrealism of legal assimilation of immigrants to Germany probably apply as much to any country in Europe which has experienced substantial immigration. From a positivist, state-centred perspective we would of course deny the fact that disaporic groups can and do operate within a framework today composed, not only of European laws, but also laws derived from other aspects of their cultural heritage. In the social and legal reality on the ground, however, it is evident that such laws have for some time now come to be part of the European legal landscape. Indeed, as Glenn (2000, 148) observes: 'The city has also emerged as a new field of inter-traditional activity, the result of massive population movement in the world, having possibly its greatest effect in Europe.'

This legal diversity and plurality requires a shift from the legal centralist mode of analysis and demands that we take on board the subjective aspect of legal experience. When faced with multiple and sometimes conflicting legal rules, individuals will have to make difficult decisions about balancing different legal values. Chiba (1998, 239) argues for just such a subjective perspective, observing:

> First, a person under legal pluralism may stand in the position of legal ambivalence between conflicting legal rules. Thus he/she is aware of being legally entitled to choose one of them and reject the others. Further, he/she is encouraged to make that choice on the ground that it is culturally justified. Finally he/she may be proud of the choice as a cultural privilege for its traditional value... In sum, being accompanied by cognition of cultural pride, the recipient's choice may produce a considerable effect upon the working of legal pluralism, whether positive or negative and manifestly or latently.

Inherent within this process therefore is a dynamic of subjective legal comparison. Comparative law itself thereby turns out to be the domain of the individual living under conditions of legal pluralism, rather than belonging to some arcane branch of academic inquiry. Such conditions require that individuals become legal navigators, screening for themselves the different messages sent to them from within and from without and deciding what to do each time, and often choosing rules based on the extent to which they support their own cultural integrity. Seen in this way, rethinking Shari'a in light of living as a European Muslim may be recognizable as an aspect of *tajdid* (renewal) (Ramadan, 2002, 211).

This process may often result in the 'wrong choice' since the state may not necessarily support it, especially where it is not sufficiently responsive to the subjective aspect of legal pluralism. Or it may be the 'wrong choice' because one's own community, or an adjacent community, does not respect that choice on the grounds that it goes against its own values. Muslims in Europe are themselves constantly engaged in such conflicts and tensions, notably revising what it means to be a 'good Muslim' (Nielsen, 2004, 116–20). Thus, legal pluralism in this sense of being an aspect of social reality is not necessarily a happy state of affairs where everyone's demands are met at all times. More realistically it is a series of uneasy compromises made by all individuals, but again bearing in mind that the greater the cultural distance between different laws the greater the possibility of conflict or personal crisis.[7]

Muslim Legal Pluralism: Searching for a Framework

We have already seen how political and public figures, as well as the dominant jurisprudential framework, make it difficult to conceive of Shari'a, whatever that means at this stage, operating in a Western environment. Lucy Carroll (1997, 105) expresses, from a scholarly point of view, the traditional positivist position with respect to Shari'a thus:

---

7 Chiba (1998) points out that legal pluralism can involve conflictual as well as harmonious situations. I have used this idea of 'legal pluralism in conflict' in my own work (Shah, 2005).

> It is important to realize that in the modern world Islamic law, *as law*, does not exist as some disembodied entity floating in the stratosphere, overreaching national boundaries and superseding national law. In the modern world, Islamic law exists only within the context of a nation-state; and within the boundaries of any particular state it is only enforced and enforceable to the extent that, and subject to the reforms and modifications that, the nation-state decrees.

Carroll here highlights the necessity of state sanction as a key issue for the existence of Islamic law as 'law'. However, state sanction almost appears to be a secondary issue if we take a Shari'a-centred mode of analysis. Thus, approaching the question of the operation of Shari'a from a position that deconstructs the received nationalist and positivist vision of law, and takes the agency of Muslims seriously, can help to explain how we can talk about Shari'a in a Western country, *whether or not* there is official recognition by the state authorities.

The conference at which this chapter was first presented was prefigured by the publication of the English version of the book *Between God and the Sultan* by Scandinavian author Knut Vikør. The publication of this text, the first potted history of Islamic law in English since the influential text by Coulson (1964), therefore provides an opportunity to test Vikør's ideas. Despite the fairly large scale presence of Muslims in Europe, Vikør's (2005) book does not specifically discuss their legal position. This gap in his work may therefore be regarded as a missed opportunity to address the jurisprudentially fraught and contested status of Shari'a in Western countries. Nevertheless, it is possible to find glimpses in Vikør's work that provide clues as to how Shari'a can exist despite the legal limitations stipulated by state boundaries in modernity. He says (at pp. 186–7):

> If we focus on the state rather than trying to find the 'civil society' outside, we may locate which social arenas the ruler controls; that is what changes when one sultan replaces another or a town is conquered by a neighbouring sultan. From this we can see that the domain of the state appears to be fairly limited in classical Muslim society. Political changes have fairly little effect on trade or economy, nor do they greatly affect the community of the learned, the *'ulamā'*. Both tend to continue their activities within their own networks where towns, trade routes and centres of learning are crucial, but the identity of the ruler or the borders between the states matter relatively little.

Thus, the Shari'a, being in the hands of the scholars, also remains unaffected by such political changes, and can reasonably be said to belong to a 'civil society' of scholars, within the limits of the four schools, but all crossing state boundaries.

This quote is packed full of important observations. Vikør is here trying to summarize a 'descriptive norm' of the Shari'a's operation sometime between 1000 and 1500 AD, so this norm is basically premised on assumptions that held during the pre-modern period. His limitation to the four Sunni schools, can of course be challenged since the Shari'a can be said to exist outside the bounds of those four schools – for Shias and Sufis too (Ramadan, 2002, 211–12). He underlines the fact that the Shari'a is essentially the domain of scholars who are not necessarily dependent on any state for their existence and activities. They can function despite changes in political leadership. So here we have a body of principles and/or rules that do not depend on their legitimation as 'law' from a political source. Applying Vikør's central observation about the autonomy of the Shari'a from political leadership in pre-modern times allows us to appreciate that, to the extent that it continues to depend on scholarly input, Shari'a can well enjoy a trans-state existence, despite the claims of modern states to have delimited its scope.

Of course in many states where Muslims are predominant (and in many where they are not) Shari'a continues to be applicable officially by state sanction, even though its provenance may lie outside the state. As Vikør (2005, 187) observes when speaking of the *qadi's* dual function: 'the Shari'a is thus an apparatus of the state, but based on a law that is outside the state's domain. This leaves the *qāḍī* in a divided situation, partly the state's man, partly, as a scholar, a member of the civil society network.' This dual function is illustrative of a specific form of Muslim legal pluralism, the interaction and integration of state agency and religio-scholastic agency. Elsewhere in his book, Vikør (2005, 168–70) gives fascinating illustrations of Muslim legal pluralism, by drawing attention to the practice by different pre-modern Muslim states where *qadi* courts were established according to different *madhhabs*. Further, he points out that the availability of a plurality of such dispute-processing bodies could lead to some 'forum shopping' among litigants who wished to secure the most favourable outcome for themselves (p. 151). As we will go on to illustrate for the British case, it is not simply through the agency of *qadis* that the Shari'a, or aspects of it, may be sanctioned by the state and much can depend on the specific character of the state's legal arrangements. However, from a legal pluralist perspective, to the extent that states do not sanction the Shari'a, it could still operate as an 'unofficial' law (Chiba, 1986), but as 'law' nonetheless.

← Muslim legal pluralism →

God's law -- Sultan's law

Figure 9.1 Vikør's dual model

One other critical issue in Vikør's book that needs further discussion is his relative silence on the question of the legal agency of society. Without using the term himself he acknowledges through his book's title that Muslim legal pluralism is basically founded on the interaction of religio-scholastic and state agency. Even though he uses the term 'civil society' (see quote above) he restricts that term to the scholar-jurists of Islam. Thus, for Vikør, Muslim legality lies somewhere between the state's or sultan's rules and the scholar-jurists' endeavours to find God's law. This can be illustrated by the following line anywhere along which the Shari'a can be found (see Figure 9.1).

In Vikør's reading, therefore, legal agency is basically an attribute of state officialdom and the scholar-jurists, perhaps best exemplified by the dual role of the *qadi*. While Vikør compares Islamic law with common and civil law systems, the lack of a globally oriented focus must lead the reader to question his conclusion about where Islamic law can be located within a comparative framework. We can contrast that with Menski's (2006) tripartite model of legal pluralism. Unlike Vikør, he incorporates the writing of other legal pluralists within his analysis to create a globally focused model of the pluralistic structure of law (see Figure 9.2).

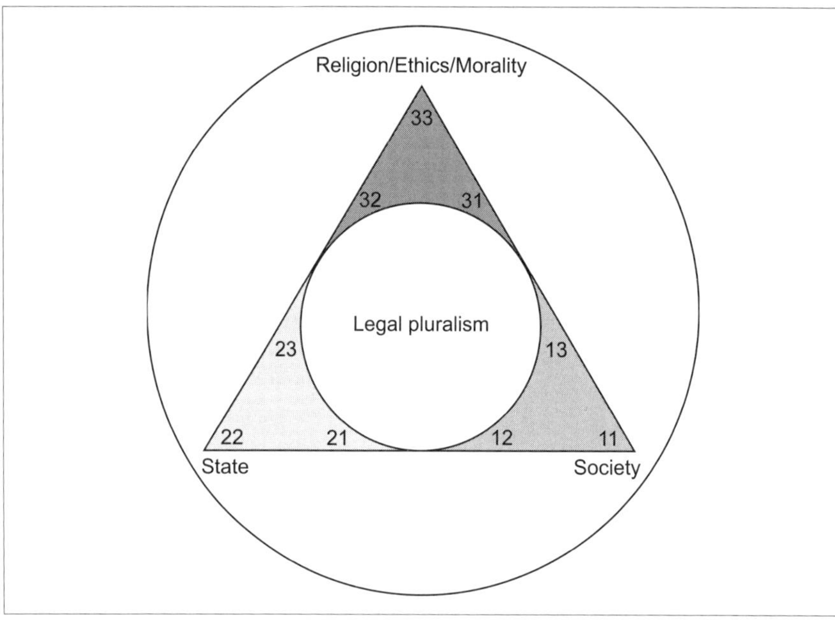

Figure 9.2 Menski's tripartite model

An advantage of this model is that it arises out of a much more rigorous comparison among different, Western and non-Western, legal traditions than Vikør is able to offer. Notably, Menski's triangular or tripartite framework of legal pluralism specifically accounts for the legal agency of the social sphere. By contrast, in Vikør's book, the agency of society at large gets very little mention. He does acknowledge the relevance of the term *urf* in the glossary, but discusses the concept minimally in the book (esp. pp. 166–7) particularly in connection with the Maliki tradition. He makes no mention of the related concept of *adat* which is not even found in the glossary, even though it is a central concept for Muslims in some South-East Asian countries (Wazir Jahan, 1992; Bowen, 2003). South Asians, meanwhile, would also be more used to using concepts like the South Asian notion of custom – *riwaj* – which is argued by Ballard (2006, 51) to be a key source of law.

Unofficial Muslim Legal Pluralism

While *riwaj* or other equivalent South Asian concepts don't get a mention by Vikør, his exposition can also be seen as basically focused on West Asia (the Middle East) and North Africa. His restricted acknowledgement of terms related to customary laws can also be accounted for by the fact that, within Islamic jurisprudence, such concepts have at best a secondary relevance, possibly because they support the argument that, ultimately, Muslim law is a very localized phenomenon. This, of course, does not suit the universalistic claims of Muslim jurists for 'their' law as having universal applicability, in much the same way as Western natural lawyers and proponents of modern human rights principles have, sometimes tenaciously, argued for the universality of their principles. For human rights this 'arrogance of universalism' needs qualification by attention to 'particularism' as Dembour (2006, 180) has recently argued. Similarly, the argument here is not that Islamic claims to universalism and global relevance are not valid, but rather that Islam and Shari'a must also find their locally adjusted solutions in light of all the founding elements of law.[8] Muslims too must adapt the global to the local, resulting in 'glocal' hybrid laws termed by Menski (Pearl and Menski, 1998, 74–7, Menski, 2001) as '*angrezi Shari'at*', Urdu for 'British Muslim law'.

Dealing first with the dynamic interaction between customs and the Shari'a as a juridico-scholastic discourse, we need to consider the ways in which British Muslims are reconstructing their legal universe, as part of *angrezi Shari'at*, by reordering the relationship between customs and Islamic rules. For Roger Ballard it is custom which turns out to be the pre-eminent source of legal ordering among South Asians. In South Asia, dispute resolution was invariably premised on local and parochial understandings of *riwaj*, rather than upon religious or state law, he continues (Ballard, 2006, 50–1):

---

8 Positions which emphasize Muslim dynamism and hybridity beyond the binary state–jurist-centred discourse are also reflected in work by Werbner (2002), Malik (2004) and, with specific reference to legal hybridity, Nielsen (2004, 108–10). Malik, like Bistolfi and Zabbal (1995), speaks of 'Islams' in Europe to underline the plurality among European Muslims. Nielsen (2004, 120) speaks of the need to 'reassemble' various components of Islam. For the argument that such adaptations depend on whether the respective rules and/or principles concern matters of *ibadat* or *muamalat*, see Ramadan (2002) and Rohe (2006).

> Hence it is in terms of the ideas and expectations arising from this locally- and community-specific sphere of *riwaj*, rather than those set out in the much more religiously and politically distant arenas of *shari'a* and *qanun*, to which South Asian settlers in Britain have turned for inspiration as they have set about establishing themselves overseas. Likewise it is to these selfsame principles (which are regularly, but mistakenly assumed to be congruent with those of the *shari'a*) to which the elders routinely turn in the efforts to achieve dispute resolution in the UK – just as they did back home in South Asia … it seems to me to be quite clear that the expectations and conventions around which South Asian settlers have organised their lives in the UK owe far more to parochial conventions of unofficial law of the communities to which they belong – or in other words to *riwaj* – than they do either to *qanun* or to *shari'a*.

Thus for Ballard, it is the sphere of custom – which he coins as *pardeshi riwaj* (overseas custom) – which remains the most dynamic and vital source of legal re-ordering in the diasporic sphere (Ballard, 2006, 51). Having said this, it is also beyond question that in the process of transplantation, customary norms are themselves undergoing reform, reformulation or, as Nielsen (2004, 120) suggests, a sort of 'reassembly'. But Ballard (2006, 52) also refers to the phenomenon of what might be termed 'Islamization' of the customary sphere. Linking it to similar processes of 'Sanskritization'[9] among Hindus, he says: 'it should come as no surprise that at least some of the principles of Shari'a orthodoxy are being actively incorporated into current understandings of *pardeshi riwaj*'.

But in which direction is this process of renegotiation pointing? At present it is difficult to provide any firm conclusions about this complex process. Certainly it involves a partial questioning of the assumptions of social order inherited from the first generation of migrants, as well as those underpinning the European social order. Islamic norms tend to be compared to such assumptions and are often seen as trumping them, notably in such contested areas as arranged/forced marriages and intra-kin or intra-caste marriages, against which the Islamic norms of free choice of marriage partner are emphasized. Much re-evaluation is directed to assumed norms of gender difference, with younger (mainly female) Muslims arguing, by reference to progressive Islamic norms, that the Prophet himself was a reformer in the direction of gender equity, a process which has since been hijacked by patriarchal forces, thereby requiring revitalization in contemporary circumstances. Thus 'culture', which is seen as the repository of 'backward' ancestral custom, is compared to the rules of 'religion' to come up with new ways of re-evaluating what is proper under God's law.

---

9 Ballard here draws upon Srinivas, who defined Sanskritization as a process 'by which a "low" Hindu caste, or tribe or other group, changes its customs, ritual, ideology, and way of life in the direction of a high, and frequently, "twice-born" caste. Generally such changes are followed by a claim to a higher position in the caste hierarchy than that traditionally conceded to the claimant caste by the local community …' (Srinivas, 1966, 6).

The predominantly South Asian cultural influences that prevailed in the earlier post-war years of labour immigration and family reunification are now also being complemented by a greater proportion of people immigrating from West Asian and African countries, providing Muslims with new opportunities to compare the different cultural and Islamic influences that have determined their own understandings of Islam. Within this dynamic it appears that Arab voices have some influence and we might even be looking at a gradual process of 'Arabization' of previously accepted Islamic positions. All this obviously requires much further study but it is quite clear that the socio-legal field remains especially dynamic in the process of creating new forms of *angrezi Shari'at*.

The process of adjustment in diaspora also involves the absorption, as well as an evaluation and critique, of the dominant Anglo-conformist culture. Returning to the issue of 'happiness', which may simply equate to 'enjoyment', Muslims are regarded as out to destroy Europeans' sexual liberty and freedom of consumption. According to van der Veer (2006) it is this basic difference in weight given to a particular value that appears to be at the core of negative perceptions of Muslims in the Netherlands. From Muslim perspectives, such perceptions of 'fun' can often seem as endorsement of hedonism and can, of course, lead to serious interpersonal and internal conflicts among Muslims navigating between different parts of the social sphere. Indeed, the image of the 'fun-less' Muslim, out to deny everybody else their liberties, may be at the core of attacks against many Muslims today in Britain too. In this sense, Muslims have a major image problem in Europe.[10] Such pressures may ironically be provoking 'Protestantized' interpretations of Islam among Muslims, in turn leading to the further stereotyping of Muslims as austere Puritans. The difficulties of balancing parental cultures and the pressures of Anglo-conformism may also have some explanatory value for the high prison population among Pakistanis and Bangladeshi origin males (Spalek, 2002). It remains to be seen whether Islamic values can positively impact upon this problem.

The Question of State Sanction and Recognition

As Vikør (2005, 2) picks up, and as borne out by the *Daily Express*'s coverage mentioned above, the 'introduction of the Shari'a' tends to evoke in newspapers the spectre of Islamic criminal law, with its gruesome punishments. However, this is hardly what most proponents of official recognition of Islamic law in Britain tend to argue for. Rather the demands voiced have been restricted to asking for the recognition of Islamic family law rules. In 1975 the Union of Muslim Organisations of the UK and Eire (UMO) presented a proposal for the recognition of a separate system of Islamic family law to be automatically applicable to British Muslims.

10 Modood and Ahmad (2007, 202) report the experience of one of their Muslim interviewees who recalled how she was made to feel like a leper at a conference on sex education because she expressed a 'pro-chastity and pro-family' position.

Menski (2001, 141) observes this to have been a response to the tightening of immigration restrictions and the drawing back of flexibility shown by the judiciary in accommodating some aspects of Muslim law, while Nielsen (2004, 114) cites as a contributory factor the uncertainty about which rules were applicable to migrants under English private international law. Private international law or 'conflicts of law' rules of course remain the chief means by which the official law accepts the application of legal rules recognized by a foreign state although, as time goes by and connections with countries of origin reduce, these laws may become less relevant. However, the perpetuation among Muslim diasporic communities of transnational connections and their tendency to often choose (though sometimes unconsciously) the rules of overseas laws in preference to British laws, as manifested by the performance of key legal acts abroad, complicates the picture tremendously.[11]

Poulter (1990, 1998, 201–21) summarized the 'possible reasons' why the UMO's proposal was refused. While arguing that English law rules were relatively flexible in many respects, he also cited the following:

1. the proposals ran counter to the English tradition of having a uniform family law system (albeit with some exceptional provisions for Quakers and Jews);
2. the problem of how to decide which schools of law would be applicable, in addition to the Sunni–Shia differences, together with the difficult situation of Ahmadis;[12]
3. the problem of which courts would enforce the provisions and whether they would be staffed by Muslims only and, if so, from which of the communities of Muslims they would be drawn; and
4. the problem of compliance with human rights treaties to which the UK was a party, in particular the provisions which guaranteed the equality of, and non-discrimination between, men and women – Muslim family law patently applied to men and women differently.

Thus, besides the uncertainty of who would apply and to whom Islamic rules would be applied, the official recognition of Shari'a in family relations seems to compromise the alleged uniformist vision of British law, and its attachment to gender non-discrimination. It is almost impossible to argue today in Europe for the institutionalization of a family law system which would have overtly different rules applicable to men and women.[13] Although the 1975 demand was rejected,

11 On how this affects the official recognition of polygamy see Shah (2003).

12 Ahmadis from Pakistan and Bangladesh, where they have been officially declared as non-Muslims, continue to feature in asylum cases in British courts, while (Kurdish) Alevis from Turkey, a group following a heterodox tradition, tended to feature prominently as asylum seekers in the late 1980s and early 1990s.

13 Having said that, in Greece a parallel system of *Shari'a* in some areas of family law is applied among the 100,000 strong Muslim minority in Thrace, who are effectively

similar proposals continued to be presented to government ministers in the 1980s and 1990s. Such demands have recently appeared in a number of surveys reported in newspapers,[14] as well as being strongly suggested in a report of the NGO, the Islamic Human Rights Commission (2006).

These developments show that some Muslim organizations and individuals in Britain continue to persist in the demand for, or at least voice views as to the desirability of, the official recognition of some aspects of Shari'a. Despite some minimal concessions locally and at a national level, for instance, as to the use of *halal* food and the building of mosques[15] Muslims have been resentful of the fact that the Race Relations Act of 1976 was interpreted not to cover them on the grounds that it did not cover religious groups. It did not help that Jews and Sikhs managed to get recognition under the same legislation, thereby leaving the strong impression that Muslims were the least favourite subjects of British laws. Some recent provision in anti-discrimination law, notably Directive 2000/78/EC,[16] extends the right to take civil legal action to those discriminated on grounds of religion in employment, while the UK's own Equality Act 2006 extends more general legal protection to those discriminated against on the basis of their religion. However, these and other recent changes come in a climate where Muslims feel under constant attack and extremely vulnerable as the prime targets of law enforcement, not least under post 9/11 anti-terrorism measures.[17] Whether these feelings are simply a consequence of perceptions or grounded in actual experience,

---

regarded as a *millet* (Tsitselkis, 2004).

14 *The Guardian*, 30 November 2004, at <http://www.guardian.co.uk/islam/>, and *The Daily Telegraph*, 19 February 2006, at <http://www.telegraph.co.uk>, both accessed 7 April 2006.

15 While Khaliq (2004, 236–40) records difficulties for Muslims as well as Hindus and Sikhs in obtaining approval for religious buildings, Gale (2007) shows that, in Birmingham, applications for mosques receive a lower rate of approval from the local planning authorities than applications by other groups for approval of religious building plans. Yet, mosques of all types are now an integral part of the country's religious landscape as any traveller to urban Britain can verify.

16 This Directive is implemented in the UK by the Employment Equality (Religion or Belief) Regulations 2003, no. 1660.

17 While it might once have been expected that South Asian Muslims would compare with their Hindu and Sikh counterparts, Hindus and Sikhs have increasingly sought a distance from the 'Asian' label so as to distinguish themselves from Muslims. Recent research (Modood and Ahmad, 2007, 203) also uncovers the feeling among some Muslims that the 'Asian' label has served as a vehicle to promote the interests of 'Hindus' or 'Indians' in Britain at the expense of Muslims. Instead, Muslims increasingly find sympathy from black people who are longstanding targets of criminalization. Many black people are of course themselves Muslims, while others have converted to Islam. Irish people also express sympathy on grounds of their own experiences of being targets of earlier British anti-terror policies.

it appears that many are reaching the conclusion that life as a Muslim in Britain is getting worse rather than better.[18]

The quite politicized matter of state recognition of Muslims in general and the more specific demands centred on Islamic family law have skewed the debate on the role of official law in a particular direction. On the other hand, Lawrence Rosen (1995, 89), who argues for the minimal possible state intrusion into the private and religious affairs of minorities in European states, favours a fall-back position which would allow courts to maintain a certain distance from Islamic law, if not altogether preventing them from referring to it. He writes:

> European courts should not be in the position of interpreting Islamic law. There will indeed be instances in which it is relevant for a court to know what, in general, is the acceptable practice among particular Muslims, but when courts try to play at being mullahs, rather than implementing political concepts of valid state intrusion that have an equal impact on all religious groups, they risk both their legitimacy in the eyes of the minorities and their role as defenders of unwarranted state power.

Rather, Rosen foresees (1995, 90) the development by the Muslims of Europe themselves of legal standards and solutions to their problems *in Europe*, including alternative forms of dispute resolution. It appears that it is this mode of adaptation which British Muslims have engaged in as they have set about creating *angrezi Shari'at*. As Menski (2001, 152) explains:

> Thus, rather than abandoning certain facets of their Shari'a, South Asian Muslims in Britain have turned tables and have built the requirements of English law into their own traditional legal structures. They follow their own, new form of Muslim law, not English law. The reconstruction of *angrezi Shari'at* is strong evidence of the continued validity of South Asian legal traditions in a new environment.

Quite apart from the larger question of systemic recognition of Shari'a rules in English law, multi-layered problems of intercultural communication persist. Noting the ignorance of Muslim issues among practising lawyers and their being misled, inadvertently or purposefully, about the extent of the problems, Menski (2001, 154) observes that disputes often reach the courts in a twisted form and judges find it difficult to ascertain the full facts and to reach an adequate verdict. Communal self-help mechanisms may partly be seen as a means of overcoming such official blockages, but partly as a resuscitation of the age-old capacity for self-regulation which Rosen and Menski refer to.

---

18 For a professional and personal account of the lives of Somalis in Britain written by a former BBC and current *Al Jazeera* correspondent see Omaar (2006).

Thus, besides living in the general consciousness of being bound by God's universal law and applying in their lives the rules of Islam and of British/European laws, Muslims are also building up informal dispute settlement processes, about which we are now finding out more. While many disputes, as Ballard (above) notes, would be dealt with at family level or by community leaders, Muslims have also been establishing so-called Shari'a councils all over Britain (Pearl and Menski, 1998, 77–80; Menski, 2001, 155–8). One prominent case is that of the Muslim Law (Sharia) Council (UK) at Ealing. Led by the late Dr Zaki Badawi, it initially became involved in legal service provision out of the concern that Muslim women were frequently being abandoned without what they felt was an Islamically acceptable divorce, thus finding themselves in 'limping marriages' and unable to move on with their lives (Badawi, 1995, Shah-Kazemi, 2001). Shari'a councils are now extending their remit to include other activities. The Ealing-based Sharia Council, for example, now also undertakes counselling at earlier stages of conflict, as well as dispute resolution (Keshavjee, 2007). These cases illustrate the fact that Muslims, as with Jews before them, have been building what H.L.A. Hart, the post-war champion of the positivist school of jurisprudence, would recognize as secondary rule systems in Britain to organize their own legal affairs to some degree.

The interaction between such communal mechanisms and the official courts is bound to be an increasingly fascinating area of study. A search of the legal databases soon reveals the number of cases that come up either for enforcement of the Beth Din's arbitral awards before the courts or as a challenge to such awards. The Beth Din's arbitration agreements stipulate that any award is made according to Jewish law and such other law as is acceptable to Jewish law. The cases range from family disputes to commercial ones. For example, the case of *Kohn* v *Wagschal and others* ([2006] EWHC 3356 (Comm), [2006] All ER (D) 350 (Dec)), heard in late 2006 by the Queen's Bench Division's Commercial Court, involved a challenge by three sisters who contested the award by the Beth Din to their brother of shareholdings which the father had, during his lifetime, transferred into the names of the sisters as a way of avoiding tax. The Beth Din had found that his real intention had not been to make a gift of the shares to his daughters. Thus deprived of their anticipated windfall, the sisters were not willing to accept the award. Their brother obtained an order from the High Court under the Arbitration Act 1996 which the sisters challenged. In the event the sisters lost the case, the Queen's Bench Division finding no illegality in the manner in which the award had been made. We thus find a communally located system in interaction with the official court system, a collaboration which appears to have functioned for a long period of time in Britain, and which hardly causes much murmur beyond the group of community insiders.

Some Muslim groups are now actively studying this model to see whether they can also use the same framework for arbitration among Muslims. The similar prospect of Muslim arbitrations being enforceable by the official courts recently resulted in an acrid debate in Canada, leading the authorities to suspend the recognition of religion-based dispute resolution under the arbitration legislation in Ontario (Bakht, 2006), which also adversely affected the position of the previously active Catholic and Jewish arbitration bodies. In reality of course such bodies can simply operate outside the state's ambit unless they conform to certain statutory demands (Bakht, 2006, 79–81). This is not only a British or Canadian phenomenon and is also taking shape in India, a country with a huge Muslim minority population. There the *ulama* are openly asking for recognition of their own legitimacy to operate courts even though the official Indian courts regularly rule on matters of Shari'a. It seems, however, that Muslim arbitration in the UK – or should we rather speak about unofficial British *qadi* courts? – would be covered by the Arbitration Act 1996 as are the Beth Din awards at present. Thompson (2005), a Muslim barrister, has already written to the effect that this is an indirect way of obtaining recognition of the Shari'a under English law. The question now is probably not whether, but when, the official British courts would eventually have to rule on matters of *angrezi Shari'at* in their efforts to tease apart the issues raised by arbitral agreements based on Muslim law principles.

We will find degrees of legal self-organization in many different minority communities in Britain besides Muslims and Jews. Muslims are to some extent singled out and picked on because of the fear of a Muslim fifth column in Britain today but also, it has to be said frankly, because some Muslim spokespersons have hardly been adept at presenting a case for their own communities in acceptable tones. The confrontational, all-or-nothing and sometimes quite anti-pluralistic positions being adopted by some of these figures without appreciation of the other side's position hardly assists in easy communication or a smooth process of interaction between the official and unofficial spheres. Having said that, there is increasing awareness of the ground shifting beneath the veneer of a uniformist, state-driven legal order. Something more complex is therefore going on which is incrementally also being taken on board by some perceptive academic commentators. Cownie et al. (2003, 24) recently noted in their textbook, *English Legal System in Context*:

> There is no single unique English legal system that structures British society. The rules, the courts, the lawyers which owe their authority to the state are a legal system in England and Wales. They are, as we will see, a very important legal system that is hugely influential in most people's lives. However, this is not the only legal system. Other forms of dispute resolution also have an impact on people's lives. What previous authors have described as being 'the English legal system' is merely one part of the English legal universe.

These writers indicate subtly that their antennae have picked up on the fact that the English legal universe can no longer be described in a monistic fashion. Specifically mentioning the existence of bodies like the Beth Din and Sharia Council (Cownie et al., 2003, 25), they indicate that notice needs to be taken of something more plural in structure and composition of the legal system. This sort of acknowledgement also contrasts with the statement by Lucy Carroll (quoted above) who would condition the application of Shari'a upon state-sanction.

Divorcing Realities

Are the above-mentioned indications of legal plurality only taken notice of in the domain of some (although not many) textbook writers and commentators? In fact things have moved further ahead that anyone wishes to admit too publicly. Let us take an illustration presented by a tiny Act of Parliament passed not so long ago. The Divorce (Religious Marriages) Act 2002, section 1(1) inserted a new section 10A into the Matrimonial Causes Act (MCA) 1973, which came into force on 24 February 2003. It reads as follows:

> 10A Proceedings after decree nisi: religious marriage
>
> (1) This section applies if a decree of divorce has been granted but not made absolute and the parties to the marriage concerned –
>
> (a) were married in accordance with –
>
> (i) the usages of the Jews, or
>
> (ii) any other prescribed religious usages; and
>
> (b) must co-operate if the marriage is to be dissolved in accordance with those
>
> usages.
>
> (2) On the application of either party, the court may order that a decree of divorce is not to be made absolute until a declaration made by both parties that they have taken such steps as are required to dissolve the marriage in accordance with those usages is produced to the court.
>
> ....

Before discussing the details of this legislation, it should be mentioned that, for a divorce to be obtained in the UK, going through official court procedures is mandatory. This applies to all communities, unlike the marriage laws where some concessions regarding solemnization methods are made to Anglicans, Jews and Quakers. Even here, the model of 'asymmetrical pluralism' (Singh and Tatla, 2006, 144) is under constant pressure to adjust (Shah, 2007).

Actually, the 2002 legislation is not the first of its type. The Family Law Act 1996, section 9(3), while not saying so explicitly, had already attempted to address the position of Jewish women who were unable to secure a *get* from their husbands by empowering the court to refuse to finalize the divorce under civil law (Pearl and Menski, 1998, 104–106). The discussions in the lead-up to the 2002 Act also primarily address the question of limping marriages within the Jewish community and the measure was presented largely as one of concern to orthodox Jews. Indeed, it does not appear to be the case that there was widespread consultation with Muslims or any other groups. However, Andrew Dismore MP, who led the discussion on the measure in its stage as a Bill through Standing Committee,[19] had this to say:

> There have been no approaches from the Muslim community about the matter, although there is a similar, but not identical, difficulty. The Bill provides a mechanism to overcome such a problem should there be an approach from the Muslim community.

Clearly enough, a court would have the power, upon application by a party to the divorce, to withhold the final official divorce if a divorce according to religious 'usages' among Muslims is not given. It was recognized in the Standing Committee's discussion that while this measure would not solve the problem of limping marriages among Jews, it would go some way towards addressing the difficult situation of wives not divorced according to Jewish law. The same might be said of Muslims, although a recalcitrant man may escape the notice of the court altogether, for instance, where a wife simply signs the official divorce papers when she is told to do so.[20] Where a Muslim man does not pronounce a *talaq* will we see wives resorting to Shari'a councils and then submitting their divorce pronouncements before the official family courts, and would these be acceptable under the mentioned 'prescribed religious usages'? Would such a divorce be Islamically legitimate as a *faskh* (Pearl and Menski, 1998, 285–6; Vikør, 2005, 313), as adapted to British requirements? It appears that a family court could demand from the parties a certificate from a 'relevant religious authority' that all steps needed to dissolve a marriage in accordance with the relevant religious usages have been taken.[21] We need further discussion and analysis of the implications of

19 Standing Committee D, Wednesday 7 November 2001, at <http://www.parliament.the-stationery-office.co.uk/pa/cm200102/cmstand/d/st011107/am/11107s02.htm>, last accessed 26 March 2006.

20 In *Akhtar v Rafiq* [2006] 1 FLR 27 the court accepted a plea by a woman who argued that a divorce granted by a court several years previously be declared void on the basis that she had never received service of the documents related to the divorce petition in the English court. One suspects that the husband was trying to use the English legal procedure without involving the wife, but the district court had, at the time, no real means of checking on the credentials of the purported acknowledgement of the service of documents.

21 This is evident from the wording of paragraph 2.45B of the Family Proceedings Rules (as amended).

the aforementioned amendment to the MCA and wait with interest to see how it will work out in practice.

Standing back a little, we can see that the new section 10A of the MCA is a response not only to the woes of Jewish women that they are in trapped marriages which have effectively broken down, since the Act patently attempts to cover usages other than those followed by Jews. I am tempted at this stage to put forward the argument that this 'sneaky' coverage of Muslims shows us some patterns of how a multicultural law is developing in Britain. First, we are not allowed to discuss Muslim issues too loudly especially if they may result in accusations that we are creating a pattern of differential official legal coverage according to the needs of various communities. Mention of Muslim law or Shari'a within legislation seems to be outside the bounds of legitimate discussion, a sort of blasphemy against the secular legal consensus or, more specifically, anti-Islamic public orthodoxy.[22] So, for the moment, we must talk about Muslims as if they are not really there – as those following 'other prescribed religious usages'. We are none the wiser therefore of how Islamic law on divorce works and still further away from discussing openly how it *should* work in contemporary Britain. At the same time, Parliament and the courts are also showing their awareness of the ground shifting underneath them if they don't take some kind of action. So a certain type of legal pluralism is at work here officially, but it is still rather muted and could be better described, as in the case of marriage solemnization, as 'asymmetrical pluralism' in a legal context.

On the other hand, the 2002 Act does nothing for wives who while travelling in, say, Pakistan are given a *talaq*. While frowned upon by the classical Muslim law, especially if it is in its 'quickie' form, such a divorce is perfectly valid according to Shari'a, and is also recognized officially in Pakistan's legal system (Pearl and Menski, 1998, 334–73). Here we see British laws *creating* another kind of limping marriage situation – where the wife is divorced under the religious law, but where such a divorce is not recognised by the official British law (Pearl and Menski, 1998, 97–104). In these kinds of cases we see another kind of legal snobbery in that actions that are not somehow connected to a state authority are simply turned down. Again little people, it is alleged, have no legal agency to control their affairs. In one case that I was consulted on recently, the Home Office claimed that the wife had effectively lied to them upon re-entry to Britain. Why had she not informed the authorities that her husband had *talaq*ed her on what was seemingly a family holiday in Pakistan? So here we have official double-speak – had the wife been applying on the basis of a remarriage she would have been told that she had not properly been divorced in a way recognized under English law, but here when she was claiming indefinite leave to remain, she is told that she is guilty of not coming clean and telling the authorities that she *is* divorced.

22 But for an exception one can refer to the Welfare of Animals (Slaughter or Killing) Regulations 1995, Schedule 12, para. 2, which specifically clarifies the meaning of 'slaughter by a religious method' as including 'the Muslim method for the food of Muslims by a Muslim who holds a licence'.

This style of what I am tempted to describe as 'official lawlessness' is harder to justify in light of other developments. In the case of *H* v *H (Queen's Proctor intervening)(validity of Japanese divorce)* ([2006] EWHC 2989 (Fam) [2007] All ER (D) 71 (Jan)) we find that a Japanese consensual divorce, known as *kyogi rikon*, is now accepted in Britain as legally valid even though state involvement in this procedure is minimal, with a simple notification to an administrative authority in Japan being enough to finalize the divorce officially. There appears to be no real court intervention here, and yet such divorces, when pronounced abroad, are now recognized by English law, again leaving the impression that, by comparison, it is Muslims who get a hard deal in British courts. Meanwhile, arguments that allege the protection of Muslim women to be a primary aim of non-recognition of Muslim socio-legal realities would appear to ring rather hollow.

New Horizons

One final case should suffice to again illustrate how Muslim law is gradually infiltrating the official legal order, and may also suggest where future efforts by Muslims and the state agencies as to official recognition may concentrate. After many years of the UK having acceded to the European Convention of Human Rights (ECHR) as a matter of international law, with effect from October 2000 it was incorporated into British law, and claims related to religious freedom under its Article 9 now frequently come up in the British courts. In *R (on the application of Begum (Shabina)* v *Denbigh High School Governors* ([2005] 2 All ER 396), the House of Lords had to rule on whether the exclusion of a schoolgirl Shabina Begum contravened Article 9 of the ECHR. The appellant school was asking for a reversal of the Court of Appeal's unanimous decision holding its exclusion of Shabina unlawful on the basis that its school uniform policy, while conceding to Muslim dress sense to the extent of allowing the wearing of *shalwar kameez* or *hijab*, did not allow her to wear the fuller covering of a *jilbab*, and that this restriction had not been properly justified as being necessary in a democratic society. While unanimously holding that the appeal should succeed, the Lords differed on the precise points of ECHR law, three holding that there had been no interference with the freedom to manifest one's religion while two found that the decision of the school, while constituting an interference, was justified. For our purposes, however, it is interesting that both the Court of Appeal and the House of Lords felt it necessary to decide whether wearing of a *jilbab* was required by Islamic law. Cumulatively, the courts consulted sources of Islamic tradition, heard several expert opinions and took into account some academic authority on the issue before the Lords finally decided that such a form of dress was not required and that the school had made adequate concessions to the Muslim sensibilities.

While hardly a unique development if one takes into consideration similar cases across different European countries and at the European Court of Human Rights (McGoldrick, 2006), cases like Shabina's do illustrate the fact that British judges are increasingly likely to have to decide themselves whether a particular issue complies with or is required by Islamic law. In so doing, one can almost see them, from an Islamic viewpoint, as acting like *qadi*s, and consulting experts who can be seen as performing the role of *mufti*s, about the history of both of which we have much to learn from Vikør (2005, 140–221).[23] In this sense, we may well be seeing a transition in the extent to which the social and religious spheres are pushing the official, state sphere to include consideration of Muslim-specific concerns within the state's scope of legality. More than that, we may now be past the point where the kinds of objections summarized by Poulter (above) are still valuable, or they will at least have to placed in juxtaposition to the continuing search for legal recognition among British Muslims. We might even be moving, under the umbrella of principles such as the 'freedom, either alone or in community with others and in public or private, to manifest his religion or belief, in worship, teaching, practice and observance', to a position where we are considering, not whether Islamic law is relevant, but whether it has been taken into account in a correct manner. Thus, Modood (2005) may well be proved right to the extent that he argues that Muslims' struggle for religious recognition may well be their lasting legacy to British multiculturalism.

However, this is far from being the end of the story, but simply new horizons opening up for us to consider in the future. Increasing official recognition and sanction by the state of Muslim law and practice will not necessarily be able to deal with all the complex disputes and legal problems that Muslims find themselves in. Even where matters are confined to problems within Muslim communities, the claim that 'Islamic' principles can fully resolve them involves what Chetan Bhatt (1997) has termed 'epistemic overreach'. This is underscored by the fact that, besides state and religious influence, openness will have to be retained to the socio-legal sphere. In other words, attention will need to be given to all parts of Menski's triangular structure of law. Furthermore, it is likely that, no matter what the level of state recognition and sanction offered to Shari'a rules principles and rules, Muslim practice will generally continue to be premised on self-regulation as opposed to state regulation. Therefore, while the state may have an important role in fashioning *angrezi Shari'at*, it will not be able to act as a replacement for the socio-religious legal order which continues to be a primary normative agent in Muslim life.

23 In *Shamil Bank of Bahrain EC* v *Beximco Pharmaceuticals Ltd* (No.1) [2004] 1 WLR 1784 the choice of court in the contract was an English court, but the choice of law clause referred to *Shari'a*. Despite expert evidence on both sides explaining the Islamic rules on banking and the taking of interest, the English Court of Appeal went ahead to decide the matter solely on the basis of English law. Among the reasons given were that the Islamic rules were really only religious principles and far too imprecise to be applied, while the international rules on the law applicable to contracts envisaged only the rules of a particular state legal system. Vikør (2005, 1–2) actually anticipates this sort of consequence when he explains that, on one view, the *Shari'a* is not really a precise body of rules.

Chapter 10
Shari'a and Secularism in France

Manni Crone

Questions related to Shari'a have generated heated debate throughout Europe in recent years. This interest is largely triggered by a vague notion of Shari'a constituting a challenge or even a threat to European 'core values'. For example, the webpage <www.sharia.dk> presents Shari'a as 'a barbaric system of law' characterized by brutal forms of punishment such as flogging, stoning, beheading and the severing of hands and feet. Moreover, it is argued that since Shari'a is 'set up by God, it is situated beyond human reason. It cannot be discussed. It cannot be subject to voting. It cannot be changed.' Such 'a barbaric system of law' obviously runs counter to values that are perceived as European, such as secularism, democracy, human rights or equality between the sexes. As French imam Tareq Oubrou has suggested, however, the pertinent question is not whether Shari'a is compatible with secularism or not, but *which* Shari'a. What normative form of Shari'a are we talking about (Oubrou, 2000, 2)?

The current unease regarding Shari'a is not, however, exhausted by this notion of 'a barbaric system of law' being sneaked in through the back-door and diluting our political modernity from within. The trouble also stems from the fact that Shari'a challenges our categories of understanding and our norms of liberal agency. Is Shari'a – as the translation 'Islamic law' suggests – a system of law? Or does it constitute a normative system, an Islamic ethos, a 'path', precepts of how to practise one's faith, a system of spirituality, a political programme or some obscure mix of all these elements? Recent debates on the practice of Islamic family law in Europe and the oft-repeated question of Islamic penal law appear to corroborate the interpretation of Shari'a as law. If Shari'a is law, however, it is indeed an unusual one, as it is neither introduced nor backed by any state in the European context.

This confusion concerning Shari'a is confirmed by the dissent in modern and postmodern scholarship. The renowned Orientalist Snouck Hurgronje famously argued that Shari'a was not a law, since it did not live up to the Western standards of the time, i.e. a positive law emanating from the political sphere and backed by state power (Hurgronje, 1916). Max Weber disagreed with Hurgronje by defining Shari'a as a 'sacred law'. He thus accorded it the status of law, but still an inferior one, since – compared to European law – it lacked in rationality. Whereas European law was both 'formally' and 'substantially' *rational*, Shari'a was 'formally' and 'substantially' *irrational* (Weber, 1972). Hurgronje and Weber thus agreed that Shari'a was a deficient mode of law, since it was characterized by a lack. The great

20th-century scholar, Joseph Schacht, broadened our understanding of Shari'a by maintaining that it was not merely a system of law but also of ethics (Schacht, 1964). However, Schacht emphasized the judicial aspect in his empirical work and more or less overlooked the ethical aspects of the Shari'a. More recently, anthropologist Talal Asad has pointed out that Shari'a introduces a distinction between 'law' and 'ethics', provided that we do not understand 'law' and 'ethics' 'in their modern, secular sense' (Asad, 2003, 248).

In this chapter, I shall refrain from providing yet another definition of Shari'a or, as Asad, pose sophisticated genealogies of concepts such as 'law' and 'ethics'. My focus is slightly different, since I want to suggest that Shari'a constitutes a form of government; not only in the sense of a technique to rule others, but also as a self-government technique. Shari'a could thus be considered not as a law in a classical positivist sense, but as a technique of 'conducting conduct' implying the elaboration and the administration of a 'regime of truth' (Foucault, 1994; Rose, 1999). Hence, there is an epistemic dimension to Shari'a-governance, since it implies the construction of a 'truth' capable of guiding practice. In contemporary Europe, however, such Shari'a-governance is unrelated to the state or state sovereignty and is therefore not backed by the use of legitimate violence. In order to be effective, it presupposes authority in the form of 'spontaneous' social recognition. The fact that Shari'a constitutes an alternative system of governance *beside* the authority of the state does not, however, mean that it is in *conflict* with the authority of the state. There is no necessary *clash* between the law of God and the laws of the state as is often presupposed in public discourse.

That which I want to suggest is the absence of a necessary contradiction between Shari'a and secularism and that Shari'a discourses and practices are currently adapting to European forms of secularism. Whether Shari'a is a fixed system of law or a flexible ethics is a topic of intense discussion. Nonetheless, the social practice of Shari'a reveals that the universal norms associated with Shari'a can at least be *contextualized*, i.e. interpreted and practised in ways accommodating the 'human laws' of the secular state. I am not suggesting that Shari'a discourses in Europe today are necessarily secularist in the sense that they explicitly comply with the secular state; rather, the focus of interest is to examine *how* some Shari'a discourses currently frame Shari'a as a technique of governance that accommodates the authority of the secular state. This is the case in France, which will be at the centre stage of this chapter. In this context, secularism will therefore be understood in its particular French version, the so-called *laïcité*, which not only implies a separation of church and state, but equally so a politics of secularism, i.e. the notion that the state possesses the right to construct and organize particular forms of religion. In France, the construction of a Shari'a compatible with French *laïcité* is accomplished by downscaling the legal aspects of Shari'a in favor of an emphasis on the ethical aspects. This 'ethicizing' of Shari'a is, at present, expressed in two main discourses that construct Shari'a as a 'morality oriented towards an ethics' and a 'morality oriented towards a code', respectively (Foucault, 1984, 37). In a discourse inspired by classical Islamic concepts, Shari'a becomes a universal ethics underpinned by a set of Islamic *values*. In a rising Salafi discourse, Shari'a is conceptualised as a rule or a moral code expressed in a simple Qur'anic distinction between what is allowed and forbidden (*halal* and *haram*).

The chapter proceeds in three steps. First, I shall consider how classical interpretations of Shari'a are currently challenged by the fact that Muslims in France constitute a minority. I will thereafter examine the French discourse of a 'minority Shari'a', which endeavours to 'acclimatize' Shari'a to French secularism. Finally, I will assess the success of the minority Shari'a and briefly consider competing Shari'a discourses that frame Shari'a as a technology of the self.

Muslims as a Minority

What is the particularity of the European context in which Shari'a is to be practised today? And how does being in a minority affect the reformulation of Shari'a in contemporary Europe? With the rise of Islamist discourses in the 20th century, Shari'a was increasingly framed as a legal matter. In countries with a Muslim majority population, Shari'a discourses often had to deal with the question of how to codify the Shari'a, i.e. of how to transform the Shari'a into the positive law of the state. The appearance of the modern nation state and the ambition of enhancing modernization processes in countries with a Muslim majority population often meant that Shari'a was sidetracked and replaced by positive laws inspired by European codes. This was the case with the Tanzimat reforms in the Ottoman Empire and the introduction of the Napoleonic code in Egypt in the 1880s. The Islamic reform movements and their intellectual heirs, the Islamists, could be considered as representing critical responses to this marginalization of the Shari'a. However, in contradistinction to the reformists and the traditional scholars (*'ulama'*), who merely claimed an Islamization of the positive laws, the Islamists more ambitiously called for an Islamization of the *state*.

However, Shari'a discourses in contemporary Europe tend to frame Shari'a differently. As Muslims in Europe today are in the *minority*, the utopia of the Islamic state no longer appears to be the most obvious solution. The question to be dealt with is no longer how to establish an Islamic state or how to ensure an Islamization of the positive laws, but more precisely how to interpret and practise a 'law' that is not backed by any state. Who has the authority to define the Shari'a, and how could Shari'a be enforced when it is not backed by the legitimate use of force? What we see in Europe at present is not the importation of Middle Eastern Islamism struggling to make Shari'a the law of the state. More precisely, we are witnessing the discursive decoupling of state and law – a process that opens up for an alternative between (1) legal pluralism, where Shari'a would be a parallel system of law beside the positive laws (the debate about personal law in the UK), or (2) an 'ethicizing' of the Shari'a, where Shari'a is no longer framed as 'law', assuming instead the form of a religious ethics (France).

Such a separation of Shari'a and state is hardly new and unheard of. On the contrary. Before the emergence of the modern nation state, and in particular the emergence of Islamist movements claiming a fusion of Shari'a and state, Shari'a and political authority were clearly separate (Zubaida, 2003). Hence, Shari'a legislation was a function of what we might today call 'civil society', since the religious scholars (*'ulama'*) and Islamic judges (*qadis*) were responsible for defining and administering the 'law' without any necessary interference from the political authorities (Vikør, 2005). But if law and state are once again being separated, then we are obviously talking about very different 'states' and 'laws'. One of the major differences between the situation of 'historical Islam' and that of contemporary Europe is the fact that the European Muslims constitute a permanent minority.

If Shari'a matters to European Muslims in a situation of minority, is it then because Shari'a is 'the way we used to do things back in Morocco, Egypt or Pakistan'? Is it because Shari'a is 'our *culture*'? And does this imply that Shari'a is the core of a *minority* identity paving the way for specific minority rights? Within the last decades, we have indeed witnessed the appearance of a politics of multiculturalism whereby different minorities have claimed political recognition and specific rights with reference to a specific culture (Modood, 2006). Such a cultural right could be the right to practise Islamic family law. As political scientist Olivier Roy has suggested, however, the re-Islamization of Muslims in Europe today assumes the form of a separation of religion and culture and the subsequent appearance of a 'pure' religion (Roy, 2007, 243). Young 'born-again Muslims' in Europe often reject the traditional 'ethno-religion' of their parents, which they perceive as being a primitive and backward form of 'cultural Islam'. If Muslim women are oppressed, it is – according to this discourse – not because of Islam (whatever that might be), but because of patriarchal North African culture.

Hence, in order to define a 'pure Islam' cleansed of any cultural imprint, young Muslims increasingly drop the legal tradition of the Shari'a (the *fiqh*) and turn directly to the Qur'an and the *sunna* (the deeds and sayings of the Prophet). Not only young Muslims, but also imams, religious scholars and Muslim intellectuals in France increasingly insist on the necessity of cleansing Islam of its cultural elements. Hence, if Shari'a matters to European Muslims today, it is not because Shari'a is a constitutive part of Middle Eastern, South Asian or North African *culture*, but because the *reformulation* of religious discourse and practice in contemporary Europe produces a 'pure' religion that is cleansed of the original cultures. What defines European Muslims as a minority today is then not culture, but precisely the practice of Shari'a, which therefore becomes a crucial matter. Although the current deculturalization of Islam leads to the discourse of a 'pure' religion that increasingly abstracts from the original culture, I would argue – together with Malika Zeghal – that such a deculturalization is accompanied by a 'reculturalization' (Zeghal, 2005). The deculturalization is followed by a recontextualization, since Shari'a must be practised within a new context. However, this raises the critical question of how Shari'a can be practised in a secularist setting in which Muslims are in the minority.

Minority Shari'a and Religious Authority

Tareq Oubrou, head of the Bordeaux mosque, has addressed this question by developing the concept of a 'minority Shari'a' (*Shari'a de minorité*). Oubrou is affiliated with l'Union des Organisations Islamiques de France (UOIF), a French Islamist organisation which, at its founding in 1983, had close ideological ties to the Muslim Brotherhood in Egypt. Nevertheless, Oubrou belongs to a new generation of French 'Islamists', who have abandoned the classical Islamist project of constructing an Islamic state in favour of a politics of reconciliation with the secular state in France. True to their Islamist heritage, these new Islamists – Oubrou, but also a figure such as Tariq Ramadan – remain situated within a political logic and have contributed with reflections about how Shari'a can be reconciled with secularism in both France and Europe (Ramadan, 2003; Oubrou, 2000). In *Les Musulmans d'Occident et l'avenir de l'islam* ('Western Muslims and the future of Islam'), Tariq Ramadan (2003) thus argues that Shari'a and secularism are compatible in the sense that European Muslims should first and foremost respect the positive laws of the European states like any other citizens.

This minority Shari'a deals explicitly with the question of how to 'acclimatize' Shari'a to secularism in a situation in which Muslims are in the minority. The term 'minority' should not, however, be mistaken for a statistical or demographic concept referring to the relative number of Muslims in France. French political discourse is indeed quite averse to the notion that French society could possibly be composed of minorities as opposed to indistinguishable French citizens – an image that haunts the French social imagination as 'communitarianism'. Hence, 'minority' is not a statistical concept, but more precisely 'a posture of spatio-temporal exception' (Oubrou, 2000). In the classical legal tradition (*fiqh*), the idea that Muslims could live as a minority under foreign rule was indeed considered to be a temporary exception that ought to be dealt with either by conquest or emigration. In this line of thought, Muslims were supposed to live either in a country where they were in the majority or – if for some reason this was not the case – at least in a country where they were in power as in Mogul India. The specific situation of being a *permanent* minority in a secular state ruled by non-Muslims thus constitutes an 'exception' that requires reconsideration on its own terms. Hence, the classical distinction between *dar el-Islam* and *dar al-harb* – the abode of Islam and the abode of war –becomes obsolete and opens up for reflections about how Europe should be characterized today, since obviously the *dar al-harb* label no longer seems appropriate.

But how is Shari'a to be interpreted and practised in this 'spatio-temporal exception'? According to the minority Shari'a, the Islamic scholars in France (*fuqaha*) should assume responsibility and formulate a Shari'a that is compatible with the political and cultural context of France. It is often argued that Europe is currently witnessing the individualization of Islam, since Islamic norms are no longer imposed by positive law or social norms (Roy, 2002). This loss of normative evidence in Europe opens up for an increased reflexivity and, at the same time, a greater autonomy of Islamic practices. Muslims who become re-Islamized in the West are assailed with new questions of how to practise their faith. Faced with innumerable questions of this kind, young born-again Muslims do not necessarily pay a visit to the local imam, consulting instead online fatwas and even studying classic Arabic in order to be able to read the Qur'an *themselves*. This enhanced autonomy and the related questioning of authority have paved the way for the proliferation of so-called 'Salafi' discourses, which reject the traditional legal schools in favour of a tight focus on the fundamental texts of Islam (the Qur'an and the *sunna*). Hence, increased autonomy and the weakening of authority not only lead to freedom and enlightened citizenship, but also to Qur'anic *bricolage* and a loss of refined ethical knowledge (el-Fadl, 2003b).

When Oubrou urges the religious scholars to assume leadership and participate in the formulation of a French Shari'a, he is in other words calling for the re-establishment of religious authority. Hence, the minority Shari'a has the ambition of governance in the precise sense that it implies the elaboration of a 'truth' intended to be normative for Muslims in France. But if the practice of Shari'a in France is to be guided by a self-proclaimed religious authority underpinned by the possession of religious knowledge, how is this authority more precisely to accommodate the authority of the secular state? How can the law of God be compatible with the laws of the secular state? And how should the minority Shari'a – in practice – co-exist with French secularism?

In order to make Shari'a compatible with French *laïcité*, Oubrou calls for an 'ethicising of Shari'a' (Oubrou, 2003a, 1). In the UK, Shari'a discourses are often framed as a legal matter. At stake in British discussions is not the question of an Islamization of the positive laws, but rather, the claim that Islamic family law should be politically recognized and thus introduced as a parallel system of law. Hence, Muslim lawyers have a prominent voice in British discussions on Shari'a, where they often argue that since a *legal* assimilation of British Muslims is impossible, the political authorities should officially recognize the practice of Islamic family law and even allow for official Shari'a courts (cf. Prakash Shah in this volume). By framing Shari'a as a parallel system of law, the British debate challenges the positivist understanding of what law is. In France, Shari'a discourses tend not to frame Shari'a as a *law* challenging the positive laws of the state, but rather as an *ethics* that is not in conflict with French secularism; Shari'a governs at a different level.

In order to transplant Shari'a to a new minority context, the minority Shari'a distinguishes between different levels of Shari'a: the law (*hukm*) and the fatwa. The 'law', which is not properly speaking a law, but rather a norm or a rule, is the outcome of textual hermeneutics; conversely, the fatwa is preoccupied with the *application* of the 'law'. Hence, Shari'a is not, as often argued, a fixed body, but a circumscribed corpus of texts whose interpretation and application are characterized by a great sensibility to a particular environment. Moreover, the universal norm of the Shari'a cannot be merely deduced from a literal reading of the Qur'an, but must be elaborated in accordance with the complex hermeneutic rules elaborated by the classical *fiqh* scholars.

When it comes to the understanding of the religious norm, Oubrou is neither a Salafi hardliner, keen on literal understandings and applications of the Shari'a, nor a liberal softie. There are indeed many more liberal reform discourses now arguing that not only the fatwa, but even the 'law' is characterized by great flexibility. These radical reformists argue that since the Shari'a was initially incarnated in a particular culture (the Arab culture of the 7th century), it is marked by this particular culture. The conceptions of punishment, women etc. as presented in the Qur'an might have been at the forefront of 7th-century norms, but this is no longer the case in the 21st century. In order to grasp the universal norms of the Shari'a, it thus becomes necessary to 'deculturalize' or 'de-Arabize' it. Human rights scholar Abdullahi Ahmed An-Naim proceeds further yet, arguing that since Shari'a is a human construction elaborated by Islamic jurists during the first centuries of Islam, it is possible to deconstruct it – and even discard it altogether – in order to develop a brand new Shari'a abreast of the times, and in particular of the human right standards of the 21st century (An-Naim, 2008). Compared to such radical reform discourses, the minority Shari'a adopts a more conservative stance, since it has its point of departure in classical *fiqh*.

To Oubrou, what matters not is that the Qur'an was incarnated in a particular *culture*, but that the Qur'an grants consideration to 'the particular *context* of its revelation' (Oubrou, 2003b, 8). In order to grasp the universal norms of the Qur'an, it is not sufficient to consider the Qur'an *in abstracto*, since the word must be considered in the light of the Qur'anic context as well as the tradition of the Prophet (the *sunna*). Therefore, according to Oubrou, one 'cannot be a good Muslim by exclusively reading the Qur'an. That's absurd!' (Oubrou, 2003b, 8). The current tendency among both Muslims and non-Muslims in Europe to focus exclusively on the Qur'an is thus flawed. If the Qur'an stipulates, say, that women should inherit only half as much as their male counterparts, one does not grasp the universal norm by following this rule to the letter or by rejecting it as an expression of old-fashioned culture. In order to grasp the universal norm, we must understand why – in the particular context of the Qur'an – women inherited only half as much as men. This could be explained by the fact that, at the time of the revelation, men were responsible for providing for their families. But since this is no longer the case, the justification for the unequal treatment in matters of inheritance has disappeared. In accordance with the minority Shari'a, Islamic feminists could even argue that in contemporary societies, where women often must provide for the family, it is women and not men who ought to inherit the lion's share.

However, this hermeneutical effort and the elaboration of the 'law' are not within the reach of everyone, since it requires specific training and the possession of specialist knowledge, including command of the four classical schools of law (*madhhab*, pl. *madhahib*). The minority Shari'a is thus 'conservative' in the precise sense that it sticks to the authority of the four legal schools. In France, there is an ongoing discussion about what should be the point of departure for the practice of the Shari'a: Islamic principles or French secularism: '*fiqh* or France'? (Bowen, 2004, 342). To Oubrou, this formulation of the question is flawed. The word of God might be absolute, but the normative aspect of the Revelation concerned with Islamic practice – Shari'a – is flexible, since it introduces the human context into its own metabolism. Hence, the question is rather how to practise an absolute rule in the particularity of my situation. If the Muslim scholars in France should – initially – stick to the beaten track of Islamic tradition and more precisely to the four legal schools (*madhahib*), they should start by considering French laws and the norms of French culture and *then* look for the Islamic legal alternative offering the best fit with these parameters. In some cases, it might be the Hanafi school of law, in others the Hanbali etc.

However, since the 'law' is to be practised in a wholly new context of French secularism, the most innovative part of the minority Shari'a is not the legal aspect (on this point, the minority Shari'a remains within the boundaries of classical *fiqh*), but reflections on the 'morphologic dimension of its social realisation' (Oubrou, 2000, 3). What matters in a French context is not merely the elaboration of the universal rule of the 'law', but the *practice* of the 'law'. How could this 'law' be practised in France in such a manner that it is 'integrative' and not in 'rupture' with the legal and cultural environment? This work of acclimatization is the task of the fatwa. In order to emphasise the flexibility and capacity of adaptation of the Shari'a, the minority Shari'a develops a true 'fatwa-panoply', i.e. a variegated and fine-meshed typology of diverse forms of fatwas granting consideration to the different aspects of the context.

Positive Fatwas and the Contextualization of the Shari'a

What is a fatwa? It might be necessary briefly to stress that a fatwa is neither a death penalty pronounced by some high-ranking ayatollah, nor a court sentence! It is not a court sentence for the simple reason that the *mufti*, who traditionally pronounces the fatwa, is not a judge; rather, he is a high-ranking scholar (that is at least the way it used to be). A fatwa is an expert's opinion most often given as an answer to a specific question in order to enlighten a Muslim on some aspect of Islamic legal tradition. A fatwa has no binding power. It is merely indicative, and a Muslim can freely choose to follow it or to ask someone else for an alternative fatwa (see art. 'Fatwa' in *EI2*). The fatwa is then an important technique of government, since it proposes a 'truth' that is supposed to guide religious practice. In order to encourage practices of Shari'a that are compatible with French secularism, however, the minority Shari'a introduces an innovative distinction between 'positive' and 'negative' fatwas. A positive fatwa is a fatwa that has been pronounced, whereas a negative fatwa refers to the curious phenomenon of a fatwa that is *not* pronounced. I shall return to this.

The aim of the positive fatwa is to fit Shari'a into the *legal* as well as *social* environment. This is why it comes in two versions: the common fatwa and the individual or 'circumstanced' fatwa. According to the *common fatwa*, a fatwa must not be in conflict with the positive laws of the state. The common fatwa is then secular, since it grants consideration to the *legal* environment and subordinates the Shari'a to the positive laws of France. Hence, the minority Shari'a introduces the positive law in the economy of the Shari'a and clearly marks a distance to advocates of legal pluralism, who urge the secular state to recognize and allow the practice of Muslim personal law. Indeed, the '*Shari'a de minorité*' has nothing to do with the '*fiqh* of minorities' (*fiqh al-aqalliyyat*), since in the minority Shari'a, Shari'a loses the aspect of law and becomes a 'morality oriented towards an ethics', which is supposed to guide Muslims in their everyday practice.

However, a fatwa should not only take into consideration the formalized legal environment, but also the secular ethos of the public sphere. This is the main function of the *circumstanced fatwa*, which is not general, but is an answer to a specific case and as such takes into consideration the particular circumstances of the individual case. After the adoption of the famous law banning visible religious symbols from public schools in France, a *mufti* should then – according to the principle of the common fatwa – encourage Muslim girls to follow the republican law and remove their headscarves when in school. But that's not all. Although headscarves are permitted in the public sphere outside of public schools, if such behaviour is contrary to cultural norms and as such could prevent a Muslim from getting a job, a *mufti* could give a circumstanced fatwa advising the particular women in the light of the particular situation to take off her headscarf in order to get the job.

Does this imply that the minority Shari'a subordinates Shari'a to French law? Must the law of God subject itself to the (all too) human laws of the Republic? And is the minority Shari'a nothing but a complete dilution of the Shari'a, since it relativizes it beyond recognition? Not really. Rather, the minority Shari'a introduces a division of labour between the two systems of 'law' that makes it perfectly clear what 'law' and what authority should be followed in different cases. The minority Shari'a remains within the classical *fiqh* distinction between *'ibadat* and *mu'amalat* – religious duties and contractual matters. *'Ibadat*, which are concerned with religious duties (praying, fasting etc.), are absolute and non-negotiable. They cannot be acclimatized or contextualized. In order to be a Muslim worthy of this name, a Muslim does not necessarily have to practise, but must at least have the possibility to practise (according to Oubrou, it is not necessary to practise in order to be a Muslim). But since the secular laws of France guarantee the freedom of religion, and thus do not interfere with *'ibadat*, Muslims can live in secularist France and freely practise their religion. This is essential. If the positive laws were against *'ibadat* and thus prevented Muslims from practising their religion, they should not abide by the positive laws, but leave the country as soon as possible. However, when it comes to the more mundane matters of *mu'amalat* – relations between people, marriage, divorce, inheritance, contracts etc. – the positive laws are primary. In *mu'amalat* matters, Muslim citizens should abide by the French laws like any other citizen. The minority Shari'a thus introduces the idea of a *hierarchy* in the Shari'a. Not every subject matter is of equal importance. Whereas *'ibadat* are absolute, *mu'amalat* can be relativized – a standpoint that is also taken by someone such as Tariq Ramadan.

Fatwa-ization of Shari'a and the Use of Negative Fatwas

The ambition of re-establishing authority and guiding Islamic practice in ways that are compatible with French secularism should not, however, lead to an authoritarian control or regulation of Muslim citizens. Hence, Oubrou is critical of the current tendency to consider Shari'a as an unambiguous norm regulating every aspect of people's lives. In contemporary Europe we witness the proliferation of Salafi discourses framing Shari'a as a strict norm framed around the simple Qur'anic distinction between *haram* and *halal* (forbidden and allowed). Since Muslims in modern-day Europe are assailed with questions of how to practise their faith in a new environment, we witness a true proliferation of demands for fatwas. When UOIF hold their annual meeting in the Paris suburb Le Bourget, they erect a fatwa-tent, where Muslims can go and get a 'face-to-face fatwa'.[1] However, most fatwas are currently provided via the internet, and the most hip Islamic websites (e.g. Islamonline) have fatwa banks where prominent (or less prominent) scholars deliver fatwas on all imaginable questions from the use of lottery tickets to masturbation. Increasingly, young Salafi Muslims in France and elsewhere try to realign their whole existence in accordance with fatwas given by Saudi sheiks (Haenni, 2006).

The negative fatwa is conceived in order to counter this 'fatwa-ization' of the Shari'a. Obviously, the minority Shari'a is not against the use of the fatwa as such, since the fatwa holds a prominent position in the minority Shari'a. The problem is not the fatwa as such, but the *scope* and the *dissemination* of the fatwa. Does 'Islam' have an answer to every possible question about how one should live? Is it the core of an Islamic ethics to answer whether one ought to eat with the left or right hand? At least the minority Shari'a takes a critical stance towards the idea that Shari'a covers every possible aspect of human existence and that subsequently every possible question is worth a fatwa. Like the reformist thinkers in Iran who insist that Shari'a does not have answers to every *political* question – and that the administration of a modern state subsequently requires secular knowledge such as economics, sociology and political science (Soroush, 2000) – the minority Shari'a insists that Shari'a does not have an answer to every *ethical* question about how to shape one's existence. When an imam is asked to give a fatwa on a subject that is

1 Personal observation.

below a certain 'triviality limit', he or she could give a negative fatwa, i.e. choose to remain silent on the matter. Hence, the negative fatwa authoritatively creates a space of autonomy, since it allows the individual Muslim to make their own decision on the matter.

Hence, the minority Shari'a not only marks its disagreement with Shari'a discourses framing Shari'a as a law, but also with rising *halal* discourses framing Shari'a as a 'morality oriented towards a code'. According to Oubrou,

> We cannot just work with fatwa, because we have to think not just normatively but in terms of theology, tolerance, the person, the society, liberty and determinism, and ethics. We are required in emergencies to respond to questions about what is *haram* and *halal*, but we have to carry out a long term effort to rethink what Islam should be in a very secularized society, as France (…). The normative has to respond to what I call the *maqasid*, the broad vision of Islam, design, objectives; this goes beyond the normative. Ethics are central to Islam (cited in Bowen, 2004, 341).

This idea of an 'ethicizing' of Shari'a is closely linked to the notion that there is a hierarchy within Shari'a, that some practices are more important than others and that, subsequently, some 'sins' are more serious than others. In opposition to the contemporary Salafi discourse, which puts every question at the same level of importance and extends religious norms to all aspects of life, the minority Shari'a restores the more complex *fiqh* distinctions between what is *required*, *forbidden*, *recommended*, *disapproved* and *permitted* (the so-called 'five *ahkam*'). The discussion of the famous Islamic headscarf could exemplify this point, since it points to the possibility that the question of the so-called headscarf is not a matter of yes or no, *halal-haram*, but a much more complex matter that is not necessarily dealt with in terms of an absolute norm, but could be only recommended or even considered in terms of values. Oubrou even claims that there is no such thing as an 'Islamic headscarf', like there are no 'Islamic shoes' (Oubrou, 2003b, 9). There is no Islamic headscarf; more generally, however, there is an 'ethics in relation to the body' (Oubrou, 2003b, 9). If the prescription to cover the head (*khimar*) is indeed to be found in the Qur'an – and thus for some Muslims acquires status of an absolute that must be followed to the letter – it is, according to Oubrou, merely a passage of minor importance that does not at all have the significance it is given in public discourse at present (see the chapter by Sensenig-Dabbous elsewhere in this volume). If a Muslim woman chooses not to wear a headscarf, she is not committing a serious sin. What is important is not to follow a recommendation to the letter, but to freely perform a particular relationship to the body that implies some kind of 'decency'. This counts for men as well as for women. Whether to wear a headscarf or not is certainly not at the same level of importance as other values such as altruism, generosity or forgiveness.

The End of Authority and the Rise of Salafism

The minority Shari'a is a theoretical discourse that ethicizes the Shari'a. Hence, it has the ambition of governing religious practice by elaborating a 'truth' that renders Shari'a compatible with French secularism. But what is the position of the minority Shari'a in French Shari'a discourse more generally? Is it a free-floating theoretical discourse formulated by some marginalized intellectual, or is it a successful technique of government? Is it a pure intellectual exercise, or does it have some impact on current practices of the Shari'a? Strictly speaking, this is not a question of a simple 'impact' on social practice. Rather, I assume that there is a dialectic between, on the one hand, Islamic practices 'spontaneously' adapting to the context of secularism and, on the other hand, a theoretical discourse that attempts to – *a posteriori* – legitimize such practices and at the same time conduct them in an integrative manner. Hence, the question to be addressed is whether the minority Shari'a is constitutive of authority. Is it a discourse which merely seeks to legitimize existing practices, or does it succeed as a technique of government?

As mentioned, Oubrou is one of the leading intellectuals in UOIF, the French Islamist organization. He is responsible for the training of imams at the Bordeaux mosque. In this capacity, he is not a marginal intellectual at, say, a university. Rather he is a 'public intellectual' (Bowen, 2004); his ideas are related to a major organization with political influence. Hence, the minority Shari'a is not just any discourse, but a discourse that has contributed to the reformulation of Islamism in France over the last decade. At its founding in 1983, the UOIF had close ideological ties to the Muslim Brotherhood in Egypt. Within the last 20 years, it has nonetheless undergone a thorough transformation, since it has abandoned the ideology of Shari'a as a system of law to be implemented in a future Islamic state (Amghar, 2006; Haenni, 2006). Since the end of the 1980s, the UOIF has scaled down its confrontational stance to the secular state and has – in the 1990s – become straightforward secularist, since it has given up the ideal of the Islamic state and has in practice accepted the secular state in France. The new French Islamists take pains with the elaboration of a French Islam (Islam *de* France) and in this perspective have initiated a politics of cooperation with the state. In 2003 they consented to participate in the newly established French Council of the Muslim Cult (Conseil Français du Culte Musulman, CFCM), which was created by the French government in 2002 in order to liaise with the state in questions of how to regulate the Muslim religion.

The minority Shari'a can thus be perceived as a discourse justifying the political evolution of the UOIF, and as such has been quite successful. Likewise, the idea of creating a centralized body responsible for the acclimatisation of Shari'a to a European context has been carried out – if not in a French context at least at a European level in the form of a European Council for Fatwa and Research (ECFR) headed by the prestigious scholar Yusuf al-Qaradawi. Although intellectuals such as Oubrou and Ramadan have been the advocates of such a central fatwa organ, they have, however, subsequently marked their distance to this council, which they consider to be too 'Middle Eastern'.

At a sociological level, the ambition of the minority Shari'a to generate centralized authority has nevertheless been less successful. First, unlike the Muslim Brotherhood, the UOIF is not a centralized organization with an uncontested leader (*amir*); rather, it is a pluralist organization. Hence, the minority Shari'a is faced with competing discourses of how Shari'a could be conceived in a French or European context. Tariq Ramadan, who has also written about about how to reconcile Shari'a and secularism, is very critical of Oubrou's focus on classical *fiqh* (Ternissien, 2003). Likewise, liberal Muslims outside the organisation have criticized the minority Shari'a for its emphasis on tradition and authority. In any case, the idea of establishing a centralized Islamic authority in a specific geographical setting is at odds with a sociological evolution that goes in the direction of globalization and fragmentation of religious authorities. As often noticed, the internet is overflowing with fatwas issued by various 'authorities' from all parts of the world (Qatar, Saudi Arabia, Egypt, US, France etc.). The ambition of the UOIF to assume centralized leadership and exercise government can thus be regarded as an attempt at countering this anarchical trend. However, such an attempt is increasingly contested – both by young 'Islamists' from the UOIF, as well as by the current rise of Salafi discourses.

Apparently, Salafi discourses are on the rise in contemporary France. According to the French intelligence service, DGST, one out of four conversions to Islam in France today are Salafi (Haenni, 2006). According to Dhaou Meskine, an imam teaching in the Paris suburb Aubervillier, there is currently a 'wind from the Orient' in France bringing texts and television programmes from Saudi Arabia. These winds are promoting Hanbali versions of the Shari'a (Bowen, 2004, 341). Today, a growing number of young Muslims in France prefer imams who teach directly from the Qur'an and the *hadith* – or at least from the Hanbali school – as opposed to those teaching from a more flexible approach to Shari'a and *fiqh*. Hence, many of the young Salafi Muslims turn their backs to the UOIF leaders, whom they accuse of bourgeoisification and becoming 'lab-Muslims' for the French state. These newly converted Salafis reject (or probably ignore) the sophisticated epistemic constructions of classical *fiqh* as well as current attempts to reinterpret classical *fiqh* in the light of the French context. Instead, they adhere to a conception of Shari'a as a fixed norm, which should not be adapted or contextualized to a French context. They take the life of the Prophet as an indispensable model to be followed in every detail. In Lyon, for example, a group of Salafis harassed and beat up a local imam, because he did not – exactly as the Prophet – pray directly on the floor (Haenni, 2006).

Apparently, the Salafi discourse is better adapted to the sociological evolution described above, since it constructs Shari'a as a decentralized technique of self-governance or as an 'aesthetic of existence' (Foucault, 1984). Indeed, this Salafi discourse frames Shari'a as a technique for shaping a pious existence by the repeated performance of embodied practices in accordance with the norms of the Shari'a. Salafis are not subjecting themselves to old-fashioned religious authorities clinging to the knowledge of classical *fiqh*. Rather, they reject such learned authorities and shape their pious existence by following a simple religious norm, which they – more or less autodidactically – can access directly through the Qur'an and the Sunna. In order to deal with questions that are not explicitly dealt with in the Qur'an, they download fatwas issued by Saudi sheiks (Haenni, 2006). Hence, Salafis reject the eclectic approach of the minority Shari'a and the idea that it is possible to mix different schools of law by picking the one offering the best fit with the legal and social context. In contrast to the minority Shari'a, which relativizes and contextualizes the Shari'a, the Salafis deliberately abstract from the particularity of the French context.

Despite the attempt to turn their back on French society and perform a decontextualized form of Islam, the Salafi conception of Shari'a fits perfectly with the ambient consumerism of the secular society they are otherwise rejecting. Although Salafi Muslims *in discourse* turn their back on secular society and are often hostile towards the secular state, their conception of Shari'a in terms of *halal* and *haram* is very conducive to a secular ethos of consumption. According to this Shari'a discourse, it is indeed possible to be a good and pious Muslim by consuming in an Islamically correct manner, i.e. by adopting strictly *halal* consumer practices. In recent years, this conception of Shari'a has paved the way for an ever-expanding global *halal* market (Fischer, 2007). *Halal* food (supermarkets, catering, fast food), *halal* soft drinks (Mecca cola, Zamzam), *halal* clothing (headscarves, Islamic street wear), Islamic financial services (interest-free loans), *halal* tourism (hotels with separate pools for men and women and no alcohol served), *halal* medicine (drugs without animal gelatin), telecommunications (mobile phones that call to prayer), toys (Islamic 'Barbies' with headscarves and decent dress), even music (Islamic rap) and so on are offered in order to satisfy a growing Shari'a-based consumer sector (Crone, 2007).

Although it is not only Salafis, but Muslims more generally, who increasingly turn to *halal* consumption, Salafis have a more intransigent attitude when it comes to the strict respect of *halal*. In 1999, the European Council of Fatwa and Research, which is dedicated to the adaptation of Shari'a to a European context, issued a fatwa allowing interest-free loans for the purchase of property in particular circumstances. Salafis refuse such a relativist stance, insisting instead on the strict Qur'anic prohibition against charging interest on loans. In order to respond to a growing number of demanding Salafi consumers, entrepreneurs and purchasers of property, we currently witness the mushrooming of new financial products offering interest-free loans (Housby, 2006). Muslims interested in buying a house close to a particular mosque or who espouse the 'new spirit of *halal*-capitalism' by becoming entrepreneurs increasingly demand financial products that comply with their conception of the Shari'a.

To people with limited education, Shari'a consumption becomes a means of acquiring direct access to the sacred. Being a good and pious Muslim no longer presupposes sophisticated legal knowledge dealing with the complexity of ethical situations, but merely sporadic contact with religious authorities through the medium of the fatwa. Shari'a-based consumer practices are obviously only one of various means by which Salafi discourses are expressed in practice. The Salafi discourse could also be expressed in, say, strictly religious practices or even in violent acts. A majority of the approximately 50 French citizens who had made an attempt to join the insurgency in Iraq in 2006, have been recruited among Salafis (Haenni, 2006). Hence, if violent Salafism is a marginal – although not insignificant – phenomenon, Shari'a-based consumption is currently becoming a mass phenomenon with a large appeal to both intellectual Islamists as well as to unskilled Muslims in the French suburbs (Amghar, 2005).

With the rise of Salafism and *halal* consumption, Shari'a is increasingly detached from classical *fiqh* and from sophisticated intellectual constructions like the minority Shari'a. Instead, Shari'a is directly expressed in social practices through profane acts of consumption. Shari'a-based consumer practices thus become a way of gaining 'good points' (*hasanat*) and pleasing God, while at the same time pleasing oneself (Boubekeur, 2005, 57). There is then a distinct this-worldly dimension to Salafi consumption. If Salafis attempt to construct a 'pure', decontextualized Shari'a by insisting on the practice of Islam at the time of the Prophet as an indispensable model, such discourses nonetheless blur the distinction between the secular and the religious, since the religious norm is increasingly expressed in profane consumer practices.

However, the Salafi practice of Shari'a in France is not merely imbued with secular culture. It is also compatible with the *political* principle of secularism; not because Salafi discourses explicitly endorse secularism, but because they – in practice – respect the separation of state and religion. While the 'new' Islamists of the UOIF have accepted secularism and have even begun to cooperate with the secular state, Salafis often turn their back on the state and political life in general. They are apolitical in the precise sense that they do not involve themselves in politics, and secularist in the sense that the practice of their religion unfolds *outside* the political sphere – in a religious, cultural or economic sphere. Nonetheless, although Salafis do not engage in traditional forms of conventional politics (parties etc.), their political engagement might assume other forms. If a very small minority engage in radical forms of politics, a much larger group increasingly use Shari'a-consumption as a political weapon, either to boycott specific products (as during the Danish cartoon crisis during the winter 2005–2006) or through a more general refusal to consume 'Western' products, when they can find proper *halal* substitutes. However, this emergence of a politicized *halal* consumption is a normal, democratic form of politics that is not contrary to the principle of secularism.

Conclusion

In this chapter, I have argued that Shari'a is not a static system of law, but a flexible normative system that possibly assumes the form of law. In contemporary France, this normative system increasingly becomes an ethics or a normative form of government. Hence, Shari'a has a great capacity to adapt to the political context as well as social practice. In present-day France, the reformulation of Shari'a revolves around two major poles: a renewed Islamist discourse framing Shari'a as a morality 'oriented towards an ethics' and a rising Salafi discourse framing Shari'a as a morality 'oriented towards a code' (Foucault, 1984, 37). Both of these discourses are secularist. The minority Shari'a and other new Islamist discourses are secularist in the sense that they 'ethicize' and relativize the Shari'a, which is no longer considered to be an absolute law to be implemented in an Islamic state, but as a flexible ethics that must respect the laws of the secular state. The main challenge to the new Islamist discourse – the Salafi Shari'a discourse – is secularist as well. Not because Salafis accept the secular culture or the political principle of secularism, but because it uses an absolute moral code as an individual technique for self-governance unfolding *outside* the political sphere.

By elaborating a minority Shari'a, the French Islamists considered that the rethinking of the classical dogma (*fiqh*) and the elaboration of a new regime of truth (the minority Shari'a) was a condition for the reform of Islamic conduct in Europe. The question, however, remains whether the encouragement of secularist Shari'a practices presupposes a theological *aggiornamento*? Everything seems to indicate that Shari'a-based practices increasingly bypass the sophisticated knowledge of classical *fiqh* and that the evolution of the Shari'a is increasingly driven not by legal knowledge or intellectual constructions, but by social practice.

Chapter 11
Divine Law and Human Understanding – The Idea of Shari'a in Saudi Arabia

Dorthe Bramsen

The law of Saudi Arabia is based on the Qur'an and the *sunna* of Muhammad and, as such, is believed by the Saudis to be in conformity with the divine law, the Shari'a. Strict rules within criminal law and for the conduct of women are applied, but the law is not codified except in some areas of *siyasa*. The Qur'an and the *sunna* are in principle open for interpretation, but the leading *'ulama'* who have legislative power tend to be rather optimistic regarding their and their predecessors' ability to discern what they believe is the true meaning of the canonical texts. Therefore the openness only rarely leads to a redefinition of the rules. In 2005, for example, when a member of the Shura Council, Muhammad al-Zulfa, suggested that the issue of women driving cars should be taken up in the council (*Arab News*, 23 May 2005),[1] the leading *'ulama'* claimed that the issue had been decided once and for all. Thus a fatwa issued by the Permanent Committee for *Ifta'* under the leadership of Ibn Baz (d. 1999), the former Grand Mufti, stated that, based on the Qur'an and the *sunna* of Muhammad, '[t]here is no doubt that [women driving cars] is not allowed' (Ibn Baz, 2002, vol. 3, 351). Consequently the issue was not taken up.

This chapter will take up the idea of Shari'a in Saudi Arabia as it is displayed in the kingdom's official discourse. How do Saudi *'ulama'* conceive of Shari'a and what exegetical or hermeneutic strategies do they make use of when identifying and defining it? Focus will be on their optimism regarding the possibility of formulating an all-comprehensive law derived from the Qur'an and the *sunna*, the question being what theological and legal theories underlies it.

The Saudi Legal System

Before expounding the legal epistemology and methodology of Saudi Arabian *'ulama'* the Saudi legal system should be sketched out. The concept of law in Saudi Arabia is based on the doctrine of *siyasa shar'iyya* as developed by Ibn Taymiyya (d.

1 Since 1990 women have officially been prohibited from driving cars in the kingdom based on a fatwa rendered by the Permanent Committee for *Ifta*, one of the two official *ifta* institutions in Saudi Arabia (Al-Atawneh, 2004, 66). The other one is the Board of Senior *'Ulama'*.

1328) and his pupil Ibn al-Qayyim (d. 1350). *Siyasa shar'iyya* means governance in accordance with the divine law, and it calls for a harmonization between the law and procedures of Islamic jurisprudence, *fiqh*, and the practical demands of governance, *siyasa*. The rationale behind the doctrine is that if the divine law is duly observed, the *siyasa* of rulers will not conflict with *fiqh* as elaborated by the legal scholars. If conflict between them appears, it is either because *fiqh* is understood too narrowly, neglecting the resources of the Shari'a for attaining the public good, *al-maslaha al-'amma*, or because rulers disregard the divine will and act unjustly. In the formulation of Ibn al-Qayyim, true *siyasa* is but a part of Shari'a (Vogel, 1997, 695). In Saudi interpretation the doctrine implies that the king may take any action needed for the public good, including legislating to supplement *fiqh*, provided that the Shari'a is not infringed thereby.[2] The call for a unification of *fiqh* and *siyasa* points to the concept of *tawhid* as defined and interpreted by Ibn Taymiyya and following him Ibn 'Abd al-Wahhab (d. 1792). Thus Ibn 'Abd al-Wahhab distinguished between *tawhid al-rububiyya* and *tawhid al-uluhiyya*, i.e. between acknowledging that Allah is the sole creator and serving Him as such, underlining that it is the last which characterizes being a Muslim. A Muslim is, seen from his perspective, a believer who acts in accordance with his belief, i.e. worships and serves nobody but Allah in all circumstances, in *fiqh* as well as in *siyasa* (Bramsen, 2007, 23–8).

The implicit structure of the formal Saudi legal system is illustrated in Figure 11.1. The structure is implicit since no formal presentation identifies it in this way, or in any other for that matter. At the top of the chart are the two spheres of the system, *fiqh* and *siyasa*; in the middle the different judicial institutions and at the bottom the different types of law.

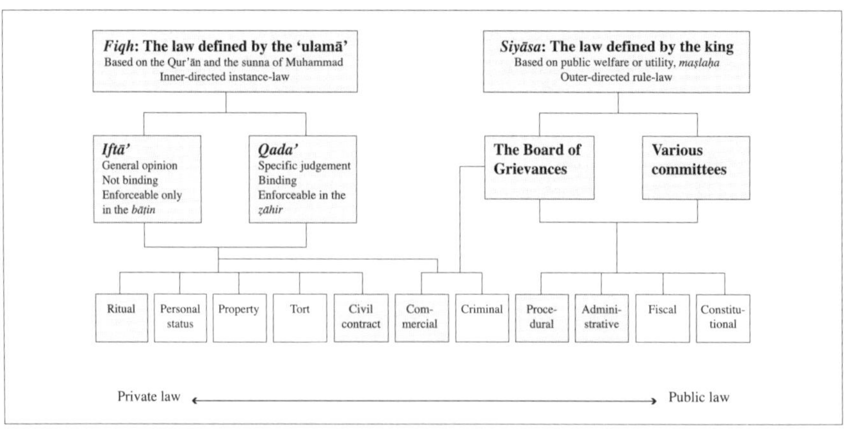

Figure 11.1 The formal legal system of Saudi Arabia

2 Cf. *al-Nizam al-Asasi*, Royal Decree No. (90A), 27 Sha'ban 1412 (March 1992), art. 55 and 67.

Fiqh, to take this first, is the law defined by the religious-legal scholars, the 'ulama', legislated and applied by *mufti*s and *qadi*s. It is a private or individual law with what Frank Vogel calls microcosmic concerns. Vogel has in his book *Islamic Law and Legal System: Studies of Saudi Arabia* given a thorough description of the Saudi legal system, and 'microcosmic' refers in his use to the 'atomic quality' of law, involving only an individual law-maker and a unique case, and to the 'hologram- or chromosome-like ability to shape and generate the legal system as a whole, encompassing both its mundane and transcendent dimensions' (Vogel, 2000, 23–4). The concept of microcosmic law is, to clarify, a combination of two rather elementary ideas: that of 'instance-law', a law that comes into being only as it is applied to a particular, concrete event, and that of 'inner-directed justification'. By the last is meant that legitimation of law arises solely from the individual conscience, as it contemplates the Qur'anic text or the *sunna*; for instance if one asks why a particular law is legitimate, the answer is given in terms referring to the encounter of the individual conscience with the canonical text (Vogel, 2000, 25). As for the law of the *mufti*s, it is general and non-binding. It is enforceable in the *batin* only; i.e. the decision of its application is left to the conscience of the person requesting a fatwa.[3] *Mufti*s render fatwas, i.e. legal opinions, from within the *Ifta'* institution. Since 1971 there have been two such official institutions in Saudi Arabia, their history and development having been thoroughly described by al-Atawneh (al-Atawneh, 2004, 21–47). The first is the Board of Senior *'Ulama'*, currently composed of 18 senior religious-legal scholars appointed by the king. It is headed by the State Mufti 'Abd al-'Aziz Al al-Shaykh and conducts studies and adopts formal fatwas on major public issues, acting either in response to an inquiry from the king or independently (Vogel, 1996, 263).

The second is the Permanent Committee for Scientific Research and Legal Opinions, in this study abbreviated to the Permanent Committee for *Ifta'*. It is made up of six members of the Board of Senior *'Ulama'*, all selected by the king. Its members work full time responding to requests from private citizens for guidance on their personal affairs and are headed by the State Mufti.

As to the law of the *qadi*s it is specific and binding. *Qadi*s are judges in the Shari'a courts which are administered by the Ministry of Justice and are the courts of general jurisdiction. These are the summary courts, the general courts, the Appellate Court or Court of Review, and the Supreme Judicial Council.[4] Contrary to the law of the *mufti*s which rests on what is given as the truth by the person requesting a fatwa, the law of the *qadi* is based on the *zahir*; i.e. the outer 'facts'. This makes it enforceable in the outer world. If a person knows in his heart that the facts of the external forum of the court do not correspond with the facts in the

3 Cf. Masud, Messick and Powers, 1996, 18–19.

4 Cf. Royal Decree No. (M/64), 14 Rajab 1395 (23 July 1975): *The Law of the Judiciary*, art. 5. For a description of the jurisdiction areas of the different courts, se Bramsen, 2007, 32–6.

internal forum of conscience, he is – at least in theory – not obliged to follow the ruling. As Muhammad said, according to *hadith*:

> You bring me lawsuits to decide, and perhaps one of you is more skilled in [presenting] his plea than another, and so I judge in his favour according to what I hear. He to whom I give in judgment something that is his brother's right, let him not take it – for I but give him a piece of the Fire. (Al-Bukhari 4:204, quoted in Vogel, 2000, 18)

Siyasa, being the other sphere of Saudi law, is defined by the king. It is a public law or a state law with what Vogel calls macrocosmic concerns. In opposition to microcosmic concerns, this means that it is an outer-directed rule-law, a law in the form of general, abstract rules issued by an external, worldly institution (Vogel, 2000, 26). *Siyasa* is composed of numerous decree-laws or regulations called *nizamat* and contrary to *fiqh* is based on the principle of *al-maslaha al-'amma*, public welfare or utility. Shari'a courts have generally refused to enforce *nizamat*, holding that they only apply the Qur'an and the *sunna*, so various *siyasa* tribunals have been set up during the years (Vogel, 2000, 175f.). These include the Board of Grievances (*Diwan al-Mazalim*) and a range of committees and are the concern of different ministries of the government. *Siyasa* includes laws such as labour relations, commercial papers, traffic rules, social security and government tenders, and is from the official Saudi point of view seen as complementary to *fiqh*, not opposed to it. Thus it renders laws or regulations that cannot be rendered on the basis of the Qur'an and the *sunna*, but are in compliance with Shari'a or in accordance with the provisions of Islam.[5] Furthermore it is based on the principle of *al-maslaha*, public welfare, which is held to be nothing but the purpose of the divine law (*Al-Daawah*, September 2004, 25; June 2005, 27). Formally *fiqh* is applied in the spheres of ritual and personal status or family law, and in public spheres of property, tort, contract, commercial and criminal law, whereas *siyasa* is applied in procedural, administrative, fiscal and constitutional law, and in commercial and criminal law along with *fiqh*.

The Character of the Law

The law of Saudi Arabia is not codified except for the *nizamat*. Within *fiqh*, which will be the area of concern in this chaper, the law is from a Saudi point of view based exclusively on the Qur'an and the *sunna* of Muhammad, as such being inner-directed. *Mufti*s are, as indicated, concerned with facts in the internal forum of conscience, their law being enforceable in the *batin*, whereas *qadi*s are concerned with facts in the external forum of the court, their law being enforceable in the *zahir* (Vogel, 2000, 17). The root principle for obedience to the law is not the

5 Cf. Royal Decree No. (90/A), 27 Sha'ban 1412 (March 1992), article 8, 55 and 67.

authority of the mufti or the *qadi*, but the religiosity and pious conscience of the individual (Vogel, 2000, 14; *al-Daawah*, Aug. 2004, 24). That the law officially is based on the Qur'an and the *sunna* implies that *mufti*s as well as *qadi*s are obliged to practise *ijtihad*, not *taqlid*. The meaning of *ijtihad* is, broadly speaking, the process by which the divine law is found by interpreting the canonical texts, and *taqlid* the adherence to transmitted codes construed by others. A *qadi* should, from the Saudi point of view and idealistically speaking, strive for the divine truth in every case that confronts him, both concerning the law and the judgment, without being bound by past opinions. There is no rule of precedent, *stare decisis*, in Islamic law as interpreted by the Saudis.

Not codified, the law and most of the rules applied today in Saudi Arabia can, however, be found in books written by medieval *'ulama'*. Most Saudi scholars adhere to traditional Hanbali legal positions, since Ibn 'Abd al-Wahhab and his followers, who founded Saudi Arabia as a state with the Saud family, acknowledged the Hanbali school and the *fiqh* books that are most often consulted are *al-Mughni* by Muwaffaq al-Din ibn Qudama (d. 1223), *Kashshaf 'an al-matn al-iqna'* and *Sharh muntaha al-iradat* by Mansur bin Yunus al-Bahuti (d. 1641) (Vogel, 2000, 9, 11, 13). According to a former deputy minister at the Ministry of Justice, Dr Hamad al-Faryan, *qadi*s are in fact required to be Hanbalis in their *fiqh*, but only as a starting point, for the sake of unification of the system. As individuals become more qualified, they may pass beyond the school's views (Vogel, 2000, 126). Acknowledging this and acknowledging that fatwas issued by the Board of Senior *'Ulama'* have a 'near legislative effect' as Vogel has documented (Vogel, 2000, 117; 1996, 262–9), does not change the ideals and claims of Saudi 'ulama' about practising *ijtihad*, however. It is just a matter of properly understanding what *ijtihad* and having a non-codified law mean according to the Saudis.

Having said this it must be emphasized that a growing number of Saudi scholars are in favour of codifying the law. But as Vogel has pointed out, codification should not only be understood in the sense of continental European civil law systems, arousing 'issues of secularization, state monopolization of legislation, demotion of non-positive sources of law like natural law or religious law, the formation of the nation state, centralization of state power, and the invention of new positive legal and constitutional institutions'. Codification, *taqnin*, he clarifies, has other potential meanings; one at the opposite extreme from the civil law model is the preparation of a simple restatement or compilation of laws covering an entire subject-matter, using clear logical organization, careful definitions, consistent terminology, numbered sections, and so forth, but having no binding force, even if it is issued by an official body. If this approach were to be used in Saudi Arabia, the Board of Senior *'Ulama'* or some other authoritative group of scholars could restate rules of *fiqh*, perhaps only as to points of difficulty or to record *'ulama'*s differences of opinion, and then publish the results. Such a code would then carry the weight of an authoritative fatwa, but nothing more (Vogel, 2000, 310f).

Recognizing this, scholars in Saudi Arabia tend to understand codification according to the civil law model, however, as codes of *fiqh* rules made binding on *qadi*s by the king's command (Vogel, 2000, 336). And as to the growing number of proponents of codification, one of them is Abdullah bin Sulayman bin Muni', member of the Board of Senior *'Ulama'*. He has, according to himself, called for a codification for more than 25 years, holding that it would 'reduce differences and would constitute a strong factor in hastening the verdict in judicial proceedings', and 'make rulings much clearer for litigants before going to court'. He does not support a codification of the penal code, however, including *ta'zir* punishments; i.e. punishments which are not clearly defined in the Qur'an and the *sunna* of Muhammad. 'The [penal] law cannot be changed, manipulated or reinterpreted', he states, and *ta'zir* punishments 'should be left to the discretion of the judge' (*Al-sharq al-awsat*, 23 March 2006).[6] Another proponent is Abd al-Muhsin al-'Ubayqan, member of the Shura Council and judiciary consultant for the Ministry of Justice. In an article in *Al-Sharq al-awsat* he states that he has experienced aggressive verbal attacks as a response to his writings concerning the codification of Shari'a. Some considered him 'a tool of neo-imperialism that aims to replace God's laws with secular laws', and others wrote: 'Sharia is strictly denoting to Quran and the Sunnah (sayings of the Prophet Mohammed). The Ijtihads of the jurists are not included as such. How could we ever codify the Quran and Sunnah? They are so great and holy that they could not be codified in legal terms and as articles of law.' In response to this he says:

> what is actually meant by codifying Islamic Jurisprudence is the writing down of its rules, which is the same as issuing Fatwas (religious edicts) deduced from Quran and Sunnah. These rules will be taken from Quran, Sunnah, and Ijmaa (consensus of jurists).
>
> Why would this be religiously prohibited? What is the difference between the books of jurisprudence and the codification of the rules? We know that books of jurisprudence contain rules directly or indirectly taken from Quran and Sunnah to make it easier to teach students and to facilitate legislation. Codification and the books of jurisprudence are the same.
>
> Thanks to Almighty God, our courts apply Sharia law. However, there are several rules and varied opinions as some verses in the Quran and Sunnah can be interpreted in many ways. In addition, the human mind is limited, which may cause conflict between opinions. It is for this reason that codification is necessary. It would contribute to establishing justice. It will facilitate a judge's work and relieve him of conducting difficult research in the books of jurisprudence. We are living in times that require rapid verdicts in accumulating cases. This process will be speeded up by codification. Codification would also be useful to end the serious matter of conflicting verdicts that sometimes occur within the same case

6 'Interview with Saudi Council of Senior Ulama Member Sheik Abdullah Al Manee', see <http://www.aawsat.com/english/news.asp?section=3&id=4254>.

and in the same city, perhaps even in the same court or that are issued by the same judge. (*Al-Sharq al-awsat*, 28 April 2006)[7]

As can be deduced from his article, the main argument of the opponents of codification is that the law of Saudi Arabia is the Shari'a in form of the Qur'an and the *sunna* of Muhammad. It is not the human interpretation of it embedded in *fiqh*. To this al-'Ubayqan remarks that, however that may be, different books of jurisprudence are in actual fact used to teach law students and to facilitate legislation; i.e. *ijtihad* might very well be the ideal, but it is not the practice.[8]

With this general outline of law and legal system in Saudi Arabia we shall turn to the legal epistemology of Saudi Arabian *'ulama'*.

Theological and Legal Theories

The epistemology of Saudi Arabian *'ulama'* is based on the classical and medieval Hanbali teaching. So much so that according to Professor Humaydan al-Humaydan, Department of Law, King Saud University in Riyadh, it is hard to find Saudi books on *usul al-fiqh* that are not editions, commentaries or simply rewritings of the old teaching (interview, 10 May 2005). Looking at a list of recommended books from the Imam Muhammad ibn Saud Islamic University in Riyadh, from where up to 97 per cent of Saudi *qadi*s hold their law degrees, it is also striking that no modern Saudi books on *usul al-fiqh* are mentioned. Only standard *fiqh* works by different prominent scholars of the past from all the four *madhahib*, including the Hanbalis Ibn Qudama (d. 1223), al-Bahuti (d. 1641) and Ibn Qayyim al-Jawziyya (d. 1350).[9]

The conformity of Saudi legal teaching with traditional Hanbali teaching means that Saudi *'ulama'* embrace what is termed the *usul al-fiqh* identified by al-Shafi'i (d. 820). *Usul al-fiqh* signifies the roots or sources of what is held to be the divine law and are the Qur'an, the *sunna* of Muhammad, *ijma'*, consensus, and *qiyas*, analogy. As Hanbalis Saudi *'ulama'* put special emphasis on the vertical aspect of the law, though, stressing the law's transcendence, i.e. that it comes from

7 See <http://www.aawsat.com/english/news.asp?section=2&id=4740>.

8 The same remarks are given by others, mainly non-Saudis, for example Prof. 'Atwa, an Egyptian scholar teaching in Saudi Arabia (see Vogel, 2000, 338–9). Notice that Vogel sees the crucial doctrinal issue regarding the question of codification to the Saudi scholars to be when, or even whether, the ruler has the power to dictate the law his *qadis* apply, implying that the majority of them reject codification. Judging, *qada'*, to them, Vogel points out, 'is nothing but *ijtihad*, the striving of the qadi's conscience to draw near God's own judgment of the case; it is microcosmic law' (Vogel, 2000, 336).

9 The list was given to me by female scholars of Islamic law at the Imam Muhammad ibn Saud University, 14 May 2005. Who wrote it is not clear, though; it was given to me as *the* list of recommended books by the university and the kingdom. I asked several times who wrote it, but my question was not considered important.

Allah. This means that in practice they claim and maintain that the law should be derived exclusively from the Qur'an and the *sunna*. The Qur'an contains in their view the uncreated and real word of Allah, having been transmitted by continuous testimony securing its authenticity, and the *sunna*, i.e. the speech, acts and approvals by Muhammad, is held to be divinely inspired and reflect the will of Allah.[10] Saudi *'ulama'* also claim at the same time, however, that the law is all-encompassing and they employ the principles of *ijma'* and *qiyas*. As the official Saudi discourse reads, Shari'a is 'suitable for all times and places' and 'can accommodate all emergent cases' (*Al-Daawah*, September 2004, 7 and November 2004, 7).[11] But as to *ijma'* it coincides in the use of the Hanbalis with the *sunna* of Muhammad, the only *ijma'* held to be legitimate being the *ijma'* of the *Sahaba* or *salaf*, the first generations of Muslims (Bramsen, 2007, 55–8). Furthermore it is held by the Saudis to be authoritative as based on the Qur'an and the *sunna* as scholars are believed to be unable to agree on anything conflicting with the content of the canonical texts.[12] As to *qiyas* it is from the Hanbali and Saudi point of view a method of interpretation and not a source of law. It is, following amongst others Ibn Taymiyya, a way of excavating the meaning of the canonical texts, nothing more but also nothing less. In the words of Ibn Taymiyya, the Qur'an and the *sunna* encompass all the legal rulings for the acts of men, and '[t]hose who deny this do so only because they do not understand the meanings [*ma'ani*] of the general texts, which are the statements of God and his Messenger …' (Ibn Taymiyya: *Majmu'at Fatawa*, vol. 19, 280, 283).[13]

10 Cf. for example al-Dawish, 2002, vol. 4, 6–12 and vol. 5, 10–11.

11 Many fatwas point to the same, underlining the horizontal aspect of the law. To a question of whether or not Muhammad completed the rules and regulations of Islam, the Permanent Committee for *Ifta'* answers, for example, that 'it was not the Prophet who enacted the rules and regulations of Islam, but it was Allah Himself', and that Allah has 'outlined in detail the Islamic constitution. Allah himself tells us that He has made our faith complete'. The committee then quotes the Qur'an: 'Today have I perfected your religion for you, and have chosen for you Islam as your religion'(3:5), underlining that these words are the words of Allah, wherefore 'no one can ever suggest that the message of Islam is incomplete or that the Islamic law does not respond to any clear human need' (*al-Daawah*, May 2005, 29). And to a question like 'What has religion got to do with fashion, cosmetics or how women dress?' the Permanent Committee for *Ifta'* answers – pointing to the law's all-comprehensiveness – 'The question of dress and fashion is not separate from Allah's law and the way of life He laid down for mankind … It has a direct relationship with the question of Lordship …' (*al-Daawah*, June 2005, 25). The last proclamation points to the dogma of *tawhid* being the cornerstone of every legal argument.

12 Cf. al-Dawish, 2002, vol. 5, 14, 43–4.

13 By 'texts' Ibn Taymiyya means 'the words of the Book and Sunna, whether the expression is of certain [*qati'*] or apparent [*zahir*] significance [*dalala*]'. The text is translated by Vogel in his material for the course 'Comparative law: The Islamic legal system', at Harvard Law School, spring 2005, 529, 531.

Qiyas is as a method of interpretation covered amongst others by the term *ijtihad*. And following the teaching of among others Ibn Taymiyya and Ibn 'Abd al-Wahhab, Saudi scholars explicitly uphold the right to employ it for everyone who is aware of its techniques. Not being unaffected by the scholarly debate about whether or not the gate of *ijtihad* was closed in the 10th century or later, many fatwas are actual responses to this debate, stating verbatim that the gate of *ijtihad* has never been and still is not closed. A short fatwa by the Standing Committee for *Ifta'* reads:

> The gate of *ijtihad* is not closed. It is open for people with knowledge of, belief and insight in the Book of Allah, the Sunna of his Messenger, the speech of the ancestors from among the companions of the Prophet and their followers … (al-Dawish, 2002, vol. 5, 18)

And a longer one reads:

> The gate of *ijtihad* to knowledge of the Shari'a rulings is still open for one who is qualified, i.e. has knowledge about what is necessary for him in the matter in which he practises *ijtihad* from among the Qur'anic verses and hadiths, is capable of comprehending them [the Qur'anic verses and *hadiths*] and making inference based on them in relation to the matter, is cognizant as to what he concludes of hadith and incidences of *ijma'* regarding the matters in which he investigates so as not to transgress the consensus of Muslims in his judgment of them, and is knowledgeable about the Arabic language to the extent that he is able to understand the texts and so that *istidlal* and *istinbat* is possible for him. Nobody has the right to speak of religion according to his own view (*bi-ra'yihi*), or to give fatwas without knowledge. It is mandatory that one consults the legal evidence, *dalil*, first and then the teaching of the people of knowledge, taking their evidences and methods of interpretation in the form of inference (*istidlal*) and logical deduction (*istinbat*) into consideration. Only after so doing can one speak or give a fatwa about what he is convinced of and is satisfied with himself. (al-Dawish, 2002, vol. 5, 17)

Like Ibn Taymiyya, Saudi scholars focus on evidence or proof, *dalil*, when speaking about formulating the divine law, not allowing statements of what the law is about, if these are not the results of individual striving. Striving in order to be valid and sufficient needs not be in the form of *ijtihad mutlaq*, i.e. absolute *ijtihad*, though; not everybody is obliged to formulate the divine law directly on the basis of the Qur'an and the *sunna*. *Ijtihad* should – as also Ibn Taymiyya emphasized – be employed according to one's ability, not more but also not less. As to laymen that have no skills in the religious and legal sciences they are naturally allowed to follow or imitate a religious scholar. As a fatwa issued by the Standing Committee for *Ifta'* reads:

> Legal rulings are based on the texts from the Book of Allah and the Sunna of his Messenger and on what has been added to these in the form of *ijma'* and sound *qiyas*. A Muslim who is incapable of deriving rules from the evidence, *dalil*, is allowed to follow or imitate, *yuqallid*, the one he trusts the most from among the 'ulama'. As Allah says: 'Ask the people who know if you are among those who do not know'. (al-Dawish, 2002, vol. 5, 14)[14]

Blindly imitating is, however, banned. As the fatwa makes clear one has to choose which scholar to follow – all *'ulama'* are, as stated again and again in the Saudi material, liable to make errors, the very reason why *ijtihad* is preferable.[15] Nobody will be punished for choosing wrong, just as the *mujtahid* will not be punished for erring in his interpretation of the law, but everybody will be held responsible. Hence, everybody should be on guard and follow from the teaching of the scholar they choose only 'what complies with the truth, *al-haqq*', rejecting what opposes it, i.e. what is not supported by the canonical texts (al-Dawish, 2002, vol. 5, 27). It is not required that one follows a scholar from a particular *madhhab*, i.e. school of law – as the Standing Committee for *Ifta'* states: 'On the contrary, one has to accept what the legal proof, *al-adilla al-shar'iyya*, requires whether this is in line with the teaching of the adhered to *madhhab* or not' (al-Dawish, 2000, vol. 5, 45).[16] All scholars, no matter which *madhhab* they belong to, can be right as long as they base themselves on the Qur'an and the *sunna*.

Identifying and Defining Shari'a in Practice

As pointed out, Saudi *'ulama'* hold the Qur'an, the *sunna* of Muhammad and *ijma'* to be legitimate and authoritative sources to the divine law. The Qur'an is held to render certain knowledge, since it is the word of Allah, and the *sunna* contained in the *hadith*s likewise when it has been transmitted by a 'large number' of people, all of whom – it is asserted – cannot possibly lie (Zysow, 1984, 16, 14).[17] As to *ijma'* it does not play a big role as it mainly accords a status of certainty to sources already used (Zysow, 1984, 199f, 205; Vogel, 2000, 45f).

But are the sources held to render certain knowledge always clear? What about the Qur'an? Is it in all cases comprehensible for humans? The Qur'an itself states:

---

14 See also vol. 5, pp. 17, 18, 25, 27, 28, 42, 43, 44, 63.

15 Cf. al-Dawish, 2002, vol. 5, 27, 28, 60.

16 See also vol. 5, pp. 21, 44–5, 57, 64.

17 How many transmitters it takes for a report to be *mutawatir* is unascertainable. Zysow notes that to deny *tawatur* as a source of certainty would be to deny that the Qur'an is of certain authenticity. It would also introduce doubt as to our knowledge of history, of geography, and even of our own place in the world: the identity of our parents, the food we may safely enjoy and those that threaten our life. See p. 20.

> He [Allah] it is Who has sent down to thee the Book; in it are verses basic or fundamental (of established meaning); they are the foundation of the Book: others are not of well-established meaning. But those in whose hearts is perversity follow the part thereof that is not of well-established meaning. Seeking discord, and searching for its hidden meanings, but no one knows its true meanings except Allah. And those who are firmly grounded in knowledge say: 'We believe in the Book; the whole of it is from our Lord:' and none will grasp the Message except men of understanding. (3:7)

The translation rendered here is the one found on the internet page of the Saudi Ministry of Islamic Affairs, Endowment, Da'wah and Guidance (<http://quran.al-islam.com>). It is close to Abdullah Yusuf Ali's, but whereas the Saudis translate the Arabic term *mutashabihat* as (verses of) not well-established meaning, Ali and also Muhammad Asad and Ahmad Ali translate it as allegorical.[18] The reason for this could be that the Saudis following Ibn Taymiyya reject that there is allegorical speech in the Qur'an. The Permanent Committee, under the presidency of Ibn Baz, has thus stated:

> Based on the definition of metaphor as defined by Arabic Rhetoricians, it is not correct to say that there are metaphors in the Qur'an, the Sunnah, nor in the Arabic language itself. This is because every phrase in the Qur'an, the Sunnah or in the Arabic language has a real meaning. ('Abdul-'Aziz, 2002, vol. 7, 80f)

The committee refers explicitly to Ibn Taymiyya's *Kitab al-Iman*, Book of Faith. Here Ibn Taymiyya argues that 'the division of languages into literal and figurative usages is a later innovation that was never advocated by the pious ancestors' (Ibn Taymiyya, 1999, 125). Every word in the language, he states, refers to something – language having its origin in Allah – if not to something particular then to an abstract universalia. It is this reference that gives the word its meaning, a meaning that is literal, *haqiqa*, as opposed to figurative, *majaz* (Ibn Taymiyya, 1999, 111–18).[19]

The Qur'anic verse cited is not equivocal, though. The Arabic text translated by the Saudis as 'but no one knows its true meaning except Allah. And those who are firmly grounded in knowledge say: "We believe in the Book …"' has no punctuation mark and reads:

18 The root of the term is *shabaha* which in 6th form means to resemble one another or to be doubtful, obscure.

19 Ibn Taymiyya does not claim that the literal meaning of a word is absolute in the sense that it is conveyed without the aid of a surrounding context. As he states, every meaning of a word is restricted and specified by the semantic context. For a thorough description of Ibn Taymiyya's view of the language and his use and understanding of the term *haqiqa*, see Bramsen, 2003, 31–41.

> wa-ma ya'lamu ta'wilaha illa-llah wa'l-rasikhuna fi al-'ilm yaquluna amanna bihi …

The punctuation mark in the translation is put after *illa-llah*, but it might as well be placed after *wa'l-rasikhuna fi al-'ilm*. The verse would then read: 'But no one knows its hidden or true meaning except Allah and those firmly grounded in knowledge. They [i.e. those firmly grounded in knowledge] say: "We believe in it …"' This would convey a completely different meaning, implying that some scholars are capable of understanding everything in the Qur'an. Various rationalistic-minded Qur'an commentators have held this last interpretation to be right, for example al-Zamakshari (d. 1144),[20] but most commentators have stuck to the first; so also the Saudis. The Saudis do not deny or neglect that the last interpretation could be right, however, which is important to notice. In a fatwa issued by the Permanent Committee for *Ifta'* represented by Ibn Ghudayyan, 'Abd al-Razzaq 'Afifi and Ibn Baz, it is claimed that both interpretations are equally valid, the interpretations referring to different aspects or levels of the Qur'anic meaning (al-Dawish, 2002, vol. 4, 170–5). The first interpretation refers to the inner Qur'anic meaning, *al-batin*, and the second interpretation to the outer Qur'anic meaning, *al-zahir*. Illustrating the case, the Permanent Committee for *Ifta'* points to the Qur'anic meaning of the divine attributes, *istiwa'* and *maji'*, sitting and coming, stating:

> The meaning (*ma'na*) of *al-istiwa'* and *al-maji'* is known by those firmly grounded in knowledge, whereas the modality or how of it (*kayfiyyat dhalik*) is known only by Allah Himself. (al-Dawish, 2002, vol. 4, 174)

In this they follow Ibn Taymiyya who also distinguished between an inner and outer meaning of the Qur'an, and at the end of the fatwa they also refer to him (al-Dawish, 2002, vol. 4, 175).[21]

The Saudi claim that the outer meaning of the Qur'an is within human reach implies that they are not much bothered by the Qur'anic statement about the verses not being well established in meaning, the *mutashabihat*. Like Ibn Taymiyya they seem quite optimistic concerning the human ability to reach an all-comprehensive interpretation of the divine message.[22] It is just a matter of methodology. Clinging to what they believe to be the prescribed methodology of sura 3:7, the Saudis are of the opinion that what is not of well-established meaning should be referred to what is, the meaning of it then becoming evident. The denotation of the term

20 See Peters, 1994, 192–4.

21 For Ibn Taymiyya's position, see Abrahamov 1995, 374.

22 Cf. Zysow 1984, 98.

mutashabihat is, to conclude, from the Saudi perspective, (verses) which are in need of interpretation.[23] The abovementioned fatwa reads:

> The Qur'an is, taken all together, well-established in meaning (*muhkam bi-hadha al-ma'na*), clear (*wadih*) without ambiguity … Thus Allah has said: 'A divine writ [is this], with messages that have been made clear in and by themselves, and have been distinctly spelled out as well – [bestowed upon you] out of the grace of One who is wise, all-aware' [11:1] … And He has said: 'Allah bestows from on high the best of all teachings in the shape of a divine writ fully consistent within itself, repeating each statement [of truth] in manifold forms …' [39:23] (al-Dawish, 2002, vol. 4, 170f)

And concerning the meaning of the verses not well-established in meaning it reads, referring to the scholars firmly grounded in knowledge:

> They are the ones who seek the truth, bringing back the not well-established verses to the well-established verses, the function of the last being to validate the meaning of the first, so that any confusion or obscurity with regard to the first's special and intended meaning is eliminated. (al-Dawish, 2002, vol. 4, 173)

The last point, which is that what is intended by the Qur'anic verses not well-established in meaning is not beyond human reach, is emphasized elsewhere in the same fatwa. It is also found in other fatwas, for example in one by Ibn Baz alone. In this Ibn Baz states that the meaning, *al-ma'na*, of the divine attributes, which is generally held to be not well established, is within the reach of *ahl al-sunna*, the meaning being what Allah intended it to be:

> The soundest is not to leave the matter about the divine attributes to Him who knows the hidden things, i.e. Allah, since He has explained it [the matter] to His servants and made it clear in His noble Book and through His trustworthy Messenger (peace be upon him) …
>
> *Ahl al-Sunna wal-jama'a* knows Allah's intention or purpose, *muradahu*, of His speech … (Ibn Baz, 2002, vol. 3, 55)

Like in the aforementioned fatwa issued by the Permanent Committee for *Ifta'*, a distinction is made between the inner Qur'anic meaning and the outer. Basing himself on the pious ancestors, Ibn Baz explicitly refutes that human beings have access to the modality or the how, *al-kayfiyya*, of the divine attributes (Ibn Baz, 2002, vol. 3, 55–8). He adheres, we could say, to the *bi-la kayf* doctrine.[24]

---

23 Other definitions of the term *mutashabihat* are non-judicial, abrogated, non-essential or changeable and ambiguous or allegorical verses. See Madigan 2004, 6.

24 For a thorough description of this doctrine, see Abrahamov, 1995.

> He [Allah] has not made the modality [of the divine attributes] clear. The knowledge of the how, *al-kayfiyya*, should be left alone, but not the knowledge of the meanings, *al-ma'ani*. (Ibn Baz, 2002, vol. 3, 55)

> The dogma behind this is that Allah has not addressed humans in a way which they do not understand. Why would He have done that? As Ibn Baz announces: 'Allah, exalted in His holiness, is far above that'. (Ibn Baz, 2002, vol. 3, 55)

The methodology that not so well-established parts of the Qur'an, i.e. the *mutashabihat*, should be interpreted in the light of well-established parts, the *muhkamat*, makes the question of which verses belong to which part important. As Daniel Madigan has pointed out it is 'a key hermeneutical tool that makes possible a variety of approaches to the question of the authority of individual verses' (Madigan, 2004, 6). A classical example in the field of theology is if sura 75:22–3: 'Some faces will on that Day [Judgement Day] be bright with happiness, looking up to their Sustainer' takes precedence over sura 6:103: 'No human vision can encompass Him, whereas He encompasses all human vision …', or if it is the other way around. If it is the first – as the Hanbalis have traditionally claimed – the meaning is that Allah will be seen by the believers on Judgement Day, while if it is the second – as claimed by the Jahmis and the Mu'tazilis – Allah will be near the believers on Judgement Day, but He will not be seen by the human eye.[25]

The question of the authority of the individual Qur'anic texts and rulings is just as fundamental when the issue is other systems of classification. As described by Zysow there are several such (Zysow, 1984, 90–8), and all of them are hermeneutical tools functioning as exegetical strategies, employed to give the Qur'an a clear and unambiguous meaning, ruling out apparent discrepancies. Here I shall mention only one, namely that the Qur'anic terms and rulings can be classified as either general or specific. A general term or ruling is referred to as *khass*, and a specific term or ruling as *'amm*. The system is based on well-defined linguistic rules, but classifying the individual entities is still a matter of interpretative choices. Is the ruling in sura 33:33 that Muhammad's wives should stay at home and not mix with men other than their relatives general, applying to all women, or is it specific, applying only to the women mentioned in the sura? The Saudis would claim the first, if asked as will be demonstrated, and others, such as for example Asma Barlas in *Unreading Patriarchal Interpretations of the Qur'an*, as the subtitle of one of her books reads, would claim the last.

Being aware that the emphasis has so far been on the Qur'an as source of the divine law – the Qur'an being '[a] divine writ with messages which have been made clear in and by themselves', 'fully consistent within itself' (sura 11:1 and 39:23) – it is important to note down that Muslim scholars agree that Muhammad's *sunna* and the sayings of his companions may be needed in order to understand the

---

25 For this discussion see for example Ibn Hanbal's *Radd 'ala al-jahmiyya wa'l-zanadiqa* translated in Seale, 1964, 112–13.

meaning of it. The *sunna* and the sayings of the *Sahaba* are from the perspective of the scholars, sources complementing the Qur'an in more than one way. As Ibn 'Uthaymin (d. 2001), who until his death was a prominent member of the Board of Senior *'Ulama'* and the Permanent Committee for *Ifta'* states in a fatwa regarding Islamic rulings:

> The interpretation of a Companion is an acceptable proof, and in terms of the interpretation of the Qur'an, it comes third in the following ranking:
>
> 1. The Qur'an explained by another verse of the Qur'an.
> 2. The Sunnah explaining the Qur'an.
> 3. The sayings of the Companions explaining the Qur'an.[26]

This note points to the fact that although Islamic hermeneutics are governed by interpretative rules and have a fully developed hermeneutical apparatus claiming that the Qur'an renders meaning in and by itself, it is like all hermeneutics empirical, not theoretical. It is governed by rules but have no 'method' if the term 'method' is used in its restricted sense as meaning 'neutral decision procedure' (Rorty, 1999, 14).[27]

Actual Methodology

Illustrating some of the hermeneutic strategies that Saudi *'ulama'* make use of when formulating an all-comprehensive law derived from the Qur'an and the *sunna*, two issues will be taken up. The first is the issue of 'protecting the nobility and chastity of women', which is an important one in Saudi Arabia. Ibn Baz, the former Grand Mufti, has taken it up, for example, in fatwas on women driving cars, women veiling, women shaking hands with non-*mahram* men, women working along with men and women mixing with men in education.[28] As to women driving cars he proclaims, as pointed out in the introduction, that '[t]here is no doubt that such is not allowed'. His argument for so doing is in part: women driving leads to many evils and negative consequences. Included among these is her mixing with men without her being on her guard. It also leads to evil sins due to which such an action is forbidden. The Pure Law forbids those acts that lead to forbidden acts and considers those means to be forbidden also. Allah has ordered the wives of the Prophet, peace be upon him, and the women of the believers to remain in their houses, to wear *hijab* and not to display their adornments to non-*mahram* males as that leads to promiscuity that overruns a society. Allah has stated, 'Stay in your houses and do not display yourselves like that

26 'Abdul-'Aziz, 2002, vol. 8, 199.

27 See also Fish, 2005, 645–6, 650.

28 For the fatwas and a thorough analysis of them, see Bramsen, 2007, 86–99.

of the times of ignorance and offer prayer perfectly and give Zakat and obey Allah and His Messenger' (33:33).

Allah also says, 'O Prophet! Tell your wives and your daughters and the women of the believers to draw their cloaks (veils) all over their bodies. That will be better, that they should be known (as free respectable women) so as not to be annoyed' (33:59).

Yet another verse states:

> Tell the believing women to lower their gaze and protect their private parts and not to show off their adornments except only that which is apparent and to draw their veils over necks and bosoms and not to reveal their adornments except to their husbands, their fathers, their husbands' fathers, their sons, their husbands' sons, their brothers or their brothers' sons, or their sisters' sons, or their women or the (female) slaves, or old male servants who lack vigor, or small children who have no sense of the shame of sex. And let them not stamp their feet so as to reveal what they hide of their adornment. And beg Allah to forgive you all, O believers, that you may be successful. (24:31)

The Prophet, peace be upon him, himself said: 'A man is never alone with a woman except that Satan is the third'[29] (Ibn Baz, 2002, 351f).

The strategy he makes use of is to argue that women driving cars 'leads to many evils', especially 'her mixing with men', which is – according to him – forbidden. Thus the Qur'an 33:33 reads: 'Stay in your houses …', and Muhammad has stated: 'A man is never alone with a women except that Satan is the third'. Within the Qur'anic context 33:33 applies to Muhammad's wives specifically, the verse preceding it reading: 'O wives of the Prophet! …', but Ibn Baz takes it to be of a general character, its ruling being applicable to all women. Thus it should from his point of view be interpreted in the light of the Qur'an 33:59 and 24:31 in which no distinction is made in terms of ruling between Muhammad's wives and the believing women. Implicitly Ibn Baz employs *qiyas* as a hermeneutic principle, arguing that the *'illa*, i.e. the effective cause behind the order that Muhammad's wives (all believing women) should stay in their houses, is that women mixing with non-*mahram* men leads to evil and is forbidden. This being the case, women driving cars is also forbidden.

As to women veiling and shaking hands with non-*mahram* men, Ibn Baz's hermeneutic strategy is the same. Thus he declares based on a Qur'anic verse that within the Qur'an deals specifically with Muhammad's wives:

> it is incumbent upon [a] Muslim woman to veil herself from every man who is not a Mahram for her and not to shake hands with them, according to the Words of Allah, Most High: 'And [as for the Prophet's wives,] whenever you ask them for anything that you need, ask them from behind a screen: this will deepen the

29 Recorded by Ahmad ibn Hanbal and al-Tirmidhi.

> purity of your hearts and theirs' (33:53). This Verse includes the wives of the Prophet, peace be upon him, and others, as [it] is fundamental regarding the address of the Lawgiver, because Allah sent His Messenger, peace be upon him, to all mankind, so it is not permissible to particularize one of them with a legal ruling without a specific evidence which proves that, and because the reason for Allah's mentioning it – which is to purify the hearts of all – and every Muslim, male and female is in need of it. ('Abdul-'Aziz, 2002, vol. 5, 200f)

His argument is, as seen, that verse 33:53 is not only about how to approach Muhammad's wives, but about how to approach women in general. As to women shaking hands with non-*mahram* men, he also makes use of another hermeneutic strategy, declaring:

> Likewise, women shaking hands with men other than their Mahrams is not permissible due to the causes of Fitnah it includes, and it has been confirmed from the Prophet, peace be upon him, that he said: 'Verily, I do not shake hands with women'. And 'Aishah, may Allah be pleased with her, said: 'By Allah, the hand of the Messenger of Allah, peace be upon him, never touched the hand of a woman. He did not accept the pledge of allegiance from women except in words.' ('Abdul-'Aziz, 2002, vol. 5, 203)

Here he argues on the basis of Muhammad's *sunna*, reasoning that what Muhammad did not do, although it would have been natural, male Muslims should not do either. Thus Muhammad's behaviour conforms to and reflects nothing but the divine law.

As to Ibn Baz's opinion on women working along with men and on mixing in education, it is found in two fatwas. In the first Ibn Baz states:

> It is a known fact that when a woman enters the fields of men, it causes mixing between the two and also seclusion of men with women. These things are very dangerous for them due to what they could lead to, and more importantly, it is contradictory to the texts of the Shari'a that order the woman to stay in her house and to perform the duties which are specific to her and which require the characteristics that Allah has created her with. The duties keep her far away from mixing with men. (Husain, 2004, 234)

He then cites the Qur'anic verses already quoted above, 33:33–4, 33:59, 24:30–1, 33:53, and some *hadith*s stating that 'the Messenger of Allah, peace be upon him, forbade a man from being in seclusion with a strange woman at any cost.' Muhammad is reported to have said for example 'the third of them is the Shaytan' (Husain, 2004, 237). All are, Ibn Baz proclaims, 'clear cut regarding the obligation to stay far away from mixing, which will lead to evil, the destruction of the family and the ruining of society' (Husain, 2004, 238). In the second fatwa, Ibn Baz proclaims, arguing against the permissibility of mixing in education:

> Islamic Law does not call for mixing (of men and women) … In fact, it forbids it with a strict forbiddance, as Allah says: 'And stay in your houses, and do not display yourselves like that of the times of ignorance' (33:33). ('Abdul-'Aziz, 2002, vol. 5, 147)

He then cites the Qur'an 33:59 and 24:31 and refers to some *hadith*s including the one according to which Muhammad said: 'I have left behind me no greater trial and temptation (*fitna*) to men than women' ('Abdul-'Aziz, 2002, vol. 5, 149). And after making it clear that it is obligatory for all Muslim women to be veiled in public, he argues on the basis of what he believes to be historical facts, proclaiming:

> The women at the time of the Prophet, peace be upon him, did not indulge in mixing with men – neither in the mosque, nor in the markets … In fact, the women in the mosque of the Prophet, peace be upon him, used to pray behind the men in the rows farthest from the men and he, peace be upon him, used to say: 'The best rows for the women are those in the rear and the worst of them those in the front, while the best rows for men are those in the front and the worst are those in the rear' – in order to warn them against trial and temptation of the last rows of the men by being in the first rows of the women …
>
> So how can it be accepted … to call for mixing and to claim that Islam calls for it and that the precincts of the university are like the mosque and that the times of study are like the times of prayer, when it is well known that the difference is great and that the distance between them is great, to anyone who understands what Allah has commanded and what He has forbidden, and knows the Wisdom if Him, Most Glorified in legislating for His creatures and the rulings and judgements which He has expounded in His Grand Book for men and women …
>
> [S]tudying time is long in comparison to prayer time and … the acquisition of knowledge from female teacher in a private place is safer for all and farther for them (i.e. the women) from the causes of trial and temptation. It also makes the men safer from being tempted by them, because the seclusion of young men from young women in educational areas – as well as being safer for them from temptation – is more likely to result in them attaining the aim of their studies and being able to concentrate on them and pay good attention to their professors and acquire knowledge from them. This is far from the distraction of looking at young women and thinking about them and the exchange of poisonous glances and words which incite immorality. ('Abdul-'Aziz, 2002, vol. 5, 152–5)

Ibn Baz's point is – it seems – that women's permission to pray behind men in a mosque does not mean that mixing between the sexes in educational institutions is allowed. On the contrary; Muhammad stated that '[t]he best rows for the women are those in the rear and the worst of them those in the front …', which indicates that mixing between the sexes is undesirable if not prohibited. The last is, to use the Islamic legal terminology, the *'illa* behind Muhammad's saying. On this Ibn 'Uthaymin agrees in a fatwa entitled 'The Danger of Mixing of the Sexes in Schools and Universities' stating after quoting the just-cited *hadith*:

> This is because the first row is close to the men and the last row is far from them. So if maintaining a distance between men and women and segregating them is desirable even in places of worship such as prayer, in which the worshipper feels that he is standing before his Lord, far removed from matters relating to the life of this world, them how will it be if the mixing is in schools? Is not maintaining a distance and abandoning mixing even more necessary? Verily, the mixing of men with women is a great trial and temptation (*Fitnah*) … ('Abdul-'Aziz, 2002, vol. 5, 156)

He clearly makes use of *qiyas*, and holds the *'illa* behind Muhammad's saying to be – like that of Ibn Baz – that mixing between the sexes is undesirable if not prohibited. To demonstrate the correctness of this he cites a *hadith* according to which Umm Salamah said: 'The Messenger of Allah, peace be upon him, would make the Taslim and the women would stand up when he finished his Taslim and he would remain in his place for a while before standing … We consider – and Allah knows best – that this was so that the women could leave before the men encountered them' ('Abdul-'Aziz, 2002, vol. 5, 157). Furthermore he cites a *hadith* according to which Abu Sa'id al-Khudri said:

> A woman came to the Messenger of Allah, peace be upon him, and said: 'O Messenger of Allah! The men have taken your sayings (Hadith), so make for us a day on which we may come to you, so that you teach us what Allah has taught you'. He said: 'Gather on such-and-such a day in such-and-such place'. So they gathered and the Messenger of Allah, peace be upon him, came to them and he taught them what Allah had taught him. ('Abdul-'Aziz, 2002, vol. 5, 157–8)

And based on this he states: 'It is clear that women should be taught separately in a specially designated place, since he [the Prophet] did not say to them: "Why do you not attend with the men?"' ('Abdul-'Aziz, 2002, vol. 5, 158).

The other issue to be taken up in order to demonstrate some of the hermeneutic strategies that Saudi *'ulama'* make use of when formulating an all-comprehensive law derived from the Qur'an and the *sunna*, is the issue of when to perform the Hajj ritual of *ramy al-jamarat*, i.e. stoning the three pillars in Mina outside Mecca. The issue has recently been raised since 363 people were killed during its performance in January 2006. According to the newspapers some 600,000 pilgrims were squeezed in at the Jamarat ramp on 12 January, where they were striving to throw stones at the three pillars representing the devil in the afternoon. A dozen of them stumbled over baggage, tripping others behind them, which caused a deadly stampede (*Associated Press*, 13 January 2006). The site of Jamarat has now been reconstructed in order to host the growing masses of pilgrims and in 2007 the ritual passed off without causing any deaths. If the problem is solved permanently remains to be seen, though.

Regarding the question of when to stone, a fatwa issued by Ibn Baz reads, simplifying the subject a little:

> stoning the pillars … is only after midday and it does not suffice to do it before that. This is because the Prophet, peace be upon him, stoned during the days of At-Tashreeq after midday and he said: 'Take your Hajj rites from me' (Muslim no. 1297). Thus, it is obligatory on the Muslims to follow him in that – may the best of blessings and peace be upon him from His Lord. ('Abdul-'Aziz, 2002, vol. 4, 246)[30]

As seen he argues on the basis of the *sunna* of Muhammad that the stoning should take place after midday, not before it. Other scholars in Saudi Arabia are of the same opinion, however inappropriate it might be. Answering a man requesting if it is permissible for him to stone in the morning because of travel arrangements, Ibn 'Uthaymin has stated, for example:

> [t]here is an opinion that permits stoning before midday, but it is not correct. The correct view is that stoning before midday is not permissible. This is because the Prophet, peace be upon him, said: 'Take your Hajj rites from me' (Muslim no. 1297). And he, peace be upon him, did not stone until after midday. If a person says: 'The Prophet's stoning after midday is simply his action and mere action does not prove obligation', we say that this is correct. It was merely an action and mere action does not prove obligation. In reference to it merely being action, this is because the Prophet, peace be upon him, did not command that the stoning be done after midday nor did he prohibit stoning before midday. In reference to the action not being a proof of obligation, yes, it does not prove obligation, because obligation can only be by a command to do an action or a prohibition of leaving it off. However, we say that this action is accompanied by something that proves its obligation. This point of view is based on the fact that the Messenger, peace be upon him, delayed stoning until the sun declined past midday, that proving the obligation. For if the stoning before midday had been permissible, the Prophet, peace be upon him, would have done it, because it is easier on the servants and more accommodating. And the Prophet, peace be upon him, was not given the choice between two matters except that he chose the easiest of them, as long as it was not a sin. Thus, the fact that he did not choose the easiest thing here, which is stoning before midday, proves that it is a sin. The second point which proves that this action is for obligation, is the fact that the Messenger, peace be upon him, stoned immediately after midday before praying the Zuhr prayer. So, it is as if he was waiting for the midday with anticipation

30 See also pp. 241–3, 248.

> to make haste with the stoning. For this reason, he delayed the Zuhr prayer even though it is better to pray it in the first part of its time. All of this was so that he could stone after midday. ('Abdul-'Aziz, 2002, vol. 4, 244f)[31]

Ibn 'Uthaymin's argument is the same as Ibn Baz's, namely that Muhammad stoned after midday and his *sunna* should be followed. He does acknowledge, however, that Muhammad's action in itself does not necessarily and always prove obligation, but he states that in this case it does. Thus Muhammad chose to stone after midday, although it would have been easier to stone before, the heat considered, and 'the Prophet … was not given the choice between two matters, except that he chose the easiest of them, as long as it was not a sin'. Furthermore, Ibn 'Uthaymin argues, Muhammad stoned immediately after midday before praying the Zuhr prayer 'as if he was waiting for the midday with anticipation to make haste with the stoning'. He delayed the Zuhr prayer, 'even though it is better to pray it in the first part of its time'. This is for Ibn 'Uthaymin a clear indication of stoning before midday being impermissible.

The strong opinion of Ibn 'Uthaymin and also Ibn Baz regardless, it is important to notice that Ibn 'Uthaymin acknowledges that there is another opinion on the question of when to stone during the Hajj. He just does not believe it is correct. It is important because after the tragedy in 2006 the Saudi Minister of the Interior, Prince Nayif, called on Saudi scholars to issue fatwas allowing pilgrims to carry out the stoning before noon to spread the crowds, emphasizing that '[t]he number of pilgrims is only going to increase in the coming years, so there must be solutions so that this sort of incident is not repeated' (*Associated Press*, 13 January 2006). As far as I know (spring 2006) no fatwas have come out yet, but according to *AFP* Abdul Aziz Al al-Shaykh has admitted that the hours for the stoning ritual could be extended as part of the efforts to avoid deadly stampedes in the future. Referring to the above mentioned fatwa referred to by Ibn 'Uthaymin according to which stoning before midday is allowed, he thus declared: 'No one can say that those who apply this fatwa are doing something wrong, since they are following the opinion of a venerable scholar' (*AFP*, 17 January 2006). His declaration points to the Saudi acknowledgment that *fiqh* and fatwas are mere interpretations of Allah's law, not necessarily being identical with it, since the Qur'an and the *sunna* do not provide clear answers to all questions. One *ijtihad* can be as good as the other – or rather, one *ijtihad* cannot overrule another – so long as it is based on the canonical texts and is the result of a 'venerable' scholar's utmost efforts.

Closing Remarks

As demonstrated, Saudi *'ulama'* by and large are quite optimistic when it comes to identifying and defining an all-comprehensive law derived from the Qur'an and the

31 See also pp. 243–4.

sunna of Muhammad. The theological and legal theories underlying this optimism are that the Qur'an contains no allegorical speech and renders certain knowledge about the divine law. The same goes for the *sunna* when it has been transmitted by a 'large number' of people. *Ijma'* does not play a big role as a source of law, but when it does it accords a status of certainty according to theory due to the fact that scholars are unable to agree on anything conflicting with the content of the canonical texts. As to *qiyas* it is not seen as a source of law, but as a method of interpretation referring to the extension of a Qur'anic or sunnaic rule established for one legal situation to another where the two situations have the same effective or legal cause called '*illa*. In theory *qiyas* does not render certain knowledge, only probable, since its legitimacy is not based explicitly on the Qur'an and the *sunna*, but in practice it can be employed with confidence. Thus, *qiyas* is, when all comes to all according to the Saudis, nothing but a way of excavating the meaning of the canonical texts.

That the Saudis are optimistic regarding identification and definition of an all-comprehensive law based on the canonical texts does not mean, however, that they do not distinguish between Shari'a as the divine law as such and the human understanding of it. Hence a distinction is clearly played out on the theoretical level by differentiating between an inner and outer meaning of the canonical texts, and on the practical level by claiming the right and obligation to practice *ijtihad* in all cases. The latter points to the law of Saudi Arabia not being codified, a fact that may not have a big impact on the way the Qur'an and the *sunna* are interpreted in daily life, as most Saudi scholars are traditionalists, basing themselves on medieval Hanbali *fiqh* manuals, but at least in principle gives Shari'a a degree of flexibility and practicability. These characteristics, however vague, will be lost once Shari'a is codified.

As to the two issues taken up in the last part of the chapter, the fatwas treating them illustrate how Saudi scholars identify and define Shari'a in practice. Ibn Baz and Ibn 'Uthaymin, who are taken to represent Saudi *'ulama'*, do base themselves explicitly on the Qur'an and the *sunna* of Muhammad complying with Saudi legal theory, but in order to formulate an all-comprehensive law derived from these sources they make extensive use of *qiyas*. This makes their formulation probable, according to their own theory, not certain, but this they do not make a show of. As scholars they are, after all, also not obliged to specify the basis of their opinion and mention their method of reasoning to non-specialists requesting a fatwa.

Chapter 12
Speaking in His Name? Gender, Language and Religion in the Arab Media

Dima Dabbous-Sensenig

> 'My sisters wear it so I will also have to and because our teacher tells us the Koran says it's the duty of the girl to wear it. I will have to. God will punish me if I don't.'
>
> (Sara, Lebanese, 12 years old, *The Daily Star*, 16 November 2006)

> 'The war on Islam is being waged nowadays through the woman.'
>
> (Male caller, *Al-Shari'a wa'l- Hayat*, 17 May 1998)

Introduction

Since the 1998 Turkish ban of the headscarf, the subsequent ban of religious symbols in France in 2004, and the more recent controversy in the UK involving a Muslim schoolteacher who was sacked for refusing to remove her face covering (*niqab*), the Muslim dress code (headscarfing or what is commonly referred to as wearing the *hijab* or headscarf) continues to make headlines in both Western and Arab media. On the one hand, it epitomizes for many Westerners the 'clash of civilizations' that exists between the secular West and the Muslim East while, on the other, its rejection by the West is perceived by most Arabs and/or Muslims as evidence of the West's blatantly discriminatory attitude towards Islam and Muslims in general. More importantly, the rift between East and West as far as the debate on *hijab* is concerned is centred on diametrically opposed views about the meaning and purpose of the headscarf. For most Muslims, the covering is ordained by God, a religious obligation (*fard*) for women, and therefore is beyond discussion. For Western societies, the *hijab* is a marker of political difference and lack of integration among Muslim immigrants in the host societies, and a symbol of (threatening) Islamic fundamentalist resurgence that is increasingly feared, especially since 9/11 (Cowell, 2006).

Although the *hijab* controversy is, among other things, an interesting case study of how religion can be instrumentalized for political reasons by all sides involved, the present chapter will deal exclusively with the theological perspectives and Shari'a discourses on the headscarf as reproduced by the Arab media following the bans in Turkey and in France. More specifically, it will examine Shari'a discourse(s) on the headscarf in a major Arab satellite channel, *Al Jazeera,* on one of its best-known and longest-running talk shows (also its only religious talk show) which has dedicated several episodes to the issue of the Muslim covering: *Al-Shari'a wa'l-Hayat*.[1] This examination of *mediated* Shari'a discourses is important for the following reasons:

- In the past few years, there has been a sharp increase in the amount of religious programming on Arab satellite stations (Basma, 2006). These religious programmes (and stations), reportedly the most popular alongside the music video channels, need to be examined in order to see which particular discourses on Shari'a and the Muslim dress code are being privileged (at the expense of others) and broadcast to tens of millions of Arab/Muslim viewers both in the Arab world and in the diaspora.
- Moreover, the present study seeks to analyse the extent to which a power struggle (for definition and control) is at the heart of the various existing Shari'a discourses on the headscarf. It will do so by examining the theological and linguistic aspects of the dominant/recurrent discourse on the headscarf as promoted by *Al-Shari'a wa'l-Hayat* and the means through which (carefully selected) guests seek to establish their particular theological views (concerning the 'appropriate' Muslim covering) as being more authoritative, more 'competent' (Hymes quoted in Deacon et al., 1999, 148), and more 'commonsensical' than all other competing discourses on the headscarf, even when they are not. Indeed, as will be argued later on, not only are these televised Shari'a discourses on the headscarf commonsensical and hegemonic, they are *also* authoritarian and present serious methodological flaws in their theological arguments, and yet are treated as authoritative and given prominence over competing discourses on the headscarf in the religious talk show studied.
- Finally, considering that the study deals with Shari'a discourses in televised talk shows, it will also examine the extent to which the talk show genre itself is particularly suited for the promotion of authoritarian religious discourses that seek to close off debate on problematic theological issues, specifically those relating to women.

Conceptual Framework: Is Shari'a Discourse a Special Type of Discourse?

Shari'a, or 'God's way' in Arabic, interpreted most commonly and narrowly to mean Islamic law, has, from a historic-jurisprudential perspective, been derived

1 The study is based on written transcripts of *Al-Shari'a w'al-Hayat* talk show episodes which are freely available on *Al Jazeera's* website. Between 4 January 1998 and 11 February 2007, there was a total of three episodes entirely or mostly dedicated to the Muslim dress code. These episodes had single guests and were broadcast on 17 May 1998 and 21 December 2003 with Shaykh Qaradawi and 5 September 1999 with Shaykh Qabisi.

by Muslim jurists primarily from Muslim scriptures (Qur'an and *sunna*), and secondarily from these scholars' interpretation of Scriptures and consensus whenever disagreements arose (*ijma'*). This body of professionals (jurists or *fuqaha'*) specialized in the construction and articulation of Shari'a, a discursive endeavour at the heart of which lies the issue of power (to construct religious reality, that is).

Considering that the present study deals with the critical analysis of those Shari'a discourse(s) on the Muslim dress code which are privileged on *Al Jazeera*, a conceptual framework and a methodology which can both account for the interplay between authority/power to define (Muslim/religious) reality on the one hand, and the expression of this power through language and the talk show format on the other, are needed. In media and cultural studies, at least two approaches or conceptual frameworks can be drawn upon for such a study, precisely because of their ability to account for the relationship between power and language/meaning, namely Gramsci's concept of hegemony and Foucault's approach to discourse, knowledge and power (for a discussion of the merits and limits of each, see Macdonald, 2003).

With regard to the present analysis, I find Gramsci's concept of hegemony particularly useful in its ability both to identify the process through which particular social constructions of reality become hegemonic, and are naturalized and turned into 'common sense', on the one hand, and its recognition that ideologies and common sense are not forever stable, even if they appear to be so, and can be contested (for details, see Dabbous-Sensenig, 2006, 62–3). Methodologically speaking, critical discourse analysis, or CDA, allows for the study of the role played by language in legitimizing/naturalizing certain social relations, because it assumes that relations of power are embedded in language structures (i.e. in lexical and grammatical choice, modality, metaphor, and so on), and is concerned with the ways in which texts 'encode relations of power, authority and status' (Deacon et al., 1999, 149).

However, I would argue that Shari'a discourse, as a particular type of discourse that has sprung out of a specific set of doctrinal/jurisprudential rules and methodologies throughout Islamic history, is not entirely comparable to other 'worldly' discourses available or circulating in a society at a particular point in time, and which are normally the subject, in critical studies, of what is referred to as discourse analysis (e.g. teachers' educational discourse, doctors' medical discourse, lawyers' legal discourse, politicians' policy discourse, etc.).

The term 'discourse', most scholars in the field agree, refers on a basic level to language use in social life. More important than the production of meaning in this language use, however, are the different social practices and relations – 'the specific frameworks of thinking' (Macdonald, 2003, 1) – which are constructed in the process, '*from* and *in* the interests of a particular point of view' (Deacon et al., 1998, 146, emphasis mine).

Generally, 'recipients tend to accept beliefs, knowledge, and opinions (unless they are inconsistent with their personal beliefs and experiences) through discourse from what they see as authoritative, trustworthy, or credible sources, such as scholars, experts, professionals, or reliable media' (Nesler et al. in van Dijk, 2001, 357). Moreover, not only are these sources competent 'linguistically', they also demonstrate mastery of 'contextual competence', i.e. mastery of the different contexts, circumstances and settings in which the linguistic competence is deployed (Hymes quoted in Deacon et al., 1999, 148).

Though Shari'a scholars can be said to belong generally to this category of 'experts', what distinguishes their discursive practices from that of the above-mentioned authoritative sources is the fact that their contextual competence goes beyond simply knowing the 'when', 'what', 'where', 'with whom' and 'how' when speaking (Hymes quoted in Deacon et al., 1999, 148). For these Muslim jurists, contextual competence is a question of authoritative legitimacy that is primarily rooted in religious texts, and of their ability to understand, interpret and relay 'Divine Will' based on scriptures. In other words, their discursive practice is not just about interpreting some legal texts using legal 'jargon' or discourse that may or may not successfully 'persuade' recipients, the way lawyers and legal scholars do, but consists mostly of purporting to express God's will through the formulation of Shari'a laws. Their social power and authoritativeness is, in that respect, derived from their ability to ground their discourse in texts that are at one and the same time legal *and* religious/sacred, to mediate and interpret the Word of God, and not just speak for themselves (or their interest group) the way other (non-religious) social actors do when interacting with others. It is indeed this dual nature of Shari'a discourse (speaking *about* God on the one hand and speaking *for* God on the other), I would argue, which places it apart from (or is it above?) strictly 'legal discourse', for instance, or from other types of 'worldly' discourses normally subjected to critical analysis using conceptual frameworks such as Gramsci's or Foucault's and CDA as the concomitant methodology. In other words, Shari'a discourse, as one category of religious discourse, is premised on belief in the Islamic religion, and a set of ensuing basic religious dogmas, the most important of which is the belief that the Qur'an is the *infallible*, *recorded* Word of God. Unless this belief and these dogmas are taken into account in the critical discourse analysis, a deconstruction of power relations as embedded in language, of the kind applied to other social discourses, will fail to fully account for the *extent* of this power and control of Shari'a discourse on the community of believers. This distinctive aspect of Muslim religious discourse, as we will see later, largely explains why some specific, key grammatical constructions, phrases and words are particularly favoured by the two main guests in the episodes studied in order to 'convince' their audience why their definition of the Muslim dress code is the only valid one, and why other definitions are to be dismissed because (supposedly) they are not from God.

For the above-mentioned reasons, an additional conceptual framework which can help in understanding and deconstructing Shari'a discourse in general, and analysing the inter-textual, almost organic relationship between (religious) power/ authority and meaning in an Arab/ Muslim context, is needed.

The Authoritative vs. Authoritarian: A New Conceptual Framework for the Critical Analysis of Shari'a Discourse

In the previous section, I argued that Shari'a discourse is not only a specific type of discourse with its own set of rules for making meaning, but, more importantly, it is a type of discourse which, by its very nature, purports to speak for God, to relay Divine Will. While the first, general aspect of this discourse is common to other types of discourses usually subjected to critical discourse analysis, the second aspect, I would argue, is unique to religious discourse in general. With regard to the Muslim Shari'a discourse in particular, not only is the analyst faced with the challenge of understanding the specific rules of this discourse, she also has to be aware of the dogmatic, 'Divine' aspect of this discourse, i.e. that the legal rulings uttered by the Muslim jurist or scholar express Divine Will. In this respect, I find the work of Islamic legal expert Khaled Abou el-Fadl highly pertinent for the present critical analysis of Shari'a discourse. It should be noted that Abou el-Fadl writes from outside the field of CDA and is exclusively interested in the ethical dimension of the Muslim legal system – an interest, which, in my opinion, is also highly problematic because of its idealization of Muslim jurists, especially early ones. However, I find his legal and ethical critique of contemporary Shari'a discourses very insightful. Being personally unaware of any existing methodologies especially developed for the critical analysis of religious–legal discourses in general and Shari'a discourses in particular, the present study is an attempt to come up with such a methodology by grafting Abou el-Fadl's critique of Shari'a discourses onto the existing methods of linguistic analysis as developed within the field of CDA, in order to more fully account for the interplay between language/meaning and power in social relations.

In his recent study entitled *Between God and the Sultan: A History of Islamic Law*, Knut Vikör points out that 'the central factor was that the law was common and had the proper authority, not necessarily what it said' (2005, 30). Indeed, Abou el-Fadl's ethical concerns are centred on what constitutes 'proper authority' in Islamic juristic discourse, which leads him to eventually distinguish the 'authoritarian' from the 'authoritative' in this type of discourse.

As Abou el-Fadl explains, in Islam, God, God's book, and the Prophet (through his *sunna*) are 'the only authorities that count' (el-Fadl, 2001, 23). However, very early on in Islamic history, Muslims were increasingly confronted with and debated the implications and meaning of the sovereignty of God and his Word, realizing that 'the real challenge [was] *discerning* what God actually said' (in el-Fadl, 2001, 24, emphasis mine). Moreover, he argues, the idea of submission to God (literally *islam*) actually 'raises a host of challenging issues', the first of which relates 'to the ability to verify that a specific command is in fact coming, directly or indirectly, from God or God's Prophet' (el-Fadl, 2001, 25). This first issue, he argues, is a matter of historical verification and authentication ('competence') of the source or text in which these commands are preserved (el-Fadl, 2001, 25). The second issue concerns the 'determination' of the meaning of the specific command, by seeking to understand both the meaning of the sacred texts and how this meaning should be applied or put into use. The third issue is one of 'agency' – of who 'bears the responsibility for ascertaining and resolving the issues of competence and determination' (el-Fadl, 2001, 25). Although these questions (related to competence, determination and agency) engaged Muslim theologians (and political leadership) for centuries, with no unified orthodox position able to emerge. Jurists (our concern in this study) argued that they were more qualified than anyone else to understand God's instructions, 'and so, effectively …stood as a *medium* between God and human beings' (el-Fadl, 2001, 27, emphasis mine). Indeed, as far as Islamic law is concerned, 'it is the juristic paradigms and categories that dominate all normative discourses on Islamic orthodoxy' (el-Fadl, 2001, 31), with the juristic concept of authority being 'a firmly embedded part of Islamic dogma'.[2]

Particularly relevant for the type of analysis undertaken here is Abou El-Fadl's conceptual distinction between the 'authoritative' and 'authoritarian' in Islamic juristic discourse. To start with, the Qur'an and *sunna* do not speak for themselves, but speak through agents who are human beings. Five 'contingencies' or requirements, he says, which are largely found in the classical juristic tradition (though not exactly the way he classifies them), should be fulfilled or demonstrated by these 'special agents' (jurists or *fuqaha'* in this case) in order for them to be considered authoritative by 'common agents' or lay people. These requirements are: honesty, diligence, comprehensiveness, reasonableness and self-restraint (el-Fadl, 2001, 54–5). Briefly, this means, first, that a 'special agent' should not pretend to know what he/she does not know (honesty). Second, he/she should exert a reasonable amount of effort to understand and derive God's instructions, and this effort should be commensurable with the importance of the law derived and the extent to which it will affect others (diligence). Third, for purposes of comprehensiveness, he/she should exhaust all possible avenues for knowing God's instructions, and not decide to neglect investigating 'certain lines of evidence (instructions) for the sake of convenience or comfort' (el-Fadl, 2001, 55), or personal interest, I would add. Fourth, special agents, when choosing and defending their (divine) instructions, should act respectfully and with reasonableness towards both the established communities of meaning and interpretation on the one hand, and towards the text itself on the other (i.e. scriptures). In other words, they should seek to 'make sense' when addressing communities of interpretation, but without 'over-interpreting', or imposing on the text the instructions that 'the reader would have liked to see' (el-Fadl, 2001, 55). As we will see later on, it is this specific problem (of imposing on the text interpretations that they or their constituencies would like to see), compounded by a lack of reasonableness and diligence, which characterizes dominant

2 See Abou el-Fadl's justification concerning this focus, and why he neglects, by comparison, socio-cultural practices and social constructions of authority, or the Qur'anic conception of authority (2001, 31–4).

Shari'a discourses on *hijab* on the talk shows studied, and which makes them authoritarian rather than authoritative. Fifth, authoritative special agents exhibit a certain degree of humility when representing the will of God. The Islamic phrase 'God knows best' (*Allahu a'alam*) forcefully represents this contingency, acting as 'an epistemological and moral disclaimer', a reminder (for both speaker and recipient) that the jurist is exercising self-restraint, and careful not to usurp the role of God, or at least is avoiding the appearance of doing so.

Finally, 'special agents' (jurists or *fuqaha'* in the case of Islam) are authoritative not because they are in a formal position of authority, but because of the '*social perception* of being authorities on the set of instructions (indicators) that point to God's Way (or *Shari'a*)' (el-Fadl, 2001, 53, emphasis mine).

Having established in detail what constitutes the 'authoritative' in Islamic orthodoxy, Abou el-Fadl goes on to define the 'authoritarian':

> [the] authoritarian tendencies co-opt the Islamic juristic tradition but essentially misrepresent and corrupt it in an unabashed result-oriented process. In other words, it is these authoritarian tendencies that *invoke and utilize the persuasive effect of the juristic tradition, and, thus, force it into the realm of the relevant and authoritative.* (el-Fadl, 2001, 31, emphasis mine)

In sum, by starting off with the basic premise that the Islamic juristic tradition is relevant and culturally/theologically authoritative (a position which precisely explains its strong persuasive power over Muslim recipients or 'the community of interpretation'), by tracing the conceptual and methodological components which make this religious tradition authoritative, and then by proceeding to distinguish the 'authoritative' from the 'authoritarian' in Islamic juristic/religious discourse, Abou el-Fadl offers a conceptual model which is suitable for understanding and eventually decoding the nature of Shari'a discourses on *hijab* in Arab talk shows. Indeed, Abou El-Fadl's model for deconstructing Shari'a discourse allows analysts to account as much as possible for the issue of power (and abuse thereof) in the construction of (religious) meaning, mostly at the micro- or linguistic level of the critical discourse analysis.

As we will see later on, the nature of the scriptural foundation of the Muslim dress code for women strongly brings to the fore all five contingencies mentioned by Abou el-Fadl when considering what God (and the Prophet) actually said and meant regarding the headscarf. On an initial broader level, Abou el-Fadl's model can be used in order to identify all types of existing Shari'a discourses on a particular issue and to assess their authoritativeness (i.e. the extent to which their internal methodology and intellectual process for deriving Shari'a rulings conform to accepted frameworks of thought). This phase or level can also provide the socio-historical context of the various discourses on the headscarf to be analysed in the media. The next step in this macro-level analysis (which can only be partially dealt with here for lack of space) involves the study of the organizational/hierarchical structure of the individual episodes, in order to identify the various interpretations/

topics reproduced and to see which of them is being privileged in these episodes and how. Then, a micro-level analysis of the grammatical, syntactical and rhetorical strategies used by individual speakers will allow the analyst to identify the linguistic means through which any given position is seeking to appear authoritative (even when it is not, from a classical juristic perspective). Both at the macro and micro levels of analysis, Abou el-Fadl's conceptual distinction between the 'authoritative' and 'authoritarian' in Muslim legal discourse can be applied in order to expose two important aspects of Shari'a discourses on the headscarf on *Al Jazeera* talk shows: first, how such discourses attempt to *appear* authoritative when instead they are authoritarian; second, how they are promoted at the expense of competing discourses in order to reproduce social dominance or hegemony with regard to headscarfing through discursive practices– an endeavour which lies at the heart of any critical discourse analysis (van Dijk, 2001, 353–4; Fairclough, 1995).

Scriptures and the Problem of Defining the Muslim Dress Code

Since any critical discourse analysis of the media requires studying 'text in context' (Titscher et al., 2000, 27), I will first briefly review Shari'a discourses on the headscarf which exist in Arab and Muslim societies, and which provide answers to the following two-pronged question: is headscarfing a religious obligation for Muslim women to start with, and if yes, how should a Muslim woman cover herself? This initial wider contextual part, by providing a range of existing interpretations on the same issue, will allow for the subsequent linguistic analysis of the Shari'a discourses on the headscarf which are promulgated in or privileged by the *Al Jazeera* episodes studied.

Most importantly for the present study, a detailed, micro-level analysis of key phrases related to the nature of the headscarf will be conducted in order to identify those syntactic/grammatical and lexical features of the texts which are used in order to legitimize some interpretations/definitions of the headscarf at the expense of other definitions (van Dijk, 1988; Halliday, 1985).

The Muslim religious dress code for women is derived from and referred to in just two Qur'anic verses: verse 31 of sura 24 (The Light); and verse 59 of sura 33 (The Clans).[3] In 24:31, the Prophet Mohammad is commanded by God to:

> Say to the believing women that they should lower their gaze and guard their modesty; that they should not display their ornaments [*zina*] except what appear thereof, that they should draw their headscarfs [*khumur*, sing. *khimar*] over their

3 The following translation is largely based on Youssef Ali's. I have introduced modifications by removing those words in the translation which are not available in the Arabic original text (e.g. beauty), and added in bracket a transliteration of the Arabic original words whose meaning is ambiguous or not fixed (e.g. *zina*, *khimar*, etc.).

> bosoms [*juyub*, sing. *jayb*], and not display their ornaments [*zina*] except to their husbands, their fathers, their husbands' fathers …

In 33:59, God says to the Prophet:

> O Prophet! Tell thy wives and daughters, and the believing women, that they should cast (draw close) their garments [*jalabib*, sing. *jilbab*] over their persons. That is most convenient, that they should be known and not molested. And God is Oft-Forgiving, Most Merciful.

A close reading of these verses, and of the widely varied classical and modern juristic literature which seeks to explain them, shows the extent to which the Qur'anic foundation (i.e. 24:31 and 33:59) for defining the Muslim dress code is ambiguous, to say the least, and is based on vague and disputed terms (*zina, khimar*, *jayb* and *jilbab*) which are nonetheless key in determining what parts of her body a Muslim woman should cover (for a detailed review of the problematic nature of the headscarf-related Qur'anic verses see Dabbous-Sensenig, 2006). Consequently, various orthodox (male) commentators (classical or contemporary), depending on the school of jurisprudence to which they belonged, have offered different justifications for what a Muslim woman can display in public (i.e. 'apparent ornaments'). Whereas for some a Muslim woman can only show the face, hands and feet – a type of covering commonly referred to as the *hijab* (Zeydan, 2004; Qaradawi, 2001), others went as far as arguing that the entire female body is 'a shameful part' and therefore needed to be covered fully with what is often referred to as the *niqab* or *burku'* (Hajjaji-Jarrah, 2003; Hamid Abu Zeid, 2000). In short, the Muslim dress code for women is inevitably varied as a result of the *different interpretations* made by religious scholars, depending largely on which established Muslim schools of jurisprudence they belong to.

More recently, a number of progressive and less restrictive interpretations of the headscarf-related verses have emerged, which not only questioned the established view, that wearing the headscarf is a basic tenet of Islam (as often argued by orthodox theologians), but also that covering the hair is an obligation for Muslim women. Indeed, these interpretations openly acknowledge the lack of any direct Qur'anic reference to covering the hair or face, and some argue for entirely new definitions of dress-related terms based on modern theories and methodologies for interpreting the Qur'an (Hajjaji-Jarrah, 2003; Shahrour, 1990).[4] For Shahrour and other non-orthodox exegetes, for instance, a Muslim woman is not defying the

4 In my opinion, the Muslim progressive position on the *hijab* is legitimate in so far as it seeks to question the theological soundness of the dominant interpretation of the Muslim dress code for women. However, it fails, both methodologically and theologically, to provide a convincing counter-argument.

word of God if her hair (to say nothing of her face) remains uncovered (Shahrour, 1990; Khalaf Allah, 1977).

Macro-level Analysis: Identifying the Headscarf-related Topics

Topics or themes are global, overall meaning structures of a text consisting of an hierarchically arranged set of macro-propositions or sentences. They can be expressed as a summary, and they define the gist of a text, thus playing a central role in the overall understanding of a text (van Dijk, 1988, 34–5). Though the hierarchical organization of topics in a text, or the ordering of the topical information (what information is presented first, and what information last) may have ideological implications (van Dijk, 1991, 121), in this section, and for the limited purpose of the present study, I will identify exclusively the three sub-topics related to defining the nature of the Muslim female dress code which are mentioned in one way or another in the television episodes studied. Once these sub-topics are identified, I will proceed with the more detailed micro or linguistic analysis of key phrases related to these sub-topics in order to analyse the extent to which religious discourse on the headscarf is both hegemonic *and* authoritarian.

Hijab *as Covering Everything except Face and Hands*

When asked by host Mansur to define the *hijab*, Qaradawi, in a long exposé, asserted that the 'matter (concerning the *hijab*) is clear', i.e. that a woman should cover everything except the face and hands. In support of this definition of the proper Muslim dress code, he repeatedly backed this assertion by mentioning the two headscarf-related verses (24:31 and 33:59), the consensus of the *umma*, the names of several transmitters of *hadith*, and Islamic tradition and history.

In the 2003 episode, asked to respond to the French intention to ban religious symbols, Qaradawi asserted that the covering was not a symbol, that 'God ordained it' (*al-khimar alladhi amara Allah ta'ala bihi*) and that the Muslim woman 'is required by God to cover up' (*al-muslima mutalaba min Allah bi-annaha tastur*). Once again, he cited the evidence behind such assertions: verse 31 in sura 24 ('that they should draw their headscarves over their bosoms'). He also added: 'this is a Qur'anic command and not even one of those things in which there was need for *ijtihad* [independent reasoning] by jurists. It is an order: "Say to the believing women and men [*sic*] that they should cast their garments over their persons".'

In the 1999 episode with Shaykh al-Qabisi, the guest put forth views identical to Qaradawi's concerning the *hijab* and *niqab* (he promoted the first and rejected the latter), explaining that 'you can wear whatever you want', as long as 'the common denominator is showing the face and hands only'. As he explained, 'there are clear orders in Islam concerning the *hijab*', 'the *hijab* is a settled matter' (*amr mafrugh minhu*), is one of the 'basic [or fixed] tenets of Islam' (*thawabit al-islam*), and is 'a command from God' and 'a command from the Prophet' (*awamir min Allah, awamir min al-rasul*). For Qabisi, any woman who does not follow these orders is a 'sinner with regards to the text' (*athima bi'l-nass*). Similarly, Qaradawi asserted in his 2003 episode that any woman who does not cover her head is disobeying God's orders (*tukhalif amr Allah*), though this does not make her a disbeliever.

Headscarf as Modest Clothing

Whereas both guests endorsed and elaborated on the Shari'a definition of Muslim dress code as an obligation to cover the body except for the face and hands (and received a number of calls from viewers who supported their views), two other definitions were also included in these episodes, though mostly via the presenter's own questions or the various interventions by callers who disagreed with the guests' definition of the headscarf. To start with, the position that the Muslim dress code is not a basic tenet of Islam but mostly a question of modesty and decency in clothing (without necessarily having to cover the hair) was represented in two episodes on the headscarf with Qaradawi. In his introduction to the 1998 episode, host Ahmad Mansur reflected on the (then) hot issue of the headscarf which had 'acquired a strong political dimension' especially in France and Turkey in previous weeks, and asked Shaykh Qaradawi whether headscarfing meant covering the hair or not, mentioning the position of some who argue that the Qur'an is open to interpretation and that it does not have any clear reference to hair.

In the same episode, a male caller complained about the show's 'obsession' with the headscarf at the expense of more urgent issues facing Muslims (e.g. the rise of fundamentalism in Islamic societies). In the 2003 episode, another male caller was similarly 'saddened' by the obsessive focus on headscarf, complaining that 'we in Egypt were not disbelievers when our women did not don the *hijab* from the 1940s through the 1980s', whereas a female caller from Germany complained that parents are forcing their young daughters to wear the *hijab*. Finally, in the 1999 episode with Qabisi, a male caller attacked Qabisi's endorsement of the *hijab* at length (19 lines in the transcript), arguing, based on his readings about the four schools of jurisprudence and early women in Islam, that the issue of *hijab* is not an Islamic but a socio-economic one and a feature of Arab nationalism, and quoted in support if his position Shaykh Tantawi of Al-Azhar University in Egypt who said that the head covering is not mandatory (*laysa fardan*).

Niqab *or the Full Covering*

The third definition of the Muslim dress code (i.e. *niqab* or total covering of face and body) was also a sub-topic of the Muslim covering, and was discussed in two of the three episodes of *Al-Shari'a wa'l-Hayat* (it was not an issue in the 2003 episode dedicated to the ban of the hair covering in France). In the 1998 episode, a male caller from Palestine wanted Qaradawi's opinion concerning the *niqab* which is being favoured by some in his hometown, prompting a rather long response from Qaradawi who explained that covering the face is not mandatory (*laysa bi-*

wajib), citing some early jurists' and his own interpretation of verse 31 of sura 24. In the 1999 episode Shaykh Qabisi, the guest on his own brought up the issue of *niqab*, rejecting it and arguing that it is unwarranted in Islam (*laysa wajiban* and *laysa fardan itlaqan*). He did so as part of his more elaborate discussion of the Muslim dress code and of intermingling between the sexes, and as an example to support his argument that the concept of *haram* (meaning 'sinful' or 'forbidden'), which is one of the five categories or values of Shari'a, is being abused by some legal scholars who attempt to control Muslim men and women with 'the whip of *haram*'.[5] Later on, several callers, male and female, expressed their dismay at Qabisi's 'very, very, very permissive rulings' (*fi ba'd al-ahkam mutasamih kathiran kathiran kathiran*) and his narrow or 'specific view' of Islam (*manzurak al-khass 'an al-islam*) as far as his definition of the Muslim dress code is concerned. One of them also attacked what he called Qaradawi's 'erroneous' views on the Muslim dress code which echo Qabisi's, and went as far as doubting Qabisi's credentials as a Muslim scholar. In support of his attack on Qabisi's views, one male caller narrated a report by Aisha (one of the Prophet's wives and a main transmitter of *hadith*) justifying covering the face and cited, as additional evidence, verse 59 from the Clans (sura 33). In the same episode, another pro-*niqab* female caller cited the same verse 59 ('they should cast their garments over their persons that they should be known [or recognized] and not molested') also in order to prove Qabisi wrong and justify the *niqab*. According to this caller 'the recognition of a woman is based on her face; that is why the face should be covered'. She then attacked Egyptian feminist Nawal Saadawi who, on another show on *Al Jazeera*, referred to the *hijab* as 'a prison', and concluded by saying that 'if my *hijab* and staying at home is a prison … then it is a very welcome one'.

So far, the summary of the three sub-topics related to the description of the Muslim dress code which appeared on the three episodes of *Al-Shari'a wa'l-Hayat* studied shows that the televised Shari'a discourses on the headscarf do, initially, include all three positions on the Muslim dress code (i.e. covering the hair, covering the face, and not covering the hair or face). These positions also exist in Arab/Muslim societies, knowing that of all three positions, the most dominant or 'commonsensical' in these societies is the one promoting the *hijab*. As such, this talk show seems, so far, to live up to *Al Jazeera*'s motto of representing 'the opinion and the other opinion' (and in this case, the third opinion). However, the mere identification of existing topics and themes related to the Muslim dress code does not reflect the value given to one position over another by the producers of the shows studied, as the following linguistic analysis at the micro level will demonstrate.

5 The five categorizations of all human actions according to Shari'a are: that which is mandatory (*fard* or *wajib*), encouraged (*mustahabb* or *mandub*), permissible (*halal* or *mubah*), discouraged (*makruh*) and forbidden (*haram* or *mahzur*).

The Headscarf in *Al-Shari'a wa'l-Hayat*: a Local/Linguistic Analysis

In the 1998 episode with Qaradawi, although all three discourses on the headscarf were mentioned, Qaradawi's responses and attitude towards the two other extreme positions (*niqab* or covering the face on the one hand and not covering the hair on the other) were significantly different. When asked by the host to comment on the anti-covering view, Qaradawi dismissed entirely, without engaging them theologically, the opinions of those who argue that headscarfing does not necessarily mean covering the hair, because they are not 'legitimate' interpreters of the Qur'an, but 'people off the street' (*nas min ard al-tariq*). In the 2003 episode, he reacted negatively towards a male caller who defended the anti-covering position, and attacked his character by saying he was 'confused' (*mushawwash*), was influenced by 'imperialist cultures' and ideas, that the *khimar* is 'an order from God' voluntarily followed by Muslim women, and that 'in reality he [i.e. the caller] understands nothing about Islam'. Qaradawi concluded his dismissal by personalizing the debate and openly denigrating the caller, saying he 'is sorry that his name [i.e. the caller's] is Muhammad Amin, and that unfortunately he has nothing of the qualities of that name' (the first name is also the Prophet's, and the second means 'trustworthy' in Arabic).

By contrast, in the 1998 episode, in response to a viewer's question about *niqab* (face covering) and whether it is obligatory, Qaradawi asserted it is not. Interestingly, unlike the utter dismissal and personal attack that characterized his response to the caller who defended the anti-covering position, his response towards supporters of the *niqab* (as another extreme interpretation of the Muslim dress code) was both tolerant and theological. He thus went through the intellectual effort of proving why the *niqab* is not a religious obligation, citing what he said earlier concerning the Qur'anic phrase 'and what appear thereof' from verse 31 in sura 24. He also cited Ibn Hazm, a religious authority from the early period of Islam, who said that the fact that God said 'they should draw their headscarves over their bosoms' is proof that covering the face is not an obligation or else God would have said: 'they should draw their headscarves over their faces'. Qaradawi then went on to give further evidence that the *niqab* is not an obligation by saying that several *ahadith* (reports about the Prophet) prove that the norm for women during the times of the prophet was not to cover the face, and that three schools of Islamic jurisprudence (he does not name them) and the majority of Muslim scholars (*jumhur*) agree that the face need not be covered. He concluded by requesting that 'countries where the face is covered like Saudi Arabia … be left alone', because the real battle is not whether the face should be covered or not, but that the woman at least cover her body except the face and hands (for more details concerning the 'battle' metaphor and the double standards applied by both guests and host when dealing with competing positions on the headscarf see Dabbous-Sensenig, 2006, 75–6).

The above brief analysis of lexical framing of the sub-topics on the headscarf, by looking at the 'surrounding features of the reporting discourse' and how these features 'can influence the way in which *represented discourse* is interpreted' (Fairclough, 1995, 83), reveals the disparate attitude exhibited in the show vis-à-vis competing definitions of the headscarf: while both competing definitions were rejected, the guests (mostly Qaradawi in this case) respected and tolerated the *niqab* and disregarded as illegitimate the progressive anti-covering position, regardless of the theological soundness of these interpretations. In the following section, in order to further understand the role of language in constructing (a specific) religious reality and promoting one interpretation at the expense of other equally legitimate (or illegitimate) interpretations, I will analyze the representational or ideational function of the text, i.e. how events and the people and objects involved in them are *represented* in the linguistic choices made in simple sentences or clauses (Halliday, 1985). This linguistic study will be, whenever possible, complemented by an intertextual analysis in order to bring out the various levels of meaning embedded in simple grammatical constructions and to connect linguistic strategies with the wider socio-religious context, using Abou el-Fadl's model for categorizing and deconstructing Shari'a discourses.

According to a functionalist approach to grammar, speakers - when representing something that happens – have the choice between various process types: they can represent it as an Action or an Event, as a Process or a State, and so on (Halliday, 1985). These choices or transformations, more importantly, *depending on the wider socio-cultural context*, may not be purely linguistic. When such choices are made *systematically*, they reflect the *intention* of the speaker and may be ideologically motivated. Two such particular, recurrent transformations are worth noting about Qaradawi's and Qabisi's discussion of the Muslim dress code in the episodes dedicated to the headscarf. In response to the central question put forth by the host about the proper definition of the *hijab*, both Qabisi and Qaradawi (independently) gave categorical answers leaving no room for doubt concerning the Qur'anic injunction that Muslim women should cover everything except the face and hands. For both men, the *hijab* ' is clear in the Qur'an' (*hadha wadih fi'l-Qur'an*), 'the Qur'an is clear' on that issue (*al-Qur'an wadih*), 'God ordained it' (*amara Allah bihi*), 'The Qur'an is the one who commands it' (*al-Qur'an huwa alladhi amara*), 'it is a Qur'anic command' (*hadha amr qur'ani*), it is a 'command from God' (*awamir min Allah*), or a 'command from the Prophet' (*awamir min al-rasul*). By looking at the syntactical nature of these (similar) key clauses recurrently used by both guests in order to justify the *hijab* or covering the body except for the face and hands, one notices first that they are all 'extreme case formulations' that offer a categorical position on or definition of the Muslim dress code. More importantly, all these formulations work to suggest that 'a phenomenon is 'in the object' or objective rather than a product of the interaction or the circumstances', or as in this specific case, of human interpretation (Pomerantz quoted in Tileaga, 2005, 612). To be specific, these extreme case formulations are constructed grammatically in such a way as to turn a *mental process of sensing*, cognition or interpretation (that can alternatively and more accurately be expressed as 'I believe/think the Qur'an to be clear on this') into a state expressed as a *relational process of being* (e.g. 'the

Qur'an *is* clear', the *hijab* '*is* clear in the Qur'an', or 'is a command from God') or Action expressed as *material process of doing* ('The Qur'an *commands* it' or 'God ordained it') (Halliday, 1985). As Halliday explains,

> in a clause of mental process, there is always one participant who is human. [...] the significant feature of such a participant is that of being 'endowed with consciousness.' Expressed in grammatical terms, the participant who is engaged in the mental process is one that is referred to pronominally as *he* or *she*, not as *it*. (1985, 108)

Precisely what is common and striking about all the above formulations used recurrently and emphatically by Qaradawi and Qabisi is that what is clearly a *mental process* which would have 'foregrounded agency, causality and responsibility' (i.e. the human act of interpretation) has been worded differently, in ways that effectively backgrounded them (Fairclough, 1995, 113). These formulations, while highly common and 'commonsensical' from an Islamic point of view, grammatically emphasize the 'clarity' of the Qur'anic verses and the Divine command with regard to the headscarf, and thus effectively elide the issue of human agency or responsibility, and the fact that religious scholars have to engage actively in interpreting the Qur'an. This is especially problematic and 'unethical' from a classical juristic perspective, considering that both Qabisi and Qaradawi are clearly dealing with not-so clear Qur'anic verses – verses whose very ambiguity resulted, historically, in varied and often contradictory interpretations by Muslim scholars and jurists.

For both Qaradawi and Qabisi, the process that links God, his word as contained in the Qur'an, and the understanding (through *fiqh*) of that word by religious scholars has simply evaporated. The Qur'an is, through language, turned into an agent. It now speaks for itself.

The Authoritarian Disguised as Authoritative: Speaking in the Name of God

In order to better understand the nature of Shari'a discourse embedded in the very simple clauses studied above, and the rhetorical and ideological significance of such formulations (at the micro level), I would like to draw on Abou el-Fadl's insightful distinction between authoritative and authoritarian discourses in Islam, introduced earlier. The basic premise for such a distinction, it should be recalled, is that there exists a religious juristic discourse which, early on, established itself as being authoritative, and is both acceptable and convincing to the recipients or community of believers (i.e. Muslim viewers in this case). By contrast, one can identify an antithetical type of religious discourse which is not authoritative (for reasons that will be explained shortly), yet claims or appears to be so nonetheless, mostly through language.

Islamic classical jurisprudence developed as an attempt to understand God's law (or Shari'a) through *fiqh* (or the process of jurisprudence by which the rules of Islamic law are derived). Whereas Shari'a as God's Will was considered to be an immutable ideal and an abstraction, *fiqh* as 'the product of the human attempt to understand God's will' was seen as imperfect and evolving (el-Fadl, 2001, 32). This conceptual distinction is reflected in the well known Arabic Muslim phrase '*wa-Allahu a'lam*' (and God knows best) with which (ethical) classical jurists, exemplifying the authoritative in Islamic jurisprudence, concluded their legal discussions or *tafsir* (scriptural exegesis). More than a rhetorical device, this invocation was a marker of humility and an attempt to show self-reflexivity and honesty (i.e. by foregrounding human agency in understanding Scripture) on the part of those jurists who were involved in the struggle to understand the word of God (*ijtihad*). It was also 'an articulation of the very epistemological foundation of Islamic law' which ultimately justified 'the practice of juristic diversity and the culture of juristic disputation' (el-Fadl, 2001, 32). Authoritarianism or intellectual despotism, by contrast, is marked by a refusal to base Shari'a arguments on evidence from the Qur'an and *sunna*, but more importantly, on an unwillingness 'to defer to the *structure of constraints* produced by the juristic interpretive communities' (el-Fadl, 2001, 96–7, emphasis mine). It refers to the acts of those who use the '*symbolism* of the juristic interpretive community in support of their arguments', *but not the methods of this community,* regardless of whether they believe in this interpretive community or not (el-Fadl, 2001, 97).

To start with, the symbolism Abou el-Fadl refers to is linguistic in nature, and often includes single terms or phrases such as *halal* (allowed) or *haram* (prohibited), *hadith sahih* or *mawdu'* (authentic or forged Prophetic reports), *ijma'* (consensus), and so on. As such, it suffices for someone claiming or wishing to appear authoritative to invoke (or utter) elements of this symbolism which characterizes the classical juristic interpretive community, and in doing so to 'co-opt the authority of juristic culture to the actor's service' (el-Fadl, 2001, 97). In the case of the Muslim dress code, for instance:

> If one says 'A Muslim woman ought to wear the hijab (cover her whole body except her face and hands)', or if one says it is immodest for a woman to reveal her hair, this assertion necessarily relies not just on some inevitable meaning of some text, but relies on the meaning constructed by the juristic interpretive community. This assertion about modesty relies on reference to a set of Qur'anic verses, Prophetic traditions, reports about the Companions and most importantly, the cumulative juristic efforts in selecting, preserving and giving meaning to these textual sources'. (el-Fadl, 2001, 98)

Seen from this perspective, the *formal* linguistic properties of both Qaradawi's and Qabisi's discourse on the headscarf seem to be an attempt to co-opt the authority of the classical juristic culture, to put it into their own 'service' and to simultaneously and definitively 'close' the meaning of the ambiguous headscarf-related verses in the Qur'an . To start with, the two guests' extreme case formulations, more than mere grammatical choices, are both rhetorical and ideological. They are rhetorical because they are calculated to win over (Muslim/Arab) audiences with the interpretations favoured by Qaradawi or Qabisi (Gill and Whedbee, 1997, 167). For the (Muslim) community of meaning and interpretation, if a divine rule or command is clear in the Qur'an (i.e. the Qur'anic definition of the headscarf in this case), then there is no need to debate it or interpret it. These extreme case formulations, moreover, are reinforced by the repeated use of the symbols and formal discursive properties and 'buzzwords' of the classical interpretive community. Thus, both Qaradawi and Qabisi recurrently cite specific verses from the Qur'an and (selective) Prophetic reports (*ahadith*) as evidence of an asserted 'correct' definition of the headscarf, in addition to using theologically powerful classical jurisprudential concepts expressed through words such as *ijma'* and *jumhur*, and invoking the authoritativeness of famed classical jurists, philosophers and imams who founded one of the four major schools of Sunni jurisprudence, *simply by listing their names*. These words, verses, names and phrases function as 'stock devices' that are 'rhetorically self-sufficient' or 'clinching' (Augustinos et al., 2005, 320) in that they draw, without further need for any logical evidence, on theological (and powerful) concepts and symbols pertaining to classical Shari'a discourses. Indeed, according to Abou el-Fadl, what characterizes most contemporary Shari'a discourses, whether Wahhabi or not, is the 'certainty of results, incontrovertibility of conclusions, and the unequivocalness of the asserted determinations' (el-Fadl, 2001, 174). These formulations are, furthermore, ideological because they seek to support, through religious consensus and public consent, existing socio-religious power relations. They attempt to 'close' the polysemic meaning of Islamic Scriptures and de-legitimize any alternative, non-misogynist interpretation or 'rethinking' of religious tradition, especially with regard to one of the last bastions of Muslim/Arab values, i.e. the female body.

Far from the methodologies of classical Islamic jurisprudence which sustained an ethos of pluralism and diversity, whereby jurists would engage in theological disputations and freely admit that 'there are disagreements over the appropriateness of one rule or another' (el-Fadl, 2001, 47), the privileged Shari'a discourse on the headscarf on *Al-Shari'a wa'l-Hayat* attempts definitively to close the text when the text itself is clearly open to interpretation, and by so doing 'violates the contingency of reasonableness as well as other contingencies' (el-Fadl, 2001, 56). With regard to the theologically disputed definition of the headscarf, both Qaradawi and Qabisi defined the Muslim dress code unequivocally and dishonestly, insisting that 'God says so' when in reality they were saying so. As such, they violated the principles or contingencies that, according to Abou el-Fadl, make special agents authoritative – honesty, diligence, comprehensiveness and reasonableness – and thus prove to be authoritarian rather than authoritative. Authoritarianism, Abou el-Fadl writes, 'refers to a hermeneutic methodology that usurps and subjugates the mechanisms of producing meaning from a text to a highly subjective and selective reading' (el-Fadl, 2001, 5).' 'It is the act of 'locking' or captivating the Will of the

Divine, or the will of the text, into a specific determination, and then presenting this determination as inevitable, final, and conclusive' (el-Fadl, 2001, 93). Commenting on Islamic law in general, Abou el-Fadl notes how 'it has become common in the modern age to use the authority of the Author (God) to justify the despotism of the reader … In essence, the reader becomes God' (el-Fadl, 2001, 265).

Is the Talk Show Format Suitable for Authoritarian *Shari'a* Discourse?

A critical discourse analysis of Shari'a discourses on the headscarf on *Al Jazeera*'s longest-running talk show has shown that, whereas the headscarf-related episodes do represent the three existing positions on the Muslim dress code, only one position is given prominence: the position which is already dominant and commonsensical in Arab Muslim societies, namely wearing the *hijab* or covering the body except for the face and hands. It has also shown how the language used was meant to reflect and consolidate existing power relations in society, and how it is sought to discredit and delegitimize counter-hegemonic ideas (e.g. the anti-headscarfing position in this case). It is worth noting here that CDA cannot go further in explaining the nature of Shari'a discourses, because, as I argued earlier, such discourses are religious and premised on the dogmatic belief that a jurist can actually relay the word of God.

I have already explained how authoritarian discourse in Islamic jurisprudence draws on a plethora of classical juristic concepts and jargon while it simultaneous disregards the internally consistent methodologies of interpretation of the juristic community which have generated these concepts. This 'gap' or disconnect between the Shari'a concepts invoked by authoritarian jurists in order to support specific interpretations of Islamic scriptures on the one hand, and the jurisprudential methodologies used to generate them on the other, is evident in the talk show episodes studied. This gap, indeed, can be detected within a single episode (e.g. the 1998 episode with Qaradawi), or when two or more episodes are considered in their totality (e.g. the 1999 episode with Qabisi vs. the 1998 episode with Qaradawi). To start with, in the 1998 episode, in order to convince his audience that the definition of the headscarf (as covering everything except the face and hands) is beyond doubt, Qaradawi repeatedly based his Shari'a discourse on two basic and powerful phrases/concepts drawn from the symbolic culture of the classical juristic community: 'The Qur'an is clear' and '*ijma'*'. In other words, to make his case, he drew *simultaneously* on the conclusive evidence of the text or Scripture *and* the role of the consensus of jurists in deciding upon the meaning of the text when the text is not clear or ambiguous. These two phrases or concepts, it goes without saying, are mutually exclusive from a rational classical juristic perspective. The existence of one precludes the other.

Ironically, Qaradawi questioned elsewhere the value of religious consensus (or *ijma'*) which he so frequently praised and invoked in his talk show episodes in order to justify the *hijab* (see printed interview in *Laha* magazine, 25 November

2006). Shaykh Qabisi went further in the 1999 episode, totally rejecting *ijma'* as a legitimate legal concept in Islamic jurisprudence: 'I said, I still do, and will still say that consensus (*ijma'*) is a myth. Whoever talks to you about 'consensus' is a liar.' Conveniently, both scholars did not denounce *ijma'* in the context of discussing their own understanding of the highly controversial and political issue of the headscarf, but in the context of discussing other, less problematic Shari'a issues. For instance, Qabisi attacked the juristic concept of *ijma'* only when he wanted to argue against the *niqab* and therefore to justify his own definition of the Muslim dress code, i.e. the *hijab*.

In another instance, in the same 1999 episode, the comments made by two callers served further to expose the internal contradiction in Qaradawi's and Qabisi's Shari'a discourse on the headscarf. Here, both Qaradawi's and Qabisi's definition of the Muslim dress code (which they had asserted was 'clear' in the Qur'an or Islam) were challenged by ultra-conservative male and female callers who were dissatisfied with these scholars' 'permissive' views on headscarfing. Interestingly, these callers justified the total covering of the face and body (or *niqab*) as being *clearly scriptural*, and cited as evidence those same ambiguous verses that Qaradawi cited in his 1998 episode in order to legitimize his opposing views on the Muslim dress code (i.e. 24:31 and 33:59). At some point in the 1999 episode with Qabisi, the host, Maher Abdallah, had to intervene and end the callers' vehement attack on the integrity of Qabisi's Shari'a discourse on various issues (the role of women in society, whether women were of lesser value and capacity than men, etc.) by reminding viewers that interpretation has always been part and parcel of Islamic jurisprudence, that each interpretation is bound by its socio-historical context and that a religious scholar should never collapse his words with those of God: 'he should not say "this is God's opinion". He must say, "this is the view of Islam the way I understand it".' Towards the end of the same episode, Qabisi, in response to the pro-*niqab* female caller who rejected his definition of the headscarf, conceded that he does not put forth 'opinions', and that instead he chooses the existing interpretation of the headscarf which he finds most fit for his generation, and asked the caller similarly to choose whichever interpretation convinces her the most. Shortly thereafter, also in response to a male caller who rejected his progressive and egalitarian views on women when interpreting the Qur'anic verse which has been historically interpreted to justify the superiority of men over women (*al-rijal qawwamun ala al-nisa'*, Qur. 4:34), Qabisi again brought up the issue of diversity or disagreement in legal tradition (*khilaf*), saying that dissent or disagreement in the Islamic juristic tradition is a blessing (*ni'ma*). Ironically, when later again he was asked about the headscarf, he seemed to have forgotten the 'blessing' of having dissent in Islamic juristic discourse, and insisted, once again, that 'it is a basic tenet in Islam that only the face and hands of the woman be shown'.

These few examples illustrate Abou el-Fadl's critique of authoritarian Shari'a discourse, by showing how this discourse is characterized by selectivity and methodological inconsistencies and is focused on results (and conclusive interpretations), at the expense of adopting a sound methodology consistent with that of the (authoritative), more pluralist, honest, and rigorous classical juristic tradition. Jørgen Nielsen, in a similar vein, critiques modern Muslim thinkers for being 'much quicker to condemn each other's views than they were in the past', when what mattered most and was considered to be legitimate or illegitimate was not the end result or 'the specific solutions or legal rulings'. 'The key', he adds, 'was rather whether they [i.e. the legal rulings] had been arrived at within the generally accepted framework of thought, using the generally accepted intellectual tools' (see Nielsen in this volume).

For the purposes of the present study on Shari'a discourses in the media, what is more important than understanding the nature of existing hegemonic *and* authoritarian Shari'a discourses is understanding the role of the media in promoting and legitimizing these discourses. The above-mentioned examples, which expose the inherent contradictions in these Shari'a discourses, also serve to question the suitability of the live talk show format for the promotion of dominant and hegemonic Shari'a discourses when such discourses are also authoritarian.

Concluding Comments

Although *Al-Shari'a wa'l-Hayat* seems to be intended structurally, thematically and discursively to 'close' the meaning of religious texts by privileging specific scriptural interpretations which appear to be legitimate, authoritative and commonsensical, it is difficult to say that it is fully achieving its goal. By the mere fact of discussing Shari'a within the (live) talk show format, by having to host different speakers to fill up airtime, and by accepting (for entertainment or commercial purposes) live phone calls from viewers with divergent views, what is happening de facto, I believe, is offering, however modestly, cautiously and (maybe) unwillingly, space for more than one theological view on the same religious dogma. This, in itself, I would contend, is a major challenge to religious dogmas and religious authoritarian discourses. Dogmas are dogmas because they are considered to be fixed, immutable, beyond justification, beyond questioning. For the majority of the Arab populations, the headscarf is what it is because it is 'scriptural', a clear command from God, period. Consequently no questions about it are asked, and no justifications for it have to be offered. Since the ban in Turkey, however, Arabic satellite media by the dozens have had to cover it, and television preachers from different traditions, schools and nationalities have had to justify it. Most of them might claim to be speaking in the name of the one and only God to win over their audiences, but each one is actually offering a different *interpretation* of the Divine Will on the same issue. This proliferation of (often contradictory) religious views per se, even if it does not live up to the expectations of those who look for genuinely alternative discourses on religion in the Arab satellite landscape, maybe carries in itself the seed for change.

Chapter 13
Shari‘a and the Constitutional Debate in Egypt

Jakob Skovgaard-Petersen

In March 2007 Egyptians voted on and adopted a new constitutional text. First introduced in 1971, the Constitution had been subjected to amendments before, but with amendments of 34 of the 211 clauses this one was the most wide-reaching. Some commentators had called for a whole new constitution, but in the end the Parliament and later the people settled on these changes, first proposed by the president himself in December 2006. The changes erased references to socialism, opened up for new anti-terror legislation and defined a new method of electoral supervision. In article 1, the concept of citizenship (*muwatana*) was included. And perhaps most controversially, a new clause in article 5 prohibited political activity or the formation of parties on the basis of religion – a move clearly directed against the Muslim Brotherhood which had just announced its intention to establish a party.

The Brotherhood and other actors on the Islamic wing of Egyptian politics could take heart, however, by the fact that despite some late campaigning from secularist activists and Copts, the famous article 2 was not subjected to any change. This article states that ‘Islam is the religion of the state. Arabic is its official language; and the principles of the Islamic Shari‘a are the principal source of legislation.’

This chapter will discuss the background, use and implications of article 2 as a major factor in determining what is implied by the notion of Shari‘a in an Egyptian political context today.

Islam in the Egyptian Constitutional Tradition

Egypt is no newcomer to constitutionalism. As part of the modernization and reorganization of courts in the late 19th century, Egypt promulgated its first constitution in 1882, on the eve of the British occupation. After some years of pressure on the British, a new liberal constitution was adopted in 1923, and the following years saw an intense period of party and parliamentary politics, even if both the king (1925, 1930) and later the British (1942) violated the constitutional arrangement (Brown, 2002, 39f). After the coup of 1952, new constitutions were adopted in 1956, 1958 and 1964, the latter stating Egypt's commitment to socialism and giving excessive powers to the president, at that time Gamal Abd al-Nasir. A return towards the liberal constitutional tradition was inaugurated with President Sadat's Constitution of 1971 which is still in effect, with a number of amendments.

The Islamic component in the constitutions has gained in significance over the years. The Constitution of 1923 introduced the clause that Islam is the religion of the state. This clause was, however, placed almost at the end, in article 149. In the Constitutions of 1956 and1964 it was moved to article 5, and now, as we have seen, it forms part of article 2, thus effectively defining the very framework of the constitutional text.

There are also other instances in the 1971 Constitution where Islam is invoked. The president must be sworn in 'in the name of God the almighty' (art. 90), as must the parliamentarians (art. 90) and the government (art. 155). It does not state, however, that he has to be a Muslim (Barnard-Maugiron, 2003, 341). The Shari'a is specifically, and defensively, invoked in article 11, stating that:

> The state shall be responsible for maintaining the balance between woman's duties towards the family and her activity in society, as well as for her equality with man in the fields of political, social, cultural and economic life, without detriment (*ikhlal*) to the laws of the Islamic Shari'a.

At the same time, the coveted article 40 states that there must be no discrimination based on race, gender or religion.

The History of Article 2

Shari'a, then, is evoked in a referential way, as a proclamation of national identity, without precise definition as to its constitutional and legal impact. This is increasingly also seen in other constitutional texts in Islamic countries. To many Egyptians, however, the reference to the Shari'a is clearly meant to have significant repercussions for the Egyptian legal system. What were the intentions of the formulation in the first place, and how has it been debated during the past 36 years?

The Constitution of 1971 must be seen as an attempt on the part of a new president, Anwar al-Sadat, to consolidate power and restart Egyptian politics on a new base. Sadat solicited suggestions for constitutional items directly from the public. A subcommittee travelled to the governorates to discuss it locally. Altogether 6832 suggestions were submitted. The one issue where there appeared to be widest disagreement amongst the proposals was the emancipation and legal status of women. Many of the proposals were concerned that Islam be declared the state religion, often coupled with the request that the constitution recognize the Islamic Shari'a as a source of legislation. Some suggested that it be the only source (O'Kane, 1972, 139). In the ensuing debate, there appeared to be widely divergent opinions as to, in how far existing Egyptian legislation was in accordance with the Shari'a or not. To most commentators it seemed clear that the Egyptian people must be the sovereign legislator. Disagreement arose as to whether the Shari'a should now be codified in a modern manner, or the principles of the Shari'a would rather mean paying attention to overall principles, but applying independent interpretations (*ijtihad*) with due consideration of the common good (*al-maslaha al-'amma*) (O'Kane, 1972, 145).

As soon as the Constitution of 1971 was adopted, private bills were introduced by members in Parliament, proposing various Islamization initiatives, such as enforced fasting during Ramadan, but these were stopped in a committee for private bills and were never debated in Parliament (Peters, 1988, 235). In 1975, sensing the general mood of Islamization, the government itself set up a committee to prepare for a legislation in accordance with the Shari'a.

Discussion in the 1970s was characterised by the slogan of 'implementation of the Shari'a' (*tatbiq al-Shari'a*), led not least by Abd al-Halim Mahmud, the Shaykh of al-Azhar, the Islamic university in Cairo, who in 1977 organized a major conference on the subject, warning against official rhetoric about a 'gradual implementation', and stressing that the implementation of the Shari'a would be the final step in the process of decolonisation (Zeghal, 1996, 150–6). The necessity of a 'gradual implementation' was voiced by more lukewarm debaters, among them Naguib Mahfouz who maintained that the introduction of severe punishments would be unfair until there was a greater appreciation of Islamic values in Egyptian society (Donohue and Esposito, 1982, 241–2). Still, with the government's approval of a commission, and a new public mode of support for Islamization, few people seemed willing to completely dismiss the idea of an implementation of the Shari'a, even if only 10 years before it would have been considered an anachronism. Al-Azhar had been working on its own proposal, but when the parliamentary committee was established that project was abandoned (Peters, 1988, 237–8).

The parliamentary committee prepared a proposal for a new penal code. In 1978, the work was continued by a higher parliamentary committee which in July 1981 presented six codes to Parliament, all formulated in modern legal terminology but specifying legal principles of the classical *fiqh* (from all schools) on which the individual clause was based. These were a civil code, a penal code, a code of trade and maritime commerce, a code of evidence and a code of process.

By 1981, however, the government had realized that the 'application of the Shari'a', as it was referred to, would also mean relinquishing power and room of manoeuvre to an Islamic sector, part of which was intent on establishing full political control of the country. When, three months later, President Sadat himself was murdered in an attempted coup d'état, the government was forced to opt for a more confrontational course towards radical Islamists and felt little inclination to pursue legal Islamization. The codes were not debated in Parliament. On 4 May1985, a general discussion about the application of the Shari'a was ended by the adoption of a resolution stating that existing laws were to be cleared of content contradicting the Shari'a, but that this must happen 'gradually and scientifically' (Peters, 1988, 240).

The debate about the implementation of the Shari'a kept on boiling throughout the 1980s. The entry of the Muslim Brotherhood to Parliament in 1984, and in greater force in 1987, meant that the issue was raised politically, and not only in Islamic media. In courts there were a number of incidents where judges decided to apply Shari'a regulations, e.g. against consumption of alcohol, even though this was not prohibited according to Egyptian law (Peters, 1988, 242–3). Also outside courts there were examples of Islamic groups taking over districts and declaring the local implementation of the Shari'a. However, the government and the state were no longer eager to affirm their commitment to any specific plans of implementation; whenever its spokesmen mentioned implementation, it would often be in uncommitted references to a scientific approach.

During the debate in the 1980s criticism of the idea of an implementation of the Shari'a became more vocal, and Iran and the Sudan were sometimes pointed to as examples of the excesses it could lead to (Peters, 1988, 240). In particular, the issue of the position of the Copts was raised with vigour (Peters, 1988, 245). And what the proponents saw as the flexibility of the Shari'a was derided by the opponents as evidence of the arbitrariness of the Islamic legal tradition. Writers such as Farag Foda (*Qabla as-suqut*, 1985) and Said al-Ashmawi (*al-Islam as-siyasi*, 1987) published outspoken and direct criticisms of the project of implementation of the Shari'a, affirming that Egypt's legal tradition was by and large in conformity with the Shari'a, and that the proponents, by contrast, were calling for a specific and intolerant version of it.

The Supreme Constitutional Court

The official and final interpretation of the Egyptian Constitution is the task of the Supreme Constitutional Court, established in 1969 but only functioning from 1979. Al-Azhar had rejected the payment of interest on a loan, claiming that art. 226 in the civil code accepting interest was in contradiction to art. 2 of the Constitution, thus raising the principal case of interpretation of article 2. On 4 May 1985 – the same day that Parliament avoided discussing the application of the Shari'a – the Constitutional Court ruled that it was incompetent to try laws that predated the latest constitutional amendment of 1980. This meant that the article 2 formulation that 'the principles of the Islamic Shari'a are the principal source of legislation' was to be understood as valid for future legislation but not as a warrant for a complete revision of existing Egyptian legislation.

This greatly diminished the importance of article 2 for the moment. But it also established that all future legislation must be in conformity with the principles of the Shari'a. It was therefore only a question of time before pieces of legislation adopted after 1981 were subjected to testing by the courts. This has now happened repeatedly since 1993, especially related to the law of personal status from 1985.

In an important verdict of 15 May 1993, the Supreme Constitutional Court establishing the basic distinction that the Shari'a is divided into:

1. Rules, the origins and significance of which are absolute (*al-ahkam al-shar'iyya al-qat'iyya fi thubutiha wa-dalalatiha*).
2. Rules that are relative and reflections of human judgement (*ahkam zanniya*).

While legislation must not contradict the first type of rules, the second type are based on *ijtihad* and may therefore be abrogated by another *ijtihad*, based on reason and the fundamental principles of Islam, if this ruling is more in line with the requirements of the age. And, importantly, this *ijtihad* can be practised by those in authority (*ulu al-amr*), such as a Parliament (Bernard-Maugiron, 2003, 350–1). Examining the cases involving an interpretation of article 2, Nathalie Bernard-Maugiron has established that during the 1990s, the Supreme Constitutional Court applied this distinction in a number of cases, so that in practice it became the court itself which was the ultimate arbiter of what were to be considered absolute and what were to be considered relative rulings. In almost all cases referred to it, it has upheld the text of the specific laws, thus establishing a very wide definition of Shari'a principles. In the process, however, it has confirmed certain basic principles of the Shari'a, e.g. that the wife has a duty to obey her husband, or that she must be decently dressed. It has also affirmed the prohibition of usury (*riba*), but rejected a ban on all types of interest (Bernard-Maugiron, 2003, 392). Another analysis, by Clark Lombardi, has demonstrated that this methodology draws on the neo-utilitarianism of Rashid Rida (1865–1935), as well as other rational tendencies of the 20th century, to the extent that it has been to reinforce the liberal constitutional doctrines it has already developed in various fields, e.g. in the area of women's rights (Lombardi, 2006, 271–2),

For our purposes it is important to stress that this is the most authoritative and applied definition of article 2. With the ruling of 15 May 1993, the Supreme Constitutional Court has formally recognized the Shari'a as not just the main source of legislation, but also as a corrective to legislation. However, the court has done this in a manner that Shari'a application activists would hardly approve of. No *'ulama'* are involved, and it never resorts to the Mufti, the Shaykh al-Azhar or the Azhar Academy of Islamic Research. It is the Supreme Constitutional Court itself which decides whether there is an absolute Shari'a principle involved, and whether it has been infringed. There are no formal limitations as to specific legal schools or texts. And there is a significant stress on modern social realities (Bernard-Maugiron, 2003, 391). On the other hand, the court has affirmed that certain basic principles have to be enforced, and it has stated some of them in rulings from the 1990s onwards. Conceivably, in the event that the court were to be staffed with more Islamist-leaning judges, this could be an important vehicle of Islamization.

The Recent Constitutional Revisions

During the years 2005–2007, the Egyptian Constitution has been amended twice. This has largely been due to a general pressure on the regime to demonstrate reform willingness, but it has also served the purpose of streamlining political procedures and paving the way for a transition from the current President Mubarak (who took over after Sadat in 1981) to a successor which the regime wants to come from the ranks of the ruling National Democratic Party.

The first amendment, approved in a referendum in May 2005, opened up for multi-candidate elections of the president, instead of a simple referendum on a candidate elected in parliament. The second amendment, approved in a referendum in April 2007, was much more far-reaching, changing the wording of 34 of the Constitution's 212 articles. An important ideological change was the excision of references to socialism, and the insertion of the notion of citizenship in article 1: 'The Arab Republic of Egypt is a democratic system based on citizenship. The Egyptian people form an integral part of the Arab world and work for the realisation of its comprehensive unity.'

Only few of these changes had Islamic implications. This was because the aim of the amendments was not a redefinition of the state, but redistributions of power (Abd al-Fattah, 2005, 81). The most conspicuous amendment was the insertion of a sentence in article 5, stating that, 'Any political activity or political parties shall not be based on any religious background or foundation or on any discrimination in terms of sex and lineage.' This change was clearly directed against the Muslim Brotherhood which was planning to launch a political party.

Beginning in the 1990s, the Brotherhood had made a series of statements affirming its commitment to a democratic political system and moderating its stand towards women, Copts and other traditional points where it had been criticized. When in 2005 the Brotherhood participated in parliamentary elections (and won 20 per cent of the seats although it had only fielded candidates in around 40 per cent of the constituencies), it produced an electoral programme stressing democratic political reforms, and not Islamization of the laws. This did not mean that the application of the Shari'a was no longer on the Brotherhood's agenda, but simply that, initially, it would prioritize democratic reforms, as it saw these as a way to a more permanent influence on Egyptian politics. In supporting democratization of the political institutions, the Brotherhood opted for a definition of sovereignty as belonging to God who had, however, delegated it to the *umma*. Making all members of the *umma* participate in decision-making, and accepting the Christians as politically equal (but numerically inferior) was therefore not in contradiction to an Islamic system. The Brotherhood was critical of the constitutional amendments which it saw as directed against it, at least in part, and inviting to electoral fraud by loosening the control of Egypt's judges over the electoral process. As it stated on its website, Egypt was moving towards a constitutional police state (<www.ikhwanonline.com>, 2007).

Article 2 Debated

The constitutional amendments were proposed by President Mubarak himself in late December 2006, and they did not include article 2. In January and February 2007, various human rights figures and organizations (The Cairo Institute for Human Rights, the Ibn Khaldun Centre, Kalima li-Huquq al-Insan) organized sessions on article 2 with the aim of bringing it into the discussion. The main protagonists for a change were secularist intellectuals and some Copts. In March, 100 public intellectuals made a petition to Parliament to amend article 2 (*Al-Masri al-Yaum*, 6 March 2007, 5).

The defenders of article 2 in its existing form were partly top members of the NDP, such as Mustafa al-Fiqi and Gamal Mubarak who defended the amendments generally and knew that the opening of the debate on article 2 would place the whole amendment process in jeopardy, and they were partly Islamic thinkers who believe that article 2 is a hard-won concession in the struggle to implement the Shari'a again.

The 100 intellectuals who called for change argued that:

- there are other religions and other civilizations in Egypt, and that they should also be mentioned;
- at least the wording must be taken back to that of the 1971 Constitution, so that the principles of the Islamic Shari'a be *a*, and not *the*, principal source of legislation;
- instead of Islam being the religion of the state, it should be referred to as the religion of the majority.

There were also a few more radical voices who wanted to insert human rights as the source instead of the Shari'a, as mentioning the Shari'a contradicted the equality of citizens before the law, established in article 40 of the Constitution.

A special point of view in the debate was that of Gamal al-Banna, an independent Islamic thinker and brother of Hassan al-Banna (d. 1949) the founder of the Muslim Brotherhood. According to Gamal al-Banna, article 2 – which he ascribed to Sadat's populism – destroys religion which by its nature is civil; while his brother introduced the slogan 'Islam is religion and state', Gamal preferred 'Islam is religion and community (*umma*)', believing that state power corrupts and that an official version of Islam, as in Saudi Arabia, becomes a straitjacket that suppresses true religious ethics. Hence, to Gamal al-Banna it would not be enough to supplement article 2 with a mentioning of Christianity; rather, the names of the religions must be omitted and the word 'justice' inserted instead (*al-Masri al-Yaum*, 14 March 2007, 13).

Article 2 was, however, also vigorously defended from several quarters. The ruling National Democratic Party, which was not intent on changing it, argued that by inserting the notion of citizenship in article 1, and prohibiting religious parties, it had effectively assured that the state be civil, not religious. Article 2 was about

Egypt's identity, and now it provided a balance to these other articles. At a hearing in the Cairo Institute for Human Rights on 8 February 2007, NDP ideologue Mustafa al-Fiqi claimed that the Copts overwhelmingly rejected a change of article 2. At the same meeting, Tharwat al-Badawy, Professor of Constitutional Law at Cairo University, stated that the move to change article 2 was driven by Copts in exile who had come under the influence of Zionism.

On the Islamic wing of the Egyptian debate, support for article 2 was almost unanimous. Official bodies such as the Academy of Islamic Research affirmed that this was indeed Egypt's identity, and that it was in no contradiction to the concept of citizenship.

The Muslim Brotherhood's parliamentarians gave various reasons for their support for article 2. At the hearing in the Cairo Institute for Human Rights on 8 February, Dr Ahmad Abu Baraka spoke out in favour of the Constitutional Court's application of article 2, recognizing the Shari'a's distinction between firm and flexible principles. The leader of the Brotherhood bloc in Parliament, Saad al-Katatni, expressed a fear that the campaign was really directed against the Brotherhood's involvement in politics.

The famous TV preacher Yusuf al-Qaradawi, who had historical links to the Brotherhood, discussed article 2 in a special session of his programme 'Shari'a and Life' on the *Al Jazeera* TV channel (18 February 2007), affirming the principles of popular sovereignty and human rights, but arguing that 90 per cent of the population wants the application of the Shari'a. To al-Qaradawi the Shari'a is an authoritative source for human legislation, and this is well expressed in article 2.

Numerous Islamic thinkers also lent their support to article 2. The prominent jurist and writer Tariq al-Bishri also saw article 2 as establishing the Shari'a as an authoritative source, *marja'iyya*, but with a somewhat different argument: by being placed at the beginning of the Constitution, Bishri argued, article 2 renders Islamic legitimacy to all the following articles of rights, duties and citizenship. If article 2 was omitted, the Islamic foundation of these principles would be lacking. Giving collective organs such as parliaments a religious identity is also warranted, in that it establishes the religious identity on a collective basis while at the same time allowing for individual participation of Christians on an equal level with Muslims (*al-Ahram*, 28 February 2007, 11).

The debate raged in January, February and March 2007. The vote took place in Parliament on March 19, boycotted by the around 20 per cent independents belonging to the opposition who said that their comments had been ignored. The 34 amendments were adopted by popular referendum on March 26, with low voter turnout, as is usual in Egypt.

Conclusions

We have seen that the debate on article 2 has been running through several phases. During the 1970s, there was a strong movement pressing for the application of the

Shari'a. Article 2, according to this movement, would reflect Egypt's identity, and finally overcome the impact of colonialism which was still felt in the legal system. It would provide the basis for a real implementation of the Shari'a, which would ensure a just and virtuous society. It would thus create a fundamentally new society. And that society, after all, would be shaped according to God's command.

Criticism of this current was somewhat muted; the press was not free, and as the government went along with the project of Islamization of the laws, not that many voices spoke out against it. Much of the criticism concentrated on the issue of *hudud*, or Qur'anic punishments which were seen by some to be retrograde. Criticism of the Islamization project became easier during the 1980s after the murder of President Sadat, and the government's harder anti-Islamist line. A freer party press, including an Islamist press, discussed the issue vigorously, and the issue of human rights was slowly gaining ground. Islamists were now more challenged to provide answers to the issues of non-Muslims and women, both holding fewer rights than men in classical Islamic jurisprudence. A few debaters were avowedly secularists, others maintained that the current laws of Egypt were by and large in conformity with the Shari'a.

The precise interpretation of article 2 was provided by the Supreme Constitutional Court which ruled that it was an obligation on future legislators but did not call for a full-scale revision of codes. By the 1990s, the Supreme Constitutional Court began its own interpretation of the Shari'a, normally to uphold existing legislation, but affirming certain guiding principles as binding along the way.

In the debate leading up to the constitutional changes in April 2007, article 2 was much debated, but it was never close to becoming altered, let alone omitted. By this time, it was the critics of article 2 who took the initiative and led the debate. Contrary to the discussions of the 1970s and 1980s, the contents of the Shari'a, including the *hudud*, were not discussed. Instead, the criticism centred on the presence of the article in the Constitution, and its negative role.

1. as defining the national identity in a divisive and exclusionist manner;
2. as contradicting the notion of citizenship, which requires full enjoyment of equal rights among all citizens.

The National Democratic Party wanted to retain article 2, probably to avoid opposition against more important changes introduces, e.g. in control of elections, but possibly also to further its religious credentials. In argued that introducing the clause on citizenship and banning religious parties would diminish the impact of article 2 by circumventing it.

The Muslim Brotherhood wanted to keep article 2 as a foundation for legislation and for the society it wants to create. But it, too, had more pressing fears and concerns in the changes proposed and ended up boycotting the parliamentary session and ensuing referendum, even though article 2 was not touched. For the Muslim Brotherhood the identity issue is crucial, but it is also very difficult, given the presence of the Copts.

Finally, a few Islamic thinkers, notably Tariq al-Bishri, saw article 2, not as a blueprint for a future and very different Islamic society based on very different laws, but as a blueprint of the actual Egyptian constitution which its various rights and guarantees.

Compared to the rigorist demands of the Islamic movements of the 1970s, then, there seems to be some convergence of opinions towards accepting a certain pluralism of identities in Egypt, while both the Muslim Brotherhood and Islamist thinkers are still very keen to affirm Egypt's Islamic identity, and the relevance of the Shari'a in it. It will be up to future struggles and negotiations to define how these two interests can be reconciled.

PART 3
Shari'a and Discourse

Chapter 14
Traditions of Interpretation within (Protestant) Christian Theology as Compared with Islam

Mogens Müller

Interpretation is at the very root of Christian theology. It is an inheritance from early Judaism from which the first Christian congregations soon separated themselves. In early Judaism we find interpretation at work in at least four areas. The first is the phenomenon called the 'rewritten Bible', i.e. a retelling of the biblical story with new theological or ideological accentuations. The second is translations such as the Greek Septuagint from the 3rd and 2nd century BCE, which contain a certain theological 'updating' and assimilation to the Hellenistic world. The third is the more explicit interpretation in Bible commentaries and other literature from Qumran, and finally the fourth is the allegorical Bible interpretation in parts of the so-called Pseudepigraphic literature and in the works of Philo of Alexandria. In all these ways early Judaism consciously developed its traditions. New situations could create new understandings as, for instance, when in the Maccabean revolt in the 160s BC on a particular occasion several thousand Jewish soldiers were killed because they would not fight on a Sabbath. This incident gave rise to a new interpretation of the Sabbath commandment allowing for resistance when forces were attacked on a Sabbath (1 Maccabees 2.29–41). One could even take this a step further and say that the different books of the Jewish Bible themselves are products of a longer or shorter interpretation process. Even the different sequences in which the books are placed in the Hebrew Bible and the Greek Septuagint respectively are the result of an overall objective with regard to meaning.

It is in the framework of such an ongoing process of interpretation that the emergence of Christianity has to be seen. Thus the Jesus of the canonical Gospels among other things is depicted as the teacher *par excellence* (see especially Matthew 23.8) and much of his teaching concerns the right interpretation of the will of God. The most instructive example is probably the Sermon on the Mount (Matthew 5–7). But perhaps the teaching of Jesus according to Mark and Matthew on the theme 'clean and unclean' is especially instructive. Here the very foundation of Jewish identity is attacked when it is taught that it is not what goes into the mouth which defiles a man, but what comes out of the mouth: evil thoughts and deeds of all kinds (see Mark 7.14–23; Matthew 15.10–20). The Gospel of Mark in a redactional note even adds: 'Thus he (Jesus) declared all foods clean' (Mark 7.19).

But the interpretation does not stop with the teaching of Jesus. The tradition about his teaching as well as about his life is also interpreted by the later evangelists with the result that the New Testament contains four different perceptions of Jesus and his significance.

It could be said that early Christianity constituted itself through a certain interpretation of the Holy Scriptures of Judaism just as later Rabbinic Judaism developed through a certain interpretation of the same tradition making it possible to exist as a religious community without the Temple. Thus, from a sociological point of view, both Judaism and Christianity could very well be defined as communities of interpretation. What at the beginning divided the two was not the question of which books should be regarded as holy but how they should be interpreted. And very soon early Christianity created its own collection of holy books to maintain its special interpretation, namely that Jesus was the fulfilment of the prophetic promise of Scripture of a divine eschatological intervention and bringer of the true understanding of God's will.

Accordingly, early Christianity understood itself as the realization of the promise in the Book of Jeremiah of a new covenant to replace the old one from Sinai (see Jeremiah 31.31–4). Only such a radical re-interpretation of what for the Christian Church became the Old Testament can explain how originally Jewish scripture became in the hands of the Church virtually a Christian book. The means to maintain this were different interpretation strategies, among which we find allegorical interpretation side by side with a construction of a salvation history allowing Judaism to be a finished and done with chapter. Thus it is said in the New Testament in the anonymous Letter to the Hebrews (8.13): 'In speaking of a new covenant he (i.e. God) treats the first as obsolete. And what is becoming obsolete and growing old is ready to vanish away.' However, it never occurred to these early Christians to abandon the Old Testament.

It is important to ascertain that what began as the interpretative effort of a community of interpretation also continued its history – consciously or unconsciously – through interpretation. The strength of much Christian theology has been its ability to adapt itself to contemporary philosophy, world view and sense of the actual. This was the case with many of the Church Fathers, and in the 16th century, the direct impetus to a new paradigm in Bible interpretation was the introduction of a new world picture by Copernicus and others claiming not the earth but the sun to be the centre of the universe. It made impossible the story in the Book of Joshua (ch. 10) of how the sun stopped its way and later also the moon, to facilitate the victory of the Israelites over the Moabites. Even if it was reluctantly, this breach in the historical credibility of the Bible gave rise to a growing historical criticism in biblical interpretation. And in the age of the Enlightenment it resulted in quite a new understanding of the Bible.

In the period of orthodoxy the Bible had thus been seen as inspired into the slightest detail, and its infallibility also in historical matters was taken for granted. And great interpretative effort was activated to keep that position. But beginning with English Deism and its aftermath in the German universities, continental

Protestant biblical scholarship soon adapted an ever more consistent historical and critical attitude. The Old Testament was treated as a Jewish collection of books created by – and meant to promote – Judaism, and the New Testament was conceived as early Christian literature trying to ascertain and elucidate the impact of the life and death of Jesus for the salvation of humankind. As a consequence it was realized that the Church came before its Scripture. In the form of philosophy known as Rationalism supernatural and transcendent traits were explained as ideas typical of the period to express divine action. Historical criticism alone was able to uncover historical facts and bound to describe mythological frameworks as means of interpretation.

Of course this called forth a reaction, for instance in the form of a fundamentalism claiming that the Bible is right in whatever it says. Fundamentalism, however, is a modern phenomenon because it means that one rejects what in the surrounding society are normally seen as facts of history and natural science and claims another reality to be real. But the Bible perceived as the very Word of God cannot be fallible. Thus fundamentalism is to live with a duality of truths, the common being subordinated to the biblical. Among the main factors for the rise of Christian fundamentalism were the theories of Charles Darwin concerning the descent of man, and it is typical of this type of fundamentalist thinking to try to legitimate its positions as scientific. This is, for instance, the case in the current controversies about 'intelligent design'.

Critical scholarship as practised at universities, however, considers the Bible as consisting of purely human documents trying to produce an interpretation of certain persons and events as revealing the will of God. To this end its authors, in their efforts to narrate their theology and ideology, often even blur the difference between 'story' and 'history'. But fundamentally the authors of the books of both the Old Testament and the New Testament act not only as bearers but also as interpreters of tradition, a tradition which without continuing interpretation would have sunk into oblivion. Thus outside the later canonized books interpretation continued in commentaries and dogmatic works. There is no such thing as tradition without reception, and there is no reception without interpretation (Hübner, 1990, 244). This is a basic condition, because consciously or unconsciously tradition is always taken over under new conditions and in new contexts which necessitate interpretation. Even fundamentalists interpret when they postulate an alternative sense of reality and thereby create a parallel world.

Being aware of this nature of reception even a theological attitude to the Bible will be fundamentally critical and understand itself as the continuation of the interpretative effort. New circumstances demand new reception and it is – or should be – a profound condition in this reception that the interpreter has no other means to persuade than arguments. In countries with free constitutions and consequently freedom of conscience it goes without saying that you are free to follow your own faith and conviction – if doing so does not violate public order. But you are not allowed under any circumstances to try forcefully to impose your faith or convictions – not to mention their consequences – upon others. Convincing arguments are the only legitimate means.

In a post-Enlightenment era the non-fundamentalist interpreter will always be distracted by the knowledge of the genesis of the biblical texts. The knowledge of the way they came into existence and about the historical events giving them their shape and content creates a certain and often high degree of alienation. At the same time it means a relativization. The effort to understanding is double: the one leading the reader back to the foreign world of the texts, the other trying to transfer the meaning, the sense of the texts, into her or his own time and world. Thus meaning, sense, is something which, in the final analysis, we bring to a text from our own horizon of understanding. If we cannot connect any sense with the content, the text will remain dead to us. Thus interpretation is not only something which we bring to the text, but the very condition for understanding and application. The text simply does not live without an interpreting audience, just as it only functions through the authority it exerts among those listening.

Christian theology has from the very beginning lived with a Bible. Thus the first Bible of the Church was the sacred writings of Judaism. Very early – and certainly with the apostle Paul – they received an interpretation which meant that all of the regulation concerning the ethnic identity of the Jewish people (circumcision, purity rules, observing of the Sabbath, etc.) was no longer valid, at least not for Christians coming from a non-Jewish background. With respect to the New Testament Scripture there always existed a sense of what was centre and what periphery. Martin Luther in the 16th century formulated it in the famous saying that the value of the individual biblical book should be valued to the extent that it made Christ grow (German: *Christus treiben*).

It means that the New Testament writings should not be taken as a law book where everything is of equal importance. They are not themselves revelation but the work of early Christian theologians trying to express their faith and its consequences. This is the case even with the Jesus tradition. It can be recognized from the fact that the New Testament contains four very different and partly contradictory accounts of the life of Jesus. What we have here are stations in a creative tradition process. Accordingly new interpretations should be allowed either to correct or even exclude those parts of the tradition which are in conflict with the centre, or must be categorized as bearing the stamp of the period and therefore not universally valid. An example here is the attitude to the status of women. But also the view on homosexuals could be mentioned. Typically these are among the questions where controversy is ardent between, on the one side, theologians who see themselves as being committed to historical criticism and, on the other side, fundamentalist Christians. Thus in at least parts of Protestant theology one finds traditions of interpretation, or should we rather say reception, abandoning positions taken in biblical books declaring them irreconcilable with the commandment of love.

With such a view of interpretation as the basic condition of understanding its Scripture, Protestant Christian theology departs radically from mainstream

Islam and its perception of the Qur'an. Thus a Christian reader of the Qur'an easily identifies the great majority of its characters, as also most of what is said about them. For her or him the material obviously stems from traditions deriving from the Old and New Testament, but also from traditions only accessible in the Pseudepigraphic Jewish literature and New Testament Apocrypha ('Isra'iliyyat', *EI2*, 4, 111–12). The former is, for instance, the case with regard to the traditions about how Abraham confronted the idolatry of his father. They are not present in the canonical Genesis, but known from the Book of Jubilees from the 2nd century BC. The story of how Jesus creates birds of clay and makes them fly, on the other hand, is not found in the canonical gospels, but known from the Infancy Gospel of Thomas originally from the 2nd century AD, which is included in the Apocrypha.

On the other hand it seems obvious that the relation of the traditions as received in the Qur'an and their biblical, Pseudepigraphic or Apocryphal original are not literal in character but that the traditions have reached Muhammad orally to be adapted to his special proclamation of what he believes to be the will of God and employed in his development as the Prophet. Thus for a biblical scholar the suras of the Qur'an are at best understood as Bible reception and in some way as a phenomenon parallel to the New Testament in receiving the traditions in an interpretation making them parts of a new religion and at the same time demanding to bring the original significance.

Where the Christian Church never gave up the Jewish Bible, but through interpretation made it the *Old* Testament, claiming that the key to the right understanding lies in the New Testament, Islamic scholarship apparently looks upon the traditions contained in the Old and New Testaments as more or less falsified or distorted, the Qur'an – as revealed to Muhammad – giving them back their original meaning. This means that the Qur'an, coming into existence in the 7th century AD, in Islamic thought becomes the only reliable source of the stories of, for instance, Abraham, Moses and Jesus; the biblical traditions are ignored.

As a consequence the study of the Qur'an is not – at least not normally – in Islamic scholarship combined with the study of the Bible to see how the traditions are formed and function here. Many of the stories in the Qur'an being somehow abrupt or operating by implication, obviously presuming the hearers or readers to be familiar with their content, one could expect that further information might be sought in the Bible. And as a matter of fact, the first centuries after Muhammad's death saw Islamic literature containing narrative supplements to the Qur'an. An Islamic edition of the Gospel of Matthew, named the Gospel of Barnabas and containing characteristics of the Islamic view upon Jesus (not dying on the cross, for instance), appeared as late as the first half of the 14th century or the second half of the 16th century. Probably many former Christians in converting to Islam contributed with their knowledge of the Bible ('Indjil', *EI2*, 3 1205–1208; Khalidi, 2001).[1] At the same time this literature meant an effective farewell to the Bible, being suspect in bringing other versions and interpretations. In other words, it is looked upon as tantamount to heresy.

Let me bring in a personal anecdote as illustration of how the Qur'an in an Islamic context is seen as the primary source to 'biblical' events. When I visited Syria in 1990 and in the National Museum saw the rebuilt synagogue from Dura Europos with its wonderful and partly very well-preserved frescoes (first half of the 3rd century CE) with motifs from the Bible, it was not yet possible to get any book about them. Five years later it was, but to my great surprise I did not find any Old Testament references, only references to suras in the Qur'an. The same also pertained to the reproductions of New Testament motifs from the church likewise excavated in Dura Europos (but transferred to Yale University), where the Qur'anic quotations were even more difficult to relate. At a new visit some years later I could buy a new edition of this book where all the references to the Qur'an were removed and replaced by very short but more adequate texts neutrally describing the motives. But still there were no references to the biblical books so obviously the sources of the painted motives. One is tempted to ask if there is any fear of contact with regard to the Bible.

Thus there exists a fundamental difference between protestant Christian theology and Islam in the view of the nature of the Bible and the Qur'an respectively with a likewise fundamental difference in the view of the role of interpretation as a consequence. It also finds its expression in the fact that where in Christianity the Bible is the Bible in the popular idiom, in Islam the Qur'an is only really the Qur'an in Arabic. Maybe it could be summarized as that where the Church (and this also pertains to the Synagogue) has its Bible, in Islam it is the Qur'an which has its followers, with little complementarity between the two.

1 As a curiosity it could be mentioned that there exists an old Danish translation of a German book about the biblical legends among the Muslims (Weil, 1855). For these references I owe thanks to Johan Hermann Rump.

Chapter 15
Rebellious Women – Discourses and Texts: Shari‘a, Civil Rights and Penal Law

Peter Madsen

> To speak of Islamic discourse today is to speak of politics: Islamic discourse is part and parcel of a contest over moral values, social norms, and political institutions at a local as well as a global level.
>
> Gudrun Krämer

Concepts of Discourse

During the last few decades the word ‘discourse’ has become ubiquitous in human and social sciences. Although this does not mean that a shared *concept* of discourse is available, the proliferation of the usage may be taken as a symptom of a shared *focus* on linguistic aspects of a variety of phenomena (a general overview of the field is provided by the introduction to Jaworski and Coupland, 1999, 1–44).

In the field of linguistics proper a shift of focus to language as a *system* contrary to the earlier predominant attention to *historical* developments is often associated with Ferdinand de Saussure's *Cours de linguistique générale* (Saussure, 1972) and later elaborations of his approach in the work of Louis Hjelmslev and Roman Jakobson. A *synchronic* analysis of *la langue* (i.e. the linguistic system) should lay bare the order and the rules governing the *use* of (Saussure: *parole*), the *common* systematic features underlying *individual* use of language. This *structuralist* approach became a stepping stone for the anthropologist Claude Lévi-Strauss in his studies not only of kinship structures but also of structures of mythical thinking (*pensée sauvage*). Again the intention was to lay bare the common system behind individual phenomena, i.e. the individual myths, yet whereas the language system generally speaking is neutral when it comes to world views the system of the myths is a *pensée*, a way of thinking. This is a crucial shift of focus that became a decisive inspiration for the work of among others A.J. Greimas in his attempts to develop structural semantics. His approach has two aspects. One is derived from lexicology, very briefly an attempt to analyse how clusters of semantic features constitute the content of single words in a manner similar to the way in which distinctive features (like voiced versus unvoiced) constitute the sounds, the *phonemes*, that go together in the expression of words, i.e. the kind of analysis Roman Jakobson developed. The other aspect is more important in the present context. By moving beyond the single word and the single sentence – traditionally the typical objects of linguistic analysis – his approach brought forward questions concerning semantic organization of linguistic sequences and series of sentences, like, for example, the semantic structure of a work of literature, a *semantic micro-universe*, as he named it. Similar to the analysis of *la langue*, i.e. the system of a given language, he was looking for recurrent features in a given limited corpus of texts, redundancy was the popular term at the time (i.e. the sixties), yet similar to what was the case in Lévi-Strauss' analysis of myths, these recurrent features defined a specific frame of mind, a world-view, an ideology, an imaginary – what might be termed a specific *discourse*.

Whereas structural linguistics worked at the basis of the dichotomy *langue-parole*, i.e. language system and individual utterance, a third linguistic object thus came to the fore: the systematic features defining, governing or recurring in a specific corpus of text. A major point in this kind of analysis is that it allows a shift of focus from ideas to structures of imagination – among them *narrative* structures are of particular importance. The corpus under scrutiny could be the result of *individual* creativity, like the works of an individual author, in that case the object could be the imaginary of this author, *l'univers imaginaire* as it was called in a different tradition (like in the work of Jean-Pierre Richard), or the corpus could be the results of a specific institutional and thus *transindividual* practice. The corpus could be even broader, such as in the work of the Canadian literary scholar Marc Angenot:

> My basic problem consists of trying to connect the literary, scientific, philosophical, political fields, etc., and, being careful not to overlook the stakes, constraints, and traditions of each of these fields, to extrapolate transdiscursive rules, to discover vectors of exchange, to set up a global topology of the prevailing sayable (i.e. what can and cannot be said), accounting for my using "Social Discourse" in the singular, and not "social discourses" as a simple coexistence and juxtaposition of genres, disciplines, and local cognitive strategies. (Angenot, 1995, 3)

Among the results of Angenot's approach were *1889: Un état du discours social* (1989) and *Ce que l'on dit des Juifs en 1889: antisémitisme et discours social* (1989). A related approach was developed by Teun A. van Dijk (an overview can be found in van Dijk, 1997). Angenot's phrasing 'the prevailing sayable (i.e. what can and cannot be said)' is very close to (as well as inspired by) Michel Foucault's programme for an archaeology of knowledge, although it should be borne in mind that there were other sources for Angenot's approach, among them Antonio Gramsci's analysis of 'hegemony' supported by a prevailing ideology.

One characteristic feature of this kind of discourse analysis is thus a focus on the governing rules of a specific linguistic practice, a specific discourse. Another characteristic feature is attention to the way in which discursive practice is embedded in institutions and broader social structures. A third important feature is an interest in the role of discourse in society and for individuals. The ambiguous title of Foucault's inaugural lecture at Collège de France, '*L'Ordre du discours*', points to the order that governs discourse as well as to the orders (commands) given by way of discursive practice, the way in which discourse regulates behaviour and self-comprehension (the English translation of the title as 'The Discourse on Language' does not hit the mark; Foucault, 1972). This way of thinking is an aspect of Foucault's general approach in studies like *Surveiller et punir* (Foucault, 1991) and *Histoire de la sexualité* (1976). Whereas it is a common understanding that 'sexuality' is 'repressed', it is Foucault's thesis that 'sexuality' rather was 'produced' in the 19th century as an effect of endless discursive practice. A striking formulation of this approach is the conclusion of one of the chapters in his book on the emergence and effects of the modern system of imprisonment:

> It is often said that the model of society that has individuals as its constituent elements is borrowed from the abstract juridical forms of contract and exchange. Mercantile society, according to this view, is represented as a contractual association of isolated juridical subjects. Perhaps. Indeed, the political theory of the seventeenth and eighteenth centuries often seems to follow this schema. But it should not be forgotten that there existed at the same period a technique for constituting individuals as correlative elements of power and knowledge. The individual is no doubt the fictitious atom of an 'ideological' representation of society; but he is also a reality fabricated by this specific technology of power that I have called 'discipline'. We must cease once and for all to describe the effects of power in negative terms: it 'excludes', it 'represses', it 'censors', it 'abstracts', it 'masks', it 'conceals'. In fact, power produces; it produces reality; it produces domains of objects and rituals of truth. The individual and the knowledge that may be gained of him belong to this production. (Foucault, 1991, 194)

The last sentence here is in a characteristic fashion quite radical: as well the individual as knowledge about the individual are effects of power, 'a reality fabricated by this specific technology of power'. In relation to questions concerning discourse Foucault formulates a similar approach in reference to his earlier work on the history of madness:

> […] on examining this new discipline [i.e. psychiatry], we discovered two things: what made it possible at the time it appeared, what brought about this great change in the economy of concepts, analyses, and demonstrations, was a whole series of relations between hospitalization, internment, the conditions and procedures of social exclusion, the rules of jurisprudence, the norms of industrial labour and bourgeois morality, in short a whole group of relations that characterized for this discursive practice the formation of its statements; but this practice is not only manifested in a discipline possessing a scientific status and scientific pretensions; it is also found in operation in legal texts, in literature, in philosophy, in political decisions, and in the statements made and the opinions expressed in daily life. (Foucault, 1972, 179)

This is one example of how discursive practice is seen as embedded in a variety of social institutions and practices. Foucault's approach to discourse has two sides: on one hand he is interested in the way in which discourse is ordered, on the other hand he is – in spite of the principle stated in *Discipline and Punish* (see above) – interested in what is excluded, what cannot be said:

> What one must characterize and individualize is the coexistence of these dispersed and heterogenous statements, the system that governs their division, the degree to which they depend on one another, the way in which they interlock or exclude one another, the transformation that they undergo, and the play of their location, arrangement, and replacement. (Foucault, 1972, 34)

Although this project to identify the *rules of formation* (Foucault, 1972, 38) governing discursive practice in a given field is spelled out in a fairly abstract manner in *The Archaeology of Knowledge,* the impact of Foucault's writings and particularly his books on imprisonment and the history of sexuality together with innumerable essays, lectures and interviews has proved immense. His work provided both theoretical underpinnings and analytical examples for critical analyses of discourses concerning race and gender. Edward Saïd's *Orientalism* (1978) may have been the most important step in this process. The debate sparked by Saïd's book also revealed problematic aspects, particularly potential untenable consequences of the linking of knowledge and power (also acknowledged by Saïd in his postscript to the second edition (1995). In any case: whereas structuralist semantic analysis could provide tools and inspirations for analyses of textual features, Foucault's approach could broadly speaking on one hand widen the horizon for a variety of textually based disciplines in the *Humanities*, since it was based on *contextualization* of discursive practice, and on the other hand enrich *Social Sciences* through the focus on *textual* or *discursive* practices.

Although Foucault's work from a so to speak methodological point of view has undeniable advantages, at the level of basic principles or philosophical underpinnings it has provoked serious objections. Among his critics Jürgen Habermas is probably the most prominent and when it comes to questions concerning discourse the most important. In his two chapters on Foucault in *Der philosophische Diskurs der Moderne* (Habermas, 1985) he points to the role of the concept of power and in general to the analytical a priori subjugation of the thinking and acting subject under discursive and social-historical structures as basic problems. From his first book on *Strukturwandel der Öffentlichkeit* (1962) through his entire *oeuvre*, democracy has been Habermas' central concern. *Öffentlichkeit*, the public sphere, was conceived as mediating between the private sphere (the market and the sphere of intimate relations) on one hand and the state on the other hand. Public debate was the medium for articulation of guiding principles for the state. Thus the ideal. The historical account of the structural changes in the public sphere was about the way in which this ideal was undercut.

In his later work Habermas has focused on communicative action and developed a new general conceptual frame. Now the dichotomy is between life world and system. System is twofold, on the one hand economic rationality, on the other hand bureaucratic rationality. The life world is the world of communication of experience, the world of socialization and transfer of culture from former generations, the world of articulation of self-comprehension. System and life world are in conflict. The life world is 'colonized' by systemic forces. On the other hand, articulations based on the life world may influence the way in which systems work. In this conceptual framework communication is again the medium for articulation of guiding principles for the forces governing the sphere of system, ideally the political sphere. Another word for communication is discourse, and it is through analyses of a number of aspects of discourse that Habermas' social philosophy unfolds. Here discourse is not the linguistic side of transindividual institutional practice (as Foucault has it), but interaction between individuals that in principle are free and equal. The contrast could not be more accentuated, in so far as the individuals, whom Habermas takes as *foundational* for society, in Foucault's view are *effects* of power and discourse, yet methodologically speaking the kind of features that are in focus for Foucault are from the point of view of habermasian analyses precisely features that encroach on the freedom and equality of individuals, as well as on conditions for discursive interaction. There is, of course, a historical side to these questions. Both Foucault and Habermas are writing about modernization and modernity. *Strukturwandel der Öffentlichkeit* was about the way in which a modern public sphere developed in opposition to pre-modern types of public display of power, and how modern historical developments changed the public sphere. Foucault's work similarly has the emergence of modern society and its various features as its object. About *Surveiller et punir* he wrote: 'This book is intended as a correlative history of the modern soul and of a new power to judge; a genealogy of the present scientifico-legal complex from which the power to punish derives its basis, justifications and rules, from which it extends its effects and by which it masks its exorbitant singularity' (Habermas, 1985, 23). Yet what for Habermas are moments in the emergence of modern democracy and emancipation of the individual, are for Foucault intimately linked to processes of disciplining, and his focus is on these processes (see in particular Foucault, 1991, 220–3).

Discourse or Texture of Discourses

As discursive practice Shari'a is obviously a complex phenomenon. Any attempt to define Shari'a as such implies a position in a controversial field. The word means path or way and 'stands for the normative order that Muslims have developed as an Islamic way of life' (Masud, 2001, 2). A common translation is 'Islamic law', yet as a set of norms Shari'a reaches beyond what is commonly understood as laws. A common understanding is that Shari'a is revealed or divine law, yet a crucial aspect is the interaction of elements derived from sources that are understood as divine or in some sense sacred (the Quran as well as the words and deeds of Muhammad) on one hand and on the other hand regulations stemming from social life and from state law. As discourse Shari'a may be said to comprise not only rulings and settled norms or law (*fiqh*), but also the interchange of interpretations behind rulings and law. In this sense Shari'a is rather a historical process and an interaction between institutions and spheres of communication than a fixed set of rules, and this process is further not just a series of interpretations and applications of sacred sources but a continuous interaction between religion, law, politics and social life, as it is stressed by, for example, Muhammad Khalid Masud (2001) and Karen A. Bauer, who shows in detail 'how exegetes draw on wide-ranging and disparate elements in their works, including the text of the Qur'an, *Hadiths*, grammatical analysis, law, previous interpretations, common cultural understanding, societal mores, historical narrative, current scientific understandings, and their own opinions [...] context is key in determining interpretation' (Bauer, 2008, 187). As discursive practice Shari'a is thus rather *a texture of discourses* of various kinds than just one type of discourse.

The ways in which Foucault and Habermas respectively analyse discursive practice, or discourse, are both relevant as analytical approaches to Shari'a, in particular under modern conditions. The interaction of discourse and institutions as regulations of social life, the order of discourse in Foucault's sense, is obviously an important aspect of Shari'a beyond the rulings of institutionalized courts, so much more as articulation and confirmation of rules have their own institutions, selection of protagonists and spheres of communication. Religious authorities and learned institutions (like al-Azhar in Cairo) together constitute the traditional cornerstones of formulation of rules. Social institutions, among them not least the family, implement the rules and courts take care of conflicts and breaking of rules. Under this aspect Shari'a is a system of authority that is upheld and reproduced (or changed) through discursive practice. Along the lines of Foucault's analysis of power and discourse this complex of factors is visible as a system of authority. Yet as soon as the impact of social norms is taken into consideration the picture becomes more complicated. Rules and laws are, it could be argued, usually not reproduced at the basis of power and discursive regulation of behaviour alone, a certain amount of consensus is necessary, in other words a certain amount of interaction with established social norms. Historically speaking Islamic ways of life were in the past introduced in areas with a variety of ways of life of different character, and the conquerors had to accommodate more or less to these ways of life or social norms. Later, modernization meant that new conditions of life prompted changes in social norms and as a consequence also endeavours to change Islamic norms and laws.

In order to gain greater understanding of the working of law in Islam, a twofold effort is necessary. On the one hand, we must examine how Muslim jurists tried to develop a balance between legal and social norms, and how they rooted the normative basis of *Shari'a* in social practices.On the other hand, we need to recognize the significance of the public space for the social construction of Islamic law (Masud, 2001, 14).

At an early stage and through the history, the formation of large political and administrative units, of states and of empires generated a need for laws and regulations of another kind than those comprised by Shari'a (as it is pointed out, e.g., in Zubaida, 2003) and in the first part of Lombardi, 2006). The 19th and 20th centuries brought a double challenge to the Shari'a heritage, when modern law systems (mainly of French origin) and political ideals became influential in Islamic areas. And recently media developments have challenged traditional institutional roles and opened up for a change in the spheres of intellectual interpretation and regulation (Stowasser, 2001). Increasingly norms and procedures that are central to Habermas' analysis of discourse – 'the public space', as Masud (2001) has it – have become prominent or at least attracted attention. The quasi-monopoly upheld by *'ulama'* and religious institutions is challenged by television and public debate, the public sphere is increasingly part of the sphere of interpretation and formation of rules. This also means that ways of life and social norms that are influenced by the process of modernization call for influence on general rules and regulations. Simultaneously the balance between restricted Shari'a practice on one hand and state law on the other hand is challenged by demands for Shari'a-based *state* law articulated by what is commonly called Islamist or fundamentalist groups. Since modernization understood as Westernization and undermining of Islamic traditions has provoked anti-modern reactions in the name of pure religious law (with Sayyid Qutb as an influential proponent and reference), questions concerning Shari'a have changed status in Islamic countries.

In another configuration *migration* has resulted in large minorities in Western countries where democratic procedures and principles of universal equality and individual rights have a long tradition; here demands for Shari'a rulings (or actual practice) represent attempts to withdraw minority communities from governing principles in society at large. How these actual or potential conflicts may develop depends, of course, on the type of interpretation of Shari'a in the particular context, and ultimately on the status attributed to the text of the Qur'an in relation to the other sources of Shari'a (several of these questions are sketched in Gudrun Krämer's eminent presentation of her project at Wissenschaftskolleg zu Berlin (Krämer, n.d.). In this historical context is seems so much more appropriate to look at Shari'a as a *texture of discourses* rather than as *one single discourse*. The patterns of interpretation depend, so to speak, on the ordering of the discursive threads. Various attempts have been made to play down the specific rules formulated in the Qur'an or by the prophet as *historical applications* of core elements in Islam rather than universally valid rules. Which means that historically specific rules are a matter of human decision making, a point of view that is contrary to ideas of pure divine law (like in Sayyid Qutb's opinion), that are prominent in fundamentalist camps. Since modernization and principles of equality and individual freedom affect not least the roles and positions of women in society and in family life, one specific verse in the Qur'an has been at the centre of attention and controversy, namely verse 34 in sura 4, 'Women'. A traditionalist interpretation of this verse came under scrutiny in a Spanish court in 2004.

Shari'a and Penal Code: Islam in Modern Spain

Already during the Franco regime private religious activity was recognized. In 1968 a law on freedom of religion was adopted (the main sources in what follows are articles in the major Spanish newspaper *El País*, references are by 'EP' and the date; the historical account is based on EP 3.12.01, Amghar et al., 2007, 192–4; Dassetto et al., 2007, 165–8, with bibliography). Between 1968 and 1971 the first Muslim associations were established, among them the Asociación Musulmana de España, headed by a naturalized Syrian medical doctor. The post-Franco democracy passed the Organic Law on the Freedom of Religion in 1980 and numerous new associations were formed. Soon an opposition emerged between organizations financed by their members and those financed by foreign sources, first and foremost from Saudi Arabia. In 1981 a mosque financed by Saudis was finished in Marbella. In 1989 Féderación Española de Entitades Religiosas Islámicas (FEERI) unified 15 organizations with a view to negotiations with the state, yet a few months later a part of the organization left and created Unión de Comunicades Islámicas en España (UCIDE).

In 1992 (five centuries after the fall of the last Muslim stronghold in Spain, Granada, and the beginning of the enforcement of conversion to Catholicism, it should be remembered) the socialist government negotiated an accord between the two organizations, unified as Comisión Islámica de España (CIS), including representatives of both organizations, on one hand, and on the other hand the government with a view to implementing *inter alia* religious education in schools (details about the accord in Herbert, 2005). FEERI regarded UCIDE as radical and related to the Muslim Brotherhood, whereas UCIDE regarded FEERI as radical since it included wahhabis. In 1992 Madrid's mosque (shorthand 'M-30' after the name of Madrid's nearby inner circular highway), amply financed from Saudi Arabia, was inaugurated. The formal unification, though, did not bring an end to numerous conflicts, and FEERI excluded representatives of M-30's Centro Cultural Islámico de Madrid.

On 19 January 2006 a change took place in the leadership of FEERI (what follows is based on EP 5.2.06). The former leader, who had negotiated the accord with the state in 1992, was put aside. 'Three out of six of the new directors get money from Saudi Arabia', confirmed one of the former leaders. The president, the Spanish *converso* Félix Herrero, underscored that the intention was to unify Spanish Muslims – 'We want the Muslims to speak with one voice' – and to support a politics of integration. One controversy is based on the absence of democratic meetings within the organization since 2000. According to the interpretation of the change put forward by the former president, 'They have not forgiven us that we brought forward a *fatwa* against terrorism, and, above all, that we have been very combative in defence of women's rights and their equality in front of the law.' Whereas former leaders and others point to the religious leader of M-30 as 'the real brain behind this operation', he refers to Islam's complex situation in Spain: 'Just like Jews and Protestants have each their unified voice in relation to the government, we want to do the same.' According to the historical leader of the other recognized Muslim organization UCIDE all the attempts to unify have been directed by the Saudis and have been opposed by him. Officials in the Ministry of Justice finds the composition of the new leadership unfortunate, since the mosque of the president, as *El País* relates, 'has been the centre of attention of a police operation against a terrorist cell. Among the arrested were individuals who acted as imams in this mosque'. The new president defends himself referring to his insistence that everybody who worked as imams should sign a document confirming their adherence to the constitution, and he insists that he feels betrayed by what has happened. Whatever the validity of the analysis and evaluations brought forward by the leaders of the various factions, what emerges from the accounts of these schisms is a fractured Muslim community and concerns about the role of particularly Saudi Arabia, but also Morocco, as opposed to attitudes of Spanish *conversos*. 'Except in the big mosques, that are supported by capital from Saudi Arabia, Syria or the Arab Emirates, practically every temple for community preaching is directed by Moroccans, normally holding a degree in Islamic sciences from Morocco, or by graduates from the religious university Al-Azhar in Cairo' (Barbería, EP 29.7.07). 'There are', according to Asesora de Asuntos Religiosos del Ministerio de Justicia, Ana Planet,

> a variety of types of conflictual discourses. The unfocused discourse of the person who arrives from Egypt and starts preaching in Fuencarral [an area in Madrid] without any knowledge of Spanish or of Spain; the discourse of the *resident* who invokes the Muslim condition in order to work against integration; or the discourse of the *clandestine antisystemic* who talks about Spain as infidel territory, all these discourses are but a single drop in a community that holds on to *convivencia* [co-existence, the term has specific historical connotations in the Spanish context] and the common heritage with the Spanish, yet we have to take these discourses into account.

According to the newspaper *Nacional* (31 January 2006) the newly elected president of FEERI explained that the new leadership planned to create a council of '*ulama*' with the task to issue fatwas at the national level and 'consisting of persons that are learned in Islamic law and not just simple believers'. The foreseen leader of this *consejo* would be the imam of M-30. It is in this complicated context that a case brought before the court in Barcelona gets its full significance.

On 12 January 2004 judge Juan Pedro Yllanes Suárez made public the ruling in the case concerning a publication (at La Casa del Libro Arabe in Barcelona) on *Woman in Islam* (*La mujer en el Islam*). The author, Mohamed Kamal Mostafa (in what follows: Kamal), was an imam at the mosque in Fuengirola (near Malaga, one of the major mosques in Spain) and leader of Centro Cultural Islámico Sohail as well as consultant or advisor for FEERI. In general Kamal is considered to be one of the most important Muslims in Spain. These capacities were crucial to the argument for the ruling: the author was an authority and thus obliged to take up a particular responsibility in his writings. The ruling (Suárez, 2004) quotes at length from the chapter in the book in which the author answers the question: 'Does the man have a right to beat (*pegar*) his wife?' His answer to this question prompted three organizations to bring the author before the court (EP 25.7.2000): Federation of Associations of Separated and Divorced Women (comprising some 10 organizations), Women's Council of the Community of Madrid (comprising about 80 organizations) and Association for the Support of Sexually Harassed Women. The lawyer representing these organizations, Maria José Varela, characterized the book as 'a clear provocation and an incentive to violence based on gender' (EP 25.7.2000) and referred to article 510 of the Penal Code. Kamal rephrases the question: 'How should the husband treat his wife, if she behaves improperly and how should the wife behave, when the husband commits a fault?' The answer takes as its starting point the steps towards reconciliation prescribed for the husband by Islam: (a) admonition, (b) if severe dialogue and reprimand do not work, the husband may use another 'disciplinary remedy: rejection (*abandono*) of the matrimonial bed.

What is at stake here is verse 34 of sura 4, Women: 'As for those [women] from whom you fear disobedience, admonish them, forsake them in beds apart, and beat them' (Dawood's translation; the proper translation of this verse is a highly contested issue, see below and for detailed historical analyses Marín, 2003; and Bauer, 2008) .Without explicit reference to this text Mostafa has mentioned two parts and presented them as *steps*. What then about the third step: 'beat them'? In order to approach the problem, Kamal brings an elaborate reflection on the phenomenon of violence among the sexes. 'Women have suffered and still suffer ill treatment and beatings from men.' This is the case in developed as well as in less developed parts of the world. The 'stress and tensions provoked by the vertiginous and ferocious rhythm of modern life' is part of the explanation. Yet there are also cases of violent acts against men from the side of women – Kamal refers to a Dutch group called the Association of Harassed Husbands. Religious and legislative measures have not been able to erase this violence. The prophet recommended avoiding marriage with a man known for violent behaviour towards women. Yet in spite of all efforts to bring a stop to violence, it is still there. On this background Kamal then approaches the third part of the verse from the Qur'an and recommends moderation in the name of Islam:

> We have to admit that the ideals laid out by the religions are in frontal clash with the predominating reality, therefore Islam intervenes in order to impose some limits that turns the beating into a simple symbolic suffering without any excess. [...] if the Qur'an in a short verse mentions physical punishment, this does not mean that Islam legitimizes it, it is rather steps in measures the men can take

> towards their wives in a positive sense, restricting themselves to their symbolic dimension by way of a series of restrictions. We should remember that God's Messenger never laid hand on any of his wives. (Suarez 2004)

The words and deeds of Muhammad are thus used with a view to an interpretation or modification of the word of the Qur'an. What follows then, in the text from Kamal's book as it is quoted in the ruling, are recommendations concerning limitations on physical punishment:

> In order to avoid major hurts one should never beat in a state of fury and blindness. One should never hit the sensitive parts of the body (face, breast, stomach, head, etc.). The strokes should be directed against a concrete part of the body like the feet and the hands with a not too heavy stick, i.e. it has to be fine and light in order not to leave wounds or haematomas on the body. The strokes should not be hard and strong, since the intention is to inflict a psychological suffering and not to humiliate and mistreat physically.[1]

Kamal concludes that, thanks to these restrictions and limitations, 'Islam has deprived physical punishment of significance as repressive means and turned it into a pure reprimand of a psychological-moral character.' And again the Prophet is invoked.

Manuela Marín notes in her extensive analysis of traditions of interpretation of Qur'an 4:34 and in particular the question of wife beating: 'The offending paragraphs in the book by M.K. Mustafa are hardly original. Similar statements can be found in Islamist literature all over the Arab-speaking world as well as in Western languages' (Marín, 2003, 6). One example is the influential scholar and television personality Yusuf Qaradawi In his book *The Lawful and the Prohibited in Islam* (1984) he wrote:

> Because of his natural ability and his responsibility for providing for his family, the man is the head of the house and of the family. He is entitled to the obedience and cooperation of his wife, and accordingly it is not permissible for her to rebel against his authority, causing disruption. [...] If the husband senses that feelings of disobedience and rebelliousness are rising against him in his wife, he should try his best to rectify her attitude by kind words, gentle persuasion, and reasoning with her. If this is not helpful, he should sleep apart from her, trying to awaken her agreeable feminine nature so that serenity may be restored, and she may respond to him in a harmonious fashion. If this approach fails, it is permissible for him to beat her lightly with his hands, avoiding her face and other sensitive parts. (quoted together with opinions by other authors in Stalinsky and Yehoshua 2004, Suarez 2004)

1 This and all following quotes from Kamalare as cited in Suraez 2004.

Similar interpretations of the verse in question are in line with ancient traditions, including the stress that beating should not be physically hurting (see Marín, 2003, and Bauer, 2008, 152–94). Yet in the context of modern Spain these instructions provoked the anger of the women's associations mentioned above. The judge agreed (Suárez, 2004) that Kamal had committed a crime against article 510 of the Penal Code, that concerns incitement to discrimination, hate or violence against groups defined by – among other criteria – gender, and against general principles of equality and human rights.

The lawyer representing the organizations behind the indictment, Maria José Varela, argued in her pleading (Varela, 2004), that Kamal had misused his position of authority towards members of the Muslim community, that his instructions were on his own account, that they represented an offence against the principles of the Spanish constitution, and that they could not be defended in reference to freedom of religion. She referred to a number of passages in the book that directly or indirectly argued for the superior status of the man in the family. Referring to a glorifying description of the traditional role of women in the family and a description of the bad situation they have been brought into in the actual situation, Varela quotes Kamal's opinion, that 'the woman – who was a respected mother, wife and companion – has been transformed into a dangerous rival and an opponent that aims at victory: and the result is, as it should be expected, a series of miseries as well for the woman as for the man'. Together with the quote above about the 'rhythm of modern life' this passage delineates an underlying narrative: modernity has created a miserable situation for the Muslim man. In the family the wife leaves the traditional role behind and tends to demand equality – or even superiority. In the wider social situation 'the vertiginous and ferocious rhythm' provokes 'stress and tensions'. In this situation of crisis Kamal's advice has a double aim: to bring women back into a traditional position and to calm down the violent tendencies created by modernity in men – light beating 'without excess' is on one hand a disciplined channelling of violent impulses, the symbolic or psychological suffering is on the other hand a way to turn the rebellious wife back into the role as 'a respected mother, wife and companion'. Islam – in Kamal's sense – is a tradition that can work as a solution in a situation of crisis for traditional gender roles and restore them. In this narrative modernity is the force that intrudes, and the solution is basically to exclude the intruder.

Behind the conflicts between man and woman in the family the confrontation in the moment of crisis is between (Kamal's version of) Islam and modernity. This is, of course, a well-known type of narrative, not only in a Muslim context, but also when the conflict is between Christianity and modernity. The interesting aspect is the psychological dimensions that delineate the contours of a tormented Muslim man. As discourse, Shari'a in this case is not only a series of principles and arguments: one of the threads in the discursive pattern is a narrative structure. Although it is, of course, not necessary to dig deep into Kamal's text in order to bring this narrative into the light of day, its presence as organizing structure underlying the statements of principles may hint at potentials in this sort of discourse analysis.

In the construction of this narrative Kamal did not take into account, though, that the principles of equality and human rights in Spanish law, i.e. modernity in its legal guise, were in force for everybody in Spain. Summarizing her analysis of Kamal's position, Varela underscored that:

> It is evident that it is the aim of the instructions in the book that those that are practising Islamic faith uphold relations of domination between men and women such that the man just by the fact of his gender holds a superior position with the tasks to correct, discipline and punish and can use physical and psychological violence against the woman that is his wife [...].

And in her conclusion she stressed: 'In defence of women's human rights, nobody should be allowed to hide behind a religious belief and commit crimes without being punished'.

Judge Suaréz underscored the role of Kamal as spiritual leader of his community, he pointed to 'a tone of obsolete machismo', considered the description of the roles of women 'incompatible with the predominant social sensibility', in particular with a view to the fact 'that the situation of women in our country was much similar in the not too distant past'. Besides the strictly judicial aspects, i.e. the application of the Penal Code, he also stressed that the law was based on 'absolute consensus among all the political forces'. During the first day of the proceedings Kamal had recognized that he had written a book that justified maltreatment of women, but said that 'he had done it because he could not go against the Qur'an and the doctrine derived from the sacred book'; EP 20.12.2003). According to Judge Suaréz, perceptions of religious duties did not excuse anything:

> In a non confessional state [...], that is integrated in the European Union and openly promoting a secular society, neither the possibility to be treated as an apostate by followers of the same religion or to be excluded, nor respect for doctrinal orthodoxy can serve as fundament for publication of opinions that provoke physical violence against women for the sole reason of gender, promoting conduct that transgresses the fundamental right to physical and moral integrity, seriously encroaching on their dignity and constituting a serious penal violation of a recent legal reform that reflects the disgust of society at any sort of maltreatment of women. (Suarez 2004)

As it appears from these examples from a very long argumentation there is more than one discourse in play: the strictly judicial discourse is interspersed with historical ('obsolete', 'the not too distant past'), moral ('machismo'), social ('predominant sensibility') and political ('absolute consensus') discourses. Not only there is a law, it is furthermore a law that was passed in total consensus. Not only has Kamal transgressed this law, his entire attitude is obsolete, and this is so much more repugnant because Spain only recently moved out of the grip of political and religious backwardness. Whereas Kamal regretted the crisis engendered by modernity, Judge Suaréz celebrates and defends the modernization of Spain, the secular state, the integration in the European Union, and the application of universal principles of human rights and equality. In both cases the roles and conditions of women are at stake. Whereas Kamal directed his discourse to members of his own religious community, the discourses of both Varela and Suarez have a double direction: towards the judicial system, and towards the public sphere. Newspapers frequently wrote about and commented on the process. After the sentence *El Païs* gave an editorial the headline 'An exemplary sentence' and wrote:

> The judicial sentence is particularly valuable in affirming that the confrontation between a presumed right to religious freedom, exercised by the imam, and the right to moral integrity of the women his discourse is directed towards should be resolved in favour of the last. […] The judiciary has not always been the most advanced, but the exemplary sentence of the judge in Barcelona is a good sign, that should be greeted with applause […]. (EP 15.01.2004)

This particular case crystallized a much broader problematic and provoked a variety of reactions from representatives of various tendencies in Spanish Islam. Kamal tried to present the case as repression of Islam: 'Since the Inquisition and Franco's times, I am the first person to be sent to prison for an opinion, for translating a sacred word from the Qur'an […] if the judges do not accept the Qur'an in this country, they should say it clearly […]' (EP 30.11.2004). According to one Muslim commentator, 'the subject of the so-called 'incompatibility of Islam and the Spanish Constitution' was frequently evoked in several newspapers, among them the right-wing newspaper *La Razón*, which is closely related to the Catholic Church (Prado, 2004 – Prado is a very active *converso*, who is among other things organizing conferences on Islam and feminism).

Before the process FEERI had issued a statement on maltreatment of women that urged Kamal to withdraw his book (FEERI, 2002). After the sentence the secretary commented on the case in an interview: 'No learning can offer us the criteria for understanding Islam […]. The understanding that each person had of the Qur'an is proportional to his love and openness to Allah. You may be a doctor in Islamic Sciences from the University of Azhar, but as the Messenger of God (peace be on him) says: "He who beats his wife is the worst of all men"' (quoted in Prado, 2004). In the statement mentioned above FEERI took up the question of how to translate Q 4:34, which was also a crucial issue at the trial. The point is, that alone in the Qur'an the word *daraba* has a number of different meanings – not to speak of the many meanings in Arabic in general, and consequently a number of possible translations of the third step in the attempts to correct a troublesome wife are at hand. Jacques Berque's '*essai de traduction*' has, for example '*corrigez*' (Berque, 2002, 101). Arguments against wife beating as part of Shari'a are of various kinds: philological arguments in the linguistic sense, arguments based on *sunna* and arguments based on historical change are obviously not the same type of arguments.

Women's Readings

From a methodological point of view female readers have insisted on a contextual reading in the sense that interpretation should not focus on isolated short passages, but rather on the overall character of the Quran. According to Amina Wadud the exegetes of the classical period 'begin with the first verse of the first chapter and proceed to the second verse of the first chapter – one verse at a time – until the end of the Book. Little or no effort is made to recognise themes and to discuss the relationship of the Quran to itself, thematically' (Wadud, 1999, 2). As Asma Barlas formulates the result: 'An inevitable, if ultimately unacceptable, result is a partial, piecemeal and decontextualised (mis)interpretation that not only fails to see hermeneutic connections between themes in the Qur'an, but which also projects patriarchal and misogynistic meanings into it' (Barlas, 2006, 262). Verse 34 in sura 4 is an obvious case in point. Barlas here refers to a discussion of this passage by Azizah al-Hibri (1982, 217–19). 'Men have authority over women …' is one translation of the first words (Dawood, 2006), Al-Hibri's version is 'Men are *qawwamun* over women …', and the basic notion of the Arabic word is 'one of moral guidance and caring'. Elsewhere (Q 9:71) equality or reciprocity is implied: 'The believers, men and women, are *awliya'* of one another.' This Arabic word, al-Hibri points out, 'means "protectors", "in charge", "guides". It is quite similar to *qawwamun*'. Since Q 9:71 clearly puts true believing men and women on equal foot as caring for or guiding each other, Q 4:34 should be read in the same spirit excluding a general idea of men as superior.

The general principle involved in this kind of reading is thus on one hand attention to polysemy, and on the other hand selection among a plurality of potential meanings at the basis of Qur'anic context. In many ways this is an approach that is similar to modern literary text analysis – and, of course, different from interpretations of isolated bits of the Quran by reference to posterior juridical literature. It is simultaneously a type of interpretation that is based on philology and attention to the text instead of knowledge of traditions of interpretation, which means that what is required is first and foremost linguistic competence, and that this hermeneutic practice is not an exclusive privilege based on education and positions:

> Yet, for the most part, this liberatory endeavour remains confined to the margins of Muslim religious discourse because of the structure of religious authority in Muslim societies, that allows only men, and only some men at that, to speak authoritatively in God's name. For this to change there needs to be a far-reaching reform of Muslim societies and communal consciousness since one cannot read

> the Qur'an for its best meanings in repressive and antidemocratic circumstances where one cannot ask some questions openly. (Barlas, 2006, 268–9)

Reading the Qur'an in reference to the Qur'an itself and its general spirit is one sort of contextualization that may underpin specific interpretations and thereby undermine patriarchal traditions. Another sort of contextualization takes the social and historical context of the presumed revelation into account. This is the basic argument in Amina Wadud's influential book on *Qur'an and Women* (1999), one of the contributions referred to in debates in Spain sparked by Kamal's book. The approach is based on a distinction between universal and particular: 'Certainly the circumstances of seventh-century Arabia set the backdrop for the Qur'an and its goal of universal guidance. Later generations of Muslims must consider how the text was restricted by the particulars of that time' (Wadud, 1999, xii). Reading the Qur'an in the light of the historical context may bring these particulars into the light and thereby sort out the universal aspects of the message. 'The implication of this patriarchal context must be understood in relation to the greater Qur'anic principles and their ultimate intent of harmonious and equitable relationships in society. It is this ultimate Qur'anic intent which reveals its true "spirit"' (Wadud, 1999, 81). The universal principles can then be applied to the readers' actual historical circumstances, repetition of the restrictions imposed by the original historical context can be avoided, and a way to reform can be opened up: 'These reforms operate outside the literal content of some Qur'anic passages and make modifications on the basis of greater Qur'anic intent […]' (Wadud, 1999, 82). One such passage Wadud discusses is the rest of verse 4.34. Setting off from linguistic arguments she reaches this conclusion: 'In the light of the excessive violence towards women indicated in the biographies of the Companions and by practices condemned in the Qur'an (like female infanticide), this verse should be taken as prohibiting unchecked violence against females. Thus, this is not permission, but a severe restriction of existing practice' (Wadud, 1999, 76). These arguments demonstrate the character and the perspective of the hermeneutic approach: in the past context, what may seem like a statement of the right of the husband to beat his wife appears as restriction, which means that later applications of the spirit of the text should go as far as possible towards restriction – implied in the present situation is, presumably, a full realization of the spirit of equality, that Wadud finds in the Qur'an.

Whereas arguments referred to above (like FEERI's) in reference to semantic arguments, Qur'anic context and *sunna* entirely reject the idea that the Qur'an allows wife beating of any sort, Wadud historicizes the content of Q 4:34 and regards it as obsolete (cf. opinions on Islam and wife beating of some prominent scholars compiled in Stalinsky and Yeshoshua, 2004; fatwas and commentaries in Islam Online and Al Tafsir; and four main tendencies in feminist readings of 4:34 analysed in Amghar, 2007; as well as for historical analysis Marín, 2003; and Bauer, 2008).

Historical Hermeneutics

Barlas closed her survey of women's studies of the Qur'an on a fairly pessimistic note: 'one cannot read the Qur'an for its best meanings in repressive and antidemocratic circumstances where one cannot ask some questions openly'. As it is well known, serious institutional interventions have taken place as reactions to attitudes to scholarly ideas about how to read the Qur'an. Nasr Hamid Abu Zayd is probably the most famous case. He has himself delineated the tradition behind his approach (Abu Zayd, 2003, 2005; cf. Wild, 1993). A major forerunner was Muhammad Ahmad Khalafallah whose PhD thesis generated public and institutional reactions. Abu Zayd summarizes the reaction:

> (1) A literary text is a composition of human imagination while the Qur'an represents the word of God that should not be compared to any human discourse.
>
> (2) To deal with the Qur'an as a work of literary art, *fann*, is to suggest that it is written by Muhammad.
>
> (3) Furthermore, claiming that the stories of the Qur'an do not present actual historical facts, as the literary approach suggests, is committing the greatest blasphemy that amounts to apostasy. It places the Qur'an in a lower position than a book of history.
>
> (4) More insulting to the Qur'an from the point of view of the traditional dogma is to claim that its language and structure is historically determined and culturally formed. It could be easily interpreted to mean that the Qur'an is a human text. (Abu Zayd 2003, 9)

Abu Zayd's own work generated a court decision in 1995 that declared him an apostate and accordingly decided that his marriage should be annulled. These were the reasons given by the court (Abu Zayd, 2003, 34):

1. In his books, the writer denied the actual existence of certain creatures, such as angels and jinn, referred to in the Qur'an.
2. He has described certain images in the Qur'an about heaven and hell as mythical.
3. He has described the text of the Holy Qur'an as a human text.
4. He has advocated the use of reason to explain the concepts derived from the literal meaning of the text of the Qur'an in order to replace them by modern, more human, and progressive terms. He applies his method of rational interpretation particularly to the texts related to inheritance, women, the Christians and the Jews (*ahl al-dhimmah*), and woman slaves.

Abu Zayd wants to emphasize the historical circumstances of the formulation of the Qur'an. He does not question the divine revelation, yet he wants to situate the formulation of the text in its historical context with a view to opening up for a contemporary application of basic aspects of the Qur'an. The Qur'an emerged in a specific cultural context and prompted the development of a new culture and a new type of society. This means that the meaning of the Qur'an was linked to the context of the first formulation and that subsequent significance of the Qur'an depends on new social and historical contexts. Abu Zayd articulates this well-known hermeneutical topic as a difference between 'the deep semantic structure of the Qur'an' and 'the surface structure' (Abu Zayd, 2003, 39). The deep semantic structure is the significance that is realized as the meaning of the Qur'an in specific cultural historical contexts:

> Since the interpretation of Islam is believed to be valid to all human beings, regardless of time and space, diversity of interpretation is inevitable. But being aware of the distinction between the original contextual 'meaning' and the 'significance', and also being aware of the necessity that the significance is to be strongly related and rationally connected to the meaning, will produce a more valid interpretation. The 'meaning' is almost fixed because of its historicity while the 'significance' is changeable. (Abu Zayd, 2003, 39)

Each social and historical context will thus bring forward its own interpretation. To Abu Zayd this interpretation is not arbitrary, there is a divine text. The provocative point is: 'If the text is historical though originally divine, its interpretation is necessarily humane' (Abu Zayd, 2003, 39). The implication being that authorities from the past are relegated to their specific historical context. 'The historical exploration of the Qur'an can provide us with the context, we have lost during the course of time, so that we can realize the meaning of the Divine message and its significance and separate what is "historically conditioned" from the "timeless' significance"' (Abu Zayd, 2005). The core of the message (the 'significance') may be transhistorical, yet the specific historical and cultural context demands a specific application of the text available, a specific historical 'meaning': 'the deep semantic structure of the Qur'an must be extracted from the surface structure. Subsequently, the deep structure must be explained in a wording which is that of today' (Abu Zayd, 2003, 39).

Conclusion

In Abu Zayd's hermeneutics the deep structure has the same position as the universal 'spirit' in Wadud's approach. Whatever the differences, their ways of reading the Qur'an both insist on historical contextualization and take distances to literalist approaches. Although Amina Wadud has not been met with court intervention in her life, she closes her preface to the American edition of her book in a combative mood: 'In the battle for gender parity, those who stand guard at the gate posts of Muslim status quo have sometimes reacted vehemently against claims for justice. The trenches are deep and the fighting often unfair, but the motivation for my entry into the struggle is nonnegotiable' (Wadud, 1999, xix).

The court decision that Abu Zayd's writings amounted to apostasy reveals the rules regulating the discourse on Islam in the Egyptian context, or at least rules agreed on by the originators of the accusation and the judges. It is about what can be said and what cannot be said about the general status and character of the Qur'anic text. This discursive order is at the level of 'social discourse' in the sense elaborated by Marc Angenot (1995). Controversies about Q 4:34 are more specific. They are about ways in which 'Islam' should regulate behaviour through not only divine sanction but also by talking women into acceptance of certain roles, in Foucault's parlance: specific interpretations of Q 4:34 serve as a discursive social 'technology' for 'production' of the Muslim wife as pious and subservient to her husband, a sort of '*mise-en-discours*' (Foucault): 'Men have authority over women because God has made the one superior to the other', as Wadud translated the first part of the verse. From the point of view of female critics an entire institutional structure supports and perpetuates this discourse: a massive collection of texts (*fiqh*), the knowledge of which is transferred through institutions (like al-Azhar University) and supports the authority of graduates from these institutions in their functions as imams in mosques (that may be financed by Saudi government or private resources, as in the case of M-30 in Madrid) and other institutional structures, all of this supporting, 'producing' or reproducing patriarchal family structures. In this context it is significant that Kamal's book was produced for distribution in mosques, i.e. within the institutional structure in which he held a prominent authoritative position, a relatively closed sphere of communication, embedded in the rest of the activities of and in the mosque. Kamal's discourse on women and Islam was linked to institutional practice and was aimed at regulation of practice. A Foucaldian approach to this discursive practice thus seems adequate. Under the aspect of the indictment and the case before the court, Muslim women were individuals in Spanish society and thus protected by Spanish law against discrimination and incentives to mistreatment. As soon as Kamal's book entered the public sphere it became an object of scrutiny from the point of view of human rights, and in as far as his discourse turned out to contradict principles of equality his entire institutional role became problematic. Here Habermas' approach seems adequate, since patriarchal institutional practice and discourse is challenged by public debate and institutionalized law as sedimentation of historical change in the public sphere and politics (cf. Masud, 2001).Wadud's, Abu Zayd's and so many other Muslims' interventions in debates concerning the proper understanding of Islam under modern circumstances, i.e. not least in relation to gender equality and human rights, take part in the same debate. The various concepts of discourse in the humanities and social sciences may thus elucidate the character of each their aspect of this field of controversies.

Bibliography

'Abd al-Fattah, Nabil 2005, Al-Dawla wa'l-Din. Al-Islah al-dusturi iadat at-tafkir fi `alaqa murakkiba', in Markaz al-Qahira li-dirasat huquq al-insan, *Nahw dustur misri jadid*, Cairo, 81–105.

'Abd al-Jabbar n.d., *al-Mughni fi Abwab al-Tawhid wa'l-* 'Adl, eds 'Abd al-Halim Mahmud and Sulayman Dunya, Cairo: al-Sharikah al-'arabiyya.

'Abd al-Raziq, 'Ali 1966, *al-Islam wa Usul al-Hukm*, Beirut: Dar maktabat al-hayah.

'Abduh, Muhammad 1999, *Tafsir al-manar*, Beirut: Dar al-kutub al-'ilmiyya.

'Abdul-'Aziz, Muhammad bin ed. 2002, *al-Musnad. Fatawa Islamiyah: Islamic Verdicts*. 8 vols. Riyadh: Darussalam

Abrahamov, Binyamin 1995, 'The bi-la kayfa doctrine and its foundations in Islamic theology', *Arabica*, vol. 42, 365–79.

Abu Zayd, Nasr Hamid 1995, *Al-tafkir fi zaman al-takfir*, Cairo: Sina.

Abu Zayd, Nasr Hamid 2000, *Dawa'ir al-Khawf*, Beirut: Al-Markaz al-Thaqafi al-'Arabi.

Abu Zayd, Nasr Hamid 2003, 'The dilemma of the literary approach to the Qur'an', *Alif: Journal of Comparative Poetics*, no. 23, Literature and the Sacred, Cairo: American University of Cairo Press, 8–47.

Abu Zayd, Nasr Hamid 2005, 'Wege zu einer neuen islamischen Methodik in der Hermeneutik', <www.muslimische-stimmen.de>, accessed 6 March 2008.

Abu Zayd, Nasr Hamid 2006, *Reformation of Islamic Thought. a Critical Historical Analysis*, Amsterdam: Amsterdam University Press.

Afsaruddin, Asma 2006a, 'Competing perspectives on *jihad* and martyrdom in early Islamic sources', in *Witnesses to Faith?: Martyrdom in Christianity and Islam*, ed. Brian Wicker, Aldershot: Ashgate, 15–31.

Afsaruddin, Asma 2006b, 'The "Islamic state": genealogy, facts, and myths', *Journal of Church and State*, 48, 153–73.

Afsaruddin, Asma 2006c, 'Obedience to political authority: an evolutionary concept', in *Islamic Democratic Discourse: Theory, Debates, and Directions*, ed. Muqtedar Khan, Lanham, MD: Lexington Books, 45–6.

Afsaruddin, Asma 2007, *The First Muslims: History and Memory*, Oxford: Oneworld Publications.

Afsaruddin, Asma forthcoming, *Striving in the Path of God: Discursive Traditions on Jihad and the Cult of Martyrdom*, Oxford: Oxford University Press.

Albertini, Tamara 2003, 'The seductiveness of certainty: the destruction of Islam's intellectual legacy by the fundamentalists', *Philosophy: East and West*, 53, 455–71.

Alvå, Jan 1997, 'Inledningsanförande', in *Domarkonferens i Lund 12–14 mars 1997: Dokumentation*, Lund: no publisher, printed at Reprocentralen.

Amghar, Samir 2005, 'Les salafistes français: une nouvelle aristocratie religieuse?'. *Maghreb/Machrek*, no. 183, 13–31.

Amghar, Samir 2006, 'Les trois âges du discours des Frères musulmans en Europe', in *Islamismes d'Occident. État des lieux et perspectives*, ed. Samir Amghar, Paris: Éditions Lignes de repères.

Amghar, Samir et al. 2007, *European Islam. Challenges for Public Policy and Society*, Brussels: Centre for European Policy Studies.

al-'Amiri, Rashed S. 2003, 'Legal maxims in Islamic jurisprudence', unpublished PhD thesis, University of Birmingham.

Angenot, Marc 1995, 'The concept of social discourse', *English Studies in Canada*, 21, 1–19.

Angenot, Marc 2004, 'Social discourse analysis: outlines of a research project', *The Yale Journal of Criticism*, 17, 199–215.

An-Naim, Abdullahi A. 1996, *Towards an Islamic Reformation*, Syracuse, NY: Syracuse University Press.

An-Naim, Abdullahi 2008, *Islam and the Secular State: Negotiating the Future of Sharia*, Cambridge, MA: Harvard University Press.

Arkoun, Mohammed 1994, *Rethinking Islam: Common Questions, Uncommon Answers*, Boulder, CO: Westview.

Arkoun, Mohammed 2003–2004, 'La condition feminine en contextes islamiques', in *Al-Nisa' fi'l-khutab al-'arabi al-mu'asir*, eds Bayoumi and Al-Kadri, 9th book, Beirut: Bahithat, 22–55.

Arold, N.L 2007, *The Legal Culture of the European Court of Human Rights*, Amsterdam: Martinus Nijhoff.

Asad, Talad 2003, *Formations of the Secular*, Palo Alto, CA: Stanford University Press.

al-'Ashmawi, Muhammad Sa'id 1990, *al-Islam al-siyasi*, Algiers: Mufim li'l-nashr.

al-'Ashmawi, Muhammad Sa'id 1998, '*Shari'a*: the codification of Islamic law', in *Liberal Islam: A Sourcebook*, ed. Charles Kurzman, Oxford: Oxford University Press, 52–4.

al-'Ashmawy, Sa'id 1987, *al-Islam al-siyasi*, Cairo: Sina.

al-Atawneh, Muhammad 2004, 'Fatwas and Ifta' in Saudi Arabia: a study of Islamic legal thought, 1971–2000', unpublished PhD dissertation, Ben Gurion University.

Augustinos, M., K. Tuffin and D. Every 2005, 'New racism, meritocracy and individualism: constraining affirmative action in education', *Discourse and Society*, 163, 315–40.

Austin, J.L. 1975, *How to Do Things with Words*, Oxford: Clarendon Press.

Babès, Leila, and Tareq Oubrou 2002, *Loi d'Allah, loi des hommes. Liberté, égalité et femmes en islam*, Paris: Éditions Albin Michel.

Badawi, Zaki 1995, 'Muslim justice in a secular state', in *God's Law Versus State Law*, ed. Michael King, London: Grey Seal, 73–80.

Ballard, Roger ed. 1994, *Desh Pardesh: The South Asian Presence in Britain*, London: Hurst & Co.

Ballard, Roger 2006, 'Ethnic diversity and the delivery of justice: The challenge of plurality', in *Migration, Diasporas and Legal Systems in Europe*, eds Prakash Shah and Werner F. Menski, London: Routledge-Cavendish, 29–56.

Bakht, Natasha 2006, 'Were Muslim barbarians really knocking on the gates of Ontario? The religious arbitration controversy – another perspective', 40th anniversary edition, *Ottowa Law Review*, 67–82.

Barlas, Asma 2006, 'Women's readings of the Qur'an', in *The Cambridge Companion to the Qur'an,* ed. Jane Dammen McAuliffe, Cambridge: Cambridge University Press, 255–71.

Basma, Ayat 2006, 'Religious broadcasters avoid confrontation', *Middle East Broadcasters Journal*, June–July 2006, issue no. 7, 27–9.

Bauer, Karen A. 2008, 'Room for interpretation: Qur'anic exegesis and gender', unpublished PhD dissertation, University of Princeton.

Bazmee Ansari, A.S. 2008, 'al-Fatāwā al- 'Ālamgīriyya', *Encyclopaedia of Islam Online*, Leiden: Brill.

BBC 2006, 'Veiled woman to give C4's speech', BBC News, 5 December, available at <http://news.bbc.co.uk/go/pr/fr/-/2/hi/entertainment/6210324.stm> accessed 18 December 2006.

Bell, John 1995, 'English law and French law – not so different?', *Current Legal Problems*, no. 48, 63–101.

Bell, John 2006, *Judiciaries within Europe*, Oxford: Oxford University Press.

Bellah, Robert N. 1967. 'Civil Religion in America', *Daedalus* 96 (Winter 1967), 1-21.

Bellah, Robert N. 1968. 'Civil Religion in America' in *Religion in America,* eds. William G. McLoughlin and Robert N. Bellah, Boston: Houghton Miffin, 3–23.

Bengtsson, Cajsa Sandgren 2008. *Möten med islam*, Uppsala: Svenska kyrkan.

Berger, Maurits 2006, *Sharia. Islam tussen recht en politiek*, The Hague: Boom.

Berman, Harold 2007, 'Comparative law and religion', in *Oxford Handbook of Comparative Law*, eds Mathias Reimann and Reinhard Zimmermann, Oxford: Oxford University Press, 745–6.

Bernard-Maugiron, Nathalie 2003, *Le politique à l'épreuve du judiciaire: la justice constitutionnelle en Égypt*, Bruxelles: Bruylant.

Berque, Jacques 2002, *Le Coran. Essai de traduction*, Paris: Albin Michel.

Bhatt, Chetan 1997, *Liberation and Purity: Race, New Religious Movements and the Ethics of Postmodernity*, London and Bristol, Pennsylvania: UCL Press.

Bierbrauer, Günter 1994, 'Toward an understanding of legal culture: Variations in individualism and collectivism between Kurds, Lebanese, and Germans', *Law and Society Review*, vol. 28, no. 2, 243–64.

Bistolfi, Robert and François Zabbal, eds, 1995, *Islams d'Europe: Intégration ou Insertion Communautaire?*, La Tour d'Aigues: Editions de l'Aube.

Bjerkaas, Ingrid 1966/2001, 'Mit kall', in *Norsk Tro og Tanke*, ed. Jan-Erik Ebbestad Hansen, vol. 3, Oslo: Universitetsforlaget, 415–20.

Blair, Tony 2006, 'The duty to integrate: shared British values', speech given at the Runnymede Trust, 8 December 2006, <http://www.number-10.gov.uk/output/Page10563.asp>, accessed 2 May 2007.

Bogdan, Michael 1993a, 'Islamisk brudpenning mahr inför svensk domstol', *Svensk Juristtidning*, no. 7, 597–600.

Bogdan, Michael 1993b, 'Anm. av Johanna Schiratzki, Muslimsk familjerätt, Lagar, seder och attityder', *Svensk Juristtidning*, no. 8, 677–8.

Bogdan, Michael 1999, 'Anm. av Sami Aldeeb och Andrea Bonomi red., Le droit musulman de la famille et des successions à l'épreuve des ordres juridiques occidentaux', *Svensk Juristtidning*, no. 10, 1008–1009.

Bogdan, Michael 2006a, 'Svensk rättspraxis: internationell privat- och processrätt 2001–2005', *Svensk Juristtidning*, no. 7, 601–44.

Bogdan, Michael 2006b, 'Anm. av Jan Hjärpe, Sharia. Gudomlig lag i en värld i förändring', *Svensk Juristtidning*, no. 1, 97–8.

Bogdan. Michael 2007, 'Något om den kollisionsrättsliga behandlingen av islamisk morgongåva MAHR', in *Rett och toleranse. Festskrift til Helge Johan Thue*, eds Torstein Frantzen, Johan Giertsen and Giuditta Cordero Moss, Oslo: Gyldendal Akademisk.

Boubekeur, Amel 2005, 'L'islam est-il soluble dans le Mecca Cola?', *Magreb/Machrek*, nr. 183.

Bowen, John R. 2003, *Islam, Law and Equality in Indonesia: An Anthropology of Public Reasoning*, Cambridge: Cambridge University Press.

Bowen, John R. 2004, 'Pluralism and normativity in French Islamic reasoning', in *Islam, Pluralism, and Democratization*, eds Robert Hefner, Princeton, NJ: Princeton University Press.

Bowen, John R. 2006, *Why the French don't like Headscarves*. Princeton, NJ: Princeton University Press.

Bramsen, Dorthe 2003, 'Ibn Taymiyya og de guddommelige egenskaber', *RVT: Religionsvidenskabeligt Tidsskrift*, vol. 42, 27–41, Aarhus: Aarhus Universitetsforlag.

Bramsen, Dorthe 2007, 'Divine law and human understanding: interpreting shari'a within the institutions of ifta' and qada' in Saudi Arabia', unpublished PhD dissertation Copenhagen University.

Brown, Gordon 2006, 'The future of Britishness', speech given at the Fabian Future of Britishness Conference, 14 January 2006, <http://www.fabian-society.org.uk/press_office/news_latest_all.asp?pressid=520>, accessed 2 May 2007

Brown, Nathan J. 2002, *Constitutions in a Nonconstitutional World,* Albany: State University of New York Press.

Cameron, David 2005, speech given at the Foreign Policy Centre, 24 August 2005, <http://fpc.org.uk/fsblob/560.pdf>, accessed 2 May 2007.

Carroll, Lucy 1997, 'Muslim women and "Islamic divorce" in England', *Journal of Muslim Minority Affairs*, vol. 17, no. 1, 97–115.

Chehata, Chafik 1971, *Etudes de droit musulman*, Paris: Faculté de droit et des sciences économiques.

Chiba, Masaji 1986, *Asian Indigenous Law in Interaction with Received Law*, London and New York: KPI.

Chiba, Masaji 1998, 'Other phases of legal pluralism in the contemporary world', *Ratio Juris*, vol. 11, no. 3 September, 228–45.

Christoffersen, Lisbet 2001, 'The changing position of the individual in Danish welfare law', in *Responsible Selves: Women in the Nordic Legal Culture*, eds Kevät Nousiainen, Johanna Niemi-Kiesilainen et al., Aldershot: Ashgate, 131–54.

Christoffersen, Lisbet 2006, 'Intertwinement: A new concept for understanding religion-law relations', *Nordic Journal of Religion and Society*, 19, 107–26.

Christoffersen, Lisbet 2008, 'Religion as a factor in multi-layered European Union legislation', in *Law and Religion in Multicultural Societies*, ed. Rubya Mehdi et al., Copenhagen: Jurist- og Økonomforbundets forlag, 111–30.

Christoffersen, Lisbet, Svend Andersen and Kjell-A. Modéer eds, forthcoming, *New Life in the Ruins. Law and Religion in the Nordic Countries in the 21st Century*.

Clarence-Smith, William Gervase 2006, *Islam and the Abolition of Slavery*, Oxford: Oxford University Press.

Clarke, J.I. 1980, 'Contemporary urban growth', in *The Changing Middle Eastern City*, eds G.H. Blake and R.I. Lawless, London: Croom Helm, 154–70.

Cohn, Margit 2004, 'Women, religious law and religious courts in Israel. The Jewish case', *Retfærd*, 107/2004, 57–76.

Coulson, N.J. 1964, *A History of Islamic Law*, Edinburgh: Edinburgh University Press.

Coulson, N.J. 1969, *Conflicts and Tensions in Islamic Jurisprudence*, Chicago, IL: University of Chicago Press.

Cowell, Alan 2006, 'Jack Straw ignites a debate over Muslim veil', *International Herald Tribune*, 6 October.

Cownie, Fiona, Anthony Bradney and Mandy Burton 2003, *English Legal System in Context*, London: LexisNexis.

Crane, Robert D. 2005, 'Shari'ah: legacy of the prophet: the role of human rights in Islamic law,' *The American Muslim*, January–March, at <http://www.theamericanmuslim.org/>, accessed 1 February 2009.

Crone, Manni 2007, 'Trendspotting. Er islamisme ved at blive cool?', *Politiken*, April 22.

al-Daawah, monthly Islamic magazine published in Riyadh by Al-Daawah Est. in collaboration with the Ministry of Islamic Affairs, Endowment, Call and Guidance.

Dabbous-Sensenig, D. 2006, 'To veil or not to veil: gender and religion on Al-Jazeera's *Islamic Law and Life*', *Westminster Papers in Communication and Culture*, 3, 2, 60–85.
Dahl, Tove Stang ed. 1985, *Kvinnerett I & Kvinnerett II. Kvinners levekår og livsløp*, Oslo: Universitetsforlaget.
Dahl, Tove Stang 1987, *Women's Law. An Introduction to Feminist Jurisprudence*, Oslo: Norwegian University Press.
Dakake, David 2004, 'The myth of a militant Islam', in *Islam, Fundamentalism, and the Betrayal of Tradition: Essays by Western Muslim Scholars*, ed. Joseph E.B. Lumbard, Bloomington, IN: World Wisdom, 3–38.
Dan, Joseph 1998, 'Jewish studies and European terminology. Religion, law and ethics' in *Jewish Studies in a New Europe*, eds Ulf Haxen, Hanne Trautner-Kromann and Karen Lisa Goldschmidt Salamon, Copenhagen: Reitzel.
Dassetto, Felice et al. 2007, *Islam in the European Union: What is at Stake in the Future?* Brussels: European Parliament.
Davies, Margaret 2007, 'Secular feminism and multi-faith legal pluralism', paper for 2007 Conference on Law and Society in the 21st Century; workshop on 'Feminism, Secularism and Religion', unpublished.
Davies, Margaret 2008, 'Pluralism in law and religion', in *Law and Religion in Theoretical and Historical Perspective*, eds Peter Cane, Carolyn Evans and Zoë Robinson, Cambridge: Cambridge University Press.
al-Dawish, Ahmad bin 'Abd al-Razzaq ed. 2002, *Fatawa al-lajna al-da'ima lil-buhuth al-'ilmiyya wa'l-ifta'*, 20 vols, Riyadh: Mu'assasat al-Amira al-'Unud bint 'Abd al-'Aziz b. Musa'id b. Jalawi Al Sa'ud al-Khayriyya.
Dawood N.J. 2006, *The Koran*, translated with notes, London: Penguin Books.
Deacon, D., M. Pickering, P. Golding and G. Murdock 1999, *Researching Communications*, London: Arnold.
Dembour, Marie-Bénédict 2006, *Who Believes in Human Rights? Reflections on the European Convention*, Cambridge: Cambridge University Press.
van Dijk, Teun 1988, *News as Discourse*, Hillsdale, NJ: Lawrence Erlbaum Associates, Inc., Publishers.
van Dijk, Teun 1991, *Racism and the Press: Critical Studies in Racism and Migration*, London: Routledge.
van Dijk, Teun 1997, 'Discourse as interaction in society', in *Discourse as Social Interaction. Discourse Studies: A Multidisciplinary Introduction*, ed. Teun van Dijk, vol. 2, London: Sage, 1–37.
van Dijk, Teun 2001, 'Critical Discourse Analysis', in *The Handbook of Discourse Analysis*, eds Deborah Schiffin, Deborah Tannen and Heidi E. Hamilton, Oxford: Blackwell.
Donohue, J. and J. Esposito 1982, *Islam in Transition*, Oxford: Oxford University Press.
Droeber, Julia 2005, *Dreaming of Change: Young Middle-Class Women and Social Transformation in Jordan*, Leiden: Brill.

Egypt 2007, The Constitution of Egypt, at <http://www.misr.gov.eg/arabic/laws/constitution/index.asp>.

EI2: *Encyclopaedia of Islam*, 2nd edition, 1954–2005, Brill: Leiden.

Ende, W. 2008, 'Salafiyya', *Encyclopaedia of Islam Online*, Leiden: Brill.

Enquist, P.O. 2001, *Lewis Resa*, Stockholm: Norstedts Förlag.

Ernst, Carl W. 1997, *The Shambhala Guide to Sufism*, Boston, MA: Shambhala.

Esposito, John L. ed. 1995, *Oxford Encyclopedia of the Modern Islamic World*, 4 vols, New York and Oxford: Oxford University Press.

Esposito, John L. and John O. Voll 1996, *Islam and Democracy*, New York: Oxford University Press.

Evans, Carolyn 2001, *Freedom of Religion under the European Convention of Human Rights*, Oxford, New York: Oxford University Press

Evans, Carolyn and Amanda Whiting 2006, 'Situating the issues, framing the analysis', Chapter 1, in *Mixed Blessings. Laws, Religions, and Women's Rights in the Asia-Pacific Region*, eds Amanda Whiting and Carolyn Evans, Leiden, Boston: Martinus Nijhoff Publishers, 1–24.

el-Fadl, Khaled Abou 2001, *Speaking in God's Name: Islamic Law, Authority and Women*, Oxford: Oneworld Publications.

el-Fadl, Khaled Abou 2002, *The Place of Tolerance in Islam*, Boston, MA: Beacon Press.

el-Fadl, Khaled Abou 2003a, *Islam and the Challenge of Democracy*, Princeton, NJ: Princeton University Press.

el-Fadl, Khaled Abou 2003b, 'The ugly modern and the modern ugly: reclaiming the beautiful in Islam', in *Progressive Muslims*, ed. Omid Safi, Oxford: Oneworld Publications.

el-Fadl, Khaled Abou 2005, *The Great Theft: Wrestling Islam Away from the Extremists*, New York: HarperCollins.

Fairclough, N. 1995, *Media Discourse*, London: Arnold.

Falconer of Thoroton, Lord 2007, 'Human rights and terrorism', speech at the Royal United Services Institute RUSI, London, 14 February 2007, <http://www.dca.gov.uk/speeches/2007/sp070214.htm>, accessed 2 May 2007.

al-Fatawa al-'Alamgiri, 3rd edition, 6 vols, Beirut: no publisher, 1973.

FEERI 2002, 'Declaración de la FEERI sobre el maltrato de la mujer', 22 April, <www.webislam.com>, accessed 14 February 2008.

Ferrari, Silvio 2000, 'Introduction', in *Islam and European Legal Systems*, eds S. Ferrari and A. Bradney, Aldershot: Ashgate.

Ferrari, Silvio 2003, 'The legal dimension', in *Muslims in the Enlarged Europe. Religion and Society*, eds B. Maréchal, S. Allievi, F. Dassetto and J. Nielsen, Leiden: Brill, chapter 6.

Fino, Dua M.A. 2004, 'The influence on the concepts of Qawama and Wilaya on the formation of the status of Muslim women in the light of Maqasid of the Shari'a', unpublished PhD thesis, University of Birmingham.

Fischer, Johan 2007, 'Feeding secularism: the halal-market in London', paper presented at the conference 'Secularism and Beyond', Copenhagen May 2007.

Fish, Stanley 2005, 'There is no textualist position', *San Diego Law Review*, vol. 42, no. 2, 629–50.

Foblets, Marie-Claire 2003, 'Muslim family laws before the courts in Europe: a conditional recognition' in *Muslims in the Enlarged Europe. Religion and Society*, eds B. Maréchal, S. Allievi, F. Dassetto and J. Nielsen, Leiden: Brill, chapter 7.

Foblets, Marie-Claire 2008, 'Marriage and divorce in the new Moroccan Family Code: implications for Moroccans residing in Europe', in *Law and Religion in Multicultural Societies*, eds Rubya Mehdi, Hanne Petersen, Erik Reenberg Sand and Gordon Woodman, Copenhagen: Jurist- og Økonomforbundets Forlag, 2008, 145–75.

Foucault, Michel 1972, *The Archaeology of Knowledge and Discourse on the Language*, New York: Pantheon Books (French original, 1969).

Foucault, Michel 1984, *L'Usage des plaisirs*, Paris: Gallimard.

Foucault, Michel 1991, *Discipline and Punish. The Birth of the Prison*, London: Penguin French original 1975.

Foucault, Michel 1994, 'La gouvernementalité', in *Dits et Écrits III*. Paris: Gallimard.

Friedman, Lawrence 2007, 'Technology and Legal Culture', in *Liber Amicorum Kjell Åke Modéer*, eds Bernhard Diestelkamp, Hans-Heinrich Vogel, Nils Jörn, Per Nilsén and Christan Häthén, Lund: Juristförlaget i Lund.

Frow, John 2006, 'Waiting for the Antichrist', in *The State of the World*, ed. António Pinto Ribeiro, Manchester: Carcanet and Fundacão Calouste Gulbenkian, 71–89.

Gadirov, Javid 2006, 'Plurality of legal systems and religious freedom', <www.strasbourgconference.org/papers>, accessed 20 April 2008.

Gale, Richard 2007, 'Planning law and mosque development: The politics of religion and residence in Birmingham', in *Law and Ethnic Plurality: Socio-Legal Perspectives*, ed. Prakash Shah, Leiden: Martinus Nijhoff, 127–44.

Gambles, Richenda, Suzan Lewis and Rhona Rapoport 2006, *The Myth of Work-Life Balance: The Challenge of Our Time for Men, Women and Societies*, Chichester: John Wiley and Sons.

Gerven, Walter van 2004, 'Codifying European private law,' in *Epistemology and Methodology of Comparative Law*, ed. Mark van Hoecke, Oxford: Hart, 137–64.

Ghannouchi, Rachid 1993, *al-Hurriya al-'Amma fi al-Dawla al-Islamiyya*, Beirut: Markaz Dirasat al-Wahda al-'Arabiyya.

al-Ghunaimi, Mohammad Talaat 1968, *The Muslim Conception of International Law and the Western Approach*, The Hague: Mouton.

Gill, A. and K. Whedbee 1997, 'Rhetoric', in *Discourse as Structure and Process*, ed. T.A. Van Dijk, Part I, London: Sage Publications, 157–84.

Gleave, R.M. 2008, 'Makasid al-Shari'a,' *Encyclopaedia of Islam Online*, Leiden: Brill.

Glenn, H. Patrick 2000, *Legal Traditions of the World: Sustainable Diversity in Law*, Oxford: Oxford University Press.

Glenn, H. Patrick 2007, *Legal Traditions of the World*, 3rd edition, Oxford: Oxford University Press.

Glenn, H. Patrick 2008, *Religion and Tradition*, unpublished paper given at the conference "Living Ruins of the Law" at Sigtuna, Sweden, January 2008.

Good, Deirdre Joy ed. 2005, *Mariam, the Magdalen, and the Mother*. Bloomington, IN: Indiana University Press.

Göle, Nilufer and Ludwig Amman eds 2006, *Islam in Public. Turkey, Iran and Europe*. Istanbul: Bìlgì University Press.

Griffiths, John 1986, 'What is legal pluralism?', *Journal of Legal Pluralism and Unofficial Law*, no. 24, 1–56.

Grillo, Ralph 2005, Backlash Against Diversity? Identity and Cultural Politics in European Cities, Oxford: COMPAS Working Paper no. 14.

Grøndahl, M., T.R. Rasmussen and K. Sinclair 2003, *Hizb ut-Tahrir i Danmark: farlig fundamentalisme eller uskyldigt ungdomsoprør?*, Århus: Aarhus University Press.

Gundelach, Peter, Hans Raun Iversen, Margit Warburg 2008, *I hjertet af Danmark. Institutioner og mentaliteter*, København: Hans Reitzels Forlag.

Gunnarsson, Åsa, Eva-Maria Svensson and Margaret Davies eds 2007, *Exploiting the Limits of Law: Swedish Feminism and the Challenge to Pessimism*, Dartmouth: Ashgate.

Häberle, Peter 1994, *Europäische Rechtskultur*, Baden-Baden: Nomos.

Habermas, Jürgen 1985, *Der philosophische Diskurs der Moderne*, Frankfurt: Suhrkamp.

Haenni, Patrick 2005, *L'Islam de marché*, Paris: Les Éditions du Seuil.

Haenni, Patrick 2006, *La France face à ses musulmans*, Report Europe no. 172, Brussels: International Crisis Group.

Hajjaji-Jarrah, S. 2003, 'Women's modesty in Qur'anic commentaries: the founding discourse', in *The Muslim Veil in North America: Issues and Debates*, eds S. Alvi, H. Hoodfar and S. McDonough, Toronto: Women's Press.

Hallaq, Wael 1990, 'Logic, formal arguments and formalization of arguments in Sunni jurisprudence', *Arabica*, 37, 315–58.

Hallaq, Wael 1999, *History of Islamic Legal Theories: An Introduction to Sunni Usul al-Fiqh*, Cambridge: Cambridge University Press.

Halliday, M.A.K. 1985, *An Introduction to Functional Grammar*, London: Edward Arnold.

Hamilton, Charles 1989, *The Hidaya*, vol. 1, Karachi: Darul Ishaat.

Herbert, Jean Loup 2005, 'Le réveil d'Al-Andalus: Un statut pionnier pour l'islam espagnol', in *Islam de France – Islams de l'Europe*, eds Alain Gresh and Michel Tubiana, Paris: L'Harmattan, 65–72.

Hershlag, Z.Y. 1979, 'Industrialisation in Arab countries: patterns, options and strategies', in *Arab Industrialisation and Economic Integration*, ed. Roberto Aliboni, London: Croom Helm.

al-Hibri, Azizah 1982, 'A study of Islamic herstory: or how did we ever get into this mess?', *Women's Studies International Forum*, 5, 207–19.

al-Hibri, Azizah 1992, 'Islamic constitutionalism and the concept of democracy', *Case Western Reserve Journal of International Law*, 1, 1–27.

Hjärpe, Jan 2005, *Sharia: Gudomlig lag i en värld i förändring*, Stockholm: Nordstedts Förlag.

Hodgson, Marshall G.S. 1974, *The Venture of Islam: Conscience and History in a World Civilization*, 3 vols, Chicago, IL: Chicago University Press.

Hourani, Albert 1962, *Arabic Thought in the Liberal Age, 1798–1939*, London: Oxford University Press.

Housby, Elaine 2006, 'Islamic house purchase loans', *ISIM-Review*, nr. 17, 28–9.

Hübner, Hans 1990, *Biblische Theologie des Neuen Testamentes, Band 1.* Prolegomena, Göttingen: Vandenhoeck & Ruprecht.

al-Hudaybi, Hasan 1965, *Du'ah la qudah*, Cairo: Dar al-fikr al-'arabi.

al-Hudaybi, Hasan 1977, *Du'ah la qudah*, Cairo: Dar al-tiba'a wa'l-nashr al-islamiyya.

Hurgronje, Snouck 1916, *Mohammedanism*, New York and London: G.P. Putnam and Sons.

Husain, Ed 2007, *The Islamist*, London: Penguin Books.

Husain, Ibn Maqbool ed. 2004, *Fatawa: Essential Rulings for Every Muslim Woman*, Riyadh: International Islamic Publishing House.

Ibn al-Humam 1970, *al-Fath al-Qadir*, vol. 3. Cairo: no publ.

Ibn 'Ashur, Muhammad al-Zahir 2005, *Maqasid al-shari'a al-islamiyya*, Cairo: Dar al-Salam.

Ibn Baz, 'Abd al-'Aziz b. 'Abd Allah 2002, *Majmu' fatawa wa-maqalat mutanawwi'a*, 19 vols, Riyadh: no publisher.

Ibn Rushd 1992, *Bidayat al-mujtahid wa-nihayat al-muqtasid*, vol. 1, Beirut: Dar Ihya al-Turath al-'Arabi.

Ibn Taymiyya, Taqi al-Din 1999, *Kitab al-Iman: Book of Faith*, Bloomington, IN: Bloomington University Press.

Ibn Taymiyya, Taqi al-Din n.d., *Majmu'at fatawa Shaykh al-Islam Ahmad Ibn Taymiyya*, compiled by 'Abd al-Rahman b. Qasim al-'Asimi, 35 vols. Riyadh: no publisher.

ICG 2005, *Understanding Islamism*, Cairo and Brussels: International Crisis Group, Middle East/North Africa Report no. 37, 2 March.

'Imara, Muhammad 1979, *Al-Islam wa al-Sulta al-Diniyya*, Cairo: Dar al-Thaqafa al-Jadida.

Islamic Human Rights Commission 2006. *British Muslims' Expectations of the Government*, London: Islamic Human Rights Commission.

<www.islamonline.net/English/In_Depth/Islam/Islam Wife Beating/index.html>, accessed 15 May 2008.

Jaworski, Adam and Nikolas Coupland, eds 1999, *The Discourse Reader*, London: Routledge.

Johansen, Baber 1988, *The Islamic Law on Land Tax and Rent*, London: Croom Helm.

Johansen, Baber 1999, *Contingency in a Sacred Law*, Leiden: Brill.

Johansen, Julian 1996, *Sufism and Islamic Reform in Egypt: The Battle for Islamic Tradition*, Oxford: Oxford University Press.

Joppke, Christian 2004, 'The retreat of multiculturalism in the liberal state: theory and policy', *British Journal of Sociology*, vol. 55, no. 2, 237–57.

Kabeer, Naila 2008, 'Marriage, motherhood and masculinity in the global economy', in *openDemocracy*, <http://opendemocracy.net/node/35680/print>, accessed 1 February 2008.

Kamali, Mohammad Hashim 1991, *Principles of Islamic Jurisprudence*, Cambridge: Islamic Texts Society.

Kane, Joseph 1972, 'Islam in the new Egyptian constitution', *Middle East Journal*, 26, 2, 137–48.

Keshavjee, Mohamed 2007, 'Alternative dispute resolution in a diasporic Muslim community', in *Law and Ethnic Plurality: Socio-Legal Perspectives*, ed. Prakash Shah, Leiden: Martinus Nijhoff, 145–75.

Khadduri, Majid 1955, *War and Peace in the Law of Islam*, Baltimore, MD: Johns Hopkins University Press.

Khadduri, Majid 1984, *The Islamic Conception of Justice*, Baltimore, MD: Johns Hopkins University Press.

Khalaf Allah, M.A. 1977, *Dirasat fi al-nuzum wa'l-tashri' at al-islamiyya*, Cairo: Maktabat al-anglu al-misriyya.

Khalidi, Tarif 2001, *The Muslim Jesus: Sayings and Stories in Islamic Literature*, Cambridge, MA: Harvard University Press.

Khaliq, U. 2004, 'Islam and the European Union: report on the United Kingdom', in *Islam and the European Union*, eds Richard Potz and Wolfgang Wieshaider, Leuven: Peeters, 219–62.

Klausen, Jytte 2005, *The Islamic Challenge. Politics and Religion in Western Europe*, Oxford: Oxford University Press.

Koch, Henning 2007, 'Det Materielle Demokrati – Rettigheder og Værdier' in *Liber Amicorum Kjell-Åke Modéer*, Lund: Juristförlaget i Lund, 335-342.

Koch, Henning 1994, *Demokrati, slå til!*, Copenhagen: Gyldendal.

Krämer, Gudrun n.d., 'Islamic discourses contested: Middle Eastern and European perspectives', presentation of sub-project, Europa in Nahen Osten – Nahen Osten in Europa, Wissenschaftskolleg zu Berlin <www.wiko-berlin.de>, accessed 21 September 2007.

Krause, Harry D. 2006, 'Comparative family law' in *Oxford Handbook on Comparative Law*, eds Mathias Reimann and Reinhard Zimmermann, Oxford: Oxford University Press, 1099–131.

Kurzman, Charles, ed. 2002, *Modernist Islam 1840–1940: A Sourcebook*, Oxford: Oxford University Press.

Layish, Aharon 2004, 'The transformation of the shari'a from jurists' law to statutory law in the contemporary Muslim world', *Die Welt des Islams*, vol. 44, 85–109.

Lewis, Bernard 1994, 'Legal and historical reflections on the position of Muslim populations under non-Muslim rule', in *Muslims in Europe*, eds Bernard Lewis and Dominique Schnapper, London: Pinter, 1–18.

Lindström, Lars 1999, 'Rättssalens aktörer. Förändrade roller och uppgifter', *Svensk Juristtidning*, no. 4, 467–75.

Lombardi, Clark B. 2006, *State Law as Islamic Law in Modern Egypt. The Incorporation of the Shari'a in Egyptian Constitutional Law*, Leiden: Brill.

Lüchau, Peter 2005, 'Danskernes Gudstro siden 1940'erne', in *Gudstro i Danmark*, eds Morten Thomsen Højsgaard and Hans Raun Iversen, Copenhagen: Forlaget Anis.

Macdonald, Myra 2003, *Exploring Media Discourse*, London: Arnold.

McGinty, Anna Mansson 2007, 'Formation of alternative femininities through Islam: Feminist approaches among Muslim converts in Sweden', *Women's Studies International Forum*, 30, 474–85.

McGoldrick, Dominic 2006, *Human Rights and Religion: The Islamic Headscarf Debate in Europe*, Oxford and Portland, OR: Hart Publishing.

Macklem, Patrick 2006, 'Militant democracy, legal pluralism and the paradox of self-determination', <www.strasbourgconference.org/papers>, accessed 20 April 2008.

Madigan, Daniel 2004, 'The blurred edges of the authoritative text: where is the authority of the Qur'an actually located', University of Copenhagen: unpublished paper for the International Conference on Qur'anic Studies: Literary and Hermeneutical Dimensions, 5–7 March.

Mahmood, Saba 2005, *Politics of Piety. The Islamic Renewal and the Feminist Subject*, Princeton, NJ: Princeton University Press.

Mahmoudi, Said and Chahandeh, Ali 2001, 'Om brott och straff i Iran', *Svensk Juristtidning*, no. 4, 347–72.

Mahmoudi, Said 2002, 'Om hedersmord', *Juridisk Tidskrift*, no. 1, 242–7.

Makdisi, George 1981, *The Rise of Colleges*, Edinburgh: Edinburgh University Press.

Malik, Jamal 2004, 'From the margin to the centre: Muslims in Europe – introduction', *Muslims in Europe: From the Margin to the Centre*, ed. Jamal Malik, Münster: LIT Verlag, 1–18.

Mallat, Chibli 2003, 'Islamic law and its philosophical basis', Lund: IVR Lund paper.

Mallat, Chibli 2006, 'Islamic legal culture' in *Oxford Handbook of Comparative Law*, eds Mathias Reimann and Reinhard Zimmermann, Oxford: Oxford University Press, 609–40

Maréchal, Brigitte, Stefano Allievi, Felice Dassetto and Jørgen Nielsen, eds 2003, *Muslims in the Enlarged Europe*, Leiden: Brill.

al-Marghinani, 'Ali b. Abi Bakr 1791, *Al-Hedaya*'; the part dealing with family law was translated by Charles Hamilton, *The Hedaya, or Guide: a Commentary on the Mussulman Laws*, London: T. Bensley.

Marín, Manuela 2003, 'Disciplining wives: a historical reading of Qur'an 4:34', *Studia Islamica*, no. 97, 5–40.

Marklund, Liza and Lotta Snickare 2007, *Det finns en särskild plats i helvetet för kvinnor som inte hjälper varandra* [There's a special place in hell for women who don't help each other], Stockholm: Pocketförlaget.

Masud, Muhammad Khalid 1977, *Islamic Legal Philosophy: A Study of Abu Ishaq al-Shatibi's Life and Thought*, Islamabad: Islamic Research Institute.

Masud, M.K. 1997, *Shatibi's Philosophy of Islamic Law*, New Delhi: Kitab Bhavan.

Masud, Muhammad Khalid 2001, *Muslim Jurists' Quest for the Normative Basis of Shari'a*, Leiden: ISIM.

Masud, Muhammad Khalid, Brinkley Messick and David S. Powers eds 1996, *Islamic Legal Interpretation: Muftis and their Fatwas*, Cambridge MA: Harvard University Press.

Mawdudi, Abu'l-'Ala' 1976, *Political Theory of Islam*, ed. and tr. Khurshid Ahmad, Lahore: Islamic Publications.

Mawdudi, Abu'l-'Ala' 1977, *Jihad in Islam*, Kuwait: International Islamic Federation of Student Organizations.

Mawdudi, Abu'l-'Ala' 1978, *Al-Islam wa-'l-madaniyya al-haditha*, Cairo: Dar al-ansar.

Mawdudi, Abu'l-'Ala' 1979, *The Process of Islamic Revolution*, Lahore: Islamic Publications.

Mawdudi, Abu'l-'Ala' 1980a, *al-Hukuma al-Islamiyya*, Cairo: al-Mukhtar al-islami.

Mawdudi, Abu'l-'Ala' 1980b, *al-Islam wa'l-Jahiliyya*, Beirut: Dar al fikr.

Mehdi, Rubya ed. 2007, *Retsudvikling & Integration*. Copenhagen: Jurist- og Økonomforbundets Forlag.

Mehdi, Rubya 2008, *Law and Religion in Multicultural Societies*, eds. Rubya Mehdi, Hanne Petersen, Erik Reenberg Sand, Gordon R. Woodman, Copenhagen: DJØF.

Mehdi, Rubya and Farida Shahid eds 1997, *Women's Law in Legal Education and Practice in Pakistan*. Copenhagen: New Social Science Monographs.

Melchert, Christopher, 1997, *The Formation of the Sunni Schools of Law, 9th–10th Centuries CE*, Leiden: Brill.

Menski, Werner 1993, 'Asian laws in Britain and the question of adaptation to a new legal order: Asian laws in Britain?', in *Ethnicity, Identity, Migration: The South Asian Context*, eds M. Israel and N.K. Wagle, Toronto: Centre for South Asian Studies, University of Toronto, 238–68.

Menski, Werner 2001, 'Muslim law in Britain', *Journal of Asian and African Studies*, no. 62, 127–63.

Menski, Werner 2006, *Comparative Law in a Global Context. The Legal Systems of Asia and Africa*, 2nd ed., Cambridge: Cambridge University Press.

Menski, Werner 2006, 'Rethinking legal theory in the light of south-north migration' in *Migration, Diasporas and Legal Systems in Europe*, eds Prakash Shah and Werner Menski, London: Routledge-Cavendish, 13–28.

Menski, Werner 2008, 'Law, religion and culture in multi-cultural Britain', in *Law and Religion in Multicultural Societies*, eds Rubya Mehdi, Hanne Petersen, Erik Reenberg Sand and Gordon Woodman, Copenhagen: Jurist- og Økonomforbundets Forlag, 43–62.

Modéer, Kjell-Å. 1994, *Den svenska domarkulturen – europeiska och nationella förebilder*, Lund: Corpus Iuris Förlag.

Modéer, Kjell-Å. 2003, 'From "Rechtstaat" to "welfare state": the Swedish judicial culture in transition 1870–1970', in *Lawyers and Vampires. Cultural Histories of Legal Professions*, eds W. Pue and David Sugarman, Oxford: Hart Publishing.

Modéer, Kjell-Å (2004a), 'Law and religion: Rätt och religion: En översikt av en senmodern rättsvetenskaplig diskurs', *Retfærd*, vol 107, 3–16.

Modéer, Kjell-Å (2004b), 'Religionsrättens källor och metoder: Konflikt och konvergens. Nordisk rättskultur i mötet med den europeiska utmaningen', in *Kirkeretsantologi*, eds Lisbet Christoffersen et al., Århus: Selskab for Kirkeret, 48–59.

Modood, Tariq 2005, *Multicultural Politics: Racism, Ethnicity and Muslims in Britain*, Edinburgh: Edinburgh University Press.

Modood, Tariq 2006, 'British Muslims and the politics of multiculturalism', in *Multiculturalism, Muslims and Citizenship*, eds Tariq Modood, Anna Triandafyllidou and Ricard Zapata-Barrero, London and New York: Routledge.

Modood, Tariq 2007, *Multiculturalism: A Civic Idea*, Cambridge: Polity Press.

Modood, Tariq and Fauzia Ahmad 2007, 'British Muslim perspectives on multiculturalism', *Theory, Culture and Society*, vol. 24, no. 2, 187–213.

Moe, Christian 2006, 'Refah Partisi the Welfare Party and others v. Turkey', *International Journal of Not-for-Profit Law*, 6, 1, 1–8 <www.icnl.org/JOURNAL/vol6iss1/rel_moeprint.htm>.

Moussalli, Ahmad S. 2001, *The Islamic Quest for Democracy, Pluralism, and Human Rights*, Gainesville, FL: University Press of Florida.

Muslim Brotherhood 2007, 'al-Ikhwan al-Muslimun wa'l-ta'dilat al-dusturiyya', at <www.ikhwanonline.com/Article.asp?ID=26051&LevelID=2&SectionID=212>.

al-Musnad, Muhammad bin Abdul-Aziz ed. 1996, *Islamic Fatawa Regarding Women*, Riyadh: Darussalam.

Nakamura, Kojiro 1975, *Ghazali on Prayer*, Tokyo: University of Tokyo, Institute of Oriental Culture.

Nasr, Vali 1996, *Mawdudi and the Making of Islamic Revivalism*, Oxford: Oxford University Press.

Nielsen, J.S. 1997, 'Muslims in Europe: history revisited or a way forward?', *Islam and Christian-Muslim Relations*, 8, 135–43.

Nielsen, Jørgen S. 1999, *Towards a European Islam*, London: Macmillan.

Nielsen, Jørgen 2004, *Muslims in Western Europe*, 3rd edition, Edinburgh: Edinburgh University Press.

Nygren, Rolf 1999, 'Domstolar och etniska hänsynstaganden', *Svensk Juristtidning*, no. 5, 521–8.

O'Kane, Joseph P. 1972, 'Islam in the New Egyptian Constitution: some discussions in "al-Ahram"', *Middle East Journal*, 26:2 (Spring), 137–48.

Omaar, Rageh 2006, *Only Half of Me: Being a Muslim in Britain*, London: Penguin.

Osman, Fathi 2002, 'Democracy and the Concept of Shura', in *Religions in Dialogue: From Theocracy to Democracy*, eds Alan Race and Ingrid Shafer, Aldershot: Ashgate, 85–97.

Oubrou, Tareq 2000, 'Introduction théorique à la chari'a de minorité', <http://www.oumma.com/spip.php?page=imprimer&id_article=7>, accessed 11 July 2007.

Oubrou, Tareq 2003a, 'La charia de minorité: contribution pour une intégration légale de l'islam', <http://islamlaicite.org/article.php3?id_article=24>, accessed 8 August 2007.

Oubrou, Tareq 2003b, 'Un bon musulman ne peut être qu'un bon citoyen', interview with Cédric Baylocq Sassoubre, <http://www.islamlaicite.org/imprimer.php3?id_article_326>, accessed 3 August 2007.

Pålsson, Lennart 1992, 'Svensk rättspraxis: Internationell privat- och processrätt 1986–1990', *Svensk Juristtidning*, no. 7, 475–503.

Pearl, David and Werner Menski 1998, *Muslim Family Law*, 3rd edition, London: Sweet and Maxwell.

Peters, F.E. 1994, *A Reader on Classical Islam*, Princeton, NJ. Princeton University Press.

Peters, Rudolph 1988, 'Divine law or man-made law? Egypt and the application of the Shari'a', *Arab Law Quarterly*, 3, 231–53.

Peters, Shawn Frances 2003, *The Yoder Case: Religious Freedom, Education, and Parental Rights*, Lawrence: University Press of Kansas.

Petersen, Hanne 1991, *Informel ret på kvindearbejdspladser: En retsteoretisk og empirisk analyse*, Copenhagen: Akademisk Forlag.

Petersen, Hanne 1996, *Home Knitted Law. Norms and Values in Gendered Rule-Making*, Aldershot: Dartmouth.

Petersen, Hanne 2006, *Retspluralisme i praksis – grønlandske inspirationer*, København: Ilisimartusarfik/DJØF.

Petersen, Hanne 2007, 'Integration i foranderlighed', in *Retsudvikling & Integration*, ed. Rubya Mehdi, Copenhagen: Jurist- og Økonomforbundets forlag, 235–52.

Petersen, Hanne forthcoming, 'Beyond national majority/minority dichotomies: towards legal traditions and religions of world society – a local example', in

Law and Religion in the 21st Century – Nordic Perspectives – New Life in the Ruins, ed. Lisbet Christoffersen et al., no publisher.

Petersen, Hanne and Henrik Zahle eds 1995, *Legal Polycentricity. Consequences of Pluralism in Law*, Aldershot: Ashgate..

Phillips, Trevor 2005, 'After 7/7: sleepwalking to segregation', speech given at the Manchester Council for Community Relations, 22 September, <http://www.cre.gov.uk>, accessed 2 May 2007.

Phillips, Trevor 2006, interview on Jonathan Dimbleby programme, ITV1, 26 February 2006.

Poulter, Sebastian M. 1990, 'The claim to a separate Islamic system of personal law for British Muslims', in *Islamic Family Law*, eds Chibli Mallat and Jane Connors, London: Graham and Trotman, 147–66.

Poulter, Sebastian 1998, *Ethnicity, Law and Human Rights: The English Experience*, Oxford: Clarendon.

Prado, Abdennur 2004, 'The Qur'an case in the Spanish courts', <www.abdennurprado.wordpress.com>, accessed 15 February 2008.

Pylkkänen, Anu forthcoming, 'Feminism and the challenge of religious truths: the case of Nordic Protestantism', in *Law and Religion in the 21st Century – Nordic Perspectives – New Life in the Ruins*, ed. Lisbet Christoffersen et al., no publisher.

Qaradawi, Youssef 2001, *Al-Niqab li'l-Mar'a*, Beirut: Ar-Risala.

Qur'an 1930, *The Meaning of the Glorious Koran: An Explanatory Translation, by Marmaduke Pickthall*, London: Knopf.

Qur'an 1955, *The Koran Interpreted*, transl. A.J. Arberry, London: George Allen and Unwin.

Qur'an 1966, *The Koran*, translated by N.J. Dawood, 2nd revised edition, Harmondsworth: Penguin Books.

Qur'an 1979, *The Qur'an: Basic Teachings*, trans. and eds T.B. Irving, K. Ahmad and M.M. Ahsan, Leicester: The Islamic Foundation, 1979.

Qur'an 1411 AH, *The Holy Qur'an: English Translation of the Meanings and Commentary*, Mecca: Presidency of Islamic Researches, Ifta, Call and Guidance.

Qur'an 2004, *The Qur'an*, trans. M.A.S. Abdel Haleem, Oxford: Oxford University Press.

Quraishi, Asifa 1997, 'Her honor: an Islamic critique of the rape laws of Pakistan from a woman-sensitive perspective', *Michigan Journal of International Law*, 18, 287–320.

Quraishi, Asifa and Najeeba Syeed Miller 2004, 'No altars: a survey of Islamic family law in the United States', in *Women's Rights and Islamic Family Law*, ed. Lynn Welchman, London: Zed Books, 177–229.

Qutb, Sayyid 1949, *Al-'Adala al-Ijtima'iyya fi al-Islam*, Cairo: Lajnat al-nashr li-'l-jami'iyyin.

Qutb, Sayyid 1982, *Ma'alim fi al-tariq*, Beirut: Dar al-shuruq.

Rahman, Fazlur 1980, *Major Themes of the Q ur'an*, Minneapolis: Bibliotheca Islamica.

Rahman, Fazlur 1982a, *Islam and Modernity: Transformation of an Intellectual Tradition*, Chicago, IL: University of Chicago Press.

Rahman, Fazlur 1982b, 'The Islamic concept of state', in *Islam in Transition: Muslim Perspectives*, eds John J. Donohue and John L. Esposito, New York and Oxford: Oxford University Press, 161–71.

Ramadan, Tariq 1999, *To be a European Muslim*, Markfield: The Islamic Foundation.

Ramadan, Tariq 2001, *Islam, the West and the Challenges of Modernity*, Leicester: The Islamic Foundation.

Ramadan, Tariq 2002, 'Europeanisation of Islam or Islamisation of Europe?', in *Islam, Europe's Second Religion: The New Social, Cultural and Political Landscape*, ed. Shireen T. Hunter, Westport, CT, and London: Praeger, 207–18.

Ramadan, Tariq 2003, Les Musulmans d'Occident et l'avenir de l'islam, Arles: Actes Sud.

Ramadan, Tariq 2004, *Western Muslims and the Future of Islam*, Oxford: Oxford University Press.

Razack, Sherene H. 2004, 'Imperilled Muslim women, dangerous Muslim men and civilised Europeans: legal and social responses to forced marriages', *Feminist Legal Studies*, 12, 129–74.

Razack, Sherene H. 2007, 'The "Sharia Law Debate" in Ontario: the modernity/premodernity distinction in legal efforts to protect women from culture', *Feminist Legal Studies*, 15, 3–32.

Reimann, Mathias and Reinhard Zimmermann 2006, *The Oxford Handbook of Comparative Law*, Oxford: Oxford University Press.

Renard, John 1988, '*Al-Jihad al-Akbar*: Notes on a theme in Islamic spirituality', *Muslim World*, 78, 225–42.

Rida, Rashid 1984, *Yusr al-islam wa-usul al-tashri'*, Cairo: Maktabat al-salam al-'alamiyya.

Rivers, Julian 2006, 'The legal status of Islam in Great Britain', *Derecho y Religión*, 1, 144–65.

Roald, A.S. 2001, *Women in Islam: the Western Experience*, London: Routledge.

Rohe, Mathias 2006, 'The migration and settlement of Muslims: The challenges for European legal systems', in *Migration, Diasporas and Legal Systems in Europe*, eds Prakash Shah and Werner F. Menski, London: Routledge-Cavendish, 57–72.

Rohe, Mathias 2007, *Muslim Minorities and the Law in Europe. Chances and Challenges*, New Delhi: Global Media Publications.

Rorty, Richard 1999, 'A pragmatist view of contemporary analytic philosophy', <http://www.stanford.edu/~rrorty/pragmatistview.htm>, accessed 1 September 2006.

Rose, Nicolas 1999, *Powers of Freedom*, Cambridge: Cambridge University Press.

Rosen, Lawrence 1989, *The Anthropology of Justice: Law as Culture in Islamic Society*, Cambridge: Cambridge University Press.

Rosen, Lawrence 1995, 'European Islam and the state', in *God's Law Versus State Law*, ed. Michael King, London: Grey Seal, 88–90.

Rosen, Lawrence 2008, 'Revision and reality in the family law of Morocco', in *Law and Religion in Multicultural Societies* eds Rubya Mehdi, Hanne Petersen, Erik Reenberg Sand and Gordon Woodman, Copenhagen: Jurist- og Økonomforbundets Forlag, 131–44.

Roy, Olivier 2002, *L'Islam mondialisé*, Paris: Le Seuil.

Roy, Olivier 2004, *Globalized Islam: The Search for a New Ummah*, New York: Columbia University Press.

Roy, Olivier 2007, 'Le découplage de la religion et de la culture: une exception musulmane?', *Esprit*, March–April, 242–52.

Ryberg, Lotti 1988, *Domarkarriären*, Stockholm: Juristförlaget.

Sachedina, Abdulaziz 2001, *The Islamic Roots of Democratic Pluralism*, Oxford: Oxford University Press.

Saïd, Edward 1978, *Orientalism*, London: Routledge Kegan and Paul; 2nd ed., London: Penguin, 1995.

Said, Mahmoudi and Chahanedh, Ali 2001. 'Om brott och straff i Iran', *Svensk Juristtidning*, no. 4, 347–72.

Santos, Boaventura de Sousa 2002, *Toward a New Legal Common Sense*, London: Butterworths.

al-Sarakhsi, Shams al-Din (d. *ca.* 1080), *Al-Mabsut*, 30 vols, Cairo: Matba'at al-Sa'ada, 1348 AH.

Sardar Ali, Shaheen forthcoming, '"Systemically closed, cognitively open"? A critical analysis of transformative processes in Islamic law and Muslim state practice.'

Saussure, Ferdinand de 1972, *Cours de linguistique générale*, new ed., Paris: Payothèque.

Schacht, Joseph 1964, repr. 1998, *Introduction to Islamic Law*, Oxford: Clarendon Press.

Schiratzki, Johanna 1994, 'Om tunisisk familjerätt – en replik', *Svensk Juristtidning*, no. 5/6, 560–1.

Schiratzki, Johanna 1997, 'Social adekvans och barnets bästa – HD om omskärelse', *Juridisk Tidskrift*, no. 2, 491–6.

Schiratzki, Johanna 2001, *Muslimsk familjerätt: i svenskt perspektiv*, Stockholm: Nordstedts Juridik.

Schött, Roland 1994, 'Tunisisk familjerättsreform – rapport och kommentar', *Svensk Juristtidning*, no. 1, 106–108.

Seale, Morris S. 1964, *Muslim Theology*, London: Luzac.

Semonche, John 1998, *Keeping the Faith: A Cultural History of the Supreme Court*, Lanham, MD: Rowman and Littlefield.

Shah, Prakash 2003, 'Attitudes to polygamy in English law', *International and Comparative Law Quarterly*, vol. 52, 359–400.

Shah, Prakash 2005, *Legal Pluralism in Conflict: Coping with Cultural Diversity in Law*, London: Glass House.

Shah, Prakash 2007, 'Rituals of recognition: Ethnic minority marriages in British legal systems', in *Law and Ethnic Plurality:Socio-Legal Perspectives*, ed. Prakash Shah, Leiden: Martinus Nijhoff, 177–202.

Shah, Prakash 2009, 'Transforming to accommodate? Reflections on the *shari'a* debate in Britain' in *Legal Practice and Cultural Diversity*, eds Ralph Grillo and Prakash Shah, Aldershot: Ashgate, 73–91.

Shah, Prakash and Werner Menski eds 2006, *Migration, Diasporas and Legal Systems in Europe*, London: Routledge.

Shah-Kazemi, Reza 2004, 'Recollecting the spirit of *jihad*,' in *Islam, Fundamentalism, and the Betrayal of Tradition: Essays by Western Muslim Scholars*, ed. Joseph E.B. Lumbard, Bloomington, IN: World Wisdom, 121–42.

Shah-Kazemi, Sonia Nûrîn 2001, *Untying the Knot. Muslim Women, Divorce and the Shariah*, London: Nuffield Foundation.

Shahrour, Muhammad 1990, *al-Kitab wa'l-Qur'an: qira'a mu'asira*, Damascus: al-Ahali li'l-tiba'a wa'l-nashr wa'l-tawzi'.

al-Shatibi, Ibrahim b. Musa 2000, *al-Muwafaqat fi usul al-ahkam*, ed. Muhammad 'Abd al-Qadir al-Fadili, Beirut: al-Maktaba al-'asriyya.

Shepard, William 1989, 'Islam as a "system" in the later writings of Sayyid Qutb', *Middle Eastern Studies*, 25, 31–50.

Shepard, William 1992, 'The development of the thought of Sayyid Qutb as reflected in earlier and later editions of "social justice in Islam"', *Die Welt des Islams*, 32, 1992, 196–236.

Shepard, William 2003, 'Sayyed Qutb's doctrine of jahiliyya', *International Journal of Middle East Studies*, 35, 521–45.

Siddiqui, Mona 1995, 'Mahr: legal obligation or rightful demand?', *Journal of Islamic Studies*, 6, 14–24.

Siddiqui, Mona 2007, 'Drinking and drunkenness in Ibn Rushd,' in *Studies in Islamic Law: A Festschrift for Colin Imber*, eds Andreas Christmann and Robert Gleave, Oxford: Oxford University Press, 281–94.

Singh, Gurharpal and Drashan Singh Tatla 2006, *Sikhs in Britain: The Making of a Community*, London: Zed Books.

Smith, W. Robertson 1885, *Kinship and Marriage in Early Arabia*, Cambridge: Cambridge University Press.

Soroush, Abdolkarim 2000, *Reason, Freedom, and Democracy in Islam*, Oxford: Oxford University Press.

Spalek, Basia ed. 2002, *Islam, Crime and Criminal Justice*, Cullompton, Devon: Willan Publishing.

Srinivas, M.N. 1966, *Social Change in Modern India*, Berkeley and Los Angeles, CA: University of California Press.

Stalinsky, Steven and Y. Yehoshua 2004, 'Muslim clerics on the religious rulings regarding wife-beating', *MEMRI The Middle East Media Research Institute, Special Report*, no. 27, <http://www.memri.org/bin/articles.cgi?Page=archives&Area=sr&ID=SR2704>, accessed 6 March 2008.

Stowasser, Barbara 2001, 'Old shayks, young women, and the internet: the rewriting of women's political rights in Islam', *Muslim World*, 91, 99–120.

Strömberg, Håkan 2001, 'Religion och mänskliga rättigheter', *Juridisk Tidskrift*, no. 2, 230–7.

Suárez, Juan Pedro Yllanes 2004, Sentencia 03/04, Jutjat Penal no 3 de Barcelona, Procedimiento Abreviado 276/03 C, available online <http://www.an-nisa.es/ensayos/igualdadfanatismomisogeno.htm>, accessed 5 March 2008

al-Suyuti 1947, Sawn al-mantiq wa'l-kalam 'an fann al-mantiq wa'l-kalam, Cairo: Maktabat al-khanji.

al-Suyuti 1993, *al-Itqan fi 'ulum al-Qur'an*, Damascus: Dar Ibn Kathir.

Sweden 2006, *The Swedish Judicial System – a Brief Presentation*, Stockholm: Regeringskansliet, Ministry of Justice.

Sweden 2006, *Statens ansvarsnämnds verksamhetsberättelse för 2006*, available at <http://www.statensansvarsnamnd.se/verksamh2006.pdf>, accessed 14 October 2007.

Sweden 2007, Redogörelse 2006/07:JO1 Justitieombudsmännens ämbetsberättelse, available at <http://www.riksdagen.se/webbnav/index.aspx?nid=3451&dok_id=GU04JO1&rm=2006/07&bet=JO1>, accessed 14 October 2007.

al-Tafsir: <http://www.altafsir.com>.

Taji-Farouki, Suha 1996, *A Fundamental Quest: Hizb al-Tahrir and the Search for the Islamic Caliphate*, London: Grey Seal.

Ternisien, Xavier 2002, *La France des mosqués*, Paris: Éditions Albin Michel.

Ternisien, Xavier 2003, 'L'islam de France entre gauche et conservatisme', *Le Monde*, 1 March.

Thompson, Hajj Ahmad 2005, 'Applying fiqh in UK arbitration law', paper presented to the Arbitration Conference, Regents Park Mosque, 11 September 2005, <http://www.wynnechambers.co.uk/pdf/RPM_Arbitration.pdf>, accessed 2 May 2007.

Tibi, Bassam 2002, 'Muslim migrants in Europe: between Euro-Islam and ghettoization', in *Muslim Europe or Euro-Islam: Politics, Culture and Citizenship in the Age of Globalization*, eds Nezar AlSayyad and Manuel Castells, Lanham, MD: Lexington, 31–52.

Tibi, Bassam 2005, *Islam between Culture and Politics*, Houndmills: Palgrave Macmillan.

Tileaga, C. 2005, 'Accounting for extreme prejudice and legitimating blame in talk about the Romanies', *Discourse & Society*, 16(5), 603–24.

Titscher, S., M. Meyer, R. Wodak and E. Vetter 2000, *Methods of Text and Discourse Analysis*, London: Sage Publications.

Tsitselkis, K. 2004, 'Muslims in Greece', in *Islam and the European Union*, eds Richard Potz and Wolfgang Wieshaider, Leuven: Peeters, 79–107.

al-Tufi, Najm al-Din 1993, *Risala fi ri'ayat al-maslaha*, ed. Ahmad 'Abd al-Rahim al-Sayih, Cairo: al-Dar al-misriyya al-lubnaniyya.

Tuori, Kaarlo 1997, 'Towards a Multi-layered View of Modern Law', in *Justice, Morality and Society. A Tribute to Aleksander Peczenik on the Occasion of his 60th Birthday 16 November 1997*, eds. Aulis Aarnio, Robert Alexy, Gunnar Bergholz , Lund: Juristförlaget i Lund, 427-442.

Tuori, Kaarlo 2006, 'Den postmoderna rätten mellan harmonisering och fragmentering', in *Senmodernitetens historiska och komparativa konstruktioner*, ed. Kjell Åke Modéer. Lund: Corpus Iuris Förlag, 19–26.

Twining, William 2008, 'Surface law', in *Paradoxes of European Legal Integration*, eds Hanne Petersen, Anne-Lise Kjær, Helle Krunke and Mikael Rask Madsen, Aldershot: Ashgate.

UNDP 2002, *Arab Human Development Report 2002*, New York: United Nations Development Program.

van der Veer, Peter 2006, 'Pim Fortuyn, Theo Van Gogh, and the politics of tolerance in the Netherlands', *Public Culture*, vol. 18, no. 1, 111–24.

Van Hoecke, Mark 2002, *Law as Communication*, Oxford: Hart Publishing.

Van Hoecke, Mark 2004, 'Deep level comparative law', in *Epistemology and Methodology of Comparative Law*, ed. Mark Van Hoecke, Oxford: Hart Publishing.

Van Hoecke, Mark, and Warrington, Mark 1998, 'Towards a new model for comparative law', *International and Comparative Law Quarterly*, vol. 47, 495–536.

Varela, María Rosa 2004, 'Acusacion letrada', available online at <www.an-nisa.es/noticias/161104imankamal.htm>, accessed 5 March 2008.

Vikør, Knut 2005, *Between God and the Sultan: A History of Islamic Law*, Oxford: Oxford University Press.

Vogel, Frank E. 1996, 'The complementarity of ifta' and qada': three Saudi fatwas on divorce', in *Islamic Legal Interpretations: Muftis and their Fatwas*, eds Muhammad Khalid Masud, Brinkley Messick and David Powers, Cambridge MA: Harvard University Press, 262–9.

Vogel, Frank E. 1997, 'Siyasa: in the sense of siyasa shar'iyya', *Encyclopaedia of Islam*, vol. 9, 694–6, Leiden: Brill.

Vogel, Frank E. 2000, *Islamic Law and Legal System: Studies of Saudi Arabia*, Leiden: Brill.

Wadud, Amina 1999, *Qur'an and Woman. Rereading the Sacred Text from a Woman's Perspective*, Oxford: Oxford University Press.

Wazir Jahan, Karim 1992, *Women and Culture: Between Malay Adat and Islam*, Boulder, CO: Westview.

Weber, Max 1972, *Wirtschaft und Gesellschaft*, Tübingen: J.C.B. Mohr.

Weil, G. 1855, *Mohammedanernes Bibelske Legender, hentede fra arabiske Kilder og sammenstillede med jødiske Sagn*, trans. C.G.V. Faber, Odense: Miloske Boghandel.

Werbner, Pnina 2002, *Imagined Diasporas among Manchester Muslims*, Oxford: James Currey.

Whiting, Amanda and Carolyn Evans eds 2006, *Mixed Blessings: Laws, Religions and Women's Rights in the Asia-Pacific Region*, Leiden: Martinus Nijhoff.

Wiktorowicz, Quintan 2000, 'The Salafi Movement in Jordan', *International Journal of Middle East Studies*, 32, 222–6.

Wild, Stefan 1993, 'Review: Die andere Seite des Textes: Nasr Hamid Abu Zaid under der Koran', *Die Welt des Islams*, new ser., 33, 256–61.

Witte, John Jr. 2002, Law and Protestantism. The Legal Teachings of the Lutheran Reformation, Cambridge: Cambridge University Press.

Woodhead, Linda 2005, 'Gendering secularisation theory', in *Kvinder, Køn & Forskning*, 14, 20–32.

Yilmaz, Ihsan 2005, *Muslim Laws, Politics and Society in Modern Nation-States*, Aldershot: Ashgate.

Zebiri, Kate 1993, *Mahmud Shaltut and Islamic Modernism*, Oxford: Oxford University Press.

Zeghal, Malika 1996, *Gardiens de l'Islam. Les oulémas d'Al Azhar dans l'Égypte contemporaine*, Paris: Presses de SCIO.

Zeghal, Malika 2006, 'Redéfinir l'islam après le 11 septembre 2001: le réformisme éclaté des musulmans américain', in *Islamismes d'Occident. État des lieux et perspectives*, ed. Samir Amghar, Paris: Éditions Lignes de repères.

Zetterholm, Staffan, ed. 1994, *National Cultures and European Integration. Exploratory Essays on Cultural Diversity and Common Policies*, Providence: Berg Publishers.

Zeydan, A. 2004, *Al-Libas wa-Zina fi'l-Islam*, Beirut: Ar-Risala.

Zysow, Aron 1984, 'The economy of certainty: an introduction to the typology of Islamic legal theory', unpublished PhD dissertation, Harvard University, Cambridge, MA.

Zubaida, Sami 2003, *Law and Power in the Islamic World*, London: I.B. Tauris.

Zubeida, Sami 2006, *Ret og magt i den islamiske verden*, Copenhagen: Vandkunsten; translated from *Law and Power in the Islamic World*, London: I.B. Tauris 2003.

Zweigert, Konrad, Hein Kötz 1969-1971, *Einführung in die Recthsvergleichung auf dem Gebiete des Privatrechts*, 2 vols. Tübingen: Mohr (Siebeck).

Zweigert, Konrad and Hein Kötz 1998, *Introduction to Comparative Law*, 3rd edition, Oxford: Clarendon Press.

Index